The Thinking Girl's Guide to the Right Guy

The THINKING GIRL'S GUIDE to the RIGHT GUY

How Knowing Yourself Can Help You Navigate Dating, Hookups, and Love

Joanne Davila, PhD
Kaycee Lashman

THE GUILFORD PRESS
New York   London

Copyright © 2016 The Guilford Press
A Division of Guilford Publications, Inc.
370 Seventh Avenue, Suite 1200, New York, NY 10001
www.guilford.com

Printed in the United States of America

This book is printed on acid-free paper.

Last digit is print number: 9 8 7 6 5 4 3 2 1

Library of Congress Cataloging-in-Publication Data

Names: Davila, Joanne, 1966– author. | Lashman, Kaycee, author.
Title: The thinking girl's guide to the right guy : how knowing yourself can help you
    navigate dating, hookups, and love / Joanne Davila, Kaycee Lashman.
Description: First Edition. | New York : The Guilford Press, 2016. | Includes
    bibliographical references and index.
Identifiers: LCCN 2015044847 | ISBN 9781462516957 (paperback : alk. paper) |
    ISBN 9781462522767 (hardcover : alk. paper)
Subjects: LCSH: Self-actualization (Psychology) | Man–woman relationships. | Love. |
    BISAC: FAMILY & RELATIONSHIPS / Love & Romance. | PSYCHOLOGY /
    Interpersonal Relations. | SELF-HELP / Personal Growth / Self-Esteem.
Classification: LCC BF637.S4 D374 2016 | DDC 646.7/7—dc23
LC record available at http://lccn.loc.gov/2015044847

Contents

Purchasers of this book can download and print larger versions of
select practical tools from *www.guilford.com/davila-forms* for personal
use or use with individual clients (see copyright page for details).

Acknowledgments

This book would never have come to fruition without the support of many people in our professional and personal lives.

I (Joanne) would like to thank:

Kaycee, my coauthor, without whom I never would have written this book. She inspired me with her passion, dedication, and creativity. It's been an amazing collaboration that's become a valued friendship.

My mentors and colleagues who fostered and supported my scientific and professional development, including Connie Hammen, Tom Bradbury, Steve Beach, Frank Fincham, Gayle Beck, and Marv Goldfried.

All of the scholars who understand the importance of close relationships and are making important contributions to our scientific understanding of them and to evidence-based prevention and intervention programs designed to improve relationships.

My colleagues from "the Bradbury Lab." You are my academic family, and I have benefited greatly from your intellect and your friendship.

My current and former students: Sara Steinberg, Kate Stroud, Melissa Miller, Lisa Starr, Athena Yoneda, Rachel Hershenberg, Brian Feinstein, Vickie Bhatia, and Jess Latack. You've all contributed to the intellectual environment that made this book possible.

My colleagues at Stony Brook University, who provided me with the practical and social support that assisted in the completion of this book. Thank you for believing in me and valuing this endeavor.

My clients, from whom I have learned an incredible amount about the power of relationships.

C. K., whose wisdom and guidance helped me personally navigate the world of relationships.

My family and friends, who have taught me the most about relationships and whose continuous support and love have given me great joy and assisted me in reaching my goals. And D. M., for giving me the opportunity to successfully live out the skills in this book.

I (Kaycee) would like to thank:

Joanne, my coauthor, without whom I never would have written this book. I marvel at the way she uses the skills and her deep fact-based knowledge about healthy relationships. I am grateful for the trust and friendship that has developed while writing this book, which I shall cherish.

Dr. Julius Licata (*www.teencentral.net*), for our many hours spent on discussions, articles, and podcasts to help teens understand healthy relationships.

My daughter and son, the root of my passion—more than anything I want the story of their lives to be one of personal power and healthy relationships.

My mom and sister (you know why).

My friends and colleagues, who through day-to-day relationships both personally and professionally have furthered my knowledge of the intricacies and nuances of how to build healthy relationships.

My husband, Terry, without whose support and understanding I would not have become a writer. He is my healthy relationship.

We would both like to thank:

Kitty Moore, Publisher of General Trade Books at The Guilford Press, who emphatically supported this book right from the beginning and convinced us that Guilford was the right home for it.

Chris Benton, our developmental editor at Guilford, who, through her insightful questions and careful editing, challenged us in ways that made this a better book.

All of the young women who reviewed earlier versions of the book and whose ideas helped us make it clear and relevant for you, the reader.

Ross Lonergan, our personal editor, who made sure that the drafts we sent to Guilford provided a clean read.

All of the staff at Guilford who made this book possible.

And, finally, all of the young women whom we interviewed for this book. We thank you for your willingness to share your stories, your candor in doing so, and your desire to have the skills for a healthy relationship. Without you, this book would not exist.

Introduction: Read Me First

If you've picked up this book, it's probably because you haven't been able to get or have the relationship you want. Whatever you're looking for, something casual or something more serious, things never seem to go the way you expect.

Maybe you feel like Maria, age 27, an accountant for a social media company, who feels like she's always picking the wrong guy. He seems to be great at the time, but then she's like, "What was I thinking?"

Maybe you feel like Rachel, age 23, a manager at an upscale restaurant, who is frustrated by confronting the same relationship problems over and over. She's facing the "Why does this keep happening to me?!" dilemma.

Maybe you're like Sarah, age 21, a junior in college. She's in a relationship, but she's unhappy. She wants it to last, but they can't seem to stop arguing and they can't get past their differences. She's constantly thinking, "How can I make it work?!"

Maybe, like Vanessa, a 31-year-old teacher, you've had so many disappointing experiences you feel like you don't even know what it takes to have a good relationship, or that it isn't even possible.

Well, don't worry. It is possible. We know what it takes, and we have solutions for your problems.

We believe that women end up disappointed with their relationships because they're trying to be what the guy wants without first having a deep understanding of

- What they want,
- Whether the guy they're interested in or in a relationship with has it, and
- Whether they have what the guy wants too (as measured by how he treats them).

So, the real problem is this: Women spend so much time wanting to be what guys want, trying to "make" guys like them, trying to fix problematic relationships. We all know women who, after every breakup, ask, "What did I do wrong? Why can't I get a guy to like me?" Or women who change their looks and likes and dislikes based on the guy they're with. So many women are trying to figure out what the "right" thing is to do, be, or say. They're Googling things like "How do I get a guy to like me?" and "Is it okay to make the first move?" and "What will he think if . . . [*fill in the blank*]?" This is a serious problem, and it's at the root of so many failed relationships and so much unhappiness for women.

A major message of this book is this: ***Stop trying to be what a guy wants you to be (or what you think he wants you to be) and start figuring out whether he wants what you have to offer—the real you. Furthermore, you need to figure out whether you really want him!***

You might think you do, but women pursue or stay in relationships that are never going to work all the time because they're not aware of what they really need (and deserve) or who the guy really is. If you want to be successful in the world of relationships, this has to change.

What Will You Learn from Reading This Book?

You'll learn how to make the shift from "Can I be what he wants?" to "Does he want what I have to offer?" and "Do I really want him?"

We'll provide you with the skills to help you know who you are and what you need, help you look clearly at who the guy is that you have your eye on or are in a relationship with, and help you figure out whether he likes the real you so you can make good relationship decisions and get what you want.

Skills are *so* important. When women ask questions like "How do I make a relationship work?" or "How do I pick the right guy?" they're really asking for skills. Well, we hear you, and that's what we're going to provide.

When it comes to relationships these days, there are all kinds of options out there for young women. The choices are yours to make, so we won't be giving you advice about what you "should" do. We'll give you the skills to develop a better sense of awareness about what is right for you, by focusing you on questions that will allow you to get to know yourself and what you want from a relationship: "What kind of relationship do I want?" "Who do I want to be with, and why?" "What's my idea of a good relationship?" "When am I ready for sex?" "When and how do you talk with a guy about what you want and where things are going?" Answering these questions will help ensure that whatever relationship choice you make will result in greater success. You won't find this in other books about relationships.

Although it's great to live in a world where women have choices, the fact is the process of choosing is complicated. The dating and sex scene is a tough one to navigate, because lots of "shoulds" keep coming at us—from society, family, friends, dating and sexual partners, even ourselves—and many of them even conflict (for example, "You should always wait for the guy to call you" / "You should never wait for the guy to call you"; "Focus on hookups in college, not relationships" / "Make sure to find a guy who is husband material while you're in college").

Women regularly read magazines, books, and online material for "dos" and "don'ts." The problem with this is those sources often provide advice and opinions based on stereotypes and judgments. Indeed, a 2011 analysis of bestselling dating advice books indicated that beliefs about gender roles—what's appropriate for men and women to do—continue to be woven throughout typical dating advice. The authors of this analysis note that these books commonly suggest women take passive roles and advise women against taking active roles because they might be judged negatively by men for doing so. What would you do if faced with a decision about whether, for example, to make the first move—a behavior typically thought of as a man's role? What if you hook up with someone and want to see him again—would you contact him or wait for him to contact you? Would you follow the prescribed gender roles? How would you decide? Do you need to be concerned with what others think is right?

The fact that you're faced with lots of questions and decisions is a major reason for developing the skills to sort through all the issues and choices thoughtfully. There are no "right" choices or hard-and-fast "shoulds" in the objective sense of these words, but there *are* right choices, or better choices, for individuals. The trick is in knowing what is right or better for you—then you'll know what you "should" do.

We also give you skills to navigate all the uncertainty and intense emotions that come with relationships. In terms of guiding our choices, emotions can be our best friends or our worst enemies. We'll show you how to deal with the intense feelings you're sure to experience and how to use them wisely. We'll also give you skills to deal with the potential for conflict that comes with every relationship. Everybody's got needs in a relationship. How do both you and your partner get your needs met when you want different things? How do you prevent this from turning into a major relationship-threatening fight? We've got skills to help here too.

Importantly, the skills we teach you are not just what we think work. They are skills we know work because they're based on scientific data. Researchers have been studying love and relationships for a long time now, and we know a lot about how they operate, what works, and what doesn't. The same is true for how to make decisions and how to manage emotions. All the skills in this book are in line with the research evidence.

By the end of this book you'll have the skills to

- Determine what your needs are in romantic and sexual relationships,
- Determine what kind of person you want to be involved with,
- Make healthy choices about entering or exiting relationships, and
- Successfully navigate issues and potential conflicts that come up in relationships and cope with the emotions they bring.

Once you know how to do these things, not only will you be able to improve your current circumstances, you'll be ensuring yourself a healthy relationship future.

Who Are the Authors?

We're a clinical psychologist and an organizational change specialist (with an EMBA) who both are passionate about helping people have healthy relationships.

Joanne, the clinical psychologist, is a professor of psychology at Stony Brook University, a licensed clinical psychologist in private practice, and an internationally recognized expert on close relationships and mental health, particularly romantic relationships among young women. Her research has been published and presented widely in both academic and popular venues. Joanne has always been interested in the welfare of young women and particularly in conducting research and providing therapies that will help them have successful relationships and good mental health.

Kaycee, the organizational change specialist, has worked in the corporate world creating business models that help companies conduct business efficiently by taking into account both employer and employee needs and creating strategies that promote smooth relationships and healthy change. She brings those skills to her understanding of personal relationships as well. She is an avid consumer of relationship science and got interested in writing this book as she watched her daughter deal with the trials and tribulations of her own relationships.

We're thrilled to have come together to write this book for you. We believe the combination of our experience—Joanne's relationship research and clinical experience and Kaycee's expertise in workplace relationships and change management—makes us a unique and good team. We know how central relationships are to people's lives, and we understand relationships from complementary perspectives. We know and can synthesize the science to develop effective solutions, and we want to give people the skills for successful change. We see this book as an important and exciting, and personally fulfilling, way to give to you what science has to offer to help you get what you want in a relationship.

And not only do we talk the talk; we walk the walk. We use these skills in our own relationships, and we know they can work. We're excited for you to try them out for yourselves.

Is This Book for Everyone?

The skills are fundamental. They can work for everyone—people of all ages, genders, and sexual orientations. We all do better in relationships when we know what our needs are, select partners who like us for who we really are, know how to handle potential conflict, and know how to manage our emotions and cope with relationship challenges.

However, the contexts in which the skills are applied and exactly how they're applied will be different for different groups of people, and we could not do justice to them all in one book. Research shows that people of different ages, genders, and sexual orientations face a number of different decisions, transitions, relationship issues, and stressors. For example, the types of relationship problems faced and the kinds of decisions that must be made differ drastically with age—youth in high school, young adults, and people with grown children are facing some pretty different situations. There are also some important differences in dating and sexual norms for lesbian, gay, and bisexual (LGB) individuals compared to heterosexual individuals, and LGB individuals face numerous stressors that are specific to their minority status and that can present unique relationship challenges. To really make the book useful for everyone, we would have needed to include all of the relevant research, and one book simply doesn't allow the space. In addition, we would have had to illustrate the skills with a much wider variety of in-depth character stories—"token" characters would do our readers a disservice—and there was no space here for that either.

Therefore, we've written the book for a very specific population, with the hope of addressing other groups in future books. For this one, we're speaking mainly to young women involved in heterosexual relationships. This is a large group, so many of whom are looking for love and want to know how to get it right. And so many of whom are stuck in that "how can I be who he wants?" trap that we want to help them get out of. The period of about a dozen years following high school is a particularly critical one for relationships. This age range is referred to as emerging adulthood, and research indicates there are different questions to be answered and choices to be made at this phase of life than at others. One of these choices is figuring out what kind of partner and relationship you want. Because so many young women during these years are either in, or about to be in, a relationship that could set the stage for what their future will look like, the decisions they make right now have the potential to be life altering, and we want them to make healthy ones.

One more thing: even though this book is for women, it does not foster hurtful perceptions of males—there is no man bashing and no "scheming" strategies for how women should deal with men. Our strategies are meant to be respectful to both women and men, even though the book is focused on women.

How Should You Use This Book?

This book is best read from start to finish, as each chapter builds on the prior one. To help you best understand how the skills are used, the book will follow the story lines of seven characters, all of whom are based on composites of real-life stories of an ethnically diverse group of young women. You'll see them deal with different types of romantic and sexual relationships, navigate uncertainty and conflicting needs in relationships, and confront difficult issues, including insecurity, jealousy, betrayal, and relationship aggression. You may not relate to every character, but each one illustrates typical dilemmas that different women find themselves in, and their diversity of experience provides a good way to understand how broadly the skills apply.

Chapter 1 introduces the characters and provides an overview of the skills. Chapter 2 helps you begin to figure out what kind of relationship you want and provides data-based information you can use in decision making. Chapters 3–5 describe the conditions that must be met for a relationship to be healthy and provide the opportunity for you to assess your own needs in a relationship. Chapters 6–10 show you how to figure out whether you're in a healthy relationship and how to use the skills to deal effectively with relationship problems. Finally, Chapter 11 demonstrates how to put the skills into action to have a healthy relationship. Throughout the chapters, we've provided opportunities for you to do your own self-assessment and to think about how you could use the skills in your own life. Several questionnaires and checklists are available for downloading from *www.guilford.com/davila-forms* in case you want to use them more than once.

One thing that's important to know is that it takes two people to have a healthy relationship. You can have all the skills in the world, and if you're with someone who doesn't have any, it may not work. In fact it shouldn't. With the skills, you'll be able to figure that out, get out, and find someone who's better for you. That's kind of the whole point of the book. And as you use the skills, you'll be able to help your partner develop and use them too.

Our wish for you is that by the time you've finished this book you'll know yourself and what you want. You'll be able to stand up and say "This is me" and select a guy who wants what you have to offer and treats you as you deserve to be treated. And you'll use the skills to make conscious choices that are right for you so you can have the healthy relationship you want—whatever that is—that meets both your needs and his.

Can I Have the Relationship I Want?

Abig dilemma for women these days is the fact that there are so many relationship and sexual choices. And for every choice there are people who will say it's appropriate and those who will say it's not. There are those who claim you should be abstinent before marriage. Others say, "Go out and have sex with as many people as you want!" Some believe you should seek a committed, monogamous relationship for life. Others suggest you go for serial monogamy or even casual relationships. The good news is that you can pretty much have anything you want; the bad news is that you really have to know *what* you want. Often we have no idea what we want, or if we do, we have no idea how to get it or what it might bring. We know we're attracted to someone, so we go with it. Maybe we have sex right away. Or maybe we wait until we get to that "something"—a certain number of dates or drinks, a promise of exclusivity or commitment, a feeling of love, or marriage. And we always think we'll be okay with however it develops, that we'll be able to deal with all the uncertainty as it unfolds.

It doesn't always work out that way.

We all have needs, and in relationships our needs often conflict with those of our partners. We also all deal with uncertainty in relationships and sex, and every one of us has decisions to make about what to do. So how do we deal with that uncertainty? How can we learn to balance needs appropriately? By knowing what makes for a healthy relationship—by learning healthy relationship skills and knowing how to use them.

Do I want a hookup, a fuck buddy, friends with benefits (FWB), a committed relationship? Who do I want to be with, and why? Should I stay in or exit my current relationship? How do I know whether casual sex is right for me? These questions, and others like them, are important. They are questions you have to answer. Questions whose answers come from knowing yourself and your needs.

In this book, we're going to introduce you to seven characters. Lauren, Anna, and Julianne are in their mid-20s to early 30s and became friends at work. Emily, Lexi, Olivia, and Mia, all in their early 20s, graduated from high school together. Their story lines will depict a variety of relationships and dilemmas, and we'll show you how they identify their needs and use the healthy relationship skills to get them met. Because no matter what type of relationship the characters are in—or wanting or considering—the skills will help them stay in touch with who they are and what they want and help them make relationship choices and decisions that are good for them.

Lauren

Lauren's a beauty inside and out. She's stunningly gorgeous, and everyone who knows her describes her as loving, kind, and caring. She's always wanted to channel those qualities into being a wife and mother. Her ideal age to get married, settle down, and have babies is 28. She's almost there, and she's feeling the pressure of her self-imposed deadline. Because of this, Lauren's always been in relationships, trying to find the one that will lead to everlasting marriage and family. And it hasn't been hard to attract men. They flock to her wherever she goes, and she likes that. That's how she met Dan, an extremely handsome and very wealthy business owner 10 years older than Lauren. He approached her at a work event and swept her off her feet.

As she spends time with Dan she learns they share the same sense of humor. They laugh together till their stomachs ache and love to set each other off again with a reminder of something that struck them both as hilarious. Lauren finds she loves spending time with him. She meets so many interesting people when she's with him. He really has a life she is interested in sharing with him. And the conversations she has with Dan are unlike those with anybody else; anything she can say to herself she can say to him. They talk about anything and everything. He becomes her go-to guy when anything good or bad happens in her life. She tells him the story of who she is, all her secrets, everything, and he responds with acceptance of her.

Dan also gives Lauren 150% of his care. If a problem comes up, he solves it. For example, if she asks, "Do you know a good dentist?" he'll call his dentist, book the appointment, calendar it, and set up how she'll get there. She likes that. And he's so attentive! Even though he's extremely busy at work, he texts her multiple times during the day, leaving messages like "Can't wait till I'm on my way. I'll pick you up at 7; we should be there by 8!" And always after he drops her off he'll text her a good-night message, such as "You make me feel so proud," "You're so beautiful," "I'm so happy to have you in my life." Although she and Dan are still officially just dating, she is starting to see how much better her life is with him.

But it's not all bliss.

One evening, Lauren wants to go out with friends. Dan's just back in town from a business trip, and he wants to go along:

Lauren: I want to go by myself.
Dan: But I'm home. I'm finally not away, and you're out with your girlfriends.
Lauren: We don't talk about guys and other stuff if you're there—I want to talk with my girls.
Dan: You should not act like this—I do everything for you, and now you're going to blow me off when I'm back in town?

Lauren hates when he talks to her like this, and this isn't the first time it's happened.

And he also gets jealous sometimes. For example, they're at a party, this guy is talking to her and gives her his business card, and a minute later Dan pulls the business card out of her hand. She thinks he's being ridiculous, but she says nothing.

She starts to wonder whether all of this is okay with her. The way he talks to her, as if she needs to do what he says. The jealousy. Can she really start a family with this man? She's feeling confused, but still she says nothing. She starts thinking that maybe she needs to continue to keep her options open. Maybe there's someone out there who is better husband and father material.

Then one day she's attending a work conference. She goes to the dinner the company is hosting. She sees a tall, handsome, well-dressed man and wonders if he could be the one with whom to keep her options open. She catches his eye. She smiles; he smiles. She likes that. She asks if he'd like to join her at the bar. He does. His name is Lucas. They get a little drunk, and before leaving she says, laughing, "We should do this again sometime—here's my card." He smiles. As she walks away, she whispers into Lucas's ear, "Call me."

Lucas does. They start texting and go out twice. It's exciting; they connect really well. And it's scary—what about Dan and his feelings, their feelings for each other? But she tells herself she's figuring out what is best for her, what she wants to work on, be committed to. She's trying to answer the question "Who do I want to be with, and why?"

Lauren goes out of town for work. While she's away Lucas stops texting. She thinks it's odd, but she's busy with work and with Dan's texts, so she leaves it. When she gets back home, she calls him:

Lauren: You stopped texting—why? I liked it when you were (*laughing*).
Lucas: There's something I need to tell you.
Lauren: Seriously. Really? (*thinking he's going to say he's married*).
Lucas: My wife and I broke up. I miss her like crazy. I'm sad. I'm not over her.
Lauren: When?
Lucas: Two years ago.
Lauren: Have you tried to get back with her?
Lucas: She's moved on.

Lauren couldn't say, "You should have told me." He just had, and after only two dates. She's sad. She wanted to see what it would be like to be with him. She feels drawn to him and connected to him. So much so that she makes a decision: "I will guide him through this—be a friend, be supportive—and this will make him love me. I will be patient, and he will come around." It worked.

Kinda.

Anna

Anna didn't go to college, and it's taken her a while to figure out what kind of life she wants. She's working and taking business courses part-time. Lately, she's been watching friends meet, get engaged, marry, and get to "happily ever after" (presumably!). Seriously, she's going to be a bridesmaid in four weddings next year, and she's constantly answering everyone's question: "When are you going to get married?" Although she knows that marriage and "happily ever after" are her next steps, there's no ticking clock for her.

Anna meets Eric while out celebrating a friend's birthday. There's chemistry, and they hook up. She's really attracted to him, he's really funny, and—she's happy to find out—the sex is amazing! The next day he texts:

Eric: Do you like to sext?
Anna: Yeah, I do.
Eric: Great, this will be fun!
Anna: :)

She loves their flirt—their texts and hookups are exciting, and they can't seem to get enough of each other.

Anna finds herself in love with Eric. Passionate. Intense. So. Much. Fun. Going out on his boat, hanging out with friends, walking the beach at sunset, late nights sitting around his fire pit—she loves it! It's only been a couple of months, but she's all in and already thinking about the future. Fast-forward to two months later: Eric stops initiating—no more texts, no calls. Anna is confused. It seems he's gone from totally into her to totally not. She calls Julianne:

Anna: Eric's stopped texting and calling.
Julianne: So call him to see what's up. You like him. He likes you.
Anna: I think I have to assume he's not interested and he's probably seeing someone else. He's obviously ignoring me.
Julianne: Maybe, but you need to find out. You need to let him know what you're thinking—you secretly think you're exclusive, don't you? You didn't tell him what you wanted, did you?
Anna: Haha—no, I didn't, and yeah, I was hoping we were exclusive. Why isn't he calling me?!
Julianne: Maybe to see if you'll call him.
Anna: I hate games.
Julianne: You're playing the game too—when will it be okay for you to call him?
Anna: When he's called me enough, I can call him.
Julianne: That's ridiculous. You're not being up front with him.
Anna: I just don't want to feel like I'm chasing him.

Anna unknowingly buys into gender stereotypes—like the guy has to be the one to pursue her—and she uses those stereotypes to protect herself. She'll let the guy initiate because that's what guys "should do," and it protects her from having to risk putting herself out there and possibly getting hurt. But it doesn't always work.

Julianne texts her later in the week: "Go to Eric's Facebook. Some girl is posting pictures with him. Haven't you called him?" (*No, she hasn't.*)

Anna takes a break at work, goes outside to call Eric. He picks up:

Anna: I saw your Facebook pix with that girl. So you're cheating on me with someone?
Eric: What? You never told me you wanted to be exclusive. Plus, I was the one who was always calling you! She's really interested in me. It didn't seem like you were.
Anna: What do you mean? I was totally interested in you. Why didn't you tell me?
Eric: Why should I have to tell you? I realized I liked Lizzie better. You and I are in different places in our lives. Lizzie and I aren't. She makes me happy.
Anna: You should have told me! You're pathetic! I'm disgusted with you. You two deserve each other!

After Anna hangs up, she feels sick. She now gets that she misunderstood what was happening. She thought he was cheating, but he was actually done with her. He wanted to see her all the time, he called her all the time, and then he didn't. What happened? She hates herself for telling him he was pathetic. She didn't want any of this to happen—she was so passionately in love with him. Why did he change?

She goes to lunch with Lauren:

Lauren: You okay?
Anna: It's crazy. I don't get it—he's totally into me, then he's not.
Lauren: What did he say?
Anna: That he didn't think I was really into him, and that we were in different places in
    our lives and he wasn't happy with that.
Lauren: What? Did you ask him what he meant?
Anna: No, I told him he was a pathetic loser. I said, "You disgust me. You two deserve
    each other." I guess I was kind of a bitch.
Lauren: He deserved it—come on, how he treated you?!
Anna: What would you have said?
Lauren: Probably the same, but I would've told him how I feel and pushed him more on
    why he wasn't happy and how come he seemed to change his mind so abruptly.
    And also why didn't he tell you?
Anna: Yeah, I guess. I just didn't want to push him. I didn't want to upset him more.

Missing Eric is debilitating for Anna. It's hard to get out of bed, hard to go to work. She goes back and forth between never wanting to see or talk to him again and desperately wishing she could see and talk with him again. Be careful what you wish for.

She runs into him at a bar while she's trying to drink the hurt away. But it seems she might not have to. He's all over her, flirting, talking, acting the way he used to when they were together. She remembers her conversation with Lauren and asks:

Anna: So, where's the love of your life? I thought you were so happy.
Eric: I was. She had a career. A stable job. And those things are important to me, but
    she turned out to be a bitch.

Anna has no words.

Anna's confused. She thinks to herself, "Huh? I don't have those things, but he's here with me flirting like we used to." She so wants him to like her, to want her, and he's acting as if he does. She just wants it to be true. When he suggests they hook up, she goes for it. Sex is awesome again, and they jump right back into the intensity of their flirtation. Fast-forward one month: she's pregnant.

Julianne

Julianne's recently finished an MBA program while working for a consulting company that rethinks and fine-tunes a client's market strategy. She loves her career and gives it priority in her life. She's trying to better balance career and life—her friends and family are always on her about this—but she knows she needs a guy who appreciates and accepts her career goals and how hard she works.

Fortunately, she meets Gregory at a mutual friend's party one Saturday night. They spark and exchange numbers. The next Friday, she has plans to go out with Lauren, who cancels. Julianne really feels like going out and doing something fun and interesting. She thinks, "I want to go out with Gregory to see if there is anything there. Hmm . . . Why not? I'm going to ask him out and see what happens." So she does, and it is great! They can't stop talking. He misses his train home, and she invites him over for a couch sleepover. The next morning they make breakfast. She says, "Last night was really fun—I really liked being with you," and he says, "Me too." YAY! She is going to Anna's for dinner that night, so she invites him, and after that they start dating regularly.

Gregory has become a welcome distraction from work, with lots of flirtatious coffee meetings at Starbucks and late-night dinners after working all day. He's as involved in his career as she is in hers. In fact, he just got a fantastic new job. He texts:

Gregory: Just left old job for new WAY BETTER job. Excited. Wanna celebrate my win?
Julianne: I'm in! When? Where?

He meets her in the lobby of the building where she works. They walk to get her car.

Gregory: Julianne, you parked in the wrong spot in the lot.
Julianne: Why do you say that?
Gregory: This spot is in the darkest place. It's not safe.

Sweet, she thinks.

Three months in: Julianne's happily working on career–love balance. She loves the sex, the cuddling, and all the things they do together. He's introduced her to his family. She's introduced him to hers. They both work a lot, so neither one pressures the other about that. But they're still working out how to be together. For example, according to Gregory she keeps getting coffee from the wrong Starbucks. And last night he complained she didn't have enough sour cream for the baked potatoes and she had green onions, not chives. Tonight she's taking him out for dinner. She gets into the car:

Julianne: Where do you want to go?
Gregory: I don't care. You pick.

Julianne: I feel like Thai, you?

Gregory: Yeah, I love Thai.

Julianne: Turn here; there's a good Thai place just up the street.

Gregory: I don't like that place.

Julianne: Okay, make a left; there's that new Thai place just up the hill.

Gregory: I went. I didn't like it.

Julianne: Okay, you care where we go for Thai food, so you pick.

Gregory: There's one out by my place. You can stay over.

Julianne: Baby, that's an hour away. I have to be at work by 6 a.m. to finish something up before my first meeting. Let's not do Thai. Let's go to that barbecue place you really like, have ribs.

Gregory: I don't feel like that either. Let's just go home.

They don't end up going to dinner. She's confused about why they can't make their way through simple decisions. Maybe he doesn't deal well with uncertainty, as though if he makes a decision and it doesn't turn out well, he'll feel bad about it. She's not sure.

Eight months in: They're on their way to an out-of-town wedding. Julianne is driving and she's already Googled directions:

Gregory: Where are you going?

Julianne: I'm following Google.

Gregory: You're going the wrong way. Turn here—we'll get to the freeway this way.

Julianne: Do you know how to get to the freeway from here?

Gregory: No, but I'll figure it out. You're driving in the wrong lane—slow down.

Julianne: Read the directions—there were three ways to get to the freeway from your house. I picked the way that had the shortest time. If we get lost, we'll be late.

Gregory: I wanted to go up yesterday. I told you that.

Julianne: I couldn't go. I had that meeting.

Gregory: Forget it. Just drive.

She does. But he can't let it go: "You've gone the wrong way." "Don't you know where you are?" "You've basically gone in a circle. You're going too slow. We'll be late." They're at a stoplight and she screams at him as if she's lost it, "Stop it! Shut up! I'm a good driver. I'm the one with the directions." They finally get to the freeway, and it's clear that Google has taken them in a roundabout way. But Gregory has to point that out again and again.

Julianne: What happened?

Gregory: You didn't listen.

Julianne: That's helpful. You didn't know where you were going. I had directions.

Gregory: If we're late, it's your fault.

Julianne: I'm trying to find a way for this not to happen again. I feel sick. I don't even want to go to the wedding, and I was so excited about it earlier.
Gregory: I wanted to leave yesterday.
Julianne: Do you think this is all my fault?
Gregory: Yes. You don't listen.

She wants to yell, call him names, she is so angry; she thinks to herself, "He makes me feel as if nothing I ever do is right or good enough." Does he want her to defer to him? Is he right? Does she not listen? Maybe she should have listened to him and turned right? She's so confused. Yet she squeezes his hand and says, "I love you. Let's just go into the hotel and get ready for the prewedding dinner." Even though she feels sick inside, she posts happy pictures of them and his friends having fun at the dinner. The comments range from "You guys look so happy—nice to see" to "When are we going to be at your prewedding dinner?"

Gregory asks Julianne to marry him.

Emily

Will is Emily's first love. They got together during their junior year in high school. She had dated before, but Will was the first guy she really connected with. They confided in each other. They helped each other through hard times. They really seemed to "get" each other, and they loved being together. They were everyone's favorite couple. As individuals, they also were smart and ambitious. They each had big college plans, but not for the same schools. Will got a scholarship to a prestigious university out of state where he'd be premed. Emily was going to a local state school with her best friend, Mia, to study business. Emily and Will talked about breaking up. They couldn't. They went for a long late-night walk and talked about how certain they were that they were going to spend the rest of their lives together. Will even kicked around the idea of their moving in together after college, the summer before he started medical school. They talked about how using Skype and FaceTime would be a lifesaver when it came to staying in touch and how seeing the other person would really make a difference. And then they left for college.

At first it was okay, but by the end of first semester Emily stopped feeling secure. She believes if a guy loves you, he'll make time for you, he'll call you, and he'll text you out of the blue to see how you are, like Will always did before he left for college. But recently Will had been doing that less and less. He said it was because he was busy with school, but she was busy too and she still made time to keep in touch, so she started to feel insecure. She started playing the "He loves me, he loves me not" game. Her constant questioning of his love for her drove them both crazy and led to a lot of conflict. They tried to work it out over winter break, but it started all over again in second semester, and finally they decided to break up. They were both hurt and angry and felt disconnected from each other and sick of the drama.

Fast-forward 18 months. It's the summer before junior year, and Emily runs into Will at a party. He had come home for the summer this year (unlike last year, when he stayed to take summer classes). They talked, and it was just like old times, the good times, where they connected so easily. They embraced, and the sexual sparks were as strong as ever. They admitted that they had never stopped thinking about each other. They spent the summer together getting to know one another again, each excited by the other's life and goals, and they decided they wanted to try again.

The first semester goes great. They're riding the high of being together again. But this is junior year—the year that really counts for med school applications—and Will's availability starts to wane again in spring semester. He's stopped replying to her texts again. Even the sexts. In the past Will loved when she sent sexy pictures on Snapchat. She would get a text-back such as "Damn! You just made my day, Baby. Love and miss you." He hasn't replied to one of those in a while. Not surprisingly, Emily's insecurity starts to resurface. That old idea that if he really loved her he'd make the time sticks in her head. The next time he fails to reply, she texts:

Emily: I. HATE. U.
Will: Sorry I haven't texted much. Extra course this semester. U. KNOW. THAT.
Emily: Why can't u take 5 minutes to text back?
Will: Do u need me to text every minute, every hour, every day to feel secure?
Emily: NO. Just reply!
Will: I am so tired. I'm sorry. I can't do this now.
Emily: Are u still coming next weekend?
Will: Yes.
Emily: Do u love me?
Will: Luv and miss u very much and can't wait to see you.
Emily: Me 2!

Emily Skypes Lexi:

Lexi: Did Will text you back?
Emily: Yes, he's coming next weekend. I can't wait.
Lexi: You didn't text him first "I. HATE. YOU." Again did you? (*laughing*) You know that pisses him off.
    (*Emily doesn't know what to say.*)
Lexi: (*laughing*) You did, didn't you!
Emily: He was being a jerk! I do kind of feel like an idiot about it, though.
Lexi: So why do you keep doing it?

Emily: Because he's so frustrating. I can't believe he can't take a minute to text me back!

Lexi: Listen, he still has med school ahead of him.

Emily: I know, but I could move with him and get a job where he is then. I hate long-distance, not him!

Lexi: But is that going to be good for your career? You're doing that great internship and you know they're likely to hire you when you graduate. I thought you said that was your dream job?

Emily: There are lots of good jobs. I wouldn't be happy without Will. Even in my dream job.

Lexi: Well, let's see if you and Will can even stay together through college first.

Lexi

She hasn't had a boyfriend since her ex from high school, Jake. Emily finally convinced her to go out with Dex, a lawyer she met, but Lexi never really gave it a real chance because she was still struggling to get over Jake. Although the relationship with Dex was short-lived (he moved away for a job), it did allow her to start to move on. That she could have fun times and good sex with another guy made her realize that maybe she was more over Jake than she thought. She's not sure how to classify the relationship with Dex: Was he really her boyfriend or just an ongoing hookup? But maybe classifying it doesn't matter. Being with Dex gave her some perspective and allowed her to recognize that it was probably time to start thinking about getting back in the dating and relationship game.

In the meantime, Lexi is living her single-girl life and pursuing her career. She's taking courses in broadcasting at a local school while working at a radio station and writing sports copy. She loves it. She misses spending time with her best friends (Emily, Mia, and Olivia, who all go to college), but they still talk as much as they can, and Mia still finds a way to keep bugging her to try casual sex (she doesn't want to; it's just not her thing). Emily keeps telling her to go out with this guy she knows at work, but Lexi doesn't have strong feelings for him. And then there's this guy she might want to date, but he doesn't seem interested. Mia finally convinces her to sign up for online dating, but then she gets to this question:

"When it comes to dating, what best describes your intent?"

1. I'm looking for casual dating, no commitment.
2. I want to date but nothing serious.
3. I want a relationship.
4. I am putting in a serious effort to find someone.
5. I am serious and want to find someone to marry.

Lexi talks to Mia about what to pick:

Lexi: What number should I put?

Mia: Four. "I am putting in a serious effort to find someone."

Lexi: I want to start off at 2: date, nothing serious.

Mia: Come on—if you'd really moved on from Jake, you'd at least want 3: a relationship.

Lexi: Maybe, but I don't even know if I want to get married or have kids, so I'm going to pick 2: date, nothing serious.

Mia: Two is fuck buddies. You're such a relationship person—pick 3.

Lexi: Is the number I pick about how you start a relationship or what you want a relationship to turn into?

Mia: (*laughing*) This is about what you secretly want—(A) not looking for any type of relationship or (B) looking for a relationship.

Lexi: I'm a B. Which one are you?

Mia: A. I don't even know what city I want to live in when I graduate. How do you expect me to choose anything regarding a guy?

Lexi: Hmm . . .

Mia: Start at 4 and then, if you want 3, change it.

Lexi's online dating profile:

Headline: Want to find out if you're for me and I'm for you?

Description: I want to be a TV sportscaster in the football locker rooms covering all of the highlights. Broadcasting is my passion. I'm attending sports events and loving my radio gig. Yoga fanatic, yes, but I love hiking to burn calories for all the cookies I like to bake. Movies are a must, *Arrested Development*, *True Blood* (Sookie should have ended up with Bill, i.e., #notteameric). Love Rihanna & Beyoncé. Salted caramels are my favorite! I don't drink a lot. I'm spontaneous, kind and smart. Athletic in my own right, I can hold my own in any given situation. You don't have to pay for everything—I'm good at sharing. Tall, dark-haired, fit are all nice, but smart, kindhearted, and honest are musts.

Ideal First Date: Meet up at a sports event.

Lexi can't believe it—she gets 150 messages. She sifts through them, short-listing six. Flirting/talking with all of them at the same time, trying to figure out which one she wants, is exhausting. Finally, she settles on James, a marketing and management grad student, because he *loves* to watch and play sports, sounds easygoing (not controlling), is physically fit, and mostly because he messaged her, saying, "I'd love to listen to your 'sports-talk' while on our first game date and, if you're good at it, on the next one."

Lexi starts thinking "Does he like me?" She texts Emily:

Lexi: So what can I say that won't scare him away?
Emily: Nothing. Ask your dad for his tickets. Invite him to the game.
Lexi: I'm not making the first move.
Emily: Why not?
Lexi: Because he's the guy. What if he doesn't like it when women initiate? I want him to like me. Not just think I want sex.
Emily: Stop it. Your profile pick was "4: I am putting in a serious effort to find someone." Text Mia. She'll know how you can make the first move without looking like you are.
Lexi: Okay.
Emily: Remember, you don't even know if you like him!

Mia suggests Lexi text James with the date, place, and start time of the game and then ask him if he wants to go. Lexi is sitting there staring at her phone, thinking, "What if he feels intimidated or is put off by me asking him out?" She decides to text him this: "I'm ready to 'sports-talk'—you ready to listen?"

Mia

If there is one thing Mia learned in high school, it's this: if you want a boyfriend, you have to find someone who wants to be a boyfriend. She's had her heart broken twice now, so she is very wary and careful and doesn't assume hookups lead to relationships. And right now, she's good with that. She doesn't want a serious boyfriend. She's in college and wants to play the field, so the hookup culture is working for her.

She'd known Corey for a while. He was a grad student and would be completing his master's soon and looking for a job. She'd hooked up with many of his friends, but not him. She didn't have any initial feelings of attraction to him and considered him just a friend. One night, after a lot of gin and tonics, she ran into him, and one thing led to another and they hooked up. It was good. It turned into a regular two- or three-times-a-week hookup. Then they started going to the movies, making dinner for each other, and staying together at his apartment. She started to wonder what he was really looking for—a serious relationship, a fuck buddy? And she started to question what she wanted too. She hadn't been hooking up with anyone else for a while now, and she was feeling comfortable with that. She wanted to make sure they had the same expectations. Honesty was key for her in any type of relationship. But before she had the chance to raise the issue, Corey beat her to it:

Corey: I have something to tell you.

Mia: (*As soon as he says this, she knows it's going to be one of two things—either "It's been nice but . . . " or "I want to be serious."*) What is it?

Corey: I love you.

Mia: Wow. (*smiling, but feeling awkward*) I guess I'm not quite there yet, but I'm feeling like I can get there. I'm ready to be exclusive, though, if that's what you're wanting too.

Exclusive. She knows that's a big step, and she wonders what this will mean for her, for them. They never had to put any limits in place or even talk about limits. They were just happy doing their thing. Neither of them had taken down their online dating profiles. She'd seen him check out other women, and she'd checked out other men. Would this need to change? In line with her desire for honesty about what they both wanted, what their expectations were, she told him, "I want you to share what you're thinking—tell me straight up. I want you to be honest, not lie to protect my feelings." Mia's request was honored a few months later. Corey got a job offer in a different city (his hometown), and they agreed he'd move, but they'd stay together. A few weeks later at dinner he said, "There's this girl from my past. When I posted I was moving home, she messaged me. She wants to hook up. How do you feel about that?" Mia felt jealous at the thought of him with another woman; then she felt aroused, so she asked some questions:

Mia: Do you want to do it?

Corey: Yeah, kinda.

Mia: Why? What does this mean for us?

Corey: It's just a way to deal with long distance. I think it will be difficult for both of us to not have sex while we're away from each other. I want to keep sharing everything with you. I don't want us to cheat, betray one another, lose our connection. That would be the worst thing for me.

Mia: Me too. So are we still exclusive or is this an open relationship or . . . ?

Corey: Yes and no. Maybe we can have some free passes where we can each have sex with someone else.

Mia: Hmm . . . I don't think I'm comfortable with you hooking up with a girl from your past. I'm afraid it won't just be sex. I might be okay with you hooking up with just a random person. Let me think about this more.

Olivia

Olivia lives in a sorority house, just as her mom did. But sorority life has been hard. When she first started college, to fit in, she tried out so many different looks, tried to be so many different people, had started to drink a lot because that's her school's culture. But she's done with that now, and she's learned to live with her sorority sisters making fun of her because she won't put out. Olivia's read Meg Jay's book *The Defining Decade: Why Your Twenties Matter—And How to Make the Most of Them Now*. She's taken to heart the idea expressed in the book that the best time to work on her marriage is before she has one. Olivia takes that to mean becoming better informed about what type of person she wants to marry, so she wants to try to figure that out. What's more, she really wants to find herself and her soul mate in college. Someone she can go through life with, wherever that may take them. But the soul mate has yet to be found.

Then Olivia's at a party. She sees this guy across the room. It's as if the stars suddenly align. He approaches her. His name is Zach. They talk, feel instant chemistry. They flirt, her knees go weak. She can't even look him in the eye. He asks her back to his room, but scared of what that would lead to, she makes a quick getaway, telling him to find her on Facebook. She goes over to where Emily is, points Zach out, and then tells her what just happened.

Emily: Hahaha, you want to make out with him right now—I can tell!

Olivia: I had to think quickly. I didn't even know what I was saying. How is he even going to Facebook me?! Fuck, he doesn't even know my full name!

Emily: Don't worry, it wouldn't take much searching to find you. If he doesn't know your name, he'll ask someone if he's really interested. Or you could just go over there right now and give him your number.

Olivia doesn't. She wants to, but she can't bring herself to do it. So Emily gets his last name, and Olivia is soon flipping through his photos from last year. She doesn't know what to do about her Zach daydreams. He's always on her mind now; he's all she can think about. Emily learns that Mia knows Zach, so Olivia purposely runs into her and brings him up. Mia smiles:

Mia: Zach. Noooooooooooooooooo. . . . (*laughing*).

Olivia: Stop it. (*laughing*).

Mia: Emily told me you're waiting for him to make the first move. Guys like him don't ask girls out in college.

Olivia: What do you mean?

Mia: Girls, *you know*, lure him in, coax him to be with them by having sex with him.

Olivia: Tell me about him.

Mia: He sits around with his roommates for endless hours drinking and playing video games and studying. He's smart, top in most of his classes.

Olivia: How can I get him to hang out with me without having to have sex too quickly?

Mia: I'd say jump him, hook up, but I know you don't do that.

Olivia: I have sex with limits. I respect myself.

Mia: What? Because I hook up, I don't respect myself? Stop judging me.

Olivia: I'm not! I don't believe in casual sex with just any guy. It's just a personal choice.

Mia: Okay. Well, I do believe in having some random sex. That doesn't mean I don't respect myself. It's consensual and a good stress reliever.

Olivia: Okay, fine. We're just different.

Mia: Anyway, I think Zach's house is having a party this weekend—they're getting a keg. Let's go together.

At the party Olivia really wants to talk to Zach, but she is scared for some reason; she's actually shaking. Reminiscent of the old days, she takes a shot to calm her nerves, and then another. Emily says, "Slow down with the liquid courage!" Olivia doesn't. Finally, she walks across the room to where Zach is and starts talking to him. He seems really nice and asks her to come up to his room to look at something. She follows him.

Good Relationships, Healthy Relationships

As you can see, each of the women is facing different relationship issues. Each of them has a dilemma to deal with. They all want to have the relationship they've always dreamed of. They all want things to work out, to have a "good" relationship. Hasn't every one of us been in that situation, where we really hoped things would work out but they didn't? Then we question what went wrong and whose fault it was. We wonder, "Why can't I have the relationship I've always longed for? How do I get what I want?" We wrote this book because we believe every one of us can have the relationship we want. We can have that "good" relationship. A good relationship is a healthy relationship, and throughout this book we're going to teach you the skills you will need to have one.

So, let's start with talking about what a healthy relationship looks like. Most women can name concepts that make for a healthy relationship. If you were to ask yourself or your friends, you would all likely name things like *respect, good communication, intimacy, security, positive regard.* And you'd be right. Indeed, women can identify concepts that make for a healthy relationship, but the problem is that concepts are abstract—they're not concrete—and this makes it difficult to know how to put them into practice. For example, are you creating healthy intimacy in your relationship? Is your partner behaving in ways that convey respect and positive regard and that allow you to feel secure? How do you know? It can be tough to know, right? In this book, we'll help you learn how to take a healthy approach to relationships so that you will know how to put the concepts into practice. And when you learn how to take that approach by using the skills in this book, you'll start to see that a healthy relationship is possible for you.

You may have noticed we didn't include love in the list of concepts that make for a healthy relationship. Is a healthy relationship about love? For sure it includes love—hopefully deep, passionate, knock-me-down love. But is love enough for a healthy relationship? No, it's not. Love is not enough to make the relationship you want work. Love without skills will render you powerless and leave what might have been an amazing relationship withering away and making you miserable.

We are going to help you learn a healthy approach to relationships by focusing on three key skills: *insight*, *mutuality*, and *emotion regulation*. Throughout this book we'll show you how these skills are used—to understand who you are, what your needs are, and what your preferences are for getting them met (Chapters 3, 4, and 5); to resolve relationship conflicts (Chapter 6); to assess whether you're in a healthy relationship (Chapters 7 and 8); to make stay-or-go decisions (Chapter 9); and to deal with feelings of lovesickness (Chapter 10). But first we'll explain what these skills are.

INSIGHT

Insight means knowing yourself—knowing who you are, what you are like, what you need, and why you act the way you do. It means learning from your mistakes. It means thinking about the potential consequences of your actions. It means looking ahead a little and seeing what the positive and negative consequences of being in a particular relationship might be. And it means knowing who your partner is too, what his needs are, and why he acts the way he does.

We're not taught how to ask—and *honestly* answer—questions designed to find out what each of us is like and what we're really looking for in a relationship. Sure, we can all reflect, to some extent, on what kind of guy we want to be with, but a lot of things get in the way of really being honest about ourselves and our partners and really knowing and sticking with our priorities. We need to look carefully at questions like these:

- "What is my idea of a good relationship?"
- "What type of relationship do I want?"
- "What kind of person am I?"
- "What do I really need from a boyfriend?"
- "What are my limits?"

We need to ask ourselves and our partners these questions, and we need honest answers, because those answers are what give us insight. Insight gives us power to get what we need and to make healthy decisions, and those things can help us have a healthy relationship.

Let's turn to Anna for an example. How did she find herself being blindsided by Eric's behavior and then hooking up with him again without even understanding why he did what he had done? The answer is she didn't use the skill of insight.

When Anna was making a boyfriend choice with Eric, she focused on the experience of chemistry, flirting, and sex with Eric, then quickly jumping into love without ever examining what Eric was feeling and wanting and what kind of person he really was. Since any guy is going to have both healthy and unhealthy behaviors, it's hard to know whether the guy you're with is right for you, especially at the beginning, when it's easy to see only the good things. Anna got swept away in the chemistry, but there were lots of questions about the kind of person Eric was that Anna didn't ask. It's easy for this to happen. At the beginning of relationships, we're often not thinking about anything other than how hot he is and how we feel when we're with him. That's an insight mistake.

What's worse for Anna is that she didn't learn from this mistake—and that's insight mistake number two. She jumped right back into love, even after he had told her that, in important ways, she was not what he was looking for. And why did she do it? Because she desperately wanted to be liked by him. She felt that she needed his love, but she wasn't focused on what she really needed in a relationship.

So let's talk needs. Needs are beautiful things. They help us understand how to apply concepts like security, intimacy, respect, good communication, and positive regard, which are key features of healthy relationships. And needs help us know how to set our standards and what to do when a relationship doesn't meet them. If Anna really knew what she needed—for example, to be with someone she could trust, who would care about her feelings—and if she had used that insight to set her standards (like "I won't tolerate being with someone who doesn't treat me in a caring, consistent way"), then she might not have tolerated the way Eric was behaving, and she might not have been blinded by their chemistry. She could have questioned him about his behavior and used that information to make an insight-informed decision about how to proceed. We'll talk about needs a lot more in the coming chapters so that you can set your own standards to guide your expectations and limits.

MUTUALITY

Mutuality means behaving in a way that takes into account the needs of both people in a relationship—in a way that conveys that both people's needs are important and in a way that ensures both people's needs are being attended to. When a relationship is mutual, both people feel respected and cared for, and they both feel as if they are getting what they need.

Julianne and Gregory struggle with mutuality. She's starting to think

Gregory always believes he's right and she's wrong, so she's not feeling respected. When he says things like "You parked in the wrong spot," "You got coffee from the wrong Starbucks," "You're driving in the wrong lane, you're going too fast/too slow, you're not going the right way, go this way," she feels as though nothing she ever does is good enough for him. And when she communicates this to him, he defends himself and says he's right. In all of these instances, Gregory is focused only on himself and his needs. He thinks he is focused on Julianne's needs, but he is trying to define her needs for her rather than listen to the ones she really has and accept her choices.

A similar thing happens when they try to plan a shared activity, like the time Julianne wanted to take him out for Thai food. He didn't want to follow through on the plans because he was focused on what was right for him (a Thai restaurant close to where he lives), not what was right for each of them (any other restaurant in the city so Julianne could be at work at 6 a.m.). And in all of these instances, their communication is problematic. Gregory ends up defending himself and blaming Julianne, and Julianne ends up yelling at him or, sometimes, steaming quietly.

Couples can't communicate well if they don't understand mutuality. Being mutual is the foundation of good communication. When people take a mutual approach to communication, they can have open, two-way conversations, where they listen without judgment, put themselves in the other person's shoes so they can see each other's perspective, take turns talking, and adjust their perspective when the other raises good points. When Julianne tells Gregory what she wants and he tells her it's the wrong thing, he's not taking a mutual approach to communication. Instead, he's communicating, "What I need is important; what you need is not." That's not healthy because it's not mutual. If either person in a relationship doesn't respect the other's feelings, needs, likes, dislikes, or goals, it's not a mutual, healthy relationship. When one partner makes the other feel less adequate, less important, less valuable, that's not mutual and it's not healthy.

Being mutual communicates respect—respect for your partner and, equally important, respect for yourself. When Gregory ignores Julianne's needs and she doesn't speak up for herself about that, she is communicating to Gregory that she doesn't respect herself. She is prioritizing his needs above hers. Now, although it's true that both partners' needs can't always be met at once, and sometimes one person's needs may take precedence (in Chapter 6 we'll tell you how to figure out the who, what, and when of this), if Julianne is compromising something that is a key need for her, such as her need for Gregory to accept her decisions, she is not engaged in a mutual relationship. If Julianne wants to be in a mutual relationship, she has to negotiate to get her needs met.

How can she do that? Julianne should clearly and calmly tell Gregory what she wants and why: "When we make a plan, like to go to dinner, and you can't have things exactly as you want, I'd like you to not criticize all of my ideas and to be willing to negotiate something that we can both accept and follow through on." Then she needs to let him know how she feels about his behavior: "I feel hurt when you find fault with all of my ideas and when you're not willing to compromise with me." Then she must listen to his reasons for not compromising and honestly evaluate those reasons. If he doesn't have any good reasons for finding fault with her choices and not compromising, reasons that are reassuring to her, then Julianne must choose between respecting her own needs—that is, respecting herself— and not respecting them. If Julianne is not able to happily accept how she is being treated by Gregory, she can use her unmet need to make a healthy exit choice.

It's hard to know when we can work things out with a boyfriend and when we can't. Will we know based on love? We can have a tendency to use "but I love him" as a reason to stay, but that can get us into trouble because we end up tolerating anything. As we said above, love is not enough. Understanding our needs and what's important to us is a better guide. When the relationship is not mutual and important needs are not being met, you have to ask yourself, "Do I stay or do I go?" Given how important it is to Julianne to have Gregory accept her decisions, she can ask herself, "What would be a good reason to stay?" and if she doesn't answer something like "I can trust that he is going to consistently negotiate with me (not just sometimes) without criticizing or shooting down all of my ideas," then she needs to develop her mutuality skills; otherwise, she'll be compromising her need to be accepted.

EMOTION REGULATION

Relationships come with many feelings—excitement, happiness, love, joy, sadness, anxiety, worry, embarrassment. Sometimes those feelings are easy to manage. At other times they feel overwhelming, even out of control. Sometimes we like feeling them. At other times we want to push them away or are afraid to have them. What we do with our feelings is called emotion regulation, and healthy emotion regulation is important to our well-being and our relationships.

Healthy emotion regulation involves being aware of your emotions, feeling in control of them (not acting impulsively), being able to keep things that happen in your relationship in perspective (low drama), and maintaining self-respect and commitment to your needs in the face of emotional challenges (like fights or breakups). Healthy emotion regulation also involves meeting your needs yourself and with others—not just your boyfriend—by turning to friends for support, engaging in active problem solving (rather than just ruminating about things), balancing "head and heart," and learning how to take care of yourself with comforting activities and healthy "self-talk." We'll tell you more about how to do all of these things in later chapters. For now, if you think you have difficulty with emotion regulation, know that you're hardly alone:

Not only was Anna struggling with low insight, but she was letting her emotions get the best of her with Eric. Her intense attraction to him and her deep desire to be loved clouded her thinking. Her heart had completely taken over her head, resulting in her trying to drink away her feelings and then dismissing her concerns so she could be with him again.

Olivia did something similar with Zach. She was so nervous about seeing him at the party that she used alcohol to try to calm herself and give herself the courage to talk with him, but it may have resulted in her doing something against her own values.

Emily has trouble with emotion regulation too. When her feelings of anxious insecurity come up, she immediately acts impulsively with Will by texting him "I. HATE. YOU." But that only makes Will upset and more distant, thereby fueling Emily's fears. In addition, Emily feels guilty and embarrassed afterward. This can hurt both her self-respect and their relationship.

With improved skill at managing their emotions, these women could make decisions that would be healthier for them and their relationships.

USING THE SKILLS TO DEVELOP YOUR PERSONAL POWER

Personal power involves knowing what your needs are, learning what it feels like to get them met, and using that self-knowledge to make deliberate choices to meet them. Women need to be able to make choices with intention. Practicing the skills—developing insight, being mutual, regulating our emotions—will allow us to get our needs met and develop a sense of personal power. In line with this, we call the skills "I/ME skills"—I for insight, M for mutuality, and E for emotion regulation. You'll see in the following paragraphs and throughout the book how "I" and "ME" will be an important focus of your attention in developing your personal power. They reflect a key message of this book: You can't have a healthy relationship without asking yourself "What do I need?" and "How well is this relationship working for ME?" Throughout the book, you'll encounter I/ME sidebars with information that will provide insight and help you use the skills to your greatest benefit.

There are three conditions that must be in place for us to develop personal power and to have a healthy relationship:

1. "I know and like myself." Knowing and liking yourself means knowing what your needs are, respecting those needs, and being able to meet those needs for yourself.
2. "I know and like him." Knowing and liking him means you are confident that he is the guy you want, and you treat him in a way that shows you like and respect him.
3. "He knows and likes me." This means you are with a guy who wants what you have to offer, and he treats you in a way that shows he likes and respects you.

These statements may sound simple, but achieving these conditions is not. A woman may think, for example, that he's what she wants, but what evidence is she using to determine that? In the coming chapters, we're going to show you how to really assess whether these three conditions exist in a particular relationship. We're going to show you how to identify and use evidence.

We're also going to show you how to use the I/ME skills to shift your focus from "Am I good enough?" and "Can I be who he wants?" to "I know and like myself" and "I can stand up and say, 'This is me and I can ask for what I want.'" Remember when Olivia was afraid to contact Zach before he contacted her because she thought he might see her as too forward? And when Anna wanted Eric to do all the initiating because she was protecting herself from potential rejection? And when Lauren didn't say anything to Dan about how his jealous behavior impacted her? They were all acting from a position of "Can I be who he wants?" That is not a position of personal power.

In the next chapter you'll start the process of developing your personal power by gaining insight into what you want and starting to know your needs. Always remember, you're responsible for building your personal power. You do that by deliberately working at understanding who you are and what you need. And then you take this personal power and use it when you're making choices, always paying attention to the consequences of your choices, both negative and positive, because doing so teaches us even more about who we are and what we need and increases our chances of having a healthy relationship.

2

What Do I Want?

In Chapter 1 you saw seven women trying to deal with uncertainty about what they wanted from their relationships and sex. They were getting involved in both casual and potentially serious long-term relationships that could define their lives, and they had some decisions to make. Take Anna, for example. After she told Eric she was pregnant, and the initial shock wore off, he proposed that they marry, and she agreed. This is a major decision. (And we'll come back to how it goes for her later.)

There are a number of different ways for women to start and conduct relationships, and they need to figure out what is right for them. Are you the type of person who wants marriage or a similar type of committed, monogamous relationship? Do you want a series of casual hookups with no strings attached? Do you want to date and get to know a few different guys at once? Do you want to hook up to see if it could lead to a relationship? Could you see yourself ending up in a long-distance relationship?

It's also important that you start thinking about what, if anything, you want to achieve before you settle down into a potentially serious long-term relationship. Do you want, for example, to finish school, land your first real job, buy a place of your own, develop financial independence, travel?

Whatever options you're considering, it's important to make an informed, thoughtful decision. There are pressures out there. Pressures from family and friends. Socioculturally driven pressures. And the media is full of stories illustrating these pressures. For instance, a July 2013 *New York Times* article provided a great set of examples of the wildly conflicting views about whether college women should focus on their education and career or on relationships. Supporters of one extreme argue that relationships are too demanding and distract women from their goals. They suggest that women get their sexual needs met through hookups and leave relationships for later. Supporters of the other extreme argue that women should use college to focus on relationships and find a guy who is husband material. People on both sides of the debate believe their choice is right and others are making a mistake. In a commentary on both, one woman voiced her concerns: "I know several students who have formed meaningful relationships. . . . some even stemming from a random hookup. . . . Many women, myself included, have maintained long-distance relationships, therefore putting in even more time and effort than in a traditional relationship. Why are academic success and serious relationships presented as mutually exclusive?" Emily's situation, introduced in Chapter 1, provides a good example of how these types of socioculturally driven pressures can affect women.

Does Emily want to maintain her long-distance relationship with Will?

She's confused. It's hard. Yes, long distance tests them. She notices herself going back and forth between "Yes, Will is the right guy for me, and we can make this work" and "No, long distance is not working for me." Her self-talk has more questions than answers: "Is Lexi right? Do I want to move to be with him? Or is the right job more important than the right guy?" She discusses this with Mia:

Mia: Right job or right guy, seriously? I'm with Lexi, choose the job.

Emily: I can find another job that's right for me *and* be with Will.

Mia: You're sacrificing *your* right-job for *his* right-medical-school. Em, make this decision for yourself, not him.

Emily: That's what I'm doing—I'm trying to balance my personal happiness *and* my professional success.

Mia: Seriously? We went together to Sheryl Sandberg's talk. Don't you remember what she said? "Lean all the way into your career." It's as if you're doing what she said not to do—leaning back by planning a life–work balance for something that's way off in the future. The right job could be here right now, and it's because of your dad's relationship with the CEO of the company you've been interning for. That could be a once-in-a-lifetime opportunity. Sure, you'll find another job, but who knows whether it will provide you with the same opportunities? And you'd be turning down this job for what? A future with Will that may not even happen?

Emily: I also heard Sheryl Sandberg say to ask yourself, "What would I do if I weren't afraid?" My answer is that I'd want to be with Will and eventually have a family. I'm in a relationship with the right guy now, and I want to lean into opportunities in both my life and my work. I know you don't see yourself settling down for like 10 years, but I want that sooner.

Mia: When do you think Will's going to want to settle down? Are you sure he wants it as soon as you do? Or will it be in 10 years, after medical school, residency, and whatever comes next?

Emily feels so much pressure. Even before she went to college, her girlfriends and even her mom said, "You're going to miss out on your college experience by not trying out new things for yourself." They said she was letting the best years of her life slip by, waiting around for Will instead of exploring the world more, but she disagrees. She's immersed herself in her major and taken all sorts of opportunities to learn, and she's made new friends, felt attracted to a few of the guys, and, yes, even hooked up with a number of guys when she and Will were broken up. She doesn't see herself as having missed out, and she continues to pursue educational opportunities that will prepare her for her career. Even though she wants to settle down, Emily's plans have always included establishing her career and maximizing her earning power prior to doing so, as well as working while raising a family. She's not prepared to give up her skill set in case something goes sideways with her marriage, and with how expensive things are she believes it's not realistic to rely on one person's income in a relationship. She reads all the time nowadays that two incomes are needed to raise a family. So even though she can't imagine her life without Will, she still wants to live her life and be self-sufficient.

Even though Emily's feeling confident that she wants to pursue a long-term relationship with Will (and she knows he wants that too), she knows that Mia makes a good point about potential differences in when she and Will want to settle down. She's been assuming— or maybe hoping— that Will wants the same things on the same timeline that she does, but she hasn't had the courage to speak directly with him about this yet. They've largely focused on the fact that they want to be together and they both want to pursue their careers and eventually settle down. That's pretty vague and not ideal for Emily, who really likes to plan things. The fact is, even though Emily wants Will to be her forever person, Will may not want to settle down until much later. She knows there is uncertainty there, and that's why she has some ambivalence about whether to pick right-job and maintain the long-distance relationship or move to be with Will and find a different job. She's just trying really hard to listen to herself and have insight into what she wants and needs. But the external pressures are there.

She recently read an article that referred to how she and Will had developed their relationship—met at a young age, dated to get to know each other, committed to being together—as being the old-fashioned way of doing things. The woman in the article said she felt as if she were breaking a social taboo by being in this kind of relationship. "Am I allowed to find the person that I want to spend the rest of my life with when I'm 19? I really don't know, it feels like I'm not." That's what Emily is feeling: pressure to behave differently inherent in the criticism that she is old-fashioned and in the implication that her desires are not right.

The bottom line is this: don't use pressure to make decisions about what you want. Why not? Because pressure is an unreliable guide. Pressure comes from what other people believe, what other people want. Even pressures that you put on yourself may have come from internalizing what others say you should be. Pressure gets in the way of your being really able to know yourself. (More on this subject in the sidebar below.)

What the Data Tell Us about Relationships Today

When you're navigating the complicated world of career ambition versus family ambition, dealing with the challenges of sex, intimacy, and relationships, and managing the complex task of choosing a partner, it's all about knowing yourself and having good information about your choices. It's important to determine what your own needs are in romantic and sexual

---

I/ME

Do You Internalize Pressure?

In her TED Talk "We Should All Be Feminists" (*www.youtube.com/ watch?v=hg3umXU_qWc*), Chimamanda Ngozi Adichie discusses how gender stereotypes prescribe how we should be rather than recognize how we are. She talks about how she's unlearning lessons of gender she internalized while growing up:

> The first time I taught a writing class in graduate school, I was worried. I wasn't worried about the material I would teach . . . I was worried about what I was going to wear . . . I was worried that if I looked too feminine, I would not be taken seriously. I really wanted to wear my shiny lip gloss and my girly skirt, but I decided not to. Instead, I wore a very serious, very manly, and very ugly suit. Because the sad truth is that when it comes to appearance, we start off with men as the standard, as the norm . . . I wish I had not worn that ugly suit that day. I've actually banished it from my closet, by the way. Had I then the confidence that I have now to be myself, my students would have benefited even more from my teaching because I would have been more comfortable, and more truly myself.

Her insights reflect how when a woman knows who she is and trusts that, instead of caving in to external pressures, she'll make healthier choices.

relationships and how to use who you are—not what other people or the media say you should be—to make decisions about what you want. To help you with this, we're going to start by providing you with data-based information that gives you insight into changing norms and about the kinds of relationships that are possible and typical today. Here are some statistics.

STAT 1: People become involved in relationships at a pretty young age, and eventually most people have one.

Romantic involvement starts early. Thirty-six percent of adolescents say they've had a romantic relationship by age 13; by age 17 it's 70%. Rates of involvement continue to grow into adulthood, with more than half of women and men marrying by age 30 and over 80% by age 40. Clearly, relationships are the norm.

STAT 2: People become sexually active pretty early on as well.

Engaging in sexual activity is the norm too. According to the Centers for Disease Control and Prevention's National Survey of Family Growth, the average age of first intercourse in the United States is 17 for both females and males, and over 40% of teenagers ages 15–18 have had sexual intercourse. If you ask unmarried women whether they've had sex with at least one male partner in the past 12 months, 39% of 18- to 19-year-olds, 58% of 20- to 24-year-olds, and 76% of 25- to 29-year-olds will report having done so. Indeed, over 85% of people ages 18–44 have engaged in sexual intercourse before marriage. The rates for oral sex are similar. Recent data on hookups are in line with these trends. Most of the data comes from surveys conducted on college campuses, which show prevalence rates in the general range of 35–50%.

STAT 3: People are getting married much later than they used to, and more people than ever before are choosing not to marry.

Even though women engage in romantic and sexual relationships at an early age, they are not rushing into marriage. Since the 1950s the average age at which women first marry has risen dramatically from around 21 in 1950 to 25 in 1990 and up to 27 in 2013. Interestingly, although relationships are the norm, more and more women also choose not to marry. The number of marriages declined from about 4.5 million in 2008 to 4.2 million in 2011, likely reflecting the growing interest in and acceptance of alternate forms of relationships. Indeed, 39% of Americans say that marriage is becoming obsolete, according to a report from the Pew Research Center.

The same report found that 25% of 18- to 29-year-olds aren't sure they want to marry, and 5% said they did not wish to marry at all. These trends suggest that women have the opportunity to explore what they want in life and in relationships prior to, and perhaps without, marriage. Women, therefore, have plenty of time to make good choices.

STAT 4: Lots of people live together before marriage.

Although fewer women are getting married, more are living with a partner. Over 50% of women ages 15–44 have cohabited with a male partner at some time in their life, compared with 40% in the 1990s. Among women ages 20–24, 30% will have lived with a male partner, and among women 25–29, over 60% will have done so. Within three years, about 25% of those cohabiting couples will continue to live together unmarried, about 25% will break up, and about 50% will marry. However, the news isn't good for all of those who go on to marry. Data show they are at greater risk for relationship problems and divorce than couples who don't live together before marriage. Why might this be the case?

Researchers who study this phenomenon have found that couples at greatest risk for later marital problems and divorce were more likely to "slide" into cohabitation rather than actively "decide" to make a firm commitment to one another in advance. Couples who live together after getting engaged but before getting married have a lower risk of divorce than those who live together without plans to marry. Furthermore, those who live together without a plan to marry may then "slide, rather than decide" into marriage as well. Researchers say it's a matter of inertia: with financial investments and social pressures making separation undesirable, some couples marry even though they may not have done so had they been living apart. Cohabiting doesn't necessarily weaken relationships, researchers have concluded; it makes relationships that are already weak more likely to turn into marriages.

So does this mean you shouldn't live together? No, not at all. It means that you should be making a conscious decision to do so when you're ready to commit to the relationship and that you need to be ready to make a conscious decision to exit the relationship if things aren't going well. This idea of conscious decision making will be a theme throughout the book and is in line with the idea of developing and using insight.

STAT 5: Lots of people get divorced.

Despite the fact that divorce rates have gone down recently, the rates are still high, with recent trends suggesting about one-third of first marriages begun in the 2000s will end in divorce.

What are the biggest risk factors for divorce? Research indicates they include poor communication and the inability to effectively resolve problems, low levels of practical and emotional support, hostile, critical, and disrespectful behavior, and verbal and physical aggression. The characters in this book will deal with each of these problems, and we will show you how to use the I/ME skills to identify them, work on them, or exit when you need to.

STAT 6: Most women will have a child sometime in their lives, but the norms for doing so are changing.

Eighty-five percent of women have a child by the time they are 40 years old, and about 55% give birth to their first child between the ages of 20 and 29. Although, historically, most children were born to married women, the number of young women who have a child outside of marriage has increased, suggesting new norms among young women. Among women ages 25–29, about 25% of those who are married give birth. A 2011 survey by the Pew Research Center finds that individuals ages 18–29 are less likely to link marriage and parenthood. For instance, they are less likely than individuals ages 30 and older to say a child needs a home with both a father and mother to grow up happily and that single parenthood and unmarried-couple parenthood are bad for society. In addition, about 20% of individuals ages 18–29 report they aren't sure they want children, and another 7% say they don't want children at all. Clearly, women have a variety of choices about having and raising children and can expect greater societal support for those choices.

So what should you take from these first six statistics?

TAKE-HOME MESSAGE 1: Engaging in romantic and sexual relationships is the norm, and your sense that you have lots of choices for doing so these days is accurate.

There's no single kind of relationship or "right" progression into a relationship or marriage. Having many options is good news for getting what you want, but it also means it's no surprise if you feel overwhelmed by the possibilities before you. Women today may have to deal with a lot of uncertainty, which can be difficult. Take Mia, for example. She was all into just having casual sex and thought she was just going to hook up with Corey. Then the relationship progressed to regular hookups. Okay. Then, seemingly suddenly, they're exclusive—that was a transition for her! Now he's moving, they're going to have a long-distance relationship, and he wants to have "free passes" to hook up with an old friend. This is clearly not a traditional relationship progression. But Mia is dealing with the uncertainty.

She's kept an open mind all along, and she's keeping her mind open about the type of relationship Corey wants. Who knows where it will end up? Will they stay together? Will it progress to an open relationship? Could they end up in a polyamorous relationship? Mia doesn't know, and that's because you can't always know. You can't always be certain.

For Mia, who was cheated on before, Corey's request for free passes may be particularly hard because she's sensitive to betrayal. "But is this a betrayal? He's asking openly," Mia thinks. Mia's not sure how she feels about all of it yet. One thing she knows for sure is she doesn't want to be diverted from her professional goals by relationship drama. She has to navigate how to set up her limits for these free passes. She wants to meet Corey's needs because she's getting lots of needs met by him, but she's also paying attention to what giving him a free pass would actually feel like for her—whether she could really be okay with it—so she can make an insightful decision. Mia is certain that Corey truly knows her and likes her by the way he treats her. She feels accepted by him and desired by him, and he's always there to support her and help her with things she needs to do. If she didn't trust in these things, she might be feeling confusion and anxiety about their relationship, but she does trust him, and she feels she's really getting her needs met with him. She's just not sure whether to set limits for these free passes or how to do it. She feels comfortable being who she is with him, so she says out loud what she's thinking:

Mia: You know, I'm still not sure whether I'm okay with the free passes. If we do try them, we have to set up some limits before you go.

Corey: I know.

Mia: I'm sensitive to seeing this as a betrayal.

Corey: It's not! I love you. I'm just interested in exploring an open relationship to deal with our long-distance relationship. Random hookups, no emotional connection—it's just sex, I promise.

Mia: Okay, as long as it's random hookups. I want us both to feel good about what you want. I don't really get jealous about stuff I know about. I may need you to tell me everything you're doing.

Corey: Okay, why do you want to know?

Mia: I think I might need it to feel connected to you, and to feel like I'm part of things— not on the outside—like if you were cheating. Plus, it'll be like our own kind of sexual relationship—describing all the dirty details. (*She winks at him.*)

Corey: Okay, I hear what you're saying. For me, I want the opposite. I don't want to know about how you're using your free passes until we're living together again. I know I get jealous, and I want the security of being together again and moving forward together in our life before I hear about what you were doing while I was gone. It will be easier for me that way.

Mia: Okay, I hear you.

I/ME

Is Mia Normal?

Do you think Mia wanting to know the details about Corey's hookups is unusual? Perhaps it's one of her sexual fantasies. A recent study had men and women rate 55 sexual fantasies. Eighty-four percent were rated as typical—meaning that lots of people have them—and over half of the fantasies were common for both women and men. So, remember, sexual fantasies are normal. If Mia wants to know the details and have dirty sex talk with Corey, and he's on board with that, then it's right for them.

Mia's trying hard to get her needs met and keep the relationship with Corey stable and satisfying for both of them. She's got enough skills to be able to do this. Which brings us to our next take-home message from the six statistics.

TAKE-HOME MESSAGE 2: It is critical to develop I/ME skills for establishing and maintaining a healthy relationship as early in life as possible.

Women get involved in relationships early on. If they don't know how to have healthy relationships, they are at risk for all sorts of poor choices and problematic outcomes. In psychologist and author Meg Jay's TED Talk "Why 30 Is Not the New 20," she noted that after she had a session with her very first client, Alex, her supervisor pushed her to confront Alex about her relationship problems. Meg pushed back: "Sure, she's dating down, she's sleeping with a knucklehead, but it's not like she's going to marry the guy." Her supervisor said, "Not yet, but she might marry the next one; besides, the best time to work on Alex's marriage is before she has one." We couldn't agree more! The story lies in the divorce statistics. Once divorce happens, the risk for subsequent divorce goes up (and up). Fortunately, women are getting married later, giving them time to learn about themselves and make healthy decisions. You can make healthy choices about entering or exiting a relationship and coping with issues that come up in relationships with the I/ME skills so that if you do want to try to make a relationship work or last, you can.

We know because the skills are based on empirical data from published psychological research on romantic relationships and effective psychological interventions for healthy relationships and emotion management. Thus these skills represent an evidence-based—not an advice-based—approach to forming and keeping healthy relationships.

So What Are Your Options?

As we've already mentioned, we are living in a day and age when women have all sorts of relationship and sexual options. On the more "casual" side are things like

- Hookups (or hanging out), defined as sexually intimate behavior outside of a committed relationship.
- Friends with benefits (FWBs, or "fuck buddies"), defined as two good friends who engage in sexually intimate behavior outside of a committed relationship.
- Casual relationships, where people date or have sex with a number of different partners without commitment.

On the more "committed" side are

- Monogamous relationships, where both partners have the intention of engaging in a long-term relationship. Even within such relationships, however, couples may differ on whether the ultimate goal is marriage or whether any form of nonmonogamy is acceptable.
- Serial monogamy, where people engage in a series of monogamous, committed relationships (including marriage) that eventually end.

In addition to dyadic relationships, there are those that involve three (or more) individuals.

- "Threesomes," which might include a couple plus one, or three individuals, none of whom are in a relationship.
- Group sex, including multiple couples or individuals.
- Polyamorous relationships, in which partners are involved in a committed relationship with two (or more) individuals, all of whom are aware of each other and accepting of the relationships.

WHAT WE KNOW ABOUT DIFFERENT TYPES OF RELATIONSHIPS

By far the greatest amount of research has been conducted on married couples and on those in committed dating relationships. Far less research exists on other types of romantic and sexual relationships. However, there are a number of findings you should be aware of.

Finding 1: Being married or in a committed relationship may be good for your mental health.

Research shows that, on average, compared to single people, those in a committed relationship or a marriage are at lower risk for depression. Of course, the "on average" part is important. It doesn't mean that if you're single you're going to get depressed. Plenty of single people are quite happy! Nonetheless, relationships seem to be good for people's mental health.

Finding 2: A bad relationship is NOT good for your health.

We just told you that being in a relationship is good for your mental health, but again, that's on average. There is ample evidence that being in a bad relationship is associated with all sorts of mental and physical health problems. By bad relationships, we mean those characterized by things like relationship dissatisfaction, poor communication, lots of conflict, a lack of support, a critical partner, a partner who betrays your trust, a relationship where you feel insecure, a relationship where one or both partners is emotionally or physically aggressive. When these things happen in relationships, women get depressed. They may feel more anxious. They may drink more alcohol or use more drugs, and their physical health may suffer as well.

Finding 3: A satisfying sexual relationship is good for you.

Research indicates that women who report satisfaction with their sex lives also experience greater psychological well-being and a greater sense of vitality than women who are dissatisfied. This may seem pretty obvious—better sex makes you feel, well, better overall. We bring it up, however, because many women are afraid to communicate their sexual needs out of fear of what their partner might think. So we want to emphasize that by not asking for what they want, they may be missing out on more than sexual satisfaction. Being able to communicate successfully with one's partner about sexual needs is also associated with greater emotional and sexual well-being.

Finding 4: Risky sex is NOT good for you.

The Centers for Disease Control and Prevention estimate there are approximately 20 million new cases of sexually transmitted infections (STIs) annually in the United States, with half of them occurring in those under the age of 24, split equally between males and females. Approximately 54% of the new cases of gonorrhea and chlamydia occur among people ages 20–29. About 40% of women ages 20–24 have HPV, as do another 30%

of women ages 25. Furthermore, in 2011 there were over 10,000 diagnoses of HIV among adult and adolescent females in the United States. Even though both men and women are affected by STIs, the potential consequences are greater for women as STIs can dramatically increase infertility rates, in addition to other negative health outcomes.

The rates of unwanted pregnancy are high as well. According to a 2014 report by the Guttmacher Institute, approximately 20% of all pregnancies were unwanted. Among unmarried women ages 20 to 29, over 70% of all first pregnancies are unplanned, and half of these end in abortion.

The best way to prevent unwanted pregnancy and STIs is to abstain from oral, vaginal, and anal sex. Since that is highly unrealistic for most women, the next best measures are birth control to prevent unwanted pregnancy and, to prevent STIs, (1) condoms and (2) oral, vaginal, or anal sex only with partners who have recently tested negative for all STIs. Sexual activity without these measures can be considered risky. Lots of people take these risks, and we're not making any judgments but want you to make thoughtful, informed choices about what is right for you.

Finding 5: Hookups and FWBs: The jury is still out.

Researchers are just beginning to study whether hooking up or engaging in FWB relationships has positive or negative consequences. Because the jury is still out, and the findings are somewhat mixed (compared to the prior two findings), we'll go into a little more detail about what the research shows to try to sort out the findings a bit for you.

First, research indicates that FWBs represent a diverse set of relationship experiences. For some people, FWB relationships focus mainly on the sex. For others, they focus mainly on the friendship. And some use FWBs to try to transition to a romantic relationship, whereas others have no interest in doing so. The good news is that both men and women report, on average, experiencing positive emotions in response to FWB relationships and being more committed to the friendship part of the relationship than the sex part. One study also found the majority of FWB relationships continued as friendships after the sexual relationship ended, and about half of people reported feeling as close to or closer to their former FWB partner. However, those people who did not remain friends were more likely to report that their FWB relationship was based more on sex than friendship, and reported feeling more deceived by their FWB partner, as well as more lonely and distressed. This is important because people have different expectations for what their FWB relationship will be. For example, for men, sex can be a more common motivation for starting an FWB relationship, whereas for women, emotional connection can be a more common motivation. Men also may be more likely to hope the relationship will continue to be a sexual one, whereas women may be more likely to want the relationship to either evolve into a romantic relationship or stay a friendship without sex.

Complicating this gender difference in desires is the finding that people in FWB relationships tend to avoid talking about important relationship issues, such as how to label the relationship, how they feel about the relationship, and the future of the relationship. Therefore, if partners are not talking about what they want and expect, and secretly they want different things, they may end up feeling deceived and unhappy.

There is one other important finding you need to know. One study found that engaging in an FWB relationship was associated with greater alcohol use, especially among women. Although we don't know which causes which, it's important to be aware of and consider the role that alcohol plays in your sexual decision making. The same study found the association between alcohol use and engaging in FWBs was weaker among women who engaged in more thoughtful decision making.

As to hookups, both male and female college students found them generally positive in one study. A study of over 1,300 young adults found no differences in psychological well-being between those who engaged in casual sexual relationships and those in committed relationships.

However, other studies suggest there may be emotional downsides to hooking up. One study of over 3,700 multiethnic, single, heterosexual college students found that engaging in casual sex was associated with greater psychological distress and poorer well-being for both men and women. Other data suggest these associations are even greater for women and that women find hooking up a positive emotional experience less often than men, particularly when sexual intercourse is involved. As in FWB relationships, compared to men, women show a stronger association between hooking up and alcohol use, and one study found that alcohol use predicted engaging in hookups in the future. Situational triggers, such as meeting someone at a bar, party, or other drinking situation, having someone attractive wanting to hook up with you, and feeling that everyone else is hooking up also predicted engaging in hookups. These findings again point to how important it is for women to be aware of the role of alcohol use in their sexual decision making, as well as other situations that may be a "pull" for them to engage in casual sex. Our message again is to act based on awareness and choice, not out of pressure or clouded judgment.

So what should you take from these findings?

THE BOTTOM LINE

Whatever the relationship, it has to be safe and satisfying, and to keep yourself safe and healthy you have to make informed, thoughtful decisions about what is good for you. How do you know what is good for you? By knowing yourself, using the information at hand—like the research we just talked about—figuring out what your key needs are (more to come on that), and then using what you know in your choices. What matters is what's right for you and you alone.

Lexi exemplifies this process and the challenges involved. Lexi's not sure she wants marriage or kids, but she does know she wants a monogamous relationship. She's not interested in casual sex. She thinks she would be one of those women who would feel emotionally distressed afterward if he didn't immediately take down his dating profile, for example. She has good insight into that, and she's using it to inform her decisions as best as she can. But it's hard. She's read that hookups can sometimes lead to serious relationships. For example, one article she read online said, "It's by hooking up that many students form these monogamous relationships. Roughly, they go from a first hookup, to a 'regular hookup,' to perhaps something that my students call 'exclusive'—which means monogamous but not in a relationship—and then, finally, they have 'the talk' and form a relationship." She wondered, "Could hooking up be a pathway into committed relationships for me? Could I tolerate the possibility that it wouldn't lead to a relationship?" She calls Mia:

Lexi: How can you handle having sex with someone and maybe never talking to the guy again?

Mia: When I get a little sad, stressed out, I want sex. It calms me down, and I can function better.

Lexi: Do you get off?

Mia: Mostly.

Lexi: Sex gets better for me with a guy the more we do it. It's not usually very good the first couple times. I feel like I need to know him.

Mia: If you're going to hook up and have it be good for you, then you have to be yourself—you have to tell him what you like, what you don't, what you need to get off.

Lexi: I need a bunch of things for that.

Mia: Like what?

Lexi: I want to feel special to him, to feel he wants a relationship with me and that maybe there's a future, and I need to be the only person he's having sex with at that time. How can you not think about the future?

Mia: (*laughing*) I do. The guy's in my head the next morning for a while. I find myself thinking, "Would my friends like him? My parents?" But then I let it go. You've got to be in reality about these things.

Lexi: That's hard for me. I start thinking about us living together, about being with him all the time, seeing myself in different scenarios with him years down the road just like I did with Jake.

Mia: You didn't do that with Dex.

Lexi: Actually, I did a little, but I knew he was going to move and I didn't want to get hurt. Plus, I did feel special with him, and we were monogamous. Anyway, now I'm really looking for something more. I'm ready for a more serious relationship.

Mia: We're so different. I'm not ready to commit to a guy, I'm not ready to settle down for years. I know that about myself, and I just remind myself of it when the future fantasies start.

Lexi: I really need to be the only one a guy I like is having sex with. And since I really want a relationship, I'm just not sure I could do what you do.

Lexi keeps coming back to this conversation as she thinks about what she'll do if James responds to her "I'm ready to 'sports-talk'—you ready to listen?" text. He does: "I'm ready to listen. Pick you up tomorrow? Text me address." She replies with "I'm ready to meet you at stadium front gates." Her profile pick was "4—I am putting in a serious effort to find someone." His profile pick was "3—I want a relationship." Do they have the same expectations? By making the first move, did she reset James's expectations to a hookup after the game? If she hooked up with him, would it lead to a relationship?

At the game, they have a couple beers and talk easily about whatever. His hand accidentally touches her leg; it feels good, and she flirts her way through her "sports-talk." Afterward, they go back to his place; he immediately gets her onto the bed. "Oh no," she thinks, "maybe he is thinking this is a hookup. I feel a connection, but no, too fast, I'm nervous, I should wait." On the other hand, she's thinking, "I want to know what he's like, and maybe this could lead to something." And then she starts thinking, "Take a breath—if you want to see where this might go, slow things down and try to get to know him first so you can figure out what he's looking for." But then she starts thinking, "What if he's not looking for a relationship? What if he's looking for a fuck buddy? What will I do?" She wants to be with him, but she doesn't want it to be just a hookup. She wants it to be the beginning of their relationship, and she's afraid to find out that he doesn't want what she wants because then she won't get to be with him and she's already "in like" with him.

There is a lot running through Lexi's mind in a really hot moment. You can see that she's trying hard to use her insight, but her feelings are getting in the way. (How often has that happened to all of us?) And this is where the skill of emotion regulation comes in—holding on to your head, your insight in the face of some very immediate pleasurable feelings and desires so you can make an informed, thoughtful decision. Look at what Lexi is essentially saying to herself: "I like him and want to be with him, so I'd rather not know whether he wants the same things I do because I don't want my fantasy to be crushed!" That is neither informed nor thoughtful. If Lexi was like Mia and could just be in it for the sex no matter what was to come next, all would be fine. But Lexi knows she wants more. She wants a relationship, and she's struggling in the moment to use her insight about herself and what she wants. We know this is a hard struggle. What Lexi has to focus on are the consequences and whether she can tolerate them no matter what. If she has sex with James and learns that he's kept his dating profile up or he just wanted a hookup, is she going to be crushed? If so, then Lexi has to use her insight to put on the brakes—to make that informed, thoughtful decision. If she puts on the brakes and he never calls her again, then he wasn't the right guy for her in the first place. This is what Lexi needs to realize—as do all women. If you act like yourself with a guy and he doesn't want to be with you, he's not the guy for you.

Lauren's story provides another good example of this reality. In addition, it brings us to another very important point: to navigate the complex task of choosing a long-term partner, not only do you need to know what type of relationship you want (monogamous, hookup, etc.); you also need to know what type of person you want and what qualities you want in the relationship. That is, you need to have a clear idea of what you consider a good relationship to be.

Lauren, like Lexi, is well aware of the type of relationship she wants. For Lauren, it's a monogamous committed relationship that will lead to marriage and children. But she doesn't have a clear picture of what a good relationship is to her. It's important to recognize that wanting a relationship is not the same as wanting to be in a relationship with a certain "who" and having evidence of "why." So in Chapter 1, even though Lauren was asking herself the question "Who do I want to be with, and why?"—a great question to ask—she doesn't really know how to answer it. Many of us don't. And when we don't know what information to pay attention to in ourselves and our potential partners, we struggle with making healthy decisions. That's why Lauren is choosing between two men, neither of whom may be right for her, rather than looking for a guy who *will* be right for her. She's focused on the outcome she wants, and on the internal pressure she feels to get there, rather than on whether Dan or Lucas is the right guy to try to get there with. Let's see how this plays out for Lauren.

Does Lauren want to be with Dan or Lucas? Remember when we left off in Chapter 1, Lauren had decided to pursue Lucas, to try to make him love her. After a few weeks of being the supportive friend, she initiated sex and he responded. Fantastic! Her plan was working. She would get him to love her. She was happy.

But then she wasn't. One night out at dinner, the food comes; they're talking, laughing, she's happy, and then she reaches over to try a bite from his plate:

Lucas: Seriously—do you really have to do that?
Lauren: Uh, I'm sorry? Does it really bother you that much?
Lucas: Yes.

Lauren's shocked but keeps quiet about it. They finish dinner, split the bill, and go home separately.

There have been a lot of these incidents lately. He gets snappy, and she feels as if he's almost annoyed by her presence. He also has lots of "rules" on which he's not flexible. He wants to eat at a certain time, she has to leave at a certain time, he doesn't want her to stay over on his work nights, and he doesn't want to walk her home. She doesn't understand this. When she first starts dating someone, she changes her schedule to accommodate him. She's flexible about what she wants to do and when she wants to do things. She makes sacrifices. Lucas doesn't.

Moreover, Lucas keeps going back and forth between "I'm happy being with Lauren" and "No, I'm sad, missing my ex-wife; this is not working for me." One night they're walking and talking when they have the biggest silent fight ever, meaning Lauren gets really upset, has a fight with Lucas in her head, but says nothing.

Lauren: What are we going to do tomorrow?
Lucas: I'm not around tomorrow. I just want to be alone.
Lauren: What's happening tomorrow?
Lucas: It's my wedding anniversary.

She is so hurt, but she says nothing. When she gets home, she sits down and cries. She starts thinking, "I'm being asked to leave him alone so he can mourn the loss of his ex-wife while we are dating. I'm starting to feel second best. It feels odd—I have never met his ex-wife, yet he expects me to honor and respect their anniversary date, and they're divorced."

She starts thinking, "What's in it for me? I can't stay over, I have to pay for my own dinner, and I'm forced to listen to him talk and talk about his ex-wife!" She feels disillusioned about Lucas. She reminds herself about how she loved her life with Dan. How he accepted her, cared about her, and helped her. She calls Dan, who travels a lot but has just gotten back from a business trip.

Dan: Glad you called! Got any plans for the weekend?
Lauren: Why?
Dan: I'm leaving for Chicago tomorrow. Let me book you a ticket, I miss you.
Lauren: You just got back!
Dan: Flying in for a friend's party—we'll have so much fun.
Lauren: Let me think about whether I can make this work.

She's not sure.
Lauren calls Anna:

Lauren: Dan wants me to go to Chicago with him for the weekend. What should I do?
Anna: (*laughing*) Don't ask Julianne. We know she doesn't like him.
Lauren: Seriously, would you go?
Anna: You can't let this guy go—he treats you so well. GO!
Lauren: What about Lucas?
Anna: Lucas doesn't care about you—he's wrapped up in his ex-wife. Dan cares about you.
Lauren: I know. Sometimes it feels as if I'm missing that. Lucas shows he cares in other ways, though.
Anna: Where? How?
Lauren: (*silence*) He talks about anything I want to talk about. God, I know I'm struggling to come up with something. I guess I don't need that much care.
Anna: Go to Chicago, Lauren.

Lauren thinks, "What to do? Who do I want?" She feels a connection to both men—in different ways. Dan is affectionate, confident, funny, generous, outgoing, a maximalist, if there were such a word (he has more expensive art than there are walls for in the house). He's always on the go, always the center of attention—and she is so all of that. She believes he could bring excitement into her life. On the other hand, Lucas is tall, handsome, a minimalist (the rooms in his apartment look like IKEA show-rooms), he's conscientious, organized, disciplined—and even though she is so none of that, she believes that it could bring structure into her life, which she wants. She's confused. But right now she's feeling disillusioned about love and mad at Lucas for loving his ex-wife more than her. She decides to go to Chicago.

She didn't have to tell Lucas, but she did. She texts him:

Lauren: Going out of town.
Lucas: Have fun.

Nothing.

And that's typical Lucas. She didn't expect him to ask any questions. He never did. He is zero control. She's used to a guy asking questions: "Where are you going?" or "When do you get back?" Or while away, "How are you?" Self-talk: "Maybe a guy only asks questions when he starts thinking, 'You're mine so you *have* to answer my questions.'" But in some ways when Lucas doesn't ask any questions it feels as if he doesn't care. She's confused.

As you can see, Lauren is trying to choose between two men who are willing to give her the type of relationship she wants—both Dan and Lucas want to marry and have children—but Lauren is not even considering the possibility that neither of these men is right for her. Yes, they both have qualities that she likes and can bring important things to the relationship. However, they both have qualities that she does not like and that are not healthy for her in a relationship. Dan is controlling and paternalistic; Lucas is so hands off that it feels uncaring. Both, in their own ways, are more focused on their own needs than on Lauren's. Yet Lauren lacks the insight to see that neither man is really right for her. She doesn't know what a good relationship would be for her. She is completely unable to make an informed, thoughtful decision that would allow her to find someone who could meet more of her needs and be in a truly healthy relationship.

How Do You Know What Your Idea of a Good Relationship Is?

Like Lauren's, Anna's decision about who to be in a relationship with was driven by an outcome she wanted. Anna is a person who links marriage and parenthood. She believes a child needs a home with both a mother and a father to grow up happily. On this premise, she accepted Eric's proposal. Here's how that went when Anna found out she was pregnant:

Anna: Can you come over? We need to talk.
Eric: What do we need to talk about?
Anna: Just come over.
Eric: We can't do this over the phone? Wait (*angrily*), did you cheat on me?
Anna: (*surprised*) What? No, not at all! Just please come over.

He gets there.

Eric: What is it?
Anna: I'm pregnant.
Eric: What??? Are you serious?
Anna: Yes, I'm serious. I'm not sure I'm ready for this, but I don't know what to do. I feel really confused. I don't know if I want a baby yet, but I know a baby needs a mother and a father who are together.
Eric: I know.
   (*They sit in silence for a while.*)
Eric: I know it's quick, but since I saw you in the bar that night when we hooked up again I just want to be with you. If we stay together and we don't have this child, how are we going to feel later, knowing that we could've had this baby?

Anna: Yeah, I know what you mean. I think I'd regret it.

    (More silence.)

Anna: Do you really want to stay with me? What about when you left me for Lizzie? And what about what you said about Lizzie? About her having a career and everything?

Eric: I know, but you're having my child now.

Anna: (smiling) I am, aren't I? You really want to be with me? Be a father to our child and a husband? Make a family together?

Eric: Let's do it, Anna. Let's get married and have this baby. I could never love anyone like I love you.

And she said yes.

Even though Anna made her decision based on an outcome she wanted, she, like all of us, can describe the kinds of things she wants in her relationship. After she accepted Eric's marriage proposal, her girlfriends threw her a pregnant-girl bachelorette party—no strippers, just dinner and a lot of talking. They wanted to know what she likes about Eric and their relationship:

Lauren: (teasing) Is Eric your *dream* guy?

Anna: (laughing) Yes. He's funny, he has a good job, we do really fun, romantic things together that we both love. And he'll be a good dad.

Julianne: What do you really like about him?

Anna: He makes me feel beautiful.

Julianne: Yes, we all see the comments on your Instagrams.

Anna: (laughing) I know, how cute is it when he says things like "Hot Babe and she's all mine!"

Julianne: What else do you like about him?

Anna: I feel safe because I know he'll financially take care of me and the baby. You know how I watched my parents struggle—I don't want that to happen to me.

Lauren: What do you think will make your relationship work?

Anna: Wanting to be a part of each other's life, caring about each other's feelings, being okay with the other making time to see friends—you guys!—and being available, reliable, like I am for him.

In this conversation, you can see that Anna is talking about her idea of a good relationship. These ideas can be understood as Anna's key needs, which she's aware of wanting to have met in a relationship (whether she gets them met remains to be seen). For example, when she said, "wanting to be a part of each other's life," she was saying that a key need for her is to have an *interesting* life that each partner wants to share in. When she said, "being okay with the other making time to see friends," she was saying that a key need for her is to pay attention to and *care* about each other's feelings.

When she said, "being available, reliable like I am for him," she was saying that a key need is to offer *support* when the other person is upset or has a problem.

NEEDS CAN HELP YOU UNDERSTAND WHAT A GOOD RELATIONSHIP IS

So, let's focus more on needs. In Chapter 1, we presented you with the three conditions that must be in place for a healthy relationship:

1. "I know and like myself."
2. "I know and like him."
3. "He knows and likes me."

Within each of these conditions there are things that Anna needs from her relationship (or from herself), and there are ways that she has to treat Eric (or herself). Then within these are specific needs. It sounds complicated, but it's really not. Each condition is met through the same needs; the needs only differ based on the perspective. For example, one need in a relationship is for *support*, which looks like this within each condition:

1. "I know and like myself." To meet her need for *support*, when faced with challenging or upsetting situations, Anna will actively problem-solve rather than avoid.
2. "I know and like him." To get *support* from her relationship, Anna will go to Eric in good times and bad times.
3. "He knows and likes me." To meet the need to *support* her partner, Anna will want to ensure that Eric can come to her in good times and bad times.

The needs can provide a way to help you find answers to the big question "What is my idea of a good relationship?" We've compiled a list of 14 needs. It's not meant to be exhaustive, but, as we'll describe throughout the book, it includes the primary things that relationship scholars have identified as critical to healthy relationship functioning. There are a few things to know when you're reading the list:

• The needs can be your guide to what makes for a good relationship. They all must be met satisfactorily, although some of them will be more or less important depending on what's important to you and the type of relationship you're in. Also, people will have different ways they prefer to get their needs met. There's not necessarily one right or wrong way. It's about what works for you and your relationship.

• You might read the list and think that we've missed important things like the concepts that make for a healthy relationship—security, intimacy, respect, good communication, or positive regard. However, as we'll demonstrate throughout the book, having your needs met results in all of these things. Therefore, getting your needs met is a way to create the very things that reflect a healthy relationship.

• If there are needs that aren't on the list that are important to you, go ahead and add them and treat them in the same way we suggest you treat the needs on the list. The list is meant to help you, so we want it to make sense to you.

• In the following chapters we are going to discuss each need in detail. For now, we encourage you to read through the list below so that you can start to understand what needs are. If you'd like, take some time to jot down a few ideas about the ways in which you may or may not be getting these needs met and write down any additional needs you think should go on your list.

The needs include but are not limited to:

Being *familiar* with yourself and your partner.

Thoughts:

Being *authentic* with yourself and your partner by deeply seeing and showing yourself.

Thoughts:

Being *attracted* to your partner and being comfortable with your own physical attributes.

Thoughts:

Desiring physical intimacy with your partner and feeling comfortable with yourself in intimate situations.

Thoughts:

Having an *interesting* life that each partner wants to share in.

Thoughts:

Supporting yourself and your partner.

Thoughts:

Caring about your own and your partner's feelings.

Thoughts:

Listening to what you and your partner really mean.

Thoughts:

Recognizing that your own and your partner's needs are *important* and must be included in choices that are made.

Thoughts:

Trusting yourself and your partner.

Thoughts:

Accepting yourself and your partner.

Thoughts:

Forgiving yourself and your partner for mistakes you've acknowledged.

Thoughts:

Helping yourself and your partner do things that need to be done.

Thoughts:

Keeping yourself and your partner *safe*, emotionally, physically, and practically.

Thoughts:

Additional needs:

Using the Needs to Develop Personal Power

At the end of Chapter 1 we told you we would continue to show you how to develop your personal power. The needs will really help you do so. Once you know what your needs are, you have the opportunity to actually get them met. And working to get them met gives you personal power.

Let's turn to Lauren again for an example. When Lauren gets back from Chicago, she arranges to meet up with Lucas. She's angry that he prioritizes his ex-wife over her, and rather than talking with him about this, she decides to "show" him. She walks in pretty, sits down, smiles, and says:

Lauren: I've decided to be exclusive with Dan.
Lucas: Is it because I wanted to mourn my wedding anniversary?
> *(Lauren's phone is on the table. When it rings, the word* Lovey *displays; it's Dan. She picks up. "Yes, I'll be another half hour, meet you there." She hangs up.)*
Lauren: I'm moving on.
Lucas: I can see that.
Lauren: If you really love your ex-wife, go to her and win her back, and don't give up on that. Be a little bit more proactive. Any time you need a female perspective, call me. I can help you.

Do you think Lauren has personal power?

Lauren is trying to have the power in the relationship, but she doesn't have personal power. If she did, she would be aware of and communicate her needs directly, for instance: "I'm hurt that you prioritize your ex-wife over me. I love you and want our relationship to work, but it's clear to me that you're not over her, so I need to move on. Unless you're ready to be fully with me—to *care* about my feelings and to view my needs as *important*—our relationship will not work."

Instead, she's trying to get back at Lucas because she's upset that she isn't the woman he wants. Lauren is focused on "Can I be who he wants?" rather than "Is he who I really want? Can he meet my needs?" If she were to ask herself the latter questions, and answer them honestly, she would see that Lucas cannot meet her needs, and then she could make a thoughtful decision about whether to stay with him or not. That is personal power.

In the next three chapters we'll delve more deeply into each of the three conditions that must be met to have a healthy relationship ("I know and like myself," "I know and like him," "He knows and likes me"), defining and elaborating each specific need so you can begin your journey to personal power.

3

I Know and Like Myself

Knowing and liking yourself means knowing what your needs are, respecting those needs, and being able to meet those needs for yourself.

Each specific need listed in Chapter 2 can be turned into a question—we call it a "needs question"—that you can ask yourself. By asking the needs questions that follow, you'll discover what your needs are, learn to respect those needs, and begin to meet them for yourself (rather than expecting others to meet them for you). You'll have the opportunity, via the characters you've already met, to see how other women go through this process. Seeing how these women are or are not successfully meeting their needs can help you clarify how you can meet your own needs. When you meet your own needs, *you* build your personal power.

Familiar: "Do I know my best and worst traits? Do I understand how they make me who I am, influence how I act, and affect the ways I get my needs met?"

To become familiar with yourself, do a trait assessment (on the facing page).

After you have done yours, let's look at Emily's trait assessment and at how she can use the results to understand how she goes about trying to get her needs met. For instance, she will be able to figure out why she texts Will, "I. HATE. YOU.", after he doesn't respond to her texts. Like Emily, many of us know what it feels like when a guy is not responsive or stops being so. Many of us know what it feels like to agonize over a text, to keep checking our phones, and, in spite of not wanting to, to keep looking and listening for the text to pop up, not being able to help ourselves. No one wants to feel ignored or unimportant. But why does Emily choose to react in the way she does?

Trait List

This list contains a sampling of traits that characterize people's personality and behavioral styles. They were drawn from the research literature and include traits thought to reflect some of the core aspects of personality. This list is not exhaustive. It is meant to be a guide so you can begin to understand yourself and your partner better. It also is not meant to imply that traits are inflexible or can't change. Think of each trait as existing along a continuum. Some people may show a lot of it—meaning they exhibit that trait across time and in many different situations. Some people may show very little of it—meaning they occasionally display the trait in only specific situations. Also, be careful not to think of people as their traits—meaning sometimes you might label someone with a trait and then see the person only as that. This would be unfair. People typically have many different traits that can explain their behavior. Use the trait list to help you understand people as fully as you can.

Go ahead and begin to figure out which traits characterize you. If you're not sure, enlist a trusted friend to help you.

	Best	Worst		Best	Worst		Best	Worst
Adventurous	☐	☐	Energetic	☐	☐	Outgoing	☐	☐
Affectionate	☐	☐	Enthusiastic	☐	☐	Outspoken	☐	☐
Aggressive	☐	☐	Even-			Passionate	☐	☐
Ambitious	☐	☐	tempered	☐	☐	Passive	☐	☐
Anxious	☐	☐	Excitable	☐	☐	Patient	☐	☐
Assertive	☐	☐	Excitement			Perfectionistic	☐	☐
Attention			seeking	☐	☐	Pessimistic	☐	☐
seeking	☐	☐	Fearless	☐	☐	Quick-		
Calm	☐	☐	Focused	☐	☐	tempered	☐	☐
Cautious	☐	☐	Funny	☐	☐	Reliable	☐	☐
Close-minded	☐	☐	Generous	☐	☐	Reserved	☐	☐
Competitive	☐	☐	Honest	☐	☐	Responsive	☐	☐
Confident	☐	☐	Impatient	☐	☐	Rigid	☐	☐
Conscientious	☐	☐	Impulsive	☐	☐	Selfish	☐	☐
Controlling	☐	☐	Inflexible	☐	☐	Sensitive	☐	☐
Courageous	☐	☐	Irresponsible	☐	☐	Shy	☐	☐
Creative	☐	☐	Jealous	☐	☐	Sociable	☐	☐
Critical	☐	☐	Kind	☐	☐	Spontaneous	☐	☐
Daring	☐	☐	Manipulative	☐	☐	Stubborn	☐	☐
Deceitful	☐	☐	Moody	☐	☐	Submissive	☐	☐
Demanding	☐	☐	Open-minded	☐	☐	Suspicious	☐	☐
Disciplined	☐	☐	Opinionated	☐	☐	Thoughtful	☐	☐
Disorganized	☐	☐	Optimistic	☐	☐	Unselfish	☐	☐
Easygoing	☐	☐	Organized	☐	☐			

Emily goes through the trait list and comes up with the following:

ME

	Best	Worst
Assertive	☒	☐
Creative	☒	☐
Honest	☒	☐
Kind	☒	☐
Opinionated	☐	☒
Outspoken	☐	☒
Passionate	☒	☐
Thoughtful	☒	☐

Emily asks Lexi's opinion about this to find out what Lexi sees in her (she always goes to Lexi for the "for real" opinion because she knows Lexi will give it without judgment). This is a great idea. Sometimes we can't see ourselves the way others see us, and openly listening to the perspective of trusted others can help us develop insight. It turns out Lexi doesn't agree that Emily is that assertive; Lexi also sees Emily as aggressive (not just opinionated and outspoken). Lexi tells Emily, "If you were assertive, you'd text Will something like 'It doesn't feel good when you're not responsive to my sexts' or 'You tell me you love me, then act like you don't care by not returning my text—I feel as if I'm not important to you. I would like you to text me back.' Instead, you text him something aggressive, like 'I hate you' or 'You. Are. An. Asshole.' Or 'Delete all my texts, please.'" How can Emily use Lexi's insight?

Although it may have been hard for Emily to hear what Lexi had to say, it's important for Emily to reflect on it if she wants to change her behavior and do better in getting her needs met. She sees that when she feels as if Will is not paying attention to her she becomes angry and aggressive in an attempt to get her needs for him to *care* about her and treat her as *important* met. By looking at *how* she behaves she is able to see *why* she behaves that way. Now that she has this insight, she can work on managing her angry emotions and being more assertive with Will, which will help her get her needs met and keep the relationship going smoothly.

When Anna ponders the question "Do I know my best and worst traits?" the main thing that comes to mind is that she can impulsively blow up when she's upset. If she's fighting with a guy, she's likely to yell, scream, cry, and call him all sorts of names—remember in Chapter 1 how she got angry at Eric and called him pathetic—and she's aware that she hates herself for doing so. Therefore, Anna wants to be able to use her trait assessment to gain insight into why she blows up and to work on changing that aspect of her character. For her best traits she chooses easygoing, sociable, and confident; for her worst she chooses quick-tempered and stubborn. These make sense to her. Stubborn: it's true, she doesn't always listen to others—her mother, Eric, Julianne all tell her that. Quick-tempered: yes, when she feels hurt, she's quick to anger ("Maybe that's why I become such a bitch," she thinks).

That Anna can see these traits in herself is really good news. Now she can understand why she behaves as she does, and that insight gives her the opportunity to change. Since she doesn't like her behavior, she can now make a choice to act differently when she feels hurt. To do this, Anna will need to use the I/ME skills (insight, mutuality, and emotion regulation). First, she will need to use insight to (1) *notice* when her anger level begins to rise; (2) *describe* her experience and the consequence she wants to avoid (for example, "I'm getting angry, and this leads me to behave in a bitchy manner, which I don't want to do"); and (3) *identify* her assumptions about the situation. For example, what is Anna telling herself about the situation that results in her saying mean things? Maybe she's telling herself things such as "He's such a jerk. How could he do this to me? He doesn't care about me. I'll show him!"

These are certainly thoughts that might make (or keep) anyone angry and make someone want to behave in a mean way. Therefore, to manage her anger she will need to use emotion regulation to calm herself down with new self-talk. If Anna's old self-talk was "He doesn't care about me. I'll show him!" her new self-talk might be something like "My feelings are hurt, but that doesn't mean he doesn't care about me. I need to talk with him calmly to find out why he did what he did and tell him how I feel." This kind of thinking will likely steer Anna away from acting out her frustration and anger. Finally, Anna will then need to use the skill of mutuality to communicate her feelings and needs clearly (and calmly) and to listen to her partner's response. If Anna uses the I/ME skills in these ways, she'll be able to change her behavior. And so can you.

Authentic: "Do I know and understand all aspects of who I am because I face whatever fears I have about doing so?"

Lauren is very open to knowing what she wants in her future. "I feel like I was born to be a mother. I know this will sound old-fashioned, but I've always wanted to be married, and I don't care what anyone else thinks about that. Maternal ambition is kinda like a career for me."

Olivia says, "Yes, I try to be authentic. It took me a long time in college to figure this out, but now I know how important it is." Olivia is referring to all that time she struggled with the pressure to be what her sorority sisters wanted her to be rather than looking at and trying to understand who she was. She was afraid to truly understand herself because others might not like the person she really was. Recognizing she was doing this was her first step in meeting her need to be *authentic*, and now she knows how important it is to continue doing so.

Lexi says, "I'm not sure how to answer this question. I really try to understand myself, but I think I still miss things. Like for a while I had myself convinced I just didn't want a relationship, but all my friends kept saying it was because I had never gotten over what happened with my high school boyfriend, Jake. I kept denying that, but finally I let myself really think about what they were saying, and you know what? They were right. Not only was I not really over him, but the relationship left me really afraid to trust, and I didn't want to admit that. Being with Dex actually helped me figure this out."

Lexi's experience is common. She's working on being authentic, but she still misses things. We all do, and that's why this is a need that has to be brought to the surface. The more deeply we can see into ourselves, the more we can make decisions that will be right for us. We've got to do our best to stop kidding ourselves about ourselves. This takes courage, and it's a process, but it's worth it, because it will allow us to get what we want in life and in a relationship.

Attracted: *"Am I comfortable with the body I have?"*

Olivia answers, "Mainly, but these hips of mine, why do they have to be so wide? Seriously, they are! I just don't even like to look at them!" Lexi answers, "Yes, I like my body. I figured out what my body type was in high school and how to feel comfortable with it. For example, my boobs are small, so I purposely don't wear low V-necks—they don't look right on me. Some girls might feel bad about that, but I don't. It's just what I've got, and that's okay."

Each of these characters is fortunate to basically like her body, although they recognize aspects of their bodies they are less satisfied with. Olivia is self-critical, however. She's not unlike many women who have very negative things to say about their bodies. A 2011 poll in *Glamour* magazine captured the number of times a day women say demeaning things to themselves about their bodies. On average, women have 13 negative body thoughts a day, thoughts like "You are a fat, worthless pig"; "You're too thin—no man is ever going to want you"; "Ugly. Big. Gross." That's nearly one negative thought for every waking hour! Now, it may simply be that women who read *Glamour* are more body image conscious and there-fore more likely to be critical in the first place. Even if that's true, research shows that women who are critical of their bodies—women with a high degree of body dissatisfaction—tend to compare themselves to others in a more negative manner, experience greater negative emotion, and have more thoughts about dieting than do women who are less critical of their bodies. Women who are critical of their bodies are also most likely to be negatively affected by the media's portrayal of thin women as having the ideal body type. This means if you don't like your body, what you see in the media can really affect you and make you like yourself even less, which may lead to feelings of shame, anxiety, and sadness and to disordered eating.

Even though the media portrays thin as ideal, in the real world everyone looks different, and there's only so much we can do about it. Lexi has taken a healthy approach. She's comfortable with the body she has. Hating your body and constantly striving to have it be something it's not is not healthy. If you're struggling with body image issues, you might want to check out the great YouTube video "Photoshopping real women into cover models" that speaks to the issue of accepting your body. In the video four women of different ages and body types participated in a photo shoot, just like is done with actual models, including photoshopping their pictures the way it's done in magazines. To see what happens, watch the full video at *www.youtube.com/watch?v=zRlpIkH3b5I*. The transcript below is the experience of one of the women:

While thumbing through a fashion magazine: "You look at yourself and you know you can never attain that ideal."

While getting her makeup put on for the photo shoot: "I'm never going to be skinny; I'm not a skinny girl."

While looking at the photoshopped pictures of herself: "Oh my God, I feel like it doesn't even look like me. I like my freckles. I think they add character and the fact that they're gone, I don't even know who that is. You look at these ads in magazines and you see these women look absolutely flawless and you think 'Ahh, I wish I could look like that,' but who really looks like this? Instead of looking at other things and aspiring to be something else we should just be comfortable in who we are and just try to be our best selves."

She's right.

Desire: "Do I feel comfortable being intimate, do I know what I'm ready for, and do I know what sex and intimacy mean to me?"

Lauren is a woman who has met her own *desire* need. Her answer to the question is "Yes, I enjoy having sex, and I'm comfortable talking about it with a guy and letting him know what I like and want. I would never pretend to have an orgasm or that I like something if I don't or that I'm in the mood if I'm not. I know my limits, and I will not do anything that I feel in my gut makes me uncomfortable. That would be disrespecting myself."

I / M E

More about Body Positivity

If you're interested in these issues, here are some interesting things you could check out:

- Jennifer Garner talking, on *The Ellen DeGeneres Show,* about accepting her body and everyone else needing to do so as well. Garner, who has had three children, was addressing the media frenzy around a potential fourth "baby bump." Garner said, "From now on, ladies, I will have a bump. And it will be my baby bump. And let's just all settle in and get used to it" (*https://ca.shine.yahoo. com/what-jennifer-garner-s-everlasting-baby-bump-means-for-women-123708570.html*).

- Laci Green's video "Sexual Objectification." The most important part of the video comes at minute 3:53 where she talks about self-objectification—how we hold ourselves to ridiculous standards: " . . . because women's bodies are subject to constant frivolous criticism, girls learn quickly to self-objectify . . . It's . . . a major contributor to mental health issues like eating disorders and depression which disproportionately affect young women" (*www. youtube.com/watch?v=H0qRDXBsoU0*).

In contrast, Anna does not have a clear sense of what sex and intimacy mean to her. Ideally, Anna doesn't want to have sex with someone she's just started dating or she's just met, but if she's drinking, sex happens sooner rather than later, and then she feels she needs to be in a relationship with the guy—even if she doesn't really like him. In fact, she's infamous among her girlfriends for ending up with what they've coined the "what-was-I-thinking boyfriend." In the past, she's talked to Julianne about this:

Anna: It's as if I trick myself into liking a guy once we have sex.
Julianne: You mean after you have drunk sex! (*giggles*)
Anna: Yeah, talking is easy, I'm really attracted to him, he's funny, and I'm drinking.
Julianne: What do you think about casual sex? Are you hooking up with these guys to find a boyfriend?
Anna: I don't know. Maybe. I don't know why I do this—I guess I get attached—I don't know.

Anna needs to use her insight skill. She needs to really ask herself the *desire* question and examine her thoughts and feelings and how they relate to her behavior. Maybe Anna is conflicted about whether it's okay to have casual sex. Maybe she's afraid she'll hurt a guy's feelings if she doesn't pursue the relationship. Maybe, as she hinted at in her conversation with Julianne, the experience of having sex makes her feel more attached to a guy, more in love, and results in a wish for closeness and intimacy that trumps the reality of who the guy is. (More on this subject in the sidebar below.)

Remember, Anna jumped right into a relationship, and then a marriage, with Eric after having sex with him, even though she didn't like how he had treated her. Was that a good decision for her? Or was she acting on a desire need into which she had no insight? If it was the latter, then she would have benefited from a lesson from Mia. Remember what she said after Lexi posed the question about casual sex: "How can you not think about the future?" Mia said, "I do. The guy's in my head the next morning for a while. I find myself thinking, 'Would my friends like him? My parents?' But then I let it go. You've got to be in reality about these things." Mia understands her *desire* need; she enjoys casual sex and knows it can lead to fantasies about the future, but she also knows it is not necessarily going to become a relationship, nor will it give her enough information about whether she wants it to become a relationship. This understanding allows her to behave in a realistic manner.

If you want to understand how to get your *desire* need met, you need to examine your beliefs about sex, your sexual behaviors, and the feelings you have in relation to experiences in sexually relevant situations (for example, when you first meet a guy, when you're out on a date, before, during, and after a sexual experience) across different types of relationships. For example, you might ask yourself, "When I think about casual sex, what are my thoughts and feelings?" Are you okay with having no idea what will happen and with knowing only that you are attracted to him? Are you okay with having to show yourself, physically and emotionally, to someone you don't know well? Are you okay with however it develops afterward, such as

---

I/ME

"Can Hormones Released after Sex Make Us Think We're in Love?"

When people have sex, their bodies release the hormone oxytocin. Oxytocin is associated with social bonding and feelings of safety and trust. Although it's just a hypothesis, people have speculated that oxytocin may, therefore, be responsible for the feelings of love that follow sex. If that's true it could explain why a woman might be likely to feel "in love" after having sex with a guy. Keep your eye on the research on oxytocin in the future to see what else develops about its role in love.

if it's just a one-time thing, or will you want more? What emotions come up for you when you're in, or as you think about, different scenarios? Are you excited or nervous? Do you feel happy or disappointed? Use the skill of insight to become more self-aware by better understanding the ways you get your needs met and then let that information guide the choices you make. This is how each of us can make informed, thoughtful (that is, conscious) decisions instead of using pressure from guys, family, or friends, or sociocul-turally driven pressures that tell us what we "should" do.

Interesting: *"Do I have a life of my own that I feel good about regardless of whether I'm in a relationship?"*

Lexi's answer to the question is "Yes, totally. I've always worked hard to get the things I wanted for myself, and I have them and feel good about them." She's living in a nice apartment, making enough money to support herself, and pursuing her dream of being a sportscaster. She fills her life with activities she enjoys, like sports and yoga and movies, and although she'd like to be in a relationship, she likes the life she's developed for herself. She's not looking to a relationship to make her life interesting. Lauren, on the other hand, is.

Lauren's answer to the question is "I have a great job in marketing, which is how I could afford to buy my own apartment, but I hate my job and I want to try something new—but what? I have no idea. Although I've put figuring out all that on hold because it's been a pretty emotional time for me with trying to figure out my Dan-or-Lucas problem. My priority has always been my relationships. On my own, there's nothing really interest-ing about my life. In addition, I struggle with motivation when I'm not in a relationship, but now that I'm with Dan, I feel so full of his love that I want to work on myself. With the knowledge that we love each other, I feel so much energy to take care of him and be the best version of myself."

This is a risky situation to be in. It means Lauren's happiness in life depends on being in a relationship. It also means she will always be living her partner's interesting life rather than her own. Lauren appears to be excessively dependent on a relationship to fulfill her need for an interesting life. Excessive dependency is defined as the tendency to look to others for nurturance, guidance, protection, and support, even in situations where autonomous functioning is possible. It is associated with stress in relation-ships and risk for depression, particularly in the face of relationship prob-lems. Because Lauren is not building a life for herself and is relying on a relationship instead, she may be setting herself up for worse problems in the future. What happens to Lauren if she finds herself on her own, without a partner? Do you know the old adage "Don't put all your eggs in one basket"? It really applies here. All of Lauren's eggs are in her relationship basket. If that basket is dropped, all of her eggs are gone and she is left with nothing but her uninteresting, unfulfilling life—a recipe for loneliness and unhappiness. When we build our own interesting life, one that is fulfilling and that we can feel good about, it will always be there for us, no matter what our relationship status is.

Support: "When I'm faced with challenging or upsetting situations, do I deal with them by actively problem-solving rather than avoiding them?"

Olivia's answer is "Yes, yes, yes. I'm definitely a problem solver. If something is wrong, I try to tackle it head on. I'm proactive so that things don't get out of hand. And if I can't come up with a solution, I run it by friends or someone I trust. I like to talk things out. It helps me get clear on what to do."

Lauren's answer is "I'm aware that when I don't know how to deal with something I run, I shut down, I block, I avoid. I also know I have a tendency to rush into things without thinking them through just to get it over with, and I find myself drinking more when I can't deal with what is going on in my relationships."

Olivia and Lauren are on opposite ends of the problem-solving spectrum. Olivia is active; Lauren avoids. That's good news for Olivia but bad news for Lauren because all evidence points to the fact that active coping, which involves taking a problem-solving approach, is healthy and results in better outcomes than avoidant coping, which involves avoiding the problem. People who are avoidant copers tend to withdraw from, ignore, or deny problems, and they may use alcohol and drugs as a way to do so. People who are active copers focus on identifying the problem to be solved, generating potential solutions, and then choosing and acting on the one that seems best. Unlike problem solvers, avoiders find their problems remain and often get worse over time, which can lead to more and more avoidance.

Olivia uses another excellent strategy to meet her *support* need. She turns to others to help her figure things out. Receiving assistance from others in the form of "instrumental" support, such as tangible help with problem solving, or "emotional" support, such as encouragement and validation, is associated with greater psychological well-being, especially decreased risk for depression. So, when you're faced with a problem to solve, the healthiest strategies are to take an active approach to the problem and to turn to your support system to help you do so.

Care: "Am I aware of how I feel, do I treat my feelings as legitimate, and do I use them to guide my behavior?"

Mia answers this question with a yes: "I'm aware of how I'm feeling all the time. Yesterday I came home really stressed out from school. I was supposed to see Corey right away—he was expecting me to join him and his friends for drinks and dinner—but I knew if I didn't unwind I wouldn't have a good time and wouldn't be able to really be present with him. So I called the campus recreation center to see if they had an opening for a massage, and they did, so I did that. I knew that's what I needed, so I called Corey and explained that I would meet him for dinner, not drinks. He was disappointed, but I knew it was for the best."

Olivia's answer: "I do care about my feelings, but sometimes I feel more concerned about someone else's feelings than my own. With my last boyfriend, when I was feeling resentful about something, I didn't show it. I went along with what he wanted to do, to make sure he was okay, like when I found out he was cheating on me. We reconciled, but I wasn't fully over it, and when we were fooling around I realized I didn't feel ready to do that, but I didn't want to upset him, so I didn't say anything. I just went along with it for him. I wanted that relationship to work."

In these scenarios, Mia demonstrates that she takes her feelings seriously and meets her care need well. Although Olivia recognizes her feelings, she says she sometimes cares about those of others more. In fact, a number of the characters do the same thing. Remember how Julianne didn't express her feelings to Gregory when he blamed her for getting lost while they were driving to their friend's wedding? Instead, she just told him she loved him and acted as if nothing had happened. And Lauren does this with Dan and Lucas too. Whenever they say something that hurts her feelings, like when Lucas talks about his ex-wife, Lauren gets really hurt and upset, but she does not give voice to her feelings. Instead she has a silent fight in her head.

Olivia, Julianne, and Lauren are all engaging in *self-silencing*. Self-silencing is a very unhealthy behavior. It involves not voicing one's thoughts, feelings, opinions, and needs out of fear of how the other person will respond, and it's associated with feelings of low self-worth and depression. When women silence themselves, they are failing to meet their *care* need, hurting themselves, and engaging in unhealthy relationship behavior. When you think about whether you're meeting your *care* need, you should ask yourself whether you silence yourself. If you do, we encourage you to face your fears and take the risk to give voice to your thoughts, feelings, opinions, and needs. Not doing so means you're still trying to be what the guy wants rather than being who you are and seeing if he wants what you have to offer.

Listen: "Do I pay attention to what my gut/intuition is telling me and use it to help me make choices?"

Lexi says, "I really try to now, but before I didn't, and I used to say, 'Ah, man, I should have listened to my gut' *all the time*. Even taking exams I'd not go with my gut instinct and I'd get the answer wrong. I'd be like 'I

should have listened to myself.' I definitely did not use my gut in my relationship with my ex-boyfriend, Jake, in high school. I'd ignore red flags even
though I kind of knew it was something I should have paid attention to,
and then later, in retrospect, I'd be like 'Ahh, I knew that. I knew in my gut
that was going to happen.'"

Mia is definitely going to have to work on meeting her need to *listen*
as she navigates her relationship with Corey. As you saw in the earlier
chapters, he's about to move back to his hometown, so they'll be in a long-
distance relationship. The "free pass" idea came up when Corey was considering hooking up, maybe having an FWB relationship, with a friend of his
who still lives there. After discussing the idea, Mia and Corey agreed that
instead of him hooking up with a former friend, they both could engage in
random hookups without emotional connections. Still, Mia is dealing with
two different sets of feelings about Corey hooking up: jealousy (because she
was cheated on in the past and still feels a bit insecure) and sexual arousal.
Part of her doesn't want him to do it. Part of her does. How is Mia going to
deal with these conflicting feelings? She's going to need to pay attention to
her deepest inner voice. She's going to have to really listen to her intuition.
This may take some time. That's okay. What's important is that Mia stay
open to what that deep-down voice is telling her so she can figure it out.
Over time, Mia may find she really cannot take Corey having sex with
another woman, that it's just too painful for her. No matter how arousing
she finds it, the pain outweighs the pleasure. Or she may discover she's
totally into open sexual experiences. That they feel liberating and exciting
and she can willingly and comfortably share the experience with Corey
and be happy about being able to help him meet his needs in this way.

Whatever it is that Mia's intuition eventually tells her, it's okay. There's
no objective right or wrong. Just what's right or wrong for her. When a
woman is courageous enough to really listen to her gut and then act on
what she knows feels right, she will make better relationship choices. These
choices may not always be easy or result in the outcome we'd hoped for. For
instance, if Mia's gut eventually tells her she can't be in an open relationship and Corey doesn't want to be monogamous, then Mia may need to exit
the relationship. That would be sad and difficult, but in the end better for
Mia because it will give her the opportunity to be in the kind of relationship that is right for her. One where her intuition tells her, "Yes, this is
right." When that happens, it's a really good feeling, and you know you're
getting the relationship you want. That's where you want to be.

Important: "Do I consider and value my needs in my choices?"

Emily's answer is "I'm really trying to! I'm trying to figure out how to balance my career goals and my relationship goals. I know I can't give up

everything to move to be with Will. It's too important to me to pursue my career. I'm just struggling with figuring out where the compromise will be, what will make me happiest."

Lauren's answer also is "I'm trying to!" However, as you can hear in the rest of her response, she is less able to do so than Emily. "I would love to see my girlfriends more. I would love to go back to school. But I can't. Dan really needs me to be there for him and go places with him. It's really important to him, and he gets really upset when I'm not available. I love him! So I make myself available. There is no other option."

As you might have guessed, the need to consider your own needs *important* is directly related to the skill of mutuality. Just as a reminder, mutuality means behaving in a way that takes into account the needs of both people in a relationship. This includes your own! There are two ways that mutuality can go wrong. One is when you are overly focused on your own needs to the exclusion of your partner's (kind of like Dan, which we'll hear more about later). The other is when you are overly focused on your partner's needs to the exclusion of your own. This describes Lauren. She is neither valuing her own needs nor attempting to get them met. If Lauren doesn't treat her needs as *important*, she will never be able to be in a mutual relationship.

Emily, on the other hand, is really trying to take her needs seriously and, consequently, to have a relationship based in mutuality. She gets the idea that both people have needs and both sets of needs have to be attended to. She values Will's need to pursue medicine at the best possible school. She values her own need to have a career. She may not yet know how to work this all out—and, in fact, it's hard when needs conflict—but she understands that she has to always try to treat her needs as *important*.

Trust: "Do I trust myself not to engage in behaviors that would betray who I am or what I need?"

Olivia has to make a decision about sleeping with Zach. Can she trust herself not to betray who she is? With regard to sex, it's not as if she's ever felt she wasn't ready for sex. She's just not a fan of casual sex. She does not want to be with someone with whom she doesn't have a relationship and an emotional connection. She was encouraged by her family to date, to fall in love, to wait to have sex until she felt that a guy was worthy of her and she loved him. She just met Zach, and people have told her he's a hookup kind of guy. But the problem is that when Olivia met him, it was love at first sight for her. In addition, he's not only the first guy she's been attracted to in this way but the first guy she's felt these kinds of sexual urges for. She's been hoping to meet her soul mate in college. Could this be him? Do these feelings signify "soul mate"? Can sex lead to a soul mate relationship?

These feelings have confused Olivia, and she's not sure she can trust herself not to betray her own values around sex. So, when Zach said, "Follow me," and she did, Olivia put herself in a high-risk situation where she would be tempted to go against what she had always believed in, and this might have emotional consequences for her, such as guilt or shame or anxiety. Why did she let herself follow Zach? In part because of her emotional reaction to him—the feelings of love, or perhaps lust, that she's experiencing may have led her heart (or other parts of her body) to take over her head, suggesting Olivia may need to work on regulating her emotions to bring heart and head back into better balance.

Another likely reason Olivia followed Zach is that she had been drinking—and purposely so. It's as if she were regulating the wrong emotions in this case. Olivia was probably anxious about being with Zach because she's not comfortable with casual sex, but instead of letting that anxiety provide the information she needs to trust herself and not do something that makes her anxious, she quelled the anxiety with alcohol, at the same time quelling what her head was telling her. In most cases, alcohol is a sure-fire way to increase the chances that we'll do something we would not normally do if put in a tempting situation. So, if you enjoy drinking, just remember you'll want to keep your *trust* need in mind.

Lexi's also in a situation where she's struggling with trusting herself. Ever since she initiated the date with James she's been second-guessing herself. She's worried that by her making the first move he'll think she's saying she wants to hook up after the game. That's not what she wants. She doesn't want a casual sexual relationship. Remember in Chapter 2, when Lexi was talking with Mia about whether hooking up could be a pathway into a relationship for her? Lexi was clear on how she preferred to get her *desire* need met when she said, "I want to feel special to him, to feel he wants a relationship with me and that maybe there's a future, and I need to be the only person he's having sex with at that time." Now Lexi can't stop thinking, "What message have I sent? What expectations have I set?" She's conflicted about whether she should have listened to Emily and Mia and put herself out there as she did or whether she should have "played it safe"—in line with traditional gender roles, where the man initiates and the woman is more passive.

The date day arrives, and as you saw in Chapter 2, she ends up on the bed with James, and she's enjoying herself. As you also saw, she has a decision to make—in the heat of the moment—which presents a challenge. Should she slow things down? Should she go with what's happening? "Ugh!" she thinks. "Why did I make the first move? What's he going to think if we don't have sex?"

In that moment, Lexi realizes she needs to trust herself. She's already in so much turmoil she's got to use her insight and get her emotions in line

---
I/ME

Do You Use Traditional Gender Role Stereotypes to Make Decisions about How to Act?

Research shows that such stereotypes still exist. For example, both women and men tend to think that the guy should be in control of the date, including initiating, planning, and paying for it.

What do you think of this idea? Do you agree with it? Do you disagree with it? Why? Make sure that you're making conscious choices based on what you need and what's right for you rather than giving in to external pressures.

---

and not betray who she knows she really is. She tells James she'd like to slow down—she prefers to get to know a guy more before she goes further. He wants to go further, but when she suggests they catch the sports wrap-up on the 11:00 P.M. news before she heads home, he agrees. On the way home, she's so happy she trusted herself.

However, the next morning, Lexi cannot get him off her mind—the way he kissed and touched her. Now what? Her mind is racing. "Is he going to want to see me again even though we didn't have sex? Should I wait to see what he does? Is he expecting me to text him? I really want him to text me!" She keeps checking her phone to see if he has—nothing. She texts Emily:

Lexi: ☺ Why hasn't James texted?
Emily: Text him.
Lexi: He should be pursuing me, though.
Emily: Then wait.
Lexi: What if he's expecting me to text since I made the first move? Ugh, I'm so confused.
Emily: Did you have sex?
Lexi: No. Told him I wanted to get to know him better first. Afraid that now he's not interested anymore.
Emily: You'll find out.
Lexi: I like him. I want him to like me and show it.
Emily: Then wait and see.
Lexi: It's hard.
Emily: You can't have it both ways.
Lexi: ☹

Lexi's confused. She doesn't know what to trust because she's not sure what she needs. Does she really need to be pursued? She's seen that being the initiator stresses her out, and she misses being pursued as she has been with other guys. At the same time, maybe being the initiator is okay. If she really wants to know whether he wants to see her again, she could ask him and find out. She already made it clear she's not in it for a hookup. So what's she got to lose? But if she texts him, is that her trying to make him like her? She knows what matters is that he like her for who she is. She'd trust that more if he made the next move.

Sometimes it can be hard to know what to trust in yourself. Particularly if you're trying something new, as Lexi did with initiating. In these cases, it's important to use your insight as best you can (use your skills to listen to your gut) to make a decision and then use feedback from the consequences to develop greater insight about what you need and what to trust. This is a very effective strategy if you are really open to what might happen and willing to learn from it. In fact, one of the ways we develop insight is by taking a course of action, evaluating the outcome, and making

---

I/ME

More about Gender Stereotypes

Hillary Clinton has said, " . . . it's important to help men and women recognize when they are crossing over from an individual judgment, which we are prone to make, have a right to make about someone (man or woman), into a stereotype, applying some gender-based characterization of a person . . ." (*www.upworthy.com/two-very-powerful-women-get-asked-about-double-standards-their-responses-probably-wont-shock-you?c=reccon1*).

Was Lexi making an individual judgment or a gender-based characterization when she feared that because she made the first move James would think she was a slut who only wanted to hook up? That was a gender-based characterization. She didn't know James well enough to make an individual judgment. However, if James was thinking that way and expecting sex, Lexi reset his expectations by trusting herself and not going further than she wanted. Now Lexi can see who James really is by how he responds to her limits rather than trying to guess who he is based on gender stereotypes.

Bottom line: Trust yourself, set your limits, and see how he reacts. That will tell you who he is and whether he's what you want.

any necessary revisions to our understanding of a situation and our behavior. For example, let's say Lexi decides to wait and see if James texts her. If a few days go by and Lexi doesn't hear from him, she might decide he's not interested and be okay with that—disappointed, but okay—and then move on. If she really is okay, then her strategy of waiting for him worked for her and she can continue to trust herself with this strategy in the future.

What if, however, she starts to feel anxious and finds herself ruminating over the idea that maybe he thinks if a girl initiates first, and if she likes him, she'll keep initiating? In that case, Lexi might want to reevaluate her original strategy now that she has insight into her own experience (anxiety and rumination), and she may want to text James to find out whether he's still interested.

Lexi could use the same process (using insight to make a decision and using feedback from the consequences to develop further insight) if she initially decided to text James rather than wait. Whatever the outcome, it would provide her with important feedback about what to trust in herself in the future.

Accept: "Do I accept who I am? Do I take responsibility for my behavior, without being self-critical, feeling ashamed, or treating myself in a harsh manner?"

Does Mia accept herself? Her answer is "I think I'm very hard on myself. Corey always points out that I am. I know this is my flaw. Yet it's something I refuse to let go of because my argument is you can always be a better version of yourself. Here's an example: If I go out and have a couple beers on a weeknight instead of studying, my self-talk is 'You should have been studying more. What's wrong with you? You're so irresponsible. Bad Mia!' And I just keep repeating this. It's miserable! I say these kinds of things to myself all the time."

Mia is highly self-critical. She judges herself and punishes herself and ends up feeling bad. She's also a perfectionist. She holds herself to extremely high standards, and she doesn't cut herself any slack. Perfectionism and self-criticism are unhealthy. They can lead to depression, anxiety, shame, and low self-worth. Self-criticism and perfectionism can also result from low self-worth—those "I'm not good enough" thoughts and feelings. It can be a vicious cycle where a woman doesn't feel good about herself, sets perfectionist standards and criticizes herself for not meeting them, and then feels even worse about herself. Does this sound like you? If so, you're not meeting your own *accept* need. To remedy this, you'll need to recognize how self-criticism hurts rather than helps you, and you'll need to work on accepting yourself as you are. This doesn't mean you can't work on changing things you're not satisfied with. Rather, you need to accept the reality that no one is perfect, develop compassion for your imperfections, recognize and embrace your strengths, and set reality-based expectations for what is really possible. Hard to do, but really necessary.

What would Mia sound like if she did accept herself? Something more like this: "I'm ambitious, perfectionistic, funny, kind, and sensitive, but I do tend to procrastinate, and I'm really disorganized. So sure, sometimes I go for a beer instead of studying, but I do get all my assignments in, and I get the kind of marks I need to get into a master's program for finance." If this were Mia's self-talk, she would feel a lot better about herself. She would be adopting a great emotion regulation strategy by using self-talk that was realistic and made her feel better rather than worse.

Olivia demonstrates another way in which a person might not meet her own *accept* need. She doesn't admit to and take responsibility for a certain aspect of her behavior. People are constantly telling Olivia she's judgmental, as Mia did in Chapter 1 when they were talking about hooking up. Yet Olivia refuses to acknowledge this. She says things like "People think I'm judging, but I'm not. I tell people what I think, but my intention is good. I can't help it if it's not received that way. If my friends tell me things and I give them another perspective, they think I'm judging them, but I'm just trying to help them deal with the situation they brought to me." Here's the bottom line: if the people who know you best *all* experience you in the same way, it's really likely they're right. When this is the case, it's important to pay attention. There is something you will need to accept in yourself and take responsibility for. If you ever find yourself in this kind of situation, you might want to go back and do a trait assessment, maybe even with the help of your friends to see which traits they're talking about. Truly taking responsibility for who you are and how you behave opens up the possibility that you could work on changing things you don't like or that hurt other people. And that will help you have healthier relationships.

There is even another way in which women might not meet their *accept* need: by not accepting what they really want. Julianne grew up watching her mother struggle financially to raise three kids after her father left. She vowed she would never let that happen to her. So she became completely career focused in part as a way to secure her financial independence. As she was pursuing her goals, she told herself she didn't need a relationship; her career was much more important. Underneath this, though, Julianne actually did want a relationship. Her fear of not being able to support herself, her drive to be totally self-sufficient, got in the way of letting her accept the fact that she was missing out on something she wanted. Over time, as her friends and family kept talking with her about whether she was dating and why she wasn't, she came to realize she needed to accept her desire for a relationship and learn to balance work life and emotional life so she could have one. Had she not realized and accepted this, she would have missed out on something that would allow her to live a more genuine life that was meaningful to her and reflective of all she truly is and what she truly wants.

Forgive: *"Do I forgive myself for mistakes I've acknowledged and allow myself to stop thinking about them and move on?"*

Lexi says, "I tend to hold on to stuff, especially about what happened with my ex-boyfriend, Jake. I was so totally in love with him. I wanted that relationship to work. I still can't forgive myself for that time that I was so angry at him that I pushed him and hit him with my purse. My emotions were so out of control. Our relationship went downhill after that, and not a day goes by that I'm not angry at myself for what I did. I will never do something like that again, but I still can't forgive myself." Lexi did make a serious mistake. As we'll discuss more in later chapters, physical aggression in relationships is unacceptable. However, she made a commitment to herself never to behave that way again and deserves self-compassion.

As you've seen, Emily has done some not-so-nice things in her relationship, such as sending nasty texts to Will when she's feeling neglected, and she feels bad about that. Now that she understands her behavior and is working on changing it, she also needs to forgive herself for what she did and move forward.

Self-forgiveness involves acknowledging the wrongdoing without condoning or excusing it, overcoming negative feelings about the self, and treating the self with compassion. Research indicates that, in romantic relationships, people who are less self-forgiving following a relationship transgression that they committed—particularly people who hold on to negative feelings about themselves—are less satisfied in their relationships, and their partners are too. This suggests that forgiving yourself—after appropriately acknowledging the transgression—is better for your relationship. So if you want a more satisfying relationship, work on self-forgiveness.

Help: *"Do I take responsibility for what needs to happen in my life and make sure it gets done?"*

Julianne balances career and life by work, work, work, see family, work, work, see friends, work, work, work, see family, and when she gets a break in one of her projects, she pulls up her mile-long to-do list and then does to-dos, to-dos, to-dos until she's followed through with all the urgent ones. It works for her; it always has. It's how she got through undergrad and her MBA and why she now gets fast-tracked for promotions at work. She always gets done what she needs to get done.

Lauren, on the other hand, struggles with this. She's had some big achievements (getting a good job, owning her own apartment), but some of the daily activities of life, like paying the bills, taking care of her car, and fixing things around the house, are things she doesn't like to do on her own. She'd like to have her boyfriend take care of those things for her. That's, in part, why she finds being with Dan so comforting. He takes care of things. The problem here is what Lauren would do if she didn't have a boyfriend to help her. What would happen to her life? This is another example of how Lauren is dependent on relationships. Turning to others for help with practical everyday things can be a healthy use of social support. Expecting or needing a partner to take care of everything is not and reflects a lack of healthy self-reliance.

Safe: "Do I recognize situations that are potentially dangerous for me (emotionally, physically, and practically) and make my safety a priority?

Julianne would probably answer yes to this question. However, if she did, she'd be lacking insight. Remember in Chapter 2, "Finding 2: A bad relationship is NOT good for your health," we noted that one of the things that makes a relationship unhealthy is having a partner who is critical of you. Gregory is highly critical of Julianne, but she has not fully realized yet that tolerating this constant criticism is not in line with keeping herself emotionally safe. Julianne is aware that nothing she ever does seems right or good enough in Gregory's eyes. She's not fully aware of the toll it's taking on her. Involvement with a critical partner is associated with relationship dissatisfaction and deterioration as well as with symptoms of depression. Julianne is, therefore, at risk for emotional distress.

Emily also failed to keep herself safe in one of her hookups during the time she and Will took a break. Emily was drunk—a common precursor to hookups as Chapter 2 showed—and the foreplay was fun and erotic, but then he seemed to lose interest in pleasing her. Instead, he wanted her to go down on him, and he was being very graphic about what he wanted. It reminded her of porn films she'd seen. At this point Emily was starting to sober up and suddenly realized she didn't want to be there. Had it been Will asking for this, she would have liked it, but with hookup guy, it turned her off. She didn't even know him. She had just met him that night. When she said she was feeling uncomfortable, he was surprised and said, "I think what I asked is fair. You wanted this as much as I did." And she thought, "Yes, it's true, I did. But now I don't." But she finished what she started— because she felt bad that she had maybe led him on. She believed that giving him what he wanted was an easy way to wrap things up and leave. She thought, "It will be over soon enough." And it was, but she didn't feel good about herself. She felt as if she had just been a player in a hard-core porn film, not an equal partner in a sexually intimate exchange, and it disgusted her.

I/ME

Did Emily Really Consent?

To understand what it really means to consent—how to ask for it, what a "No" sounds like (even after you've started), and what a "Yes" sounds like—watch the video "Wanna Have Sex? [Consent 101]" by Laci Green, *www.youtube.com/watch?v=TD2EooMhqRI*, who is doing her part to create a consent culture where all the sex that is had is sex that is wanted.

And if you want to open people's eyes to the difference between sex and porn, check out Cindy Gallop's TED Talk (*www.youtube.com/watch?v=FV8n_E_6Tpc*) and her website "Make Love Not Porn" (*http://makelovenotporn.com/pages/landing*).

Here's one of her examples:

Porn world: Men love coming on women's faces and women love having men come on their faces.

Real world: Some women like this, some women don't. Some guys like to do this, some guys don't. Entirely up to personal choice.

Emily didn't keep herself safe in this situation. She engaged in an activity she didn't want to participate in, with someone she barely knew, and she felt bad about herself afterward. Thankfully, it wasn't worse for Emily. What if he had insisted on having intercourse without a condom? What if he had wanted to tie her up or restrain her in some way? Would she have done it? If she had, she would have been putting herself in both

---

I/ME

How Do You Keep Yourself Safe When You Hook Up?

Part of the allure of a hookup, even with someone you think you know, can be the spontaneity and novelty of the situation. Unfortunately, that's also what can make it unsafe, because you don't know who the guy really is, what he's looking for, and whether he's got an STI.

As difficult as it is, it's always important to find out. You may not want to "break the spell" of the moment, but you'll wish you had if you end up with an STI. Furthermore, know your limits—what you will and won't be part of —and communicate those clearly.

If you want to read more about how to talk about sex, check out the website "It's Your (Sex) Life" (*www.itsyoursexlife.com/stds-testing-gyt*).

---

practical and physical danger—she could have contracted an STI, and he might have hurt her physically. She didn't even know him and therefore had no way to assess what he was capable of. By failing to keep herself safe just because she bought into the idea that she had led him on, Emily prioritized his needs over hers. She became what he wanted, rather than being herself and taking care of her need to be *safe*. If Emily had personal power, she would have said, "Yeah, you're right, I did want this, but now that I'm sobering up, I don't. I'm not comfortable with what you're asking for. I know you feel I led you on, but I have to do what I have to do."

How Does Meeting the "I Know and Like Myself" Needs Give You Personal Power?

Meeting these needs gives you personal power because doing so allows you to know, accept, and respect yourself, to be autonomous enough to take care of yourself, and to be open to genuine intimacy with someone who wants what you have to offer. Think of the 14 needs as 14 ways to increase your personal power. Fourteen guiding principles you should always be working toward. The more you can meet your own needs, the more you'll be able to have a healthy and mutual relationship. We want you to know yourself, like yourself, understand yourself, and be able to put the concept of personal power into practice in your life and in your relationships.

4

I Know and Like Him

Knowing and liking him means you are confident he is the guy you want and you treat him in a way that shows you like and respect him.

In the last chapter we showed you how to identify and meet your own needs whether you're currently in a relationship or not so that you can develop your personal power. The next step in the journey is to begin assessing your needs specifically in relation to the guy you're interested in or in a relationship with. Developmental psychologists—those who study how people develop over their life span—tell us that one of the key questions people need to figure out is this: Given the kind of person I am, what kind of person do I wish to have as a partner? Therefore, in this chapter, we focus on the question "Who do I want to be with and why?"

On the dating/sex scene, it can be very easy to focus solely on the question "Does he want to be with me?" We can get caught up in wondering things like "Does he really like me?" and "Am I hot enough for him?" and "How can I make him want to be with me?" Refocusing on the question "Do *I* want to be with *him*?" shifts your perspective to your needs, not just his, so you can really decide whether *you* know and like *him*. This is a more mutual, healthy way of approaching relationships.

Many women think they really know and like a guy (that is, they're confident he is the guy they want) after they meet him in a bar or read his profile or creep on his Facebook page or even after a date or two. When asked to describe him they might list things like "He's smart and has a job," "He's got good father potential," "He's kind and attentive," "He's physically fit," "He's so much fun," or "We're so alike." These are all good things, but they don't really cover the bases on meeting potential needs. Furthermore, some of them are things you can't truly know about a guy until you have more data—until you really observe his behavior and get to know him over time and across situations. Doing so will help you develop insight you can use to decide whether a guy is really the one you want.

To help you with this, we're going to describe each "I know and like him" need and provide examples from the seven women's story lines as they assess and observe their guys' behavior. As we do this, think about each need and start to select ones you think might be key for you (use the checkboxes we provide). In a healthy relationship, all the needs are met satisfactorily. However, you might find there are some that are priorities for you. You may not know which they are. In fact, you may not figure this out until you see they're not met. Don't worry about your answer being right or wrong; just use your gut, and if you're not sure, that's okay. You'll have plenty of time throughout the rest of the book to fine-tune your Key Needs List (provided at the end of this chapter) as you see how each need plays out in the women's relationships and, if you're in a relationship, as you start to assess whether they're actually being met in yours. As you do this, you'll be further developing personal power and increasing the chances of being with the guy who is really right for you.

At the end of the description and illustrations of each need, we offer a space for you to jot any thoughts you have about that need to help you figure out whether it might be key for you.

Familiar: "Do I know his best and worst traits? Do I understand how they make him who he is, influence how he acts, and affect the way he gets his needs met?"

Mia's answer reflects insight into Corey. For best traits, she says, "Corey is really funny, extremely considerate, and one of the most passionate people I know. His passion drives him to want to engage fully in things, but his considerate nature lets him recognize other people's needs. Like this issue we're dealing with about him wanting to hook up with other women. He's really into the idea, but he gets that it's important to consider my feelings about it too."

For worst traits, Mia says, "He's not that patient, so he can get frustrated with things sometimes. For example, he was making pie once, and it was taking a long time to work the dough, so he started to curse out the pie. Then, of course, he calmed down and realized he was being impatient. I see this with his behavior with me sometimes. Like one night, before he moved, we were leaving to go meet up with friends, and he wanted to take the recycling out on our way. Well, it's my job to sort it out, and I hadn't done it yet, and when he saw that he got really annoyed and was like 'What the fuck? The recycling isn't separated, and now we're gonna be late! Can you just hurry up and do this! I really want to get out of here!' So I just told him to relax—it's just one bin of stuff—and I did the job quickly, and I knew in a few minutes he would calm down and see he was being impatient, just like he did with the pie, and that's exactly what happened. I know not to take it personally because it's not personal. I just let it go."

Mia is able to use what she knows about Corey to understand him—both the good and the not so good—and she has factored all of it into her decision about whether to be in a relationship with him. Lauren, on the other hand, is not insightful about her partners' traits, especially their worst ones, nor does she know how to use them to make relationship decisions.

Lauren/Dan/Lucas Recap: When Lauren was struggling to decide whether she wanted to be with Dan or Lucas, she was confused; she felt a connection to both, but in different ways. She used what she was familiar with: "Dan is affectionate, confident, funny, generous, and outgoing." She believed he could bring excitement into her life. "Lucas is conscientious, disciplined, and organized." She believed he could bring structure into her life. So Lauren felt as if she was trying to choose between two different positives, excitement and structure.

However, Lauren wasn't focusing on Dan's and Lucas's negative traits, or at least not considering them in her decision. Negative traits may not be apparent at the start of a relationship, but we all have them, and if you're looking for them (which you should be) you'll see them. For example, Dan's worst traits are that he's jealous (remember in Chapter 1 how he pulled the business card out of Lauren's hand when she was at a party?), demanding (he expects her to attend all of his events), and controlling (he insists she do what he says). Lucas's worst traits are that he's rigid and self-focused (he lives his life in a particular way with no interest in modifying it for Lauren, including his ongoing attachment to his ex-wife).

If Lauren was focusing on these traits and factoring them into her decisions, she might understand, for example, how in getting structure from Lucas she also has to live with the fact that he may be interested in only his own structure. Or in getting excitement from Dan she also has to live with the fact that he may want full control of her. Are either of these situations what Lauren really wants? Might she find someone whose best traits can result in excitement and structure and who doesn't come with worst traits that hurt her? If Lauren was truly familiar with Dan's and Lucas's best and worst traits, she might be making different decisions.

What are your guy's traits (use the checklist on the facing page)?

Authentic: "Is he fully open to showing all aspects of himself and to facing whatever fears he has about doing so?"

❏ KEY NEED?

"Yes. Corey is 100% real with me," says Mia. "I've asked him to be real with me from the start because I know it's a key need for me. I told him, 'I want

	Best	Worst		Best	Worst		Best	Worst
Adventurous	☐	☐	Energetic	☐	☐	Outgoing	☐	☐
Affectionate	☐	☐	Enthusiastic	☐	☐	Outspoken	☐	☐
Aggressive	☐	☐	Even-			Passionate	☐	☐
Ambitious	☐	☐	tempered	☐	☐	Passive	☐	☐
Anxious	☐	☐	Excitable	☐	☐	Patient	☐	☐
Assertive	☐	☐	Excitement			Perfectionistic	☐	☐
Attention			seeking	☐	☐	Pessimistic	☐	☐
seeking	☐	☐	Fearless	☐	☐	Quick-		
Calm	☐	☐	Focused	☐	☐	tempered	☐	☐
Cautious	☐	☐	Funny	☐	☐	Reliable	☐	☐
Close-minded	☐	☐	Generous	☐	☐	Reserved	☐	☐
Competitive	☐	☐	Honest	☐	☐	Responsive	☐	☐
Confident	☐	☐	Impatient	☐	☐	Rigid	☐	☐
Conscientious	☐	☐	Impulsive	☐	☐	Selfish	☐	☐
Controlling	☐	☐	Inflexible	☐	☐	Sensitive	☐	☐
Courageous	☐	☐	Irresponsible	☐	☐	Shy	☐	☐
Creative	☐	☐	Jealous	☐	☐	Sociable	☐	☐
Critical	☐	☐	Kind	☐	☐	Spontaneous	☐	☐
Daring	☐	☐	Manipulative	☐	☐	Stubborn	☐	☐
Deceitful	☐	☐	Moody	☐	☐	Submissive	☐	☐
Demanding	☐	☐	Open-minded	☐	☐	Suspicious	☐	☐
Disciplined	☐	☐	Opinionated	☐	☐	Thoughtful	☐	☐
Disorganized	☐	☐	Optimistic	☐	☐	Unselfish	☐	☐
Easygoing	☐	☐	Organized	☐	☐			

you to share what you're thinking—tell me straight up. I want you to be honest, not lie to protect my feelings.' And he does what I asked. He tells me what's in his head about everything—when he wanted to be exclusive, when that girl from back home contacted him, that he was moving but wanted to stay together with me, that he wants to move to whatever city I move to after graduation, that he wants to explore the idea of free passes. He told me he did not want to hurt me, he cares about me, and he knew how difficult it would be for both of us not to have sexual experiences, which is why he brought up the idea of free passes. He wanted to continue to be honest about what was going on in his life while in our long-distance relationship. Even though he felt he was taking a big risk telling me everything he thought, he did so because he loves and really cares about me."

Corey's authenticity allows Mia to know him and, importantly, to trust he will be open and honest. Consequently, she doesn't have to worry that Corey will lie to her, say one thing and then do another, or keep some

deep-down secret hidden from her, or that she'll get blindsided by something she didn't expect. Being with someone who is authentic helps a person feel a sense of security and satisfaction. When Lauren was with Lucas
she didn't have the benefit of being with someone who was fully authentic.
He sent her mixed messages by staying with her while at the same time
continuing to express his wish to be with his ex-wife. A lack of authenticity
on the part of your partner, particularly when it manifests in mixed messages, can be crazy-making. Why? Because it results in your questioning
his honesty and wondering what he really thinks or who he really is, and
because it can then lead to your questioning yourself, your own feelings,
and your own sense of reality. You might find yourself thinking, "He says he
wants to be with me, but then he says he needs his space. I don't really feel
loved, but he tells me he loves me. What's real? Is he being honest with me?
Am I missing something? Is it me? I don't understand! I don't get him!" If
you find yourself ever saying these kinds of things to yourself, it's a sure sign
that your partner is not being *authentic* with you.

Thoughts:

Attracted: "Do I like his physical appearance just as it is without wanting it to change?"   ☐ KEY NEED?

Olivia answers, "I love Zach's physical body. He's very attractive—blond
hair, beautiful blue eyes, his hands, his smile—all man. He's exactly what
I want."

Lexi has a thing for athletic guys with broad shoulders who play sports.
She really likes it when a guy plays hockey so she can watch how his body
moves when he skates. That is so not James! But she's absolutely okay with
James's body: "He works out every day. He takes good care of himself, and
he always looks good. Yeah, he doesn't have broad shoulders or play hockey,
and his body type is not what I actually envision as the body type I'm most
attracted to, but he is who he is, and I'm happy with that."

Both Olivia and Lexi are meeting their need to be *attracted*. Olivia is
fortunate to be with someone who meets her exact physical ideals. Lexi is
not, but she recognizes that not everyone will do so, and she's happy with
James's appearance. Lexi's example shows that there may be multiple ways
to get one's need met. For Lexi, having a broad-shouldered hockey player is

an extra goodie—an ideal way of getting her need to be attracted met, but not a necessary way. We call these ideal preferences for the ways to get a need met "pet wants"—great if we can get them, not a problem if we can't. If it turns out you're not willing to get your need met in any way other than your ideal and your partner can't meet it, it might be an unreasonable demand in your relationship (we'll give you more examples of this in Chapter 6).

Can you imagine what would happen if athletic guys with broad shoulders who play sports were not an extra goodie but a necessary requirement for Lexi and she wasn't happy with James's body? We can, and it isn't pretty. First, she might not enjoy being sexually intimate with him. If that were the case and she stayed with him anyway, then she would be sacrificing her satisfaction in an important area. She also might be sending subtle, or not so subtle, signals to James—like not wanting to have sex often or not touching him in certain ways—that might make him feel confused or hurt. Even worse, if she tried to change him by asking him to lose weight or work out more—or even just conveyed that he didn't meet her ideals—it would likely lead to James feeling judged and hurt and, ultimately, to conflict in the relationship. The moral of the story: if you're not attracted to a guy's looks or body, just the way he is, right from the beginning, you'll want to think carefully about your decision to enter a relationship with him. For example, if Olivia likes only blond-haired, blue-eyed guys, then that's who she should date.

Thoughts:

Desire: *"Do I want to be sexual with him, and do I feel comfortable telling him about my sexual interests and needs?"*

Olivia says, "After I followed Zach to his room and he got me on the bed, I was really into what was happening. I loved touching him, being touched by him, feeling close to him. I had never even made out with a guy I wasn't in the 'seriously talking about love' phase with. Then he started to move too fast for me, so I worked up the courage to pull away and say, 'I usually don't do this, move this fast.' He said, 'Do you want to slow down?' and I told him I did. I told him I was a virgin. He said, 'You just need to be clear with how far you want to go when we're hooking up.' And then he backed off and we kissed for a while and went back down to the party together and hung out the rest of the night."

It took courage, but Olivia voiced her preferences. She knew she wanted to be sexual with Zach, and she also knew and communicated her limits, and he respected her, although it could have gone the other way, with Zach not being respectful. And Olivia doesn't know how he will ultimately respond—he is known as a player. Olivia is getting clear on what she needs and on being able to say it. So far, so good, Olivia!

Julianne's answer to the *desire* need question is "Sometimes." Sex with Gregory is moving from great to just okay. That's what typically happens with Julianne because she's not comfortable at the beginning telling a guy about her preferences and interests. She starts a relationship, and the sex seems great because it's new and she's so into him, and then it moves to okay because she hasn't voiced her preferences and therefore she's not getting them met. Remember the research from Chapter 2 about how being able to successfully communicate your sexual needs is associated with greater well-being? Julianne is a great example of someone who isn't following the research because she's afraid of what Gregory will think. Therefore, she doesn't give herself the opportunity to see if successful sexual communication is even possible. Every time she starts a new relationship she *promises* herself she's going to share what sex and intimacy mean to her. She likes reading sex stories in erotica books, and she likes to have a clitoris orgasm, which can take some time for her. Yet so far in this relationship, she hasn't told Gregory.

Worse yet, she's led Gregory to believe that he gives her clitoris orgasms *all the time*, when in fact he doesn't. The first time Gregory played with her clitoris she said, "I really like it when you touch and kiss me there." He was into it, and he likes to do it with 69s, so they did that, but it's hard for her to focus on herself in that position. Not surprisingly, then, he came first. Her self-talk was "OMG! I need to come; I'm taking way too long; he's probably

I/ME

Necessary Requirements or Extra Goodies?

Julianne doesn't know whether erotica or clitoris orgasms are extra goodies or necessary requirements—things she really needs. Until she figures this out, she won't expect to get them and she won't be able to set her standards. When we don't understand our own needs, we can't communicate them to others, and that hurts mutuality.

thinking there is something wrong with him. I have to fake it—*no, don't do it!*" She fakes it. And then he thinks everything is great.

Needless to say, there are things she's afraid to tell and ask Gregory. For example, "I've been faking orgasms with you all along. I'm sorry, I was afraid to tell you. Can we start over with that?" And "I like to read stories about other couples having sex. I find it arousing. Wanna try that, see if you like it too?" Until she does communicate clearly with him, she won't be meeting her own *desire* need, and she will never find out whether Gregory can meet her sexual needs.

Thoughts:

Interesting: "Am I interested in his life (whatever it happens to be), and do I want to be a part of it?"

□ KEY NEED?

Emily is really trying to use her feelings and needs to be honest with herself, and her answer is "Yes and no. Even after all this time, I wake up every single day with him in my head feeling excited about him. It's as if I'm under some sort of spell or something! I really feel we're lucky to have found each other." In addition, she finds Will's premed major fascinating. She loves to hear about what he's studying, and she enjoys the conversations they have about his coursework. She feels like she learns a lot from him. At the same time, even though she knows she wants to be with him in the long run, she's worried she'll feel as if her personal life is on hold if they live together while he's in school. He'll always be studying and working, and they probably won't have a lot of time to see friends and have fun together. Despite the fact that she'd be working and focusing on her career too, she's really not that interested in the med-school girlfriend lifestyle, but she knows that's what it might take to get to the life she is interested in sharing with him. So Emily is really conflicted.

Lexi is not conflicted as she thinks about her relationship with James. They've been dating for six months, and the first few were great—he played sports with her, they went to a lot of games, and once it became clear that he did, in fact, want a monogamous relationship, they had a lot of good sex. But things changed over time, as sometimes happens. Now she says, "I'm finding I'm not really into James's lifestyle. He and his friends just do nothing. They go to someone's house, drink, watch sports, and get hammered.

It just doesn't feel fun for me. It's nice sometimes, but lately he always wants to do the same thing, never something new and exciting. I like to get out and do things more, like we did at the beginning. It's as if he and his friends are stuck in a rut." Lexi's need to find James's life interesting is clearly not being met, and, if this is a key need for Lexi, this does not bode well for their relationship.

Anna's answer to the question is "Yes." First of all, she enjoys all the things Eric likes to do—boating, going to the beach, taking long walks together, going camping—she loves sharing those parts of his life. She also loves his plan for family life. After they decided to get married and have the baby, there were so many exciting things to talk about, plan, and do—a wedding, buying a house, moving in, setting up things for the baby. Doing so became their complete focus. Right at the beginning, Anna and Eric spent time talking about how they each viewed life with a baby, and Eric was clear he wanted to spend time with and provide for his family—that this was his first priority. As soon as Anna heard that she was thrilled and told him she would be very happy to stay at home to take care of the baby so he could focus on making money. Eric seemed so pleased that she was interested in sharing his goals, so they left it at that and went forward with getting everything in place. Anna remembers Eric's expression when Emma was born—she'll never forget his face, how happy he was. Now she loves being in the wife/mom role that complements Eric's husband/dad role.

Emily, Lexi, and Anna are all in different places with regard to their need to find their partner's life *interesting*. At the moment, Anna's the one whose need is most well met. Emily is conflicted, and Lexi is seeing that her need to be interested in her partner's life is not being met. When this need is not being met, it may signal that you and your partner don't want the same things in life. Research shows that partners feel less close to one another and experience more conflict and greater relationship dissatisfaction, as well as reduced individual well-being, when the things they like to do or the goals they have for themselves are mismatched or conflicting. This suggests that getting this need met is an important component of a healthy relationship.

Research also shows that people who are bored in their relationships become more dissatisfied over time. Their boredom leads them to feel less close to their partners and, consequently, less satisfied.

Another reason the need to feel *interested* in your partner's life is important comes from self-expansion theory. This theory, developed by Art and Elaine Aron, social psychologists who study love and relationships, says that people are motivated to expand their sense of self by learning new things and engaging in new activities, and when the self is expanding in these ways people are happier. One way in which people engage in self-expansion is through their partners, by including aspects of the partner and the partner's life in their own sense of self. For example, if your partner is an avid wine collector and teaches you all about wines (and, of course, if this is of interest to you), then you will include these aspects of your partner in your sense of self ("I know a lot about wine now too"), increasing your personal growth and your sense of excitement about your partner and making your relationship more fulfilling.

Lexi is a good example of someone who feels bored and has no sense of self-expansion in her relationship. This is a recipe for dissatisfaction. But if you have found yourself in a similar situation, don't despair. The research shows that when couples actively engage in novel, exciting activities together, they can feel more satisfied—energy returns. So if you can get your partner to engage in this way, hope remains for meeting your *interesting* need.

Thoughts:

Support: "Is he my go-to person in good times and bad times?"

U KEY NEED?

Emily knows *support* is one of her key needs, but she doesn't feel Will is being her go-to person right now. If a guy is your go-to person, you include him in your day-to-day life, so he knows what's going on with you. When something really great—or not so great—happens, he's one of the first people you call to share it with or work through it. But Will's not that available right now. He's always in class or studying, and she knows he doesn't always have the time or energy for her. Emily knows this isn't good for their relationship in the long run, so she finally decides to raise the issue with him. This is a good idea. Being honest and asking direct questions will help Emily determine whether she's going to be able to get her needs met:

Emily: I got that test back the other day but didn't call you. I called Lexi instead.
Will: What?! How'd it go? Why didn't you tell me you had gotten it back?
Emily: Lately, I stop myself when I feel like calling or texting you a flirty message, an exam mark, anything.
Will: Why? What's going on?
Emily: I don't feel like you're my go-to person anymore. You're not available. You have so much else going on.

Will: Emily, I have your back. Let's talk about this when I get there.

Emily: I want to talk about this now.

Will: Do you not want me to come next weekend?

Emily: Of course I want you to come.

Will: If we talk about this now, we may fight. I don't want that. I'd rather talk in person. I need to see you. I miss you. I love you.

Emily: I know you say that, but I need your support. I don't feel like myself with you anymore.

Will: I want to be your go-to person. I get that it looks like I'm not because that's how I'm acting. But I want to be.

Emily: Agghh! I want you to be, but you've got to act it!

Will: Please, let's work this out when I see you next weekend.

Emily: Okay, I can wait until then, but we need to keep talking about this. It's really important to me and our future.

Emily is right that it's important to their future. Research shows that support from one's partner is one of the most important relationship qualities that predict whether couples will be satisfied and whether they will stay together. When people are not good at providing support and when their partners don't experience them as being supportive, both partners are less satisfied. So getting the support you need from your partner is really important.

Mia definitely sees Corey as her go-to person. For example, when her cat died, she took it really hard, and he was right there for her, holding her when she cried and helping her cope with the loss. Now that he's moved away, depending on what the issue is, Emily or Lexi serves as her go-to person because he's not physically there, and Mia is just fine with that. Corey is still a support person over the phone, and in texts and e-mail, but Mia is comfortable turning to her friends if Corey isn't available. She never gets upset with him about this and doesn't have particularly high expectations about his availability in this regard. *Support* is not that key a need for her. In this way, she's very different from Emily. This is a good example of how there's no right or wrong when it comes to what people need in a relationship. People have different key needs. What matters is knowing what yours are so you can make sure you're getting them met. And getting the amount of support from your partner that is right for you is what's important.

Thoughts:

I/ME

Why Do People Have Different Key Needs?

Because each of us has different ideas of what a good relationship is and key needs reflect your idea. Clearly you can see how much work Emily is putting into getting her support need met. It's part of her idea of a good relationship, but it's not for Mia.

Care: *"Am I attuned to his feelings and do I respond in a helpful rather than hurtful way?"*   ⊙ KEY NEED?

Emily says, "Yes, I deeply care about Will's feelings. Early on in our relationship, Will told me, 'It's really hard for me to communicate how I feel. I need you to know that about me.' He was so right! For example, I used to think that we'd moved on after an argument because he would drop the subject, but he hadn't moved on at all. He just wasn't able to tell me how he was feeling, even if I asked. And then I remembered what he had told me, so I realized I needed to learn Will's nonverbal signals for when he's upset. I now see that if I say something that upsets him he'll get quiet and his responses will get short. If he's really upset, he'll take a shower. Now that I know these things, I can go to him and tell him I know he's upset, rather than asking him. It really helps our communication. I also know better what makes him upset, so I can predict when it will happen, like if he doesn't do well on an exam. And I know what's important to him, so I don't bring up things that I'm unhappy about before an exam because I know he won't sleep, and that will get in the way of him doing well, which only makes things worse. So even though he doesn't voice his feelings, I've learned how he does communicate them."

Emily provides a good example of being really attuned to her partner's feelings. She's learned how to identify them—which was not a straightforward process and took some time—and she really shows Will she cares by being willing and able to modulate her own behavior in a way that respects his feelings.

Mia provides a good example of a lapse in care. Mia answers the care question with "Um, I think sometimes I'm a little bit too honest. I say things without thinking about how Corey will feel. The other day he posted a photo, and I made some comment about how he had gained some weight since moving. I think it hurt his feelings. I said I was sorry, but there was nothing I could do to take it back. Ultimately he said, 'You're right,' but I still feel bad that I didn't consider his feelings more before saying it." These kinds of lapses can happen. When they happen frequently or in areas of particular vulnerability for your partner, they can be very damaging and leave your partner feeling extremely hurt. For example, if Corey was very sensitive about his weight or appearance, such a comment from Mia could have a very negative effect on him and how he feels about Mia. We show our partners we like them by being aware of their feelings, particularly their vulnerabilities, and not saying or doing things that will hurt them.

Lauren presents an interesting case of the *care* need gone awry. Lauren's answer to the care question is "I completely care about Dan's feelings. I always ask how he's doing, how he's feeling. I won't push him to get what I want, and if I hurt him by doing something inadvertently and he points it out to me, I'll make sure to stop." That sounds really caring, right? Well, Lauren also says if she's feeling hurt or angry at or confused by Dan, she doesn't care about his feelings at all and will purposely ignore them. Lauren goes to extremes with her care behavior. For her, it's all or nothing: she is either in excessive care-giving mode or in full ignore mode. Neither of these is healthy. Excessive care-giving can lead to feelings of resentment in the caregiver because it often means she is sacrificing herself in the process. Eventually that leads to anger and resentment, which then can lead, as it does in Lauren's case, to a hostile lack of care.

Why does someone engage in excessive care-giving? Most of the time it's because she wants to be liked and believes her behavior will keep her in her partner's good graces. This type of care-giving is not driven by a healthy "I know and like him" process. It's driven by an unhealthy "I want him to like me" process. If you engage in excessive care-giving and sacrifice your own needs, and then find yourself feeling resentful, it will be important to examine the motivations for your behavior and work toward a more balanced, healthy approach to caring for your partner's feelings.

Thoughts:

Listen: "Do I try to hear what he is expressing and what he means in order to understand who he is?"

Julianne cares about Gregory. She doesn't want to hurt him. She knows she is hurting him right now by taking so long to get back to him with an answer to his "Marry me?" question. She's listened to him carefully all along so that she can really understand him.

At the beginning of their relationship, out of the blue at dinner one night Gregory had suggested they each ask the other questions they wouldn't dream of asking this early in a relationship. She was so in:

Gregory: What are you looking for in a guy?

Julianne: Someone who appreciates and accepts my career goals, how hard I work, and wants an equal relationship. Someone with a similar intellect, background, and interests.

Gregory: Do you see yourself ever settling down and being a mom, a wife?

Julianne: I'm not sure. If I find the right person and I want to have a family with that person, then settling down would be right for me. You?

Gregory: I used to think I'd be married and settled down after I put a couple of years into my career, but I got really invested in it and realized it was worth making sure I was stable work-wise and financially given that I do want to settle down. So now I'm seriously looking for a long-term partner to get married and have a family. That's what I really want.

So Julianne was not surprised by his proposal, and she knows he's serious and deserves an answer. She just is not certain she wants to marry him—there are so many good things and also so many problems—and as much as she'd like to tell him he caught her off guard with his question, and that's why it is taking her so long to decide, she knows that wouldn't be honest. She heard him loud and clear from the beginning, and she really does understand.

Remember when Lauren was with Lucas and after two dates he stopped texting her and told her it was because he was still not over his ex-wife? Lauren did not hear Lucas loud and clear. If Lauren were really listening and trying to understand Lucas, she would have realized he wasn't ready for a relationship with her. He was giving her that information by continually talking about his ex-wife and through his inconsistent behavior, like when he kept going back and forth between "I'm happy being with Lauren" and "No, I'm sad missing my ex-wife. This is not working for me."

When you start a relationship with someone who doesn't want to be with you, what do you think is the most likely outcome? And how would being with someone who loves someone else make you feel about yourself? If you said you'd feel terrible and that, most likely, the relationship would not work, you'd be right. But Lauren couldn't see that because she was not listening to Lucas. She was paying attention only to herself and where she was. She wanted him to love her, and she set about trying to make that happen. Out of her own need to be loved she pursued a person who was really telling her he was not looking for a serious relationship with her.

Had she listened to and heard him, she would have had the opportunity to decide whether she really wanted to be with someone who was in love with someone else. Instead, she acted from a place of "I will make him love me," which leads to the faulty assumption "I need to be who he wants" rather than "I know and like him." In doing so, she relinquished her personal power.

Thoughts:

Important: "Do I consider and value his needs in my choices?"

`◐ KEY NEED?`

Mia says, "When Corey brought up the idea of an open relationship, I decided to consider what he wanted. I valued our relationship. If I had immediately said no, who knows what would have happened? We probably would have continued our relationship, but maybe Corey would have cheated. When I feel connected to a person, I don't feel jealous of what I know about; it's when I stop feeling connected that I feel jealous. Or maybe I would have cheated. When I get stressed, I want sex because it calms me down. Either of us cheating would have been a much bigger mistake and much harder to deal with than trying to work out an open relationship."

Lexi answered, "With some things I definitely do, but other things are harder. For example, we live 45 minutes apart, and we always have trouble figuring out who is going to drive to who, especially on weekdays. James has to get up earlier than me, so he likes me to come to him. But I work later than he does—I get off at five, and he gets off at two—so I think he should drive to me. He says I'm being selfish, but if the tables were turned, I'm sure he'd want me to come to him." However, when Lexi told him this he said, "Actually, I'd want to balance things out. Neither of us loves the long drive, so it's only fair we share it. So yes, I'd want you to come to me sometimes, but I'd also be willing to come to you."

"Oh," Lexi thinks to herself, "maybe I haven't really been thinking of him in this situation. He's right. It is only fair if I go to him sometimes. If he doesn't want to drive out because it's a long drive, maybe I shouldn't get mad."

Lexi realized she wasn't treating James in a way that showed him his needs were important. This is critical information for Lexi. If she really likes James, she has to consider his needs in her choices. This is where the skill of mutuality comes in. Maybe they can compromise, trading off on who drives so that it equals out over the week or the month.

Thoughts:

Trust: "Do I trust in his availability, consistency, and commitment, and do I trust him not to treat me in whatever way would be considered a betrayal in our relationship?"

Relationship scholars all agree that trust in your partner is at the core of security in a relationship. As you saw in Chapter 1, when Emily stops feeling secure, she starts playing the "He loves me, he loves me not" game. Whenever there's a lapse in Will's communication, Emily goes to the worst-case scenario: "He doesn't love me as much as I love him. I can't trust his feelings for me." Emily doesn't trust Will to follow through on her plan for them to communicate daily, but Will also has been clear he doesn't actually agree with her plan and he *can't* follow through on it because of how busy and exhausted he is.

Therefore, the first step for Emily and Will, if they want to work this out, is to clarify their commitment to the relationship and define what a betrayal would be in a way they can both agree and act on. Will needs to be clear about what he is capable of and follow through with it so Emily can develop trust. Emily needs to work on not going to the worst-case scenario as her default. She needs to develop realistic self-talk about the situation, such as "I may not like Will's behavior, but it's not an indicator that he doesn't love me or can't be trusted." Emily also needs to assess with herself whether daily communication is an unrealistic expectation and whether what Will can offer is enough to meet her *trust* need. If not, she needs to consider whether this is the right relationship for her.

Mia also is struggling with trust issues with Corey as they navigate their free-pass situation. The free-pass plan sounded like an adventure to Mia—a way for her and Corey to work through what they wanted from sex and love, with respect and mutuality, and a way to build trust in their relationship. They've had to work on figuring out and revising their limits with the plan. The initial plan was that free passes would be hookups with no emotional connection. However, last night Corey Skyped Mia and asked for a big compromise. He wants to be able to have drinks, talk, get to know a woman, feel mutual attraction and desire, find her interesting, and feel a small emotional connection. Mia wasn't sure she was comfortable with this, but she agreed, and he told her to check out his OkCupid profile so she would feel included in what he was doing, just like she asked.

When Mia read the profile, she felt a little better. She was pleased to see he was clear that he is looking for a casual relationship. He explained that he has a girlfriend with whom he is in a long-distance open relationship and that the plan is to move to his girlfriend's city once she graduates. Still, she's just not sure about his need for a "small" emotional connection—what's small?

Mia's not sure Corey's request is a betrayal of trust—it sounds as if he wants an FWB relationship, but her concern about him doing that with the friend who originally suggested it to him was how they ended up deciding on hookups with no emotional connection. Plus, an FWB relationship is the way she and Corey started out. Might his having an FWB relationship with someone else lead to more? Can she trust his commitment to her? Corey and Mia have always been open and honest with one another; they have always met each other's need for *authenticity*. They're going to really need to keep doing that now. And Mia is going to have to consider carefully whether she can take the risk to trust Corey.

Mia and Emily are both dealing with serious issues pertaining to trust. They are asking good questions about whether they can trust, and this is a reflection of their awareness of how important it is to accurately assess whether their *trust* need is being met. They are also both trying, as hard as they can, to figure out how to best weigh what their partners say and what they do. Mia and Emily are trying to make sense of the real evidence they have for trust. It's extremely important to do this. One mistake people can make is just to use their feelings of love or lust as a basis for trust. Olivia is a good example of this mistaken trust. She trusted Zach was committed to her without their having any kind of conversation about the nature of their relationship and despite the evidence that he's a self-described player. Anna also is a good example. Despite the fact that Eric treated her poorly in the first go-around of their relationship (remember how he was so into her and then just stopped calling her and started seeing someone else?), Anna trusted he was committed to her this time—enough to marry him—after just hooking up. She completely ignored potentially important evidence that speaks to whether her *trust* need could be met. Indeed, Eric is now starting to show some confusing behavior. Remember how he said his priority was to provide for his family? Now he wants her to go back to work because he wants a new truck, despite the fact that his "old" one is only two years old. Anna is confused by this, and rightly so. They made a plan together, and Eric is not following through on the commitment he made. This should be a big signal to Anna that her *trust* need is not being met.

Thoughts:

Accept: "Can I let him be who he is and not try to change him or make him into something he's not, doesn't want to be, or can't be?"

Relationship scholars also agree that acceptance of one's partner is a key factor in making a relationship work. Emily swings back and forth between accepting and not accepting how focused Will is on schoolwork. It's contributed to his academic success. However, it also has resulted in his losing sight of other things when he's focusing on work—like staying in contact with Emily the way she wants him to. It's the reason he doesn't take five minutes to call her or to check in with a quick text to say "Good night and I love you" after he's finished studying or even in between periods of studying. The following is a typical conversation:

Emily: I don't understand why you do not take five minutes to call me to say good night after you've finished studying.

Will: I just don't think like that.

Emily: But you know I want you to, so you should be making the effort. Don't you care about what I need?

Will: Yes. It's just hard for me. I'm focused on my studies right now.

Emily: (*interrupting*) I know. It's because you're so focused—you give 110% to anything you do and you forget about everything else when you're doing it. Then you probably feel so spent afterward that you just want to zone out, watch TV, listen to music, recharge. Let's forget about it. Can we talk about something else?

Will: Why? You can't forget about it! You are always wanting to fix me or change me.

Emily: I don't think you're broken! I think you're amazing, and I'm trying to accept you. It's just that the thing that makes you successful is also something that hurts me, and I don't know how to handle that.

Emily wants to accept Will for who he is, but she's having a hard time with it. And Will has tried to make some changes, but he can't sustain them. So what to do? If Will really cannot or does not want to change, despite knowing his behavior has a negative impact on Emily, Emily has a decision to make. Can she accept him for who he is, or is his behavior a deal-breaker? If it's not a deal-breaker, then Emily may want to work on better regulating her emotions so she can handle Will's behavior in a healthier manner. For example, if her self-talk continues to be something like "He's doing it again! He doesn't care about me. I'm not important to him!" then Emily will never be able to accept Will, and she and their relationship will suffer. They'll have the same argument over and over for the rest of their lives. However, if Emily uses what she knows about Will and his perspective on things, her new self-talk could be something like "He's acting pretty distant again, but it has nothing to do with me. It's just that exams are coming up and he's focused on his goals for the future. It's not a sign that he doesn't care about me or that I'm not important. He loves me and shows me that in many other ways." If Emily can do this, not only will she feel better— her hurt and angry emotions will be calmed—but Will will feel better and their relationship will be strengthened because of it.

Julianne answers the *accept* needs question with a yes and no. Gregory had told her right from the beginning he was devoted to his career and that other women he had dated hated how focused he was on it, but Julianne is totally accepting of that. She understands the need to work late, the last-minute canceled plans when a work crisis comes up, and the recurring out-of-town trips. It's all part of the business, and she gets that in a way that Gregory's other girlfriends have not. It is not an issue in their relationship at all. However, she is starting to realize that she cannot accept the way he criticizes her for everything. As she's worked on the *familiarity* need, Julianne's recently recognized that one of Gregory's worst traits is being critical, and he uses it to get his needs met:

Gregory: You don't know how to make the bed right!

Julianne: Okay, show me how *you* make the bed.

(*Gregory shows her how he folds the corners tight so his feet stay inside the covers at night.*)

Julianne: How come when I do something different from you it's wrong?

Gregory: It's wrong for me.

Julianne: It's as if you expect me to do things the way you do without knowing how. I generally do what's expected of me, but when you're critical I feel as if I want to do the opposite of what you want.

Gregory: Don't you want to tuck in the sheets for me so I can sleep right?

Julianne: Of course I do. Try asking, "Can I show you how I tuck in the sheets? I wake up if they come untucked in the night" rather than telling me that I'm doing something wrong.

After this conversation, Julianne can tell he's trying. For example, instead of saying, "You're in the wrong lane," Gregory asked, "Can you drive in the slow lane unless you're passing?" She's trying too. When he is critical, instead of thinking, "He makes me feel as if nothing I do is good enough," which makes her angry, she's regulating her emotions by using new self-talk, saying, "He just doesn't know how to turn that criticism into a request." Still, it's hard for both of them, and they fall into the same old pattern:

Gregory: You don't know how to handle people.
Julianne: What?! Okay, tell me *how to handle people!*
Gregory: What I meant was you handled that conversation with your client all wrong.
Julianne: I have an MBA, I run a team, I get high marks in my performance reviews, and you think you can teach me how to handle people?
Gregory: I'm looking out for your best interests!
(And then it gets ugly; it goes around in circles. This is so not her. She doesn't want such a conflict-ridden relationship.)

In the end, Julianne knows that when she defends herself by saying things like "I have an MBA. I run a team," she's having the same old experience—"I feel less than I am. I feel not good enough, and I'm angry about it." Can Julianne let Gregory be who he is without feeling less than she is? Can she accept him without it hurting her? That's the key question to ask. If a woman cannot accept her partner without hurting herself, then she cannot get the *accept* need met.

Thoughts:

Forgive: *"Do I forgive him for mistakes he has acknowledged and move on?"*

Research shows being able to forgive one's partner contributes to greater relationship satisfaction and sincere amends lead to greater forgiveness. Mia and Corey's situation is a good example of this.

Mia's concern about what might result from Corey wanting a "small" emotional connection is proving valid. On OkCupid, Corey met Other-

Woman, and they now have an FWB relationship. They get together at least weekly, and Mia has the sense that their interactions reflect much more than a small connection, at least more than what Mia thought a small connection would be. For example, one night Corey suggested to Mia they include OtherWoman on their Skype call and engage in some "Skype sex." Mia was intrigued. She thought to herself, "I don't know my limits on this until I test them out," so she agreed. When OtherWoman kissed Corey and they started to make out, Mia felt really, really aroused. She really liked it. However, in watching Corey and OtherWoman interact, Mia was aware of their emotional connection and wasn't comfortable with it. Mia then learned that Corey and OtherWoman were frequently texting and sexting. It happened when Corey was next visiting Mia. She asked if she could look at his OtherWoman texts. They had a minor spat, but he finally agreed. She saw all the texts from OtherWoman, which pushed her concerns over the edge, and she confronted Corey, saying "Is this what you meant by a 'small' emotional connection? It really seems to me that you two are much more emotionally involved than you let on and this is not what I thought I was agreeing to."

Corey heard the pain in Mia's voice. He apologized that very moment, saying he was sorry he had hurt her, and telling her the texts were reflective of the newness of the physical connection with OtherWoman and nothing more. He told Mia that OtherWoman was in a poly relationship with two other people to whom she was committed, and he reassured Mia that he was completely committed to her. He also told her he would decrease the frequency of the sexting and the texting because he could see it hurt her. He said he didn't want to keep doing something that would increase her fears of his developing a more serious relationship with OtherWoman. Initially Mia was stunned and hurt. Yet Corey immediately and genuinely acknowledged he had made a mistake. He showed that he understood and cared about her feelings. Given all of this, how could she not forgive him? So, although it was hard at first, she did forgive him, and it gave them the opportunity to refine their limits on free passes and to understand each other's needs better.

Thoughts:

I/ME

What Does a Genuine Apology Look Like?

Check out this video to find out!

In "Getting Called Out: How to Apologize" (*http://everydayfeminism. com/2013/11/how-to-apologize*), Franchesca "Chescaleigh" Ramsey says, "A real genuine apology is made up of two parts: the first part is you take responsibility for what you've done, and then the second part is you make a commitment to change the behavior."

The problem she's dealing with (what to do when you say or do something that upholds the oppression of a marginalized group) isn't relevant to this book, but the process of how to apologize definitely is.

Help: *"Am I willing to respond to his requests for help with things he has to do?"*

Mia's answer: "Yes. Corey's not very organized with his personal papers and finances, and I tend to be really organized with mine. He asked me to help him make a budget so he can follow through with his plans to move here once he gains some experience and he can find a job in my city. I did." Mia's willingness to respond when Corey asks for help shows she likes and respects him.

Lexi is struggling with whether she's willing to help James as much as he wants. Lexi likes helping people, and with James she's always been willing, but lately she finds herself feeling ambivalent about being helpful. For example, the other day they were going to her parents' house for dinner and he asked her to pick up flowers because he was running late, but she didn't want to do it. In these types of situations, it's important to use the insight skill to examine your motives. Why wouldn't Lexi want to get the flowers when it seems easier for her to do it? If Lexi just wants James to do it so she doesn't have to, she's not treating him as though she likes and respects him. But of course there may be other reasons she doesn't want to help him. It turns out Lexi is concerned that James isn't meeting his own *help* need. She thinks he's not self-reliant enough, not taking responsibility for what he needs to get done in all sorts of ways in his life. So she now feels resistant to anything he asks for help with. If Lexi wants to treat James as if she likes and respects him, she might want to work on separating appropriate requests for help from less appropriate ones. She can then respond positively to the former—picking up the flowers so they're not late to her parents' dinner—and talk with him about the importance of meeting his own *help* need when his requests seem inappropriate.

> Thoughts:

Safe: "Do I make choices to help keep him emotionally, physically, and practically safe?"

Mia and Corey are working hard to navigate the challenges of their long-distance relationship and free-pass agreement. Corey had told Mia he didn't want to know any of the details about how she was using her free passes because it would make him jealous and be emotionally painful for him. Mia, however, found it extremely difficult not to share information with him. She felt inauthentic, which led her to feel emotionally disconnected. In an attempt to feel more connected to Corey, she told him all about her OtherGuy (like Corey, she started hooking up regularly with one person). What she didn't realize was that in doing so she was putting Corey in an emotionally dangerous situation, one where he didn't feel safe because he was left to deal with serious jealousy. As you will see in the coming chapters, Mia's "He knows and likes me" need to be *authentic* with Corey and her "I know and like him" need to keep Corey *safe* have come into conflict. This can happen; needs often conflict. In Chapter 6 we're going to tell you a lot more about how Mia and Corey handle conflicting needs; for now, it's important to see that Mia's choice did not keep Corey safe.

Lauren says she wants to keep Dan safe, but her behavior is not consistent with her words. When Dan gets upset with Lauren or treats her in a way that she's unhappy with, she threatens him with ending the relationship, and sometimes she even does it. However, the break is always temporary; she'll go right back to him to make up. Take the following example:

Lauren is out with Julianne and Anna for dinner. They're catching up, laughing, and drinking. Her phone rings:

Dan: Where are you?
Lauren: I told you, I'm out to dinner with the girls.
Dan: I can tell you're drunk. I'll send Michael [his driver].
Lauren: I don't want that. I'm fine. We're having fun.

(Julianne and Anna are both yelling in unison while laughing, "We're planning the wedding—leave her alone!")

Dan: I'm sending Michael!

Lauren: I gotta go, talk to you tomorrow.

Dan: What do you mean? You live with me. I want you home safely.

Lauren: I don't even want to come home! I'll spend the night at Julianne's.

Dan: Lauren, what are you talking about?

Lauren: You're treating me like a child. I'm not coming home. Maybe I never will.

Dan: What?!

Lauren hangs up and turns off her phone. Later that night she looks out the window from Julianne's and sees Dan's car parked outside and him staring at the window making sure she's inside. The next day she goes home, takes him a present, and tells him how much she loves him.

Lauren is playing the breakup/makeup game with Dan, and she does so repeatedly. Imagine how this might feel for Dan. He's likely to start to fear that at any minute Lauren might leave him. He may become anxious about this, angry at her, and fearful of making any "wrong moves." When this happens repeatedly, it erodes the partner's—in this case Dan's—sense of safety in the relationship, leading to insecurity and an emotional rollercoaster. A sense of security is one of the keys to a healthy relationship, and it cannot exist when a partner does not feel safe.

Thoughts:

I/ME

Do You Think Lauren's Behavior Could Make Dan Rethink His Behavior?

How could it? Dan thinks Lauren is being unreasonable. He has no idea she thinks he's being controlling. She's not told him, so no mutual problem solving is going on. Neither person is walking away with a deeper understanding of what the other person wants. That's why her behavior won't lead to change in his.

How Does Meeting the "I Know and Like Him" Needs Give You Personal Power?

Simply put, when you're confident you really know and like your guy and you treat him in a way that shows that, you're another step closer to being able to have a relationship that meets your needs and another step closer to having that relationship be a healthy one.

In this chapter, we drew your attention to the question "Who do I want to be with and why?" By reading this book you are now well on your way to having the tools to answer that question. First, in Chapter 3, you began to learn about yourself—about what your best and worst traits are, about your needs, and about how to meet them for yourself. In this chapter, you began to learn about what to look for in a partner so that you can set your standards to guide your expectations. You learned about how knowing who he is can help you understand his behavior, about the kinds of needs you may have that you want him to meet, and about how your treatment of your partner reflects whether he is the kind of person you really want to be with. You can now start to assess "identity fit," which reflects a personalized connection with a partner: Does who he is fit with who you are? Does what he has to offer meet your needs? And given who you are, do you want him as a partner? If you haven't done so already, this might be a good time to start to answer these questions. We encourage you to start completing your Key Needs List, and if you're in a relationship, the needs that are and are not getting met. Doing so will prepare you for the next step in assessing identity fit and taking that next step to personal power.

KEY NEEDS LIST

Needs	I know and like him. (I am confident that this is the guy I want, and I treat him in a way that shows that I like and respect him.)	Key need?	Being met?
What I need:			
Familiar	Do I know his best and worst traits? Do I understand how they make him who he is, influence how he acts, and affect the way he gets his needs met?		
Authentic	Is he fully open to showing all aspects of himself and to facing whatever fears he has about doing so?		
Attracted	Do I like his physical appearance just as it is without wanting it to change?		
Desire	Do I want to be sexual with him, and do I feel comfortable telling him about my sexual interests and needs?		
Interesting	Am I interested in his life (whatever it happens to be), and do I want to be a part of it?		
Support	Is he my go-to person in good times and bad times?		
How I treat him:			
Care	Am I attuned to his feelings, and do I respond in a helpful rather than hurtful way?		
Listen	Do I try to hear what he is expressing and what he means in order to understand who he is?		
Important	Do I consider and value his needs in my choices?		
Trust	Do I trust in his availability, consistency, and commitment, and do I trust him not to treat me in whatever way would be considered a betrayal in our relationship?		
Accept	Can I let him be who he is and not try to change him or make him into something he's not, doesn't want to be, or can't be?		
Forgive	Do I forgive him for mistakes he has acknowledged and move on?		
Help	Am I willing to respond to his requests for help with things he has to do?		
Safe	Do I make choices to help keep him emotionally, physically, and practically safe?		

5

He Knows and Likes Me

Knowing and liking you means a guy wants what you have to offer and treats you in a way that shows he likes and respects you.

Just as every woman deserves to get "I know and like him" needs met, every guy deserves to get "I know and like her" needs met. He too is looking for someone to be *attracted* to, to *desire*, to *accept*, and so on. You have your key needs, and he has his. A guy who knows and likes you should be able to meet your needs to feel that way—that he's looking for what you have to offer and treating you that way. If he doesn't, he's not the guy for you.

Recently, there's been some media coverage of people posting *very* specific criteria on online dating sites about the type of person they're looking for. These posts look something like this:

Are you the one for me? Here's what I'm looking for:

You want to be in a committed monogamous relationship.

You're fair-skinned with blond hair and blue eyes (green is okay too), and you're thin and keep yourself in really good shape. Overweight girls need not apply.

You like wearing short skirts and high boots, tight jeans and spiked heels, and yoga clothes for casual days.

Red lipstick is hot, but too much eye makeup is not.

You're a liberated woman with a good job who is willing to pay her way.

Promiscuous women—now or in the past—are not for me. Anything over five past sexual partners is too many.

You like to dote on your man with lots of attention and romance.

You don't want kids or cats. Small dogs that don't bark much might be possible.

Now there's a guy who knows what he wants and is being very clear about it. If you read his criteria, you wouldn't have much trouble figuring out the answer to the question "Does he want what I have to offer?" If your answer was no, you'd have to rule him out, or you'd be entering a fantasy world where you'd have to try to make him like you. This would undoubtedly compromise your self-esteem, because you'd always feel "less than." You would end up with no personal power in this relationship. Nor would the relationship likely last long.

Even if you don't like what the guy above is looking for or what he values about women, you can see that at least he was being honest enough for women to evaluate whether they meet his criteria. However, rigid criteria like his are often not met in relationships, and he probably would not be a very accepting person in a relationship—bad sign for sure. But back to the point, let's imagine the following scenario:

Say by happenstance you meet this guy in a Starbucks line, not on an online dating site, so you don't know his very specific criteria for a girlfriend. You're a naturally skinny blonde with bright blue eyes. You're wearing a miniskirt and high boots, so he's immediately attracted to you. He flirts. You flirt back. You hang out later in the week. He asks, "What are you looking for?" You share, "A monogamous long-term relationship," and then you pick up the bill.

So far it seems to both of you that you're what he wants. You feel giddy and start to envision the future with him. *But wait.* There's a lot you both don't know yet. Have you ever found yourself saying about a relationship, "We had differences that weren't apparent at the start"? Until you really know his needs and he knows what you have to offer, you can't make any decisions about whether he's the guy for you. For example, what if you've slept with more than five guys? What if, after the initial flurry of calls, texts, flowers from him and little gifts from you, you both start to settle down a bit, and you're okay with the shift but he expects you to act like it's love's first blush every single day or he pouts? As soon as these revelations arise, you and he will experience conflict in your relationship.

In this chapter, we help you figure out whether the guy in question knows you and likes you well enough to make the kind of relationship you want with him possible. When you do this, you cut off any instinctive urge to try to *become* what he wants just to resolve the uncertainties and assure yourself that this relationship *will* work.

As in Chapter 4, check off anything that you think might be a key need for you and use the spaces at the end of each description to enter any thoughts you have about that need.

Familiar: *"Does he know my best and worst traits? Does he understand how they make me who I am, influence how I act, and affect the way I get my needs met?"*

Olivia says, "I'm not sure. It hasn't even occurred to me to think about whether he knows my best and worst traits. It's not as if he's ever said anything to me like 'You're really funny and generous and well intentioned.' I do know I can completely be myself with him, and he's never commented on anything negative. He's also told me, 'I love it when you laugh or sing when you're happy.' But I guess I don't know if he ever thinks more deeply about who I am."

That Olivia doesn't know whether Zach is really familiar with her has the potential to be a problem. If he really doesn't know her, he's less likely to understand her needs and her behavior, and that's definitely going to be a problem. Moreover, he may find out something about her later that he really doesn't like or doesn't know how to deal with. How many times have you, or someone you know, said, "Wow, I didn't see that coming! I thought he was so [*fill in the blank with whatever idealized view of the person you may have had*]!"

In Julianne's relationship with Gregory, he's pretty familiar with her traits, but he doesn't really understand how they make her who she is. Julianne says, "Gregory would say my best traits are being assertive, organized, honest, passionate, kind, and affectionate. When we started seeing each other, he told me he loved how I had my life together, that I knew what I wanted, and that I was honest and didn't play games. I was happy I reflected all those things to him because I do feel they're strengths of mine. However, lately he sees my ability to be organized as controlling, which makes me think he really doesn't understand this part of me. I like to plan. That's how I got where I am. If he likes that I'm organized enough to have my life together, I'd like him to understand it means I do like to have some control over things. That helps to reduce my anxiety and keep me feeling on top of my life. I really need that, but when I try to explain this, he just labels me an overorganized freak."

As you can see, Gregory's inability to use his awareness of Julianne's traits to really understand her is getting in the way of her getting her *familiar* need met. It's not enough for a guy to be able to describe what you're like. It's important that he really "get" you—that he see how and why your traits are manifested in what you need and what you do, and that he doesn't just slap a negative label on you. Otherwise, you'll end up feeling misunderstood, which can lead to reduced intimacy and greater conflict.

Thoughts:

Authentic: *"Am I fully open to showing all aspects of myself and to facing whatever fears I have about doing so?"*

☐ KEY
NEED?

Lexi says, "There are so many things I don't say to James, particularly what I'm unhappy about in the relationship. For example, I haven't told him I want to stop hanging out with his friends so much." She's self-silencing, which is the antithesis of authenticity. If you silence yourself, it's nearly impossible to let a guy deeply see you.

Lexi also says, "I've kind of stopped being me in certain ways. I've started doing the things he likes even though they're not natural for me. He likes meat and eats a lot of it. Guess what I do? I eat a lot of meat now too. Before him I ate more like a vegan. This is the most I have ever weighed in my life. What is wrong with me? Why am I doing this?" Lexi is right to ask herself these questions. She needs to think long and hard about whether she can be herself in this relationship and face any fears she has about finding out that he doesn't really want what she has to offer.

Anna also has trouble being authentic, especially at the beginning of a relationship. She says, "You know how you always show a guy your best at the beginning? That's what I do. For example, when Eric and I first started dating, I was passive. I didn't speak up about things because I wanted to make sure not to rock the boat. Totally not me, but I just really liked him and I wanted him to really like me too! So I don't think Eric knew, for a while anyway, that I was as stubborn or independent as I am. I do not like to be told what I can do, when I can go out, who I can talk to, or how much I can work, but I didn't want him to know that right away. I don't think he would have liked that very much. Most guys don't. They want a passive, agreeable woman."

Anna based her approach to this relationship on "Can I be who he wants?" rather than on "Does he want who I am?" leaving her in a place of low personal power. She employed a strategy that, without her realizing it, could come back to hurt her, because it was based on inauthenticity in two different ways. First, by pretending to be something she wasn't just to get Eric to like her, she left herself with a relationship that wasn't based on truth about herself. What's going to happen when she gets tired of pretending? And what's going to happen when he finds out who she really is? Surprise, confusion, conflict. Those do not bode well for a relationship. Second, by making an assumption about Eric based on a gender stereotype (that men like passive women), she was failing to ensure that she knew Eric at all. If it turned out Eric actually liked assertive women, her strategy would have backfired.

Thoughts:

Attracted: "Does he like my physical appearance just as it is, without wanting it to change?"   ☐ KEY NEED?

Mia's attraction need is definitely being met. In response to the question she says, "Yes, for sure! Corey's told me he likes my size, my shape, the way I move, that he finds my body intriguing, appealing, and exotic, that he loves how on the one hand I can be very graceful and precise in my movements and on the other hand clumsy at times and that it's the combination of these two that he finds so appealing. It makes me feel really good and really comfortable with him."

For an example of what it looks like when the *attraction* need is not met, let's return to our hypothetical story about the guy above and the girl he met at Starbucks. They're six months into the relationship. They're spooning in bed, and he starts to play with and lightly pinch her tiny bit of belly fat. She slaps his hand away and they laugh. But the next time she's hugging him, he does it again. Her self-talk is "This is making me feel so uncomfortable, but what do I say? I don't want him pointing out my belly fat! I mean, it's not that bad. I don't love it, but he loves to go out and eat, and I've been indulging with him because of it. Still, maybe I should get to the gym more. I wonder what he's thinking about my weight since he keeps pointing it out."

StarbucksGirl: Do you think I'm fat?

Guy: I notice your stomach is a little rounded. Do you think you've put on a few pounds?

StarbucksGirl: Maybe five pounds at most. I'm going to make time to go to the gym again. I've just been so busy with you (*giggles*).

Guy: Honestly, I haven't been as attracted to you lately. It looks more like 10 pounds.

StarbucksGirl: (*She doesn't know what to say.*)

Guy: You know, a woman being overweight is a total deal-breaker for me.

StarbucksGirl tells her best friend what happened. Her friend begs her, "Don't let him tell you you're fat and you need to lose weight. You look fantastic and wear, what, like a size 6?! *Please*, I know you have strong feelings for this guy, but if he's not attracted to who you really are, forget him! He's being a jerk." (Yay, friend! She understands the *attracted* need, as well as how hurtful his behavior is.) However, StarbucksGirl says, "I'm not comfortable with my belly fat either, so we're both not. I've noticed he wants affection and sex less frequently. I want him to feel attracted to me, so I'm happy he told me! I'm just going to lose the weight, and everything will be better."

The guy who posted is looking for a thin woman to meet his need to be attracted. StarbucksGirl never read his profile, and he didn't tell her up front because she fit his weight criterion at that time. So now she finds herself having to deal with a boyfriend who is no longer attracted to her. Taking care of yourself physically is healthy for you and for your relationship, and we all benefit when we can willingly do things that our partners find attractive. However, there are limits to this, limits that can be hard to define. For example, what if a guy you liked asked you to wear your hair a different way or not to wear your glasses when you went out with him? What if he asked you to get a boob job or fix your teeth? Are these healthy ways for you to take care of yourself? Can you do these things willingly? If your efforts to meet his *attraction* need require you to change something about your body that you accept and are comfortable with (remember your "I know and like myself" *attracted* need), and if you're doing so out of fear of criticism or rejection by him, it's time to recognize that you're not really what he wants and, consequently, he should not be who *you* want.

Thoughts:

Desire: "Does he want to be sexual with me, and can he comfortably tell me about his sexual interests and needs?"   `▢ KEY NEED?`

Anna has no problem getting her *desire* need met with Eric. "Eric really likes sex, and it's amazing!" says Anna. "I can easily tell he loves sex with me, and he's very open about telling me exactly what he likes and wants. He initiates sex often and is very affectionate. He'll text me during the day: 'thinking about you naked and wet just out of the shower, be home soon.' Or we'll be lying on the bed, cuddling, and he'll tell me, 'I think about you all day long. I can't wait to get home every day. I've never been with anyone like you.' He really makes me feel desired."

Olivia is certain Zach *desires* her, but he's begun to send mixed messages about what his real interests and needs are. Initially he never wanted to do anything beyond her limits, but lately he's been testing them. Last night he asked her if they could get naked:

Zach: I adore your body. You're so damn beautiful. I need to feel my skin against yours.
Olivia: I don't know if I'm ready yet.
Zach: Trust me—we won't go all the way.
Olivia: I'm not sure we should be doing this. (*She strips down.*)
> (*They're making out hard.*)
Zach: (*He stops, looks her in the eyes.*) You okay?
Olivia: Yes. (*She goes back to kissing him.*)
Zach: Should I go get a condom?
Olivia: No. I don't know if I'm ready yet.
Zach: Are you not sure of your feelings for me?
Olivia: It feels as if you're trying to get me to go further than I'm comfortable with even though you said you wouldn't. I don't know what you really want.
Zach: (*sounding frustrated with himself*) I don't want you to go further than what you're comfortable with. I'm sorry. I'm just being human. (*He jumps up and starts getting dressed.*)

Emily was always sure Will desired her, but she was less sure of whether he was really comfortable telling her about all of his sexual interests. Then one day, out of the blue, Will called Emily saying he wanted to tell her about a sex dream he'd had. He started off, "If you feel uncomfortable in any way, say stop." She was nervous and excited at the same time, and also confused because six months ago she had asked him what kind of fantasies he had and he said he didn't have any. But it turns out he had lied, and he now wanted to tell her about his fantasy of a threesome. That he was finally comfortable doing so made Emily really happy and excited too that it could take their intimacy—both sexual and emotional—to a higher level.

The next time they were on the phone they discussed this new disclosure:

Emily: Why did it take you so long to open up with me?

Will: (*laughing nervously*) I thought you would think I was some sexual deviant.

Emily: I don't. I love you. I feel safer with you now that I know what's in your head, and you're being genuine and sharing it with me. I think this can really bring us closer than before. If I sent you texts that describe you, me, and another girl in a three-way, would you like that?

Will: Yes, very much. And would it be okay if we talked about specific three-way fantasies when we were having sex? Would you like that too?

Emily: Definitely!

Will: I love you so much.

As Will became more able to open up with Emily, the two felt closer, and they were able to build on an already good sexual relationship in ways they both enjoyed.

Julianne has not had this kind of experience with Gregory. Although they had a good sexual relationship early on, it has become clear that Gregory does not want to have sex as frequently as Julianne would like, and he doesn't speak about his sexual interests and preferences even when Julianne asks. That Julianne and Gregory can't comfortably discuss sex and intimacy and that they have different interests suggests they may not be sexually compatible. This does not bode well for their relationship, as couples who perceive themselves to have lower sexual compatibility report lower relationship satisfaction. Perhaps another obvious-sounding research finding, but one that should be taken seriously.

Thoughts:

Interesting: "Is he interested in my life (whatever it happens to be), and does he want to be part of it?"   ☐ KEY NEED?

Mia says, "Definitely! I'm studying finance, which I'm super passionate about. Some people find it boring and have no interest in it, but not Corey. He so gets my passion for it, and he loves that I'm financially savvy because he so isn't! So he feels like he can really learn from me. It's so great to know

I'll be able to come home when we're living together and he's actually going to want to hear about my work. From the beginning Corey also made it clear he was really interested in the kind of lifestyle I lead and want to have in the future. I'm not sure I want children, and that scares off some men, but Corey was happy about it because he's not sure either."

Julianne also says yes. "Right from the beginning, Gregory has always been so interested in my life. He tells me that my being a career person gives him even more energy for his career, and he can't wait to hear about my work at the end of the day. He's like an excited little kid sometimes. It's so cute! And on special occasions he really shows me how happy he is to be with me. He created such an amazing birthday for me this year, all of his own doing." She posts:

> Thanks, everyone, for all the awesome birthday love. Especially Gregory for spoiling me with lovely gifts, a delicious dinner, and to a lesser extent the hangover I am suffering from today. He's making up for that last part with a bacon and pancake breakfast in bed.

Mia and Julianne are clearly getting their *interesting* need met. Let's take a look at Lexi and Anna now.

Lexi says, "No, not really. James doesn't want to go to yoga with me, and he doesn't want to hike or swim. I say, 'I love yoga. I want to share that experience with you.' He says, 'I like to work out at the gym; that's it.' That's what he says! Lately, I've also had to drag him to my family get-togethers. He pouts all the way there, saying, 'Do we really have to go?' And once we get there he's like, 'Can we leave yet?' He makes it so obvious that he doesn't want to be there, that it's not his choice, and that he isn't enjoying it. He only wants to do what he wants to do." If you remember from Chapter 4, Lexi was not getting her need to find James *interesting* met, and she's not getting her need for him to find her *interesting* met either. The more needs that go unmet toward the three conditions for a healthy relationship, the worse the prognosis.

Anna is finally starting to realize she doesn't have a life Eric is interested in sharing. Remember in Chapter 1 when Eric stopped calling and started dating Lizzie? He later told Anna it was, in part, because Lizzie, unlike Anna, had a stable job and career and he liked that. Anna missed that red flag—he was not interested in Anna's life. And, once they got back together and she got pregnant, she focused on what he told her then—that he was happy being the breadwinner and having her stay at home, and she confirmed that for herself in the early days when he acted so appreciative of all she did. Indeed, in Chapter 4 you saw she wanted to share in the life he had presented to her. However, because she missed the original red flag, Anna is now stunned to hear him suggesting she go back to work so he can get a new truck. Eric is demonstrating that he's not really interested in being a part of her stay-at-home-mom life. Anna didn't see this was going to be the case, and maybe Eric didn't either, but it's becoming very clear now. So she goes back to work.

Thoughts:

Support: "Am I his go-to person in good times and bad times?"

○ KEY NEED?

Being his go-to person means your boyfriend includes you in his day-to-day life—you know what's going on. When something really great—or not so great—happens, you're one of the first people he calls to share it with or work through it. As we noted in the last chapter, being able to go to a partner for *support*, for both stressful and positive, happy things, is healthy for the relationship and, importantly, responding in active, validating, helpful ways is good for relationships too.

Mia says, "I posed this very question to Corey right before he moved. I asked him, 'What can I do to support you?' He said, 'Nothing. I just want you to be here with me until I go. I want to go to sleep with you every night, and I want to wake up next to you every day.' I think that means our intimacy is what supports him. He's also told me he feels so good knowing I'm here to tell him he can do a presentation at work and nail it. Even though he knows he can, for him it's knowing he has me to reflect that back to him—this is key for Corey."

Lauren says, "Dan talks to me about everything—his mother, his work, his dreams—absolutely anything. I'm the first person he calls no matter what."

Olivia says, "I can't really say I'm Zach's go-to person at this point. He hasn't called in the last few days. I heard from a mutual friend that Zach just found out his mom was diagnosed with breast cancer and so he's been out with his friends for the last two nights drinking heavily and partying. I've sent him a couple of texts letting him know I've heard about his mom and I'm here if he needs to talk. Nothing in response. I think it's a little weird he hasn't come to me. His go-to person is still his best guy friend, who he plays video games and drinks with. Anyway, I'm hoping as we go further down the relationship path, he'll come to me for support."

In these examples, Mia and Lauren are getting their *support* need met—they are the go-to people for their guys. That doesn't seem to be the case in Olivia's relationship. Even if it's just that what Zach needs at a time like this is someone he knows well to be around without talking about what's on his mind, doing what they always do together, the fact that he chose his old friend for this rather than Olivia says he doesn't think she can do this for him. Whether he'll realize she can and make her his go-to person is unclear, so Olivia should be thinking about whether this is a key need for her.

Thoughts:

Care: "Is he attuned to my feelings, and does he respond in a helpful rather than hurtful way?"

☐ KEY NEED?

Olivia feels good that she's getting her *care* need met with Zach. "When I talk to Zach about how I'm feeling, I can tell he listens. The other day I asked him about his number of sex partners—it went like this:"

Olivia: How many women have you had sex with?
Zach: Guess.
Olivia: Less than 10?
Zach: Guess again.
Olivia: Tell me.
   (*He starts to work it out in front of her; she hears him list off Ashley.*)
Zach: 40.
Olivia: When you said Ashley—is it the same Ashley that's in some of your classes and that you hang out with? The one you study with who's an avid sports fan and watches all the games with you and your friends?
Zach: Yes.
Olivia: She's a prior FWB?
Zach: Yes. *Prior* being the keyword there.
Olivia: What happened?
Zach: We started hanging out?
Olivia: I feel uncomfortable with how you're friends with a prior FWB, especially as she's always hanging around you at parties.

"I could tell Zach cared about what I said because the next party we went to, when Ashley came up to him to talk, he put his hand on my back and pulled me into the conversation. He showed her we were together, and that made me feel better."

Whether Lauren sees it or not, neither Dan nor Lucas has shown consistent evidence of caring for her feelings. Lauren and Dan got engaged, and she moved in with him and quit her job, at his request, so she could accompany him on his trips and to his work and charity events. He provided her with a living allowance, as well as access to his personal assistant, driver, chef, and cleaning staff. Lauren was responsible for nothing. Despite the fact that Dan takes care of Lauren by providing her with tangible resources like money and personal staff, he does not attend to her feelings. At first Lauren loved the traveling and their social life, but going out almost every night started to be too much for her. Dan adjusted their lifestyle for a week or so, and then it was right back to the old pattern. As for Lucas (when they were together), despite the fact that his hands-off, no-questions-asked style provided Lauren with some freedoms, it also led her to struggle to come up with evidence that he actually cared about her feelings. This hands-off behavior, coupled with his clear disregard for her feelings about his persistent grief over his divorce, is an indicator that Lauren's *care* need was not being met. Lauren is again acting more on "Can I be who he wants?" than on "Does he want what I have to offer?"

Thoughts:

Listen: "Does he hear what I am expressing and what I mean and use it to understand me?"

☐ KEY NEED?

"James absolutely does not listen to me," says Lexi. "This really comes up about money. I've expressed to him repeatedly that I'm concerned about money right now, but he just does not hear and understand me. I just bought a new car—which I really needed because my old one died on me—and it cost more than I had planned. I'm feeling stressed out because my budget is tight and I don't want to go into further debt. I've told him this, but he doesn't understand. For example, he expects me to pay for everything because I make more money than he does, and he keeps talking about how he wants to go away for another ski weekend and blames it on me that we can't when he doesn't have the money either! He's not understanding the financial stress I'm under."

In Chapter 1, we talked about how Gregory doesn't listen to Julianne's needs. Instead, he tries to define them for her, constantly telling her what she should want and how she should do things, and why doing things "his way" would be best for her. Even when she tells him she feels nothing she does is ever good enough for him, instead of really listening to her and trying to understand what she means, he defends himself and invalidates what she is trying to communicate. This pattern continues to be reflected in discussions about the future of their relationship:

Julianne: I'm not ready to get married.

Gregory: Why not? We've talked about our ultimate relationship goals—we both want the same things. I'm ready to start a family now.

Julianne: But I'm not. I'm not sure how to tell whether someone is meant to be with someone forever. Marriage is difficult, Gregory. I don't want to get married, have a child, and then get divorced. I need to be sure.

Gregory: I can't imagine not being with you forever, not having a family with you.

Julianne: I hear that you're feeling certain, but I'm not certain. I just don't feel as if we know each other well enough to assess "forever." I want to really understand the commitment we're making. I want to take more time with this.

Gregory: What are you saying—do you want to break up?

Julianne: No! I'm not saying that. Aren't you listening to me? I just know I'm not ready to get engaged. Let's continue to see how our relationship develops without making any major commitments—

Gregory: (*interrupting*) Let's move in together, take the physical and emotional distance out of our relationship. That will reduce any doubts you have and save a lot of money on expenses.

Julianne is still confused. She thinks, "I just said I didn't want any major commitments!" But she knows that he'll keep pressing the issue, so she agrees.

Neither Julianne nor Lexi is getting her *listen* need met. Lexi is well aware of this. She's right that James is not listening to her. If he were truly listening—and thus understanding—he would not be asking her to buy things and blaming her for the fact that they can't afford expensive extras right now. He would recognize that spending over budget would put her in a difficult financial position and cause her stress.

Julianne has not fully recognized her situation as one in which she is not getting her *listen* need met. Consequently, she is giving in to Gregory to avoid confronting the fact that he doesn't listen to her. Unfortunately, giving in will only reinforce his behavior and further entrench the pattern of his not listening, his defining her needs, and Julianne giving in. Julianne needs to consider whether this is what she wants and whether Gregory really knows and likes her.

Thoughts:

Important: *"Does he consider and value my needs in his choices?"*

Emily has been struggling with whether she's getting her *important* need met with Will. Because they're long distance, Emily really wants to spend as much time with him as possible when they're together, but this doesn't always happen. Take this example:

Will comes for the weekend to see Emily and to meet up with Dr. Robinson, a family friend who is advising him on applying to medical school. The night before he's due to arrive, Emily texts: "I can't breathe—so excited to see you." The next day, she meets him at his hotel. She brings a special lunch to have in the room, and they have sex and cuddle. They watch movies, swim in the hotel pool, laugh, talk, giggle, and reconnect. Will goes to dinner with Dr. Robinson that night, as planned, and Emily stays in the hotel and studies. Early Sunday morning, Emily wakes up in Will's arms. She watches him sleep, tries to imprint his face in her mind. She can see he's so tired. She starts thinking about her exam on Monday, thinking it's now 5:30 and he doesn't leave till 9:30. "I'll get up, grab a coffee, get some studying in." As she's getting dressed, he rolls over and she kisses him on the cheek, a lover's kiss. She says, "Text me when you're up and we'll have some fun together before you leave," and then she grabs her iPad. Her plan is to study at Starbucks until he texts so she doesn't disturb him. She keeps checking her phone—no text. She gets back to the room at 7:00 A.M.; he's up, showered, and ready to leave. She's stunned.

Emily: Why are you up and dressed, and you didn't text me?
Will: Dr. Robinson called. He wants to have breakfast. I'll be back at 8:30ish. He's got some more ideas for me about preparing my applications.
Emily: (*She's disappointed.*) I would have stayed in bed with you if I knew you were going for breakfast.
Will: I didn't know.
Emily: But you knew we would only have 30 minutes to hang out before you left.

Will: (*He comes and sits down in front of her on the ottoman, takes her hands. She can't look at him.*) Are we okay?

Emily: No, you do not prioritize me. You know it's important to me for us to spend as much time together as we can when you're here!

Will: Look at me. I'll be back, and we'll have at least a half an hour.

Emily: Forget it. I'll just go. I can't wait for you. I have to stop waiting.

Will: You're talking to me, but you won't look at me—why?

Emily: I can't. I just want to go. (*She does, and then she runs back to hug him tight; she doesn't want to regret not feeling what it's like for him to hold her tight.*)

Later, she's back in her dorm room, and Will texts her when he gets back from breakfast: "Back in the room. Miss you, love you . . . " She calls him.

Emily: I want to come back to see you before you leave. Can you get a later train?

Will: I can't. I want to, but I can't.

Emily: (*She starts to cry and tries to tell him why she left.*) I'm sorry, Will. When I get hurt, I run. I feel like I have to leave the situation. You know that I wouldn't trade one minute with you for anything else, and when I see you acting like you don't care about our spending time together, I don't feel important. I think that you don't love me.

Will: But you were the one who left this morning. You went to grab coffee and to study.

Emily: I know. It was because I wanted to let you rest and I thought we'd still have time together. Did I hurt you?

Will: I missed being in bed with you. (*Silence, then . . .*) Listen, it was a complicated situation, I guess. I'll come back sooner rather than later, I promise. I love you.

Will's right. It is a complicated situation. Getting one's needs met often is. Clearly, being *important* is a key need for Emily. Will knows this, but his own needs, as well as external demands (like school), make it hard for him to meet Emily's need as consistently as she would like. Will and Emily will continue to have to negotiate this, which you'll see them do in future chapters. The good news is they can talk about the situation. They both have genuine intentions to work it out. Whether a resolution can happen is the question, and Emily will need to be prepared to make a decision about what she can and cannot live with.

Unlike Emily, Anna finds herself in a situation where Eric has no intention of even trying to meet her need to be *important*. Anna was talking to him about how they would spend Thanksgiving. They both believe family is important, and Anna believes it's particularly important to spend the holidays with the extended family because she knows everyone will want to see Emma and she thinks it's good for Emma to have everyone around. She knows Eric doesn't feel the need to spend Thanksgiving with his own family, but she would like for them to spend it with hers.

Anna: My parents invited us for Thanksgiving. I'd really like to go. What do you think?

Eric: No. I just want it to be the three of us this year.

Anna: Why? Holidays are for being with all the ones you love.

Eric: Yes, and I love you and Emma. I just want it to be us three.

Anna: If we don't go, their feelings will be hurt. They've been so good to us with the wedding and helping us out with things. I don't want to make them feel like we don't appreciate them. Plus, I think it will be great for Emma to have her first Thanksgiving with all of us.

Eric: (*angrily*) No. This year it's just going to be the three of us. End of story.

Anna doesn't know what to say. She sees how angry Eric is. So she tells her parents that they've decided to stay at home just the three of them for Emma's first Thanksgiving. She makes it sound like it was a joint decision.

If Eric was treating Anna as if he knew and liked her, he would at least be willing to consider her needs in this situation, but he's not. At all. Bad sign.

Thoughts:

Trust: "Does he trust in my availability, consistency, and commitment and trust that I will not treat him in whatever way would be considered a betrayal in the relationship?"

Corey has had complete trust in Mia's commitment to him. He's never had any reason not to. Until recently, that is. Their free-pass situation is getting in the way and resulting in confusion about whether Mia has betrayed him and in an erosion of trust.

LIMITS RECAP

Mia's limits for Corey	Corey's limits for Mia
No emotional connection	No telling me any details
Always use a condom	Always use a condom
No excessive texting/ sexting OtherWoman	No having sex anywhere in the apartment but the bed
	I always want to know when you have plans to see OtherGuy

First there was Mia telling him details about OtherGuy when he didn't want to know. Then she had sex with OtherGuy in Corey's shower (she's living in his apartment). Now Corey's wondering, "What else has she done that I've asked her not to do? What other limits has she crossed?" That his mind goes to these questions is a sure sign that he's questioning whether he can trust her. He's also starting to question whether Mia still finds him desirable. Corey calls Mia:

Corey: How is the sex with OtherGuy? Like you say, just be straight with me. I want you to be honest, not lie to protect my feelings.

Mia: The sex is sufficient, but it's not the same as when we're together. He just doesn't measure up to you.

Corey: Are you saying that to make me feel better, or is it actually true?

Mia: No. You are amazing. You are the one that I love and want to be with.

Mia knows he's wondering if she is starting to like OtherGuy more than she's let on.

Corey: I guess what I'm really afraid of is that you'll have a sexual experience that is so much more interesting and gratifying than sex with me.

Mia: That's not what I'm afraid of (*giggles*).

Corey: Is sex with OtherGuy more gratifying than with me?

Mia: No. Not at all!

Corey: I mean what if it was? Would you just say, "Oh, I really enjoyed it" or "*You* can't replicate it"?

Mia: I'd tell you. You know I need to tell you what's in my head! What can I say to help you trust me?

Mia is hearing, loud and clear, that her boyfriend cannot trust her and she wants him to be able to. If Mia can clarify the issues that feel like betrayals and resolve those, hopefully Corey will be able to trust her. If Corey can never rebuild trust, then Mia will need to consider whether he will be truly able to like what she has to offer.

Mia behaved in ways that compromised Corey's ability to trust her. Let's look at an example where there is no reason for a guy not to trust.

Before they were married, when Anna wanted to go out with her friends, Eric was usually okay with that, but now things have changed.

Anna: It's Lauren's birthday next Friday, and we're planning a special girls' night out. Okay?

Eric: I don't know. What time will you be home?

Anna: What do you mean you don't know? My mom will watch Emma, and she'll stay as late as needed. She's happy to do it so that you can do whatever you want that night too.

Eric: What time will you be home?!

Anna: I don't know exactly! Probably late! Does it matter? We all just want to go out and have fun together. Plus, I would love to have a break, just a little fun, like before the baby came.

Eric: Don't come home late!

Friday comes, and Anna goes out. She, Lauren, and Julianne are having a great time talking and laughing and catching up. Her phone rings. She sees that it's 1:00 in the morning. Her heart misses a beat. It's Eric. "He's going to freak!" she thinks. He does. When she gets home he yells, "Why didn't you call?"

Anna: Why do I need to?! You're not my parent!

Eric: You should have called me!

Anna: Why? I'm not doing anything wrong.

Eric: Why should I believe that?! (*He grabs her phone out of her hand and throws it. It smashes all over the kitchen floor.*) No more going out without me!

Anna: (*Horrified, she stares at her broken phone in disbelief.*) What are you doing? I feel like I should be able to go out and have fun without you being there.

Eric: Why do you need to just do things without me? We're married now. We need to do things together.

Anna: Of course I want to do things with you! I also want to be able to do things with my friends sometimes. It's not that often that I go out with them.

Eric: You're a drunken slut. You can't be trusted. I've always known in the back of my mind you just couldn't be trusted. I know the person you are, and people warned me about you.

Anna: What are you talking about?! Where on earth is this coming from? Who warned you about me and what did they say? I've never given you any reason not to trust me! This is crazy!

She doesn't know what else to say. This whole thing seems to have come out of the blue.

In Chapter 4, we told you trust in your partner is at the core of security in a relationship. When for no reason a guy does not trust you, there is no way your *trust* need can be met. He will never be happy with what you have to offer.

Thoughts:

Accept: "Can he let me be who I am and not try to change me or make me into something I'm not, don't want to be, or can't be?"

Lauren believes Dan *accepts* her fully. However, Dan's behavior often indicates otherwise. For example, Lauren loves to dance, and she's always been the first on the dance floor with her girlfriends. Dan won't allow this. He doesn't want her to dance with anyone but him, and he doesn't want her to dance when he's not with her. Another example: Lauren doesn't enjoy going out every night and to every one of Dan's events. She's made this clear, and although he says he understands, he continues to expect, and even insist, she go with him. If Dan really accepted Lauren, exactly for who she is, he would respect her needs and how she lives her life. If a guy doesn't want to accept who his partner is, then he should not be in a relationship with her.

What if, like Julianne, one of your boyfriend's traits is that he's critical? Say he nitpicks at you with things like "Why do you run the dishes through when the dishwasher isn't full?" "Why do you keep your toothpaste on the counter rather than in the drawer?" "You shouldn't bite your nails." "Why do you have to eat so slowly?" He's always telling you how you should have said or done something in a different way, and he's always telling you why his way is better. Does a guy who behaves like this accept you for who you are? Well, definitely not in the ways we've just pointed out (although maybe he does in other ways). Is that okay with you? Julianne confronts Gregory:

Julianne: Can you please try to stop getting me to be you? I'm me. I do things my way. Just because I do some of them differently from you, what's wrong with that?

Gregory: I'm just trying to help you do things right. Do things in the best possible way that will be good for you and good for us. I just want to make things better and easier for you! If you do things the way I suggest, things will be better.

Hmm . . . Really?!

One of the most common complaints that couples bring to therapy is the desire for the partner to change. If the partner agrees that change is needed and is willing to work on it, great! Obviously, though, people don't always want to change or can't change in the dramatic ways their partners want to see. And if they try to change for the other person, especially in response to someone telling them what to do, it's experienced by both partners as not genuine: "You're just doing that because I asked you to! You don't really want to do it!" or "I'm only doing this because you said I have to! I don't really want to do it!"

Because of problems inherent in trying to make someone change, relationship experts now stress the importance of accepting one's partner, as noted in Chapter 4. We're all different and unique. Our partners will never be exact replicas of us, and that means they will always do certain things differently and have different needs. Being accepted by your partner, fully, for exactly who you are, is one key to relationship success. Being accepted feels loving and compassionate and brings partners closer together and more willing to meet each other halfway. That doesn't mean your partner has to agree with or like every single thing you do. Instead, it means your partner should not judge you critically—he has to want to be with the person you are, as you are. If your partner cannot accept who you are, you're not the person for him.

I/ME

What Does It Really Mean to Accept People as They Are?

For an interesting take on this, listen to what Dan Savage has to say in his video "The Price of Admission" (*www.youtube.com/watch?v=r1tCAXVsClw*).

Here's an excerpt:

> There is no settling down without some settling for. There is no long-term relationship without not just putting up with your partner's flaws, but accepting them and then pretending they aren't there. And we like to call it, in my house, "paying the price of admission." . . . Your boyfriend who chews with his mouth open, you can say, "Chew with your fucking mouth shut," and hopefully he'll get there. But if he never does, him chewing with his mouth open might be the price of admission. . . . "

It can be hard to figure out what to accept and what not to accept. Keep reading—we help you use the skills to figure this out in Chapters 6, 7, and 8.

Thoughts:

Forgive: "Does he forgive me for mistakes I've acknowledged and move on?"

☐ KEY NEED?

Mia's not sure Corey forgives her for not keeping him safe when she told him about OtherGuy. She can see he's having a hard time with it. Even though she's apologized to him, in practically every conversation they have, Corey keeps coming back to it, saying something like "I just wanted the security of living together and moving forward together in our life before we talked about how you've been using your free passes. I just didn't want to know while we have this distance between us. We agreed on this." And Mia just continues to apologize. On Skype, Corey's checking in with her, or she should say he's checking up on OtherGuy:

Corey: When are you seeing him next?
Mia: I'm not sure.
Corey: Since you've told me about him I need to know when you spend time with him. I hate it when you leave me wondering if you're going to see him. In my head it's difficult for me to imagine you, the person I love, being with another man.
Mia: I know. I'm so sorry.
Corey: When are you seeing him next?
Mia: I don't know, maybe tonight.
Corey: Are you going to see him tonight or not?
Mia: His last text said, "If I finish up this paper, wanna see you." As I said, I'm not sure he'll finish up his paper, so I don't know.
Corey: I hate this! This is why I told you I didn't want to know anything! Why did you tell me?
Mia: I know. I'm sorry. In hindsight I see how it hurt you. I don't want to keep hurting you.

Corey is struggling with knowing more than he wanted and not being able to get it off his mind, and it's fueling his masochistic curiosity. He's worried he's damaging their relationship. But he's fixated on when Mia's going to meet up with OtherGuy next. He's jealous, he's upset. He hears Mia apologizing, but he just can't get past what happened.

OtherGuy continues to be part of every conversation Mia and Corey have, so finally she straight-up asks Corey:

Mia: Can you forgive me for telling you about OtherGuy?
Corey: Yes, I want to. It's hard, though. I know I was naive to think you weren't using the free passes. It was just so hard to face the reality. I want us to stay connected, and I know that means talking more about our day-to-day life. I want us to work on how we can do that.
Mia: You sound so angry all the time. Are you going to stay angry?
Corey: I don't want to. I can appreciate your circumstances. I'm across the country. OtherGuy wants to meet your sexual needs, and he can. I want to meet those needs, and I can't. I can see things from your perspective because I'm living it too.

Corey's self-talk is "I know she loves me and wants to be with me. I'm seeing selfishness in her that may always be there in our relationship, but then I have my own FWB. I've made mistakes too! How can I blame her? And I can understand why she told me even when I told her I didn't want to know. She just wanted to connect."

Mia: Do you want to break up with me?
Corey: No. Absolutely not.
Mia: Do you think you can stop saying in every call "This is why I didn't want you to tell me"?
Corey: I'll try. I love you. I want to forgive you. I'm working on it. I want us to work this out.

Emily also has done some apologizing in her relationship, and she's really working on her emotion regulation skills, but she's not sure Will forgives her for aggressively and repeatedly accusing him of not caring about her. Will has said things such as "Do you need me to text you every minute, every hour, every day to feel secure? What about that makes me feel secure? How do you think I feel when you're mean to me or when you run out and leave me? Do you think that makes me trust you?"

Emily: You know how I text you "I hate you"?
Will: Yes.
Emily: I know it upsets you. You hate drama. I'm sorry. I've been trying not to do it lately.
Will: I've noticed.
Emily: Do you forgive me?
Will: Why do you do it?

Emily: I start thinking things like "If he doesn't initiate texts or text me back within a reasonable time period, it means I'm not important to him or he's bored with me or he doesn't care about my feelings," and then it makes me so angry that I lash out. But I'm really working on that. I'm trying not to get stuck on those thoughts.

Will: Em, you have to start trusting me. I love you.

Emily: I know you say you love me. It's hard to hold on to that sometimes when I'm not getting what I feel I need. Remember that time you broke up with me—just saying that you felt disconnected from me? Then I start thinking about that, how we broke up because of the same reasons, and it scares me.

Will: That was the past.

Emily: Yes, I try to remember that. Do you forgive me?

Will: Yes. Yes. Yes.

Emily: You're sure?

Will: Yes. I don't like your "I-hate-you" crazy drama texts, and I really appreciate your efforts to stop them, but I do understand you are feeling hurt because I'm not being as responsive as you want. I'm happy you're working on not going to the worst-case scenario—the idea that I don't love you—because that's just not true. Let's keep doing our best to work this out together.

Will is willing to forgive Emily. He understands how her unmet need results in hurt feelings and how that leads to anger and to her aggressive behavior. He's made it clear that he would like her to stop that behavior, and Emily recognizes she must do so. Therefore, Will is able to forgive her, which will allow them to move forward in a healthy way. Importantly, Emily developed insight into her behavior and recognized the need to develop her emotion regulation skills. Her active work on not getting stuck in negative self-talk about Will can allow her to keep her hurt from turning into blinding anger, which will reduce her aggressive acting out.

Both Mia's and Emily's relationships are great examples of how the *forgive* need works. When a woman can acknowledge a transgression and takes steps toward repair and her guy understands, has compassion, and forgives, it shows he knows and likes her.

Thoughts:

Help: *"Is he willing to respond to my requests for help with things I have to do?"*

Mia answers, "Corey nailed *help* for me when he was here before he moved. I don't like owning up to the fact that women are less physically strong than men, but in the case of Corey and me, it's true. He's also much taller than me. So at his place there were a lot of kitchen cupboards I couldn't reach and he'd help get things, or when we were taking groceries back to the apartment it was so much easier for him to grab a whole bunch of bags and carry them in. And he would always take the heavy trash and recycling bins to the basement. Those are the things I loved to have him help me with. Also, I cook, but I don't enjoy it, so he actually did most of the cooking and cleaning up because I don't really like that either. I'm kind of lazy! With our status changed to long distance I miss him not being here to *help*, which I now know is key for me in a relationship. Just last night we were talking; I was upset, stressed out, and he was like 'How can I help?' and I yelled at him, 'You can't help! You're not here to make me dinner or help me clean up!' We got a good laugh out of that because we both know how true it is!"

Anna isn't sure whether Eric can fully meet her *help* need. Since Emma was born, even though he said things like "Don't worry, together we'll be able to take good care of this baby," he hasn't come through. She remembers after she gave birth she was exhausted. Instead of saying, "I'll take care of the baby; you just went through a gazillion hours of labor," Eric fell asleep. She threw a pillow at him and said, "Can you get up and help me with the baby?" He said, "Oh yeah, sorry" and then fell right back to sleep in the chair once he was holding Emma. It's continued like that since. Yesterday, Anna raised this with Eric:

Anna: I really need help with child care and housework stuff. It's really hard to work all day and do everything else myself.
Eric: I work harder than you do. How do you expect me to help?
Anna: Seriously?
Eric: I'm up earlier and my job is more mentally demanding than yours.
Anna: I still need help. Some nights I might have to work late—you'll have to pick up Emma.
Eric: I can't commit to that. You'll just have to make sure you get off on time.
Anna: You're the one who made me get this job.
Eric: We need the money. It's not my problem. Make it work.

Clearly, Eric is not willing to help Anna with child care despite the fact that she really needs it. Eric sees providing the child care and taking care of the home as Anna's role. Therefore, in Eric's mind he's already done his job and he shouldn't have to do Anna's too. He's not willing to help because he believes she should not even be asking for help. Given this, Anna will need to carefully consider how important it is to her to get her *help* need met. Does she want to be with a guy who won't help her with child care?

Thoughts:

Safe: "Does he make choices that help keep me emotionally, physically, and practically safe?"

□ KEY NEED?

Lauren and Julianne have both had experiences where their safety was not protected. Lauren continued to find it stressful to have to go out every night and work the room with Dan at all of his events. This led to Lauren becoming depressed. She'd wake up late in the morning. Dan's assistant would bring her food. She'd go back to bed for as long as she could until the driver showed up to take her to a four o'clock hair appointment followed by a five o'clock makeup appointment, and then her personal shopper would show up with her dress for the evening. Lauren was miserable. She started to develop panic attacks, and she started to feel depressed. She spoke to Dan about this again, and he was immediately concerned and tried to make some changes to their schedule, but again after a short time, things went right back to how they used to be. So even though Dan was concerned and initially responsive, he could not sustain making longer-term choices that would keep Lauren emotionally safe. That's important information for her. She needs to decide whether safety is a key need for her. Does she like this aspect of Dan? Does it matter to her that he can't keep her safe in this way? Perhaps Lauren should be thinking about whether she is meeting her own "I know and like myself" *safety* need as well. Should she keep herself in a situation that makes her feel depressed?

Julianne had an experience with Gregory that resulted in her feeling very unsafe as well. In an effort to meet her *desire* need, Julianne decided to tell Gregory about her interest in reading erotica. She loves when guys tell her about their sexual interests and needs, and she hopes Gregory will love hearing about hers. She's nervous, but she decides it is important to her to take the risk:

Julianne: So I got this book for us. It's got erotic stories in it that I thought might be fun for us. (*She hands the book to him.*) How do you feel about this?

Gregory: What do you want to do with this?

Julianne: I was thinking you could lie back, close your eyes, and I'll start reading out loud. You can tell me how you feel, and we can see where things go.

Gregory: How do you expect me to feel?

Julianne: Aroused?

Gregory: Why do you think that?

Julianne: I feel aroused when I read these stories, so I thought it might be fun for us together. Listen, at any time if you feel uncomfortable we don't have to do this. Just tell me to stop.

Gregory: Okay, go ahead.

Julianne: (*She starts reading.*)

Gregory: Stop. Just stop. I'm not into trash. That's trash! (*He grabs the book, starts ripping it up, and throws it into the garbage.*)

Julianne: (*The expression on her face is horrified.*) What are you doing? It's not trash. It's two people having sex. I think it's pretty tame actually, and I like the detailed description. That's what I find arousing.

Gregory: Well, I don't. I think it's disgusting, and I don't want to be part of it.

Oh no. Now Julianne does not feel safe being who she is sexually. She exposed herself personally, and he shamed her. She feels as if Gregory thinks there's something wrong with her. She's horrified. He was so harsh. She might have felt safer if he had said something like "Julianne, I'd prefer if we stopped. I'm sorry, but I don't feel comfortable with this. I know you like it, but I'm not into it. Maybe we can find another way to get you aroused. What else do you like?" That would have been disappointing, but she probably would not have felt so bad about him and herself. But he didn't say that, and now she doesn't know how to be with him sexually, how to tell him what she likes. She feels vulnerable and alone. She thinks she's going to have to just keep things to herself, as she was doing before. Wait, is that a good idea?

Not only is Julianne not getting her *safety* need met; she's also not sure she's getting her *desire* need met. Julianne will have to decide how important those needs are for her. If they are important, she may want to take a further risk and talk more about her sexual preferences with Gregory. It may not work out, just as her initial attempt here did not. Things not working out the way we hope they might is just the reality of life sometimes, and we need to be okay with that. We will take risks to try to get our needs met, and our partners may not be able to meet those needs. Although such an outcome may be disappointing, it does give us information—information that we must use to decide whether he is the right guy for us.

Thoughts:

How Does Meeting the "He Knows and Likes Me" Needs Give a Woman Personal Power?

When a woman has her "He knows and likes me" needs met, she can be sure her guy is with her because he likes what she has to offer, not because she's trying to be what he wants—and that gives a woman personal power. When you stand up and say, "This is me," and he says, "You're who I want!" and he treats you accordingly, he could be the guy for you. If instead he says, "Actually, I'd like you better another way," run for the hills! You will never have personal power in that relationship, because you will always be trying to make him like you, and that will erode your self-respect and the quality of your relationship. Not healthy.

You now have information about all three conditions that must be in place for you to develop personal power and to have a healthy relationship. By focusing on what your key needs are in each condition and on whether you're getting them met, you will be able to more fully assess fit and determine whether he's the kind of partner you really want. Be sure to complete the next Key Needs List at the end of this chapter.

One thing you may have started to notice in the last couple of chapters is that needs often conflict in relationships—your own needs may conflict with one another and they may conflict with those of your partner. In the following chapters, we deal directly with the issue of conflicting needs, and we show you how I/ME skills can help you, particularly the skill of mutuality. If your guy knows how to have a healthy relationship, he should be assessing his needs as well, and the two of you should be working to see whether both sets of needs can be met in as balanced a way as possible—that's mutuality. Of course, it's hard to know how to balance needs. Throughout the rest of the book, we'll use the characters to illustrate how the skills can help you make stay-or-go decisions based on whether your needs are being met.

KEY NEEDS LIST

Needs	He knows and likes me. (He wants what I have to offer, and he treats me in a way that shows he likes and respects me.)	Key need?	Being met?
What he needs:			
Familiar	Does he know my best and worst traits? Does he understand how they make me who I am, influence how I act, and affect the way I get my needs met?		
Authentic	Am I fully open to showing all aspects of myself and to facing whatever fears I have about doing so?		
Attracted	Does he like my physical appearance just as it is without wanting it to change?		
Desire	Does he want to be sexual with me, and can he comfortably tell me about his sexual interests and needs?		
Interesting	Is he interested in my life (whatever it happens to be), and does he want to be part of it?		
Support	Am I his go-to person in good times and bad times?		
How he treats me:			
Care	Is he attuned to my feelings, and does he respond in a helpful rather than hurtful way?		
Listen	Does he hear what I am expressing and what I mean and use it to understand me?		
Important	Does he consider and value my needs in his choices?		
Trust	Does he trust in my availability, consistency, and commitment and trust that I will not treat him in whatever way would be considered a betrayal in the relationship?		
Accept	Can he let me be who I am and not try to change me or make me into something I'm not, don't want to be, or can't be?		
Forgive	Does he forgive me for mistakes I've acknowledged and move on?		
Help	Is he willing to respond to my requests for help with things I have to do?		
Safe	Does he make choices that help keep me emotionally, physically, and practically safe?		

6

Unhappy about How Things Are Going?

U nhappiness in a relationship is a sure sign of unmet needs. So if you're unhappy about how things are going, it's time to take a look at what needs are not being met. Doing so can be challenging, because it might not be just your own needs that are languishing. Both partners have needs, and they can conflict. Woman wants guy to do *x*. Man wants woman to do *y*. They both feel unhappy. As we mentioned in Chapter 1, both partners' needs can't always be met at once, and sometimes one person's may take precedence. Figuring out when to give in versus when to hold your ground is difficult. How does each partner get her or his needs met while helping the other do the exact same thing?

In this chapter, we're going to show how using the I/ME skills can help you figure this out. We'll take you through each skill and provide you with a series of steps you can take. First we're going to sum up three of our characters' needs, because we'll be demonstrating the use of the I/ME skills through their stories.

Needs Recaps

EMILY AND WILL

Does Emily know and like Will? Emily's conflicted about her need to be interested in Will's life—does she want to live a med-school girlfriend life-style? Yet after all this time she still wakes up thinking about him and feeling excited about him every day. She doesn't always feel as supported as she'd like because so much of his time is spent in class or studying, and therefore he's not always available, but she cares about him deeply and has even learned his nonverbal signals of being upset. Can she trust his commitment to her? She finds that long-distance makes it hard to always feel connected to him due to his spotty communication. So she swings back and forth between accepting and not accepting how focused he is on schoolwork.

Does Will know and like Emily? She knows he desires her, but she struggles with whether she is really important to him because his own needs and ambitions, as well as the external demands of school, make it hard for him to prioritize her as consistently as she'd like. Given her struggle with this, can he trust her? She knows he forgives her over-the-top reactions, such as her nasty texts, because he understands how her unmet needs result in hurt feelings and how those feelings lead to her anger and aggressive behavior. However, he's not sure how to deal with Emily's expectations for how much contact she needs.

What is the needs conflict? With Emily and Will it's pretty straightforward. Emily feels that Will is treating her as if she is not important to him (by not staying in contact with her as frequently as she would like). Will does not feel that Emily can accept who he is (focused) and his decisions (to dedicate himself to school).

MIA AND COREY

Does Mia know and like Corey? She's familiar with him, and he's authentic with her. She is able to use what she knows about Corey to understand him—both the good and the not so good—and she has factored all of it into her decision to be with him. She loves helping him. She also cares about him, and he is important to her. That's why she considered and agreed to the free-pass situation. However, she's struggled with whether to trust Corey after, driven by his own desire need, he wanted to change his random free passes into an FWB relationship, but she's forgiven him for pushing the limits of his relationship with OtherWoman with lots of texting and sexting. In addition, Corey's told her she's not keeping him safe when she tells him things about her own free passes that he doesn't want to know. He told her it would make him jealous and be emotionally painful for him, but she told him anyway—her need to be authentic with him outweighed her need to care about his feelings.

Does Corey know and like Mia? He's attracted to her and desires her, and he is interested in sharing her life. He loves her passion for finance and that she's financially savvy where he isn't. He also feels supported by her, but he's not sure he can trust her. To meet her own desire need, Mia engaged in sexual activity with OtherGuy that Corey had asked her not to. Although she apologized, Corey is struggling with forgiving Mia.

What is the needs conflict? Compared to Emily and Will, Mia and Corey's needs conflict is a little more complicated. First, there is the conflict between Mia's need to be authentic with Corey and her need to keep him safe. She wants to tell him everything to feel connected to him, but he's made it clear it hurts him deeply to know the details of her relationship with OtherGuy. Then there is the conflict between their desire and trust needs. Both want to get their desire need met not only with each other but with other people as well. Although they have agreed to the free-pass arrangement, it's resulted in breaches of trust for both of them. Consequently, they feel jealous and insecure.

JULIANNE AND GREGORY

Does Julianne know and like Gregory? She likes that he's authentic. Early on he told her he's seriously looking for a long-term partner with whom to get married and have a family, which she appreciated knowing right away. She desires him, and she enjoys sex with him, but she's lied about his ability to bring her to orgasm, and when she told him about her interest in reading erotica together he freaked out. Now she doesn't feel safe being who she is sexually. She cares about his feelings, but she's not sure she can accept his tendency to be critical. She feels he criticizes everything she does and tries to control her behavior.

Does Gregory know and like Julianne? She knows he's attracted to her, although she wonders how much Gregory desires her. He doesn't want to have sex as frequently as she would like, and he doesn't speak about his sexual interests and needs. She does know that he's interested in her life. He loves her hardworking, ambitious career orientation, which is part of why he feels so excited to be with her. However, she's not sure he's completely familiar with her. For example, he sees her tendency to be organized as controlling, but she doesn't think he really understands that part of her. She likes to make plans. That's how she got to where she is in her life. Gregory seems to care about her feelings, but he does not listen to her needs. Instead, he tries to define them for her, constantly telling her what she should want and how she should do things and why those things would be best for her.

What is the needs conflict? The simplest way to understand Julianne and Gregory's needs conflict is this: neither of them can really accept who the other one is, how they treat each other, and the decisions that each makes. Gregory doesn't understand how she gets her needs met, and he doesn't accept her choices. Julianne cannot accept his critical and controlling nature, and she wants him to change.

Using the I/ME Skills to Resolve Needs Conflicts

Now we're going to take you through each skill and provide you with a series of steps you can take to identify and resolve needs conflicts like the ones faced by Emily, Mia, and Julianne. As illustrated by these three women, even though the skills and steps are listed in a particular order, they do not necessarily progress in exactly that order when you're working with them.

INSIGHT

Insight means knowing yourself—knowing who you are, what you are like, what you need, and why you act the way you do. It means learning from your mistakes. It means thinking about the potential consequences of your actions. It means looking ahead a little and seeing what the positive and negative consequences of your choices might be (steps 1–4 focus on these things). And it means knowing who your partner is, what his needs are, and why he acts the way he does (steps 5 and 6 focus on this).

Step 1. Use unhappiness as a sign that you are not getting a need met.

An important function of emotions, such as sadness, anger, fear, and boredom, is signaling that something is wrong. Sometimes emotions go awry and send us the wrong signals—we'll deal with that problem in the emotion regulation section a little later in the chapter. But generally speaking, feeling unhappy is a signal you should pay attention to.

Step 2. Identify what that need is.

You may know, but if you don't or you're not sure, go back to the needs questions and assess which needs are being met and which ones are not. Make sure you figure out whether the ones not being met are key needs.

Step 3. Identify the thoughts and feelings that arise in response to your unmet need and identify the behaviors you use to try to get that need met.

It's important to be able to identify the thoughts and feelings you experience and the behaviors you engage in when your needs are not getting met. You must ask yourself, "What am I thinking? What am I feeling? What am I doing?" Our thoughts, feelings, and behaviors are all connected, and they all affect one another.

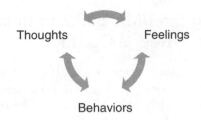

Thoughts   Feelings

Behaviors

As the diagram above shows, what we think can affect how we feel. How we feel can affect what we think. They both can affect how we behave, and how we behave leads to more thoughts and feelings. So let's say you're unhappy because your boyfriend isn't meeting your help need— he's not helping you take care of some basic chores around the apartment as you've asked. If you felt frustrated by this, you might think, "He's just a lazy slob who doesn't care about my needs or how the apartment looks!" Then you might feel angry and think, "Well, then I'm not going to help him with the next thing he asks me to do." So because of how you thought about the situation and the feelings you experienced, you selected a tit-for-tat behavior that you hoped would get him to meet your need.

A lot of times we don't stop to observe and think about our thoughts, feelings, and behaviors. They come up automatically, and we don't even question them. Unfortunately, we can't identify and negotiate a needs conflict unless we develop insight into how we're trying to get our need met by looking at the pattern of our thoughts, feelings, and behaviors. To negotiate a needs conflict, we need to fully understand our part in it. So when you're unhappy about something, when a need is not being met, you need to slow yourself down and take a look at what you're thinking, feeling, and doing.

Take a minute now and think about a time when you weren't getting what you wanted in a relationship. Write your thoughts, feelings, and behaviors to identify your pattern:

The situation was:

I was thinking:

I was feeling:

I was doing:

Can you see your pattern now?

Step 4. Determine the consequences of your behaviors.

Once you've identified the pattern of thoughts, feelings, and behaviors that occur when your need is not being met, you need to assess the consequences of that pattern. Does what you typically do result in getting your needs met? Does it do so without hurting you and your partner? If yes, great! If no, then you need to make some changes. We will demonstrate how to do so when we discuss mutuality and emotion regulation. For now, just remember that if your current plan of action—that is, the way you are trying to get your need met—is not working, it means you will need to develop a new plan. Repeating the same old patterns over and over again makes things worse in relationships, not better. Hitting your head against a wall doesn't move the wall. It just hurts your head.

Go back to the pattern you identified in the previous step. What were its consequences?

Did you get your needs met?

Step 5. Identify whether your need conflicts with a need that your guy has.

There are two primary reasons you might not be getting a need met in a relationship. One is that you have never expressed it or asked for it to be met. If that's the case, then you must communicate your need to your guy to see if he can meet it. If he can, great. You're all set. If he can't, then you need to understand why. That leads to the second reason you might not be getting a need met: it conflicts with a need that he has. Use your insight about him to determine what that need is or develop your insight about him by asking him—gently, lovingly, and in an open and curious manner—what that need is and whether it is a key need for him. (More on communication styles in a little while.) It also might be that he just doesn't care about your need or want to meet it. If that's the case, he's got a mutuality problem, which we discuss later in the chapter.

Step 6. Use your knowledge about who your guy is to attempt to understand his need.

Once you know what need of his conflicts with your need, it will be important to be open to understanding his need. Doing so requires you to draw on the need to be familiar with your partner. Remember, this need asks *"Do I know his best and worst traits? Do I understand how they make him who he is, influence how he acts, and affect the way he gets his needs met?"* The more familiar you are with him, the more you can use that information to understand his need. In addition, if you "know and like your boyfriend," not only will you become familiar with him, but you will also care about his feelings and really listen to what he means. And that brings us to the next skill.

MUTUALITY

Mutuality means behaving in a way that takes into account the needs of both people in a relationship, conveying that both people's needs are important and ensuring that both people's needs are being attended to. When a relationship is mutual, both people feel respected and cared for, and both feel as if they are getting what they need.

Step 1. Remember that both people in relationships have needs that they deserve to have met.

You're going to have to remind yourself of this, perhaps over and over, so that you don't get stuck flipping back and forth between the two of you on who is to blame, who is right or wrong, whose needs matter more. You both matter, and so do your needs, and if you want to be in a mutual relationship you have to believe this and act on it.

Step 2. Take your guy's perspective.

This step goes hand in hand with insight step 6. In addition to understanding your guy's need, you must put yourself in your guy's shoes to identify what he may be thinking and feeling and why he is behaving the way he is. Try to see things from his perspective to understand him and to empathize with how he may be feeling. This can be very difficult to do. When we are not getting a need met, it can be very hard to see things from anything but our own perspective. Getting stuck in our own perspective will not do us any good—in most cases (we will discuss exceptions to this rule in Chapter 8). Just as you want and deserve to have your guy understand your need and empathize with you, he wants and deserves the same from you.

Step 3. Unify with your guy against the problem.

Relationship scholars say that partners will be more successful at dealing with a needs conflict if they unify with each other against the problem. When needs conflict, partners tend to blame one another, dig in their heels, and defend themselves. They see each other as the problem, and this leads them to polarize against one another. And then they are stuck. Couples can become unstuck if they can shift from seeing their partners as the problem to seeing the needs conflict as a problem they must work on together. This means moving the focus from "him against me" to "us against the conflict." To do this, partners must use insight steps 3 and 4 to become fully aware of their own and one another's need-driven thoughts, feelings, and behaviors, as well as the consequences of how they are trying to get their needs met, so that they can clearly see the dysfunctional interpersonal cycle that they must unify against. When partners are unified, working toward a shared goal that takes both of their needs into account, they have a much greater chance of actually getting their needs met. Importantly, both people need to be able to effectively do step 2 (take your partner's perspective) for step 3 to work.

Step 4. Communicate your needs clearly, directly, and calmly.

Research has identified a number of strategies that allow you to communicate in a clear, direct, and calm way and that are effective in reducing couple conflict:

• Use "I" statements to tell your partner what you need and to ask for those needs to be met. An "I" statement is one that describes your own experience and needs without blaming your partner. For example, "I feel hurt when you say that. I would like you to speak to me in a kinder fashion" rather than "You hurt me. You need to stop doing that."

• Be specific in what you say. Don't use generalities. No one likes to be portrayed as "always" or "never" doing something or being a certain way (for example, "You always do that . . . You never treat me well"). It's rarely true, and it makes people defensive. In addition, being overly general is a disservice to yourself because your partner may not know exactly what you want or need. He'll understand "I would like it if you asked me how my day was when I come home" better than "Why can't you be more interested in me?"

• Focus on "soft" emotional expressions. Anger is one of the most typical feelings we have when our needs are not getting met. However, underneath anger there is often hurt, fear, and/or sadness. These underlying feelings are referred to as soft feelings. They are feelings that convey vulnerability, sensitivity, or tenderness. Love is a soft feeling as well. With soft emotional expressions you show your vulnerable, sensitive, or tender side rather than your angry, hostile, blaming side. Remember when Lexi suggested to Emily in Chapter 3 that instead of texting Will something aggressive like "I hate you" or "You. Are. An. Asshole," she say, "You tell me you love me, then act like you don't care by not returning my sext—I feel as if I'm not important to you. I would like you to text me back." That's exactly what we're talking about.

Here's an example that uses all three communication strategies: "I feel scared that I might lose you when you don't stay in contact with me. I need contact because it makes me feel safe. I would like to find a way for us to be in better contact."

Compare how that sounds to "You never care about how I feel. You're off doing who knows what without any regard for me. You're only focused on yourself!"

Which statement do you think is going to make your guy better understand your perspective and be more able to empathize with you? Owning and expressing your needs clearly and calmly, without being defensive, increases the likelihood that your guy will understand your need and want to meet it.

Try It for Yourself

Try to remember the last time you reacted from anger. Write down what you said:

Now write how you might say it using an "I" statement, specifics, and soft feelings:

Step 5. Listen to what your guy has to say in response and about his needs.

Once you've expressed your need, it is important to give your guy the opportunity to respond, as well as to express his need. Respect him by listening—really listening—to what he has to say, without judgment. Do not interrupt. Do not defend yourself. Do not blame him. Do not jump to conclusions. Just listen. And then reflect back what he has said, without judgment, to show that you heard him and that you understand (for example,

"So you're feeling . . . , and you want . . .). You'll see Emily learn to do this with Will later in this chapter.

Step 6. Engage in mutual problem solving.

If you (and your guy) can complete the first five steps (we know, it's hard, and it takes a lot of practice), you'll be more able to engage in mutual problem solving. Mutual problem solving is what you need to resolve conflicting needs. It's all about "Let's find a solution together." Here's what it involves:

- Come up with a range of ideas about how to meet each other's needs together.
- Take turns talking.
- Be open to adjusting your perspective when your partner raises good points.
- Think through the consequences of each possible solution.
- Pick a solution and commit to trying it out, giving it time, and assessing how it is working.

Mutual problem solving requires mutual understanding and, often, the willingness to compromise. Indeed, compromises are definitely needed in relationships given that we all have different key needs and preferences for how we get them met. Compromises are, however, different from giving in. If it feels as if you're giving in, then something is going wrong, and you will need to go back to your insight skills to make sure you're familiar with yourself and your partner and know your key needs and how you like to get them met. In doing so, you should consider the following three possibilities for why it feels as though you're giving in.

- You don't have a partner who understands mutuality—or who understands you and is willing to empathize with you. You'll see this aspect of mutuality play out in Julianne's story later in this chapter. If you've expressed your need clearly, directly, and calmly, and you've listened to and understood his need, but he hasn't listened to or understood yours, or just doesn't care about it or want to meet it, you will not be able to have a mutual relationship with him.
- The only way you can get your need met is through a "pet want." We all have the same needs, but as we said in Chapter 4, we each have ideal ways in which we like to get our needs met. We called these ideal preferences "pet wants." Sometimes pet wants are extra goodies, but when your pet want is the only way you're willing to get your need met, this can lead to unreasonable expectations and result in excessive demands. You'll see this play out in Emily's story later in the chapter, but we'll give you one

example here so you can see what we mean. Let's take the care need in "He knows and likes me": does the guy in your life pay attention to and care about your feelings? Let's say you want to be able to talk with him about your feelings at the end of the day because you've been under a lot of stress at work. That's a legitimate preference, especially if he's your go-to guy for support. However, lately you've been unhappy because when you talk with him it doesn't seem that he's really paying attention and showing he cares. That's a legitimate concern. He doesn't seem to be meeting your need. However, if the guy's absolute favorite thing is baseball and you insist on telling him about your day during a baseball game he's watching, that's your pet want. You want him to forgo his favorite thing to meet your need. That's not fair. You and he have to figure out in a mutual way how to meet your need without relying on an unreasonable pet want.

Can you think of any unreasonable pet wants that you have?

• You're being asked to compromise a key need or a legitimate prefer-
ence. You'll see this come up in Mia's story later in this chapter. Giving up getting a key need met is not compromise, nor is giving up a legitimate preference. For example, you should never ditch your "I know and like myself" needs. It is not a compromise, no matter what your relation-
ship status is with a guy, where it's *you* that has to be ready to accept all the consequences that come with giving in. Let's say you're involved in a one-time hookup. You both really want to be together, but the guy won't use a condom, and he tries to convince you why you should be okay with that even though you've made it clear to him that it's important to you to practice safe sex. You're unlikely to ever see him again, and you're the one who could get pregnant or contract an STI. You're the one who has to live with the consequences. This is not a compromise situation. This is not a time to give in and give up your own safety. If you were talking about giving in to see a movie he preferred or about what playlist to listen to, that's different. There must be no giving in if you're compromising your well-being. You also should never ditch your legitimate preferences. Let's go back to the care need we were just talking about—you want to be able to talk with your guy at the end of the day because of your work stress—that's legitimate, especially if you're flexible on how and when that happens. What if he says he doesn't have any time to talk with you or doesn't even see why

it's important to you? Do you give in and ditch what you want? Giving up legitimate preferences is how you end up in a relationship with no limits, where you'll always feel that you're giving in.

Can you think of any key needs you would never compromise?

How about any legitimate preferences?

What are your limits in relationships?

EMOTION REGULATION

Healthy emotion regulation involves being aware of your emotions, feeling in control of them, being able to keep things that happen in your relationship in perspective, and maintaining your self-respect and commitment to your needs in the face of emotional challenges.

Step 1. Create new self-talk.

As we noted earlier, our thoughts have an effect on how we feel. This means that if you think differently about something you will feel differently about it. Therefore, one way for us to regulate our emotions is by changing the way we think about things—by developing new self-talk, the stuff we tell ourselves in our head. If you've completed the third insight step, which involves identifying the thoughts, feelings, and behaviors that arise in response to your unmet need, you already know what some of your self-talk is. (Remember the example, "He's just a lazy slob who doesn't care about my needs or how the apartment looks!" That's self-talk.) You'll want to identify your existing self-talk really clearly, because you won't be able to develop new self-talk unless you know what your current self-talk is. And you need to recognize that self-talk happens at every step along the way to seeing and navigating conflicting needs. There's always something going on inside your head as you're trying to negotiate your needs and those of your partner. We'll demonstrate this in the character story lines later in the chapter, but let's look at an example here.

Let's return to the situation of not getting your unreasonable pet want met. If your self-talk is something like "Baseball is more important to him than I am. He doesn't care about my feelings. How could he care more about the game than he does about me?!", then you are likely to remain extremely hurt and angry and perhaps demand that he stop watching, even throw a tantrum when he's watching, maybe even threaten to break up with him. None of this is productive. New reality-based self-talk might sound something like "He loves baseball and he loves me. My insisting that he pay attention to me during baseball games sets me up to be disappointed. If I speak with him before or after the game, or even during commercial breaks, he'll pay attention. I need to be okay with that. I need to remember that he really does love and care about me. Otherwise I'm letting my pet want get in the way of things." This kind of self-talk will help you feel less hurt and angry, and it opens up the possibility for you to get your need met in a mutually satisfying way.

Can You Come Up with New Self-Talk?

Think about the unreasonable pet want you listed earlier. What are you telling yourself about it? What could your new self-talk be?

New self-talk:

Notice that we referred to reality-based self-talk. This is important. Negative self-talk is what we typically do when we're upset. It functions to amplify our negative emotions and to keep us stuck. You might think, therefore, that the opposite of negative self-talk is positive self-talk. Not necessarily. No one feels any better when trying to think positively if there is no basis in reality for it. It is not helpful to tell yourself that your boy-friend cares about you or that everything is going to be okay when you have no evidence for that. It won't make you feel better and could even contribute to your staying in a situation that's bad for you. What you tell yourself has to have a basis in reality. So in the example about unreason-able pet wants, the new self-talk will work only if it actually reflects what your boyfriend feels and what he's willing to do.

Was the new self-talk you created above reality based? Check and make sure. If not, see if you can come up with something more realistic.

Reality-based self-talk:

When you and he understand and empathize with one another, and when you engage in mutual problem solving, you can use your insights and your problem-solving plans to come up with reality-based self-talk that will help you manage your feelings as you work to get your needs met and to help your partner get his met.

Step 2. Tolerate difficult or intense feelings.

When needs conflict in relationships, people experience lots of intense, difficult feelings. Even when couples are working at mutual problem solving and learning how to meet each other's needs, negative feelings can come up. Learning how to tolerate these feelings—how to engage in what thera-pists call distress tolerance—is extremely important. When we can tolerate experiencing an unpleasant or frightening feeling, we're better able to:

- Refrain from behaving impulsively.
- Refrain from extreme displays of emotion.
- Use our new self-talk.
- Stay reality based and have hope for the future.
- Communicate effectively and meet our own and our partner's needs.

So how do we engage in distress tolerance? Well, if you're working on emotion regulation step 1 by developing new self-talk, then you're already helping yourself. Reality-based self-talk can help, as can self-talk that affirms your ability to cope. Recruit your logic resources—your head—to help you calm your emotions. That doesn't mean you try to deny or avoid your emotion, and it doesn't mean you punish yourself for having your emotion—quite the opposite. You want to validate your experience and have compassion for yourself and allow yourself to disengage gently from getting wrapped up in your emotion. To illustrate this, let's keep going with the unreasonable pet want example. Even with your new self-talk about how your boyfriend really cares, you're likely to feel those pangs of intense hurt, especially at the beginning, after you've just begun mutual problem solving. At those times, you might tell yourself things like "It's okay that I'm feeling this. I don't need to act on it. I can just notice what I'm feeling and let it be there. This is hard work, and I'm going to feel these things. That's normal. I don't want to let pet wants get in the way of my relationship and the other ways I can get my needs met. The hurt will get easier to deal with over time."

> Try writing some new, compassionate self-talk that affirms your ability to cope with a distressing situation:

Step 3. Get in touch with and convey soft feelings.

We defined soft feelings in mutuality step 4. Getting in touch with them is a great way to help you regulate your emotions. Take the example of a woman who gets angry at her boyfriend for not spending more time with her. Underneath that anger is hurt that he is not choosing to be with her, fear that he will leave her, a sense of sadness that comes from missing the person she loves. If the anger were all she was aware of and conveyed to her boyfriend, her behavior would reduce the chances of his meeting her need and make it more difficult for her to tolerate her feelings. The more she becomes aware of her soft feelings, the less anger she will feel and the more she can directly and clearly convey her feelings and needs accurately. This is what we were referring to in the fourth step in mutuality when we suggested communicating soft feelings. Of course, expressing soft feelings doesn't guarantee a positive response, but it increases the chances of one. If your guy doesn't have a positive response, that's important information for you.

Think of a time you were angry at a guy. What were the soft feelings that were underneath?

How could you have conveyed those soft feelings to him?

Using the Skills

Let's take a look now at how the characters could use the skills in situations of conflicting needs.

EMILY AND WILL

When Will makes time, he and Emily communicate daily in some way and she feels connected. However, when he doesn't initiate contact or respond to a text, or he fails to call her back or misses a call, she doesn't feel he's treating her as if she's important to him. She wants to feel like a priority in his life, and Will's lack of contact gets in the way of this.

Fortunately, both Emily and Will have good insight into this problem. In line with insight step 3, Emily has been able to identify her thoughts, feelings, and behaviors and how they are connected. She knows that when she feels her need to be important to him is not getting met she feels hurt. She starts thinking he doesn't care about her, and then she gets angry. And once angry, she'll send him a nasty, aggressive text, or, if they're together, she'll say something mean and run out of the room. She is acutely aware of her pattern now, and both she and Will can predict its emergence. Emily also knows the consequences. Her pattern never works to get her need met. It just leads to an argument and erodes their trust in one another.

Emily and Will also have been very successful in identifying their needs conflict. Through many discussions, in line with insight steps 5 and 6, Emily has been able to gain insight into how important school is to Will and how focused Will is on his work. Take the example we presented in

Chapter 4, where Emily is working on being able to accept these aspects of Will. This is a typical conversation we related there that Emily and Will have had as they've tried to gain insight into their needs conflict.

Emily: I don't understand why you do not take five minutes to call me to say good night after you've finished studying.

Will: I just don't think like that.

Emily: But you know I want you to, so you should be making the effort. Don't you care about what I need?

Will: Yes. It's just hard for me. I'm focused on my studies right now.

Emily: (interrupting) I know. It's because you're so focused—you give 110% to anything you do and you forget about everything else when you're doing it. Then you probably feel so spent afterward that you just want to zone out, watch TV, listen to music, recharge. Let's forget about it. Can we talk about something else?

Will: Why? You can't forget about it! You are always wanting to fix me or change me.

Emily: I don't think you're broken! I think you're amazing, and I'm trying to accept you. It's just that the thing that makes you successful is also something that hurts me, and I don't know how to handle that.

As this conversation shows, Emily has been struggling with how much she can empathize with Will's need and accept him. She has been trying to use reality-based self-talk and emotion regulation as she and Will make an effort to engage in mutual problem solving. Using emotion regulation step 1, she reminds herself of the reality—he loves her *and* he needs to focus intently on his work—and she tells herself that his work behavior has nothing to do with how important she is to him. When she starts to feel hurt, she tries to talk herself down so the hurt doesn't lead to anger. But it's not easy for her.

Sometimes, when Will is particularly unresponsive (like when he's got major exams), or if Emily is feeling lonely at school, her old patterns start to resurface. The old thoughts take over and the hurt becomes anger, and she can't believe Will really cares about her. One time she Googled, "Why has your boyfriend started ignoring you?" All the advice is the same—"He's just not as into you as he used to be, he doesn't want the relationship to progress, he doesn't respect you." Well, that's all Emily needed to see! That completely undid her hard work at emotion regulation. She decided she had to make a "talk-and-text plan" with Will where she would insist they communicate every day. At first she felt kind of embarrassed about it—like, really? Who has to do that with her boyfriend?! But she answered her own question with this: "A woman who has a boyfriend who doesn't respect her!"

Uh-oh. Bad plan! This is not mutual problem solving, and it's based on negative thinking and poor emotion regulation. Let's see how that worked out for her.

Emily: Part of me can't believe I want to do this—but I do—let's make a Skype-and-text plan so that we can communicate every day (*giggles*).

Will: Seriously?!

Emily: Yes. When you don't respond to my texts, I start thinking you're not that into me, that you don't respect me because I'm not important to you, and you don't care. I've told you how I feel about you not texting me back, yet you ignore my feelings.

Will: I cannot believe we are having this conversation again! This is not all about you, Emily! I've told you, until I finish what I'm doing—an assignment or studying for an exam—I block everything out. If I stop what I'm doing and text you, I lose my train of thought, and my mind starts going in circles. Why can't you accept me?! You're so confusing. Sometimes you're okay with who I am, and sometimes you're not.

Emily: I know. I want to give you what you need. Sometimes I'm okay with you being focused, but other times I think I'm compromising what I need to give you what you need, and then I end up feeling that you're treating me as if I'm not important to you.

Will: I know this is hard for you, but why do you repeatedly demand I have to change who I am for you to feel secure?

Emily: To feel important I need to have you communicate with me every day! I mean, why am I the only one who has to work at changing? I respect you—why can't you respect me?

Will: This has nothing to do with respect! So, what? I should fail and not get into medical school so you can feel *respected*? Let's just end this conversation. I don't even know what to say.

After Emily hangs up, she feels anxious and confused and is afraid that he's going to break up with her. She wonders whether she's being unreasonable.

Clearly, that didn't work out so well. They repeated the same old argument. Why did this happen? The main reason is there was a failure of mutuality on Emily's part right from the beginning, and that led to a cascade of problems. Emily deserves to get her need to be important met. That will not happen if she demands that Will change in a way he's not willing to because it compromises his own need to an extreme degree. Emily certainly could choose to end the relationship if she determines she can't feel important unless Will communicates with her every day. That is her choice to make. If she truly cannot accept his behavior, she should exit. However, if she really wants to work this out with Will, she will have to use mutual problem solving, not make a unilateral decision and insist he follow it. You may also be seeing that Emily feels her need to be important to Will can be met in only one way—through daily communication. Perhaps this is an unreasonable pet want? Emily must consider whether her need can be met in any other way. And she will need to marshal her emotion regulation skills to be able to do this. Emily decides to give it a try.

The weekend after the "talk-and-text plan" fight, Will comes to visit. They're always happy when they're together. It makes them both remember how much they love each other and mean to each other. Friday night and Saturday are always bliss. Now it's Sunday, and Will is leaving later in the day. They're in the danger zone, because Will always has to do some work on Sunday to be prepared for his Monday classes. Emily always starts to anticipate their separation and fears their impending lack of contact, and her emotions start to intensify. In the past, this has often led to a fight on Sunday night. The same old fight. Emily decides she's going to try something different this time. She's been thinking about Will's needs and trying to understand them. She's been practicing some new self-talk: "Will is stressed about school. I need to give him the space he needs. It makes him love and respect me more, not less, and that's what I want. I can trust in his love for me." She's been focusing on her soft emotions, and she's been using her logic to see the reality of Will and his feelings for her. Let's see how it goes.

It's Sunday morning. They wake early, have sex, and take some time to just be with each other. She does a coffee run (she knows he loves that). She gets back to the room, and he's working on a paper, still naked (he knows she loves that). She notices herself getting angry that he's working, but instead of expressing that and complaining he's not paying attention to her, she kisses him and says:

Emily: I love you so much. I know you have work to do. I just wish we could spend every minute together till you go.
Will: I want to, but I can't. I just need 30 minutes, and then I will.
Emily: (*Practicing emotion regulation, she says to herself, "He's so focused that if I push him with 'Please!' his mind will go in circles, and then he won't be able to finish what he needs to do—he's told me so." She smiles, gives him another lover's kiss.*) You got 30 minutes, Babe! (*She pulls out her own work.*)

In 30 minutes she sends him a text: "Tick, tock :)"

Will: (*looks over and grins*) Five more minutes—almost done.
Emily: (*Grins back.*)

In five minutes, he's still typing furiously. She starts to feel angry again; it's as if he's not making time for her, not prioritizing her. Her mind goes to "Why does he not respect my time?" But she stops herself from saying anything and instead focuses on expressing her soft feelings—feelings of love and desire rather than anger—and sends another playful text: "Is it sex time again yet? :)"

Then he looks up and smiles:

Will: Do you ever feel like everything is so busy in your mind that if you don't finish up what you're thinking you'll lose it?

Emily: Yes, all the time. (*And she really means it. She knows exactly what he's talking about. She gets it.*)

Will: That's how I feel right now. You okay with me being 15 more minutes, and then I'm all yours? I promise.

Emily: Absolutely, yes (*looking over at him and grinning*).

Will: Thank you. Thank you so much. I feel like you really get me right now.

At that moment, Emily felt emotion well up inside of her; those I-feel-so-connected-to-him feelings radiated warmth throughout her body, similar to how she feels after sex with Will. She felt as if Will was showing his love to her by telling her who he is. And she felt as if she was showing Will her love by letting him be who he is, by giving him what he needed. It felt so great to her. She did it! She didn't repeat the pattern! So much better than fighting. And they went on to have a fantastic afternoon together.

Later on, they had the following conversation where Emily initiated mutual problem solving:

Emily: When I listened to how you needed to finish up what you were working on, and I really understood and I was able to give you that, I felt really good about it, really good about us. I wanted to give you what you needed. It was different from before.

Will: I know. I really appreciated it. That's how I feel when we're apart. And it's happening all the time. I have so much work to do. I don't even know how I manage it!

Emily: Can we talk about how we're going to handle things when we're apart? Like, really try to figure out together how to do this? I want to give you your space. I also want contact. How can we make this work?

Will: I'm not sure.

Emily: Well, let me ask you this. Did you ever feel like you just wanted to know you were loved, that someone was thinking of you, that you were important?

Will: Of course. Doesn't everyone want that?

Emily: Right! Exactly! That's how I feel. I know maybe I feel that more than you do, or maybe more than other people, but that's just how I am. Like you're a focused person, I'm a person who likes to know that I'm important. So, how about this? What if I leave you alone more, or at least let you know that I know you're busy? Could you let me know you're thinking about me more?

Will: Hmm . . . That's not a bad idea. I guess we could try it. I'm kind of afraid that I won't meet your expectations.

Emily: Well, I'll try to work on mine and keep my emotions in check. (*She thinks to herself, "No more Googling crazy things!"*)

The next day Emily works on showing Will she understands him and texts him using soft emotions to communicate: "I know you're probably focused on something right now, just wanted to say hi, I love you. Stay focused—nail that paper! Love, your sweet chatty baby, who misses you being inside of her."

Later that day Will reciprocates with the following text: "On break between classes. Awoke thinking of you, as I do every day, wishing you were beside me. Miss you."

"Okay, so far, so good," Emily thinks. "He listened, he's trying. Now I just need to remember what he said. He thinks of me every morning, whether he texts me or not." Emily is right. She does need to remember what he said. That could become part of her realistic self-talk. If she could remember that, it would certainly help her regulate her emotions. Hard work, but necessary. In addition, as Emily works on this new way of getting her need to feel important met, she will become clearer on her standards for what a good relationship is. She can try it and see how she feels, and this will give her insight into whether she can really let go of what she once thought was the only way she could get her need met.

In doing this, Emily is not sacrificing or giving up her need. Instead, she's willingly compromising, by giving up her pet want, to see if she can get her need met another way. Doing so increases the likelihood that they'll be able to resolve their needs conflict in a mutually satisfying way. If they can keep up their use of the skills, they will be meeting each other's needs and will eventually develop a new, more adaptive cycle of relating with one another.

MIA AND COREY

Mia and Corey have conflicting needs, and although Mia started out trying to deal with their needs in an insightful and mutual manner, she hasn't

---

I/ME

Do You See What Emily Is Doing?

She's using the skills to identify an unreasonable expectation, which she used to think was a legitimate preference. You can reset your expectations for any one of your key needs this way. Indeed, identifying your limits by distinguishing between pet wants and legitimate preferences is a way to get the insight you need to know what you can or cannot compromise on in the spirit of mutuality.

been able to truly implement the I/ME skills in a way that will help her navigate their needs conflicts. As a result, she keeps repeating the same patterns with Corey. Let's take a look at how this all comes up when Mia goes to visit Corey for Christmas.

This is the first time Mia is going to meet Corey's family, and she's excited about that. It's a sign to her that their relationship is strong. However, it will also be the first time she meets OtherWoman and one of her partners who is male. Corey really wants them to meet and to explore a sexual experience together, and she's both excited and nervous. Because Corey has been open about his desire need, Mia knows he's aroused by the thought of her being with him and another woman (although uncomfortably jealous at the thought of her being with another man). They've discussed these things extensively, and she's been clear with him that she gets aroused by the thought of watching him with another woman and that she's open to experimenting sexually with another woman. Sounds like good insight into one another's needs, right? Let's see how it goes.

Corey picks Mia up at the airport. She runs into his arms at baggage claim, tearful:

Mia: I've missed you so much! I love you so much!

Corey: Me too! Are you okay, though? Why are you crying? You look so upset.

Mia: I am. I'm not feeling very well today. I had a lot to drink last night.

Corey: (laughing) Don't worry, you'll feel better soon. We'll get you some water and something to eat—

Mia: (interrupting) No, it's not that really. I was with OtherGuy last night, and I was so drunk that I don't remember what happened, and I think I may have done something you didn't want me to. I'm so sorry. I love you so much.

Corey: Really?! Is that the first thing you're going to tell me when you get off the plane?! Not only are you telling me something I don't want to know, but you're telling me you violated our agreement—again! I can't believe it!

Mia: (crying) I know. I'm sorry. I just couldn't live with myself during this trip and really be with you fully, especially with OtherWoman, without being genuine.

Corey: But what about me?! Maybe I can't live with you now during this trip because of it! Again, you show no regard for my feelings! Now I'm going to be thinking about this the whole time.

Mia: I'm so sorry. Please let's just try to connect and enjoy one another. Please!

They drive to Corey's place in silence. When they arrive, he takes her in his arms and says, "Everything will be okay. Let's just have our visit as planned. I love you, and I know you love me."

Oh boy—not a good start to the trip. Mia and Corey reenacted their typical authentic-safe needs conflict, with Mia needing to be authentic to feel connected to Corey while disregarding Corey's need to feel safe with her. Even though Mia knows about Corey's need (insight step 5), she doesn't have insight into her thoughts, feelings, and behaviors (insight step 3). If she did, she would be able to clearly identify that she thinks things like "I can only feel connected to Corey if I'm fully authentic." She feels sadness about the potential loss of connection, guilt for not being honest with him, and fear that their relationship might not work, and then she tells him everything no matter what. Furthermore, she has not used insight step 4 to assess the consequences of her behavior. If she had, she would have realized Corey feels unsafe and her behavior leads to conflicts and breaches of trust that harm the relationship. Mia also is unable to regulate her emotions with regard to her authenticity need. That is, she has no distress tolerance for the negative feelings that arise when she considers not acting on her authenticity need (emotion regulation step 2), and she has no healthy self-talk to help her tolerate her feelings (emotion regulation step 1). In line with this, she is unable to approach the situation in a mutual manner. She and Corey don't even make an attempt anymore to engage in mutual problem solving (mutuality step 6). They just move on without further discussion. Therefore, her need to be authentic ends up trumping her ability to keep Corey safe, so on and on the cycle goes.

The night Mia meets OtherWoman and her boyfriend things go basically as planned for the sex part. Mia and OtherWoman make out and explore each other's bodies. Then Corey and OtherWoman's boyfriend join in with them, and eventually they couple up, each with his or her own partner, and have sex in the same room but separately. Everyone seems to have enjoyed this, and afterward they go to a bar to meet up with OtherWoman's friends. Once there, Corey starts complaining about how he feels ignored by OtherWoman:

Mia: You feel ignored?

Corey: Yeah, she's not spending any time with me or us.

Mia: So what? Why are you pining for attention from her? I'm right here!

Corey: It's not that I don't want to be with you. I am so happy you're here. I am! It's just that I'm used to spending one-on-one time with her and not sharing her with her friends.

Mia: It's as if you're jealous and hurt. You probably didn't like that she just had sex with her boyfriend. You care about her. Admit it! What else am I supposed to believe?

Corey: The jealousy I feel about you is different than with OtherWoman. It creates different feelings in me. I react in a different way. With you it's as if you're cheating, and with her it's like "Hey look at me, I'm here too!" I don't know what else to say.

Mia: I just don't get it, Corey. C'mon, let's just have our own good time together. That's what I'm here for, right? (*She kisses him playfully and pulls him onto the dance floor.*)

This interaction left Mia feeling jealous. She's questioning Corey's desire need as it's butting up uncomfortably against her trust need. She's not sure she can trust Corey's feelings for OtherWoman. Yet she's happy to be there with him and she wants everything to be all right, so it's another pattern repeated and another missed opportunity for mutual problem solving.

They spend Christmas with his family. They have a wonderful time, and she's so happy. It reminds her of why they're together. The next day Mia is leaving to go back home. As she's getting out of the shower, Corey comes in reading out loud OtherGuy's last text message to her: "I miss you! Can't wait to see you. What time does your flight get in?" He's angry:

Corey: "I miss you"?—What the fuck?!

Mia: It's sweet.

Corey: You're downplaying how you feel about him to me!

Mia: No, I'm not.

Corey: I don't text OtherWoman things like "I miss you." I consider that intimate. You have no respect for me.

Mia: I respect you. (*She's confused.*) You're taking that phrase to mean a lot more than it does. Besides, he's the one saying he misses me. I didn't say that to him.

Corey: You agreed to no talking about your free passes, but you did! You agreed to not engage in things that I didn't want you to do with him, but you did those things! How can I trust you?

Mia: Yeah, well you agreed to no emotional connection, and you clearly have one. The other night you got jealous! And I checked out your texts too. You were talking with OtherWoman about your jealous feelings—what the fuck??? Anything else you want to tell me?

Corey: I have no problem with you looking at my phone, but I'd like you to do that when I'm there. I feel upset that you went behind my back. There's no reason for you to do that.

Mia: I couldn't help myself. I was so upset about how jealous you were when you didn't get her attention. But don't change the subject! You are emotionally connected to her!

Corey: Stop! I know we trust each other not to hurt the other intentionally, but we are hurting each other. We have to stop these conversations, these "you agreed to this, but you actually did it anyway!" arguments.

Mia: Do you want to break up with me?

Corey: No. Lately, I've been thinking I want to marry you one day. You are the most important person in the world to me.

Corey is right. They have to stop these conversations. All they do is play out their conflicting desire and trust needs over and over again. So what should they do instead? Mia needs to use the skills, right from the very beginning. Let's start with insight. Mia knows she's unhappy (insight step 1). She knows she and Corey have conflicting needs. She even knows what those needs are (insight steps 2 and 5), but as we noted earlier with regard to their authentic–safe conflict, she's not aware of the pattern of her thoughts, feelings, and behaviors with regard to her need, nor is she aware of their consequences (insight steps 3 and 4). Let's outline these for the desire–trust conflict to show what Mia would see if she were using the insight skills. Mia's thoughts include "He's emotionally connected to OtherWoman. He's betraying a commitment we have by not respecting the limits we set. He doesn't love me. He wants to break up with me." Consequently, her feelings include jealousy, anger, and fear. This leads her to check his texts behind his back and to argue with him angrily and in a blaming manner. The consequences of this are that Corey defends himself, turns the conversation to what he perceives as her betrayals of him, and argues back in an equally angry and blaming fashion, ultimately rendering them stuck in a cycle of conflict and distrust.

As you can see in Mia and Corey's story, both their desire–trust needs conflict and their authentic–safe needs conflict result in repeated cycles of fighting and breaches of trust. And as we've shown, Mia needs to develop insight into this cycle by examining the pattern of her thoughts, feelings, and behaviors, as well as their consequences, to make any progress toward resolution. Once that happens, Mia and Corey can work toward getting out of their dysfunctional cycle by using the mutuality skills. Mia and Corey have a serious problem, but they are not unified in solving it (mutuality step 3). Right now they see each other's behavior as the problem. However, the real problem is that their free-pass situation is not working as planned, and they need to come together to deal with that. Mia needs to do a better job of putting herself in Corey's shoes to understand his experience (mutuality step 2). In addition to expressing her needs clearly (mutuality step 4), she needs to listen carefully to Corey (mutuality step 5), and, to see if mutual problem solving is possible, she needs to consider why he can't meet her needs and she can't meet his (mutuality step 6). She also needs to work on her emotion regulation skills to create new self-talk (emotion regulation step 1) and to better tolerate and soothe her negative feelings (emotion regulation step 2). Let's look at how she would use these skills, first considering the authentic–safe conflict.

In this situation, the first thing that Mia needs to do is ask herself "Why is it so important for me to choose to meet my authenticity need over keeping Corey safe?" This is an important question, and it's the place they need to begin, because their attempts at mutual problem solving have failed due to Mia's inability to make the compromises required. Why is this? There are two possibilities. First, perhaps authenticity is a key need for Mia, meaning that compromising it would feel like compromising her sense of self and her self-respect. As we stated earlier, giving up getting a key need met is not a compromise. If authenticity is a key need for Mia, then she needs to find a partner who wants her to be fully authentic at all times. Corey is not the guy for her.

On the other hand, perhaps the way she wants to get her authenticity need met is a pet want. Given that disclosing every detail of every part of her life is not realistic with Corey, if Mia wants to resolve this needs conflict, she will have to see whether there are other ways she can feel authentic and connected in their relationship. If Mia wants to consider this, she needs to use emotion regulation and mutuality skills to deal in new ways with her feelings of discomfort that arise from not telling Corey about her free passes. For example, if she feels guilty for not being honest, she might use new self-talk to remind herself that by keeping free pass information private she is actually being kind and giving to Corey. This new self-talk would rely on Mia's using her mutuality skills to really listen to Corey, put herself in Corey's shoes, and understand his perspective. If Mia feels sad and afraid that she'll feel disconnected and lose the relationship, she could use emotion regulation skills and try to focus on all the other ways in which she and Corey are connected. In addition, using insight about the consequences of her behavior, she could remind herself with new self-talk that her current behavior is already threatening their connection and the stability of their relationship, which is exactly what she does not want. This new self-talk would need constant repeating, but it will help Mia keep her sexual experiences to herself, feel less distressed by doing so, and be more able to focus on the connection that she and Corey do have. If Mia were to use the skills in these ways, she and Corey would be more successful at resolving their authentic–safe needs conflict.

Mia can also apply these ideas to the desire–trust needs conflict. Corey is obviously emotionally involved with the other woman, so now Mia must determine whether her preference that he avoid emotional involvement is a pet want or a clear limit for her. She also needs to revisit a more basic insight question: is she truly comfortable having her partner engage in sexual relationships outside of theirs? Maybe in theory she is, but in practice it may pose too great a threat to her sense of security. If so, she'll need to communicate this clearly and directly to Corey. If Corey prefers to be in an open relationship and Mia in a monogamous one, a mutually satisfying resolution is unlikely, and the relationship won't work.

If, however, Mia decides she can be in an open relationship, she and Corey will have to use insight skills to take a long hard look at themselves to determine their key needs (and associated preferences and limits), their thoughts, feelings, and behaviors associated with their need, and the consequences of how they behave, to see how the ways they keep violating each other's limits hurt the relationship. They will need to use mutuality skills to put themselves in each other's shoes to really see how the other is feeling about the limit violations and to decide whether they can accept one another's limits and behave accordingly. If they cannot, they are not treating one another as if they know and like each other, and they should not be together. If they decide to give it a go, they'll need to examine their own limits carefully—are they truly limits or pet wants? Does a violation of those limits really mean what each fears it means? For example, if Corey wants attention from OtherWoman, does that mean he no longer wants to be with Mia, as she fears? Or if Mia engages in off-limits sexual behaviors with OtherGuy, does that mean that she's cheated on Corey, which is how it feels to him? Mia and Corey have to ask themselves and each other these questions and really listen to the answers. In doing so, they're going to need a lot of self-talk about the importance of mutuality and a lot of emotion regulation to manage their feelings of desire for others and their jealousy.

JULIANNE AND GREGORY

Julianne and Gregory's needs conflict—their inability to accept one another for who they are—intensified after Julianne's "slide" into living with Gregory. Even in planning for the move, their conflict was evident. They had decided that Gregory would move in with Julianne, so she asked him to make a plan with her for deciding what to keep, purge, and pack away before he moved in. Gregory didn't agree:

Julianne: I want us to make a list, to figure out what you'll bring before you move in.
Gregory: I don't see why we need to do that right now.
Julianne: It doesn't have to be right now. How about on the weekend? The move is coming up soon.
Gregory: I just don't think that's really necessary.
Julianne: But we only have so much space. Wouldn't it be easier to only bring what you want and need?
Gregory: Stop with the overorganization! I'll figure out what to bring.

He brought everything.

They both want to be equal partners, and they are equal with regard to upkeep of the house and paying the bills, yet the natural conflicts that arise from living together continue to exacerbate their needs conflict. For example, when they used to stay over at each other's house, they both behaved more as guests and acted accordingly. Sure, Gregory's house was always a mess, and hers was neat and tidy, but he used to clean up his own yogurt bowl, and he didn't leave stuff just lying around her house. Now that it's their house, he leaves stuff all over the place, as he did in his own place.

Julianne has asked him to be more mindful of putting his things away to keep the house tidy, but to no avail.

Gregory: Where's my coat?

Julianne: I put it in the hall closet. It was taking up space on the dining room chair, and no one could sit there.

Gregory: I told you—don't put my stuff where I don't want it to be!

Julianne: I don't like having to put your stuff away, but I've asked you to please hang your coat when you come in. Is that too much to ask?

Gregory: Yes, in fact it is. I'll put my coat wherever I want it. I don't see why I have to hang it up when I'm just going to use it again in the morning.

This kind of thing goes on every day, and Gregory goes on and on about how she shouldn't move his stuff.

Julianne also finds herself fighting with Gregory over the timing of household tasks. For instance, she'll be cleaning out the fridge, and he'll want her to go grocery shopping with him. IN. FIVE. MINUTES. If she doesn't go, she'll hear about it for days. And when she finally decided to organize the closets, which she wanted to do before he moved in, their dysfunctional cycle of Julianne taking or proposing an action followed by Gregory criticizing or dismissing it continued:

Julianne: I'm going to sort through my stuff in the closets, purge, and then drop it all off at the women's shelter.

Gregory: I don't want you to do that. I want to do the closets with you. Plus, there are more important things to do.

Julianne: Like what?

Gregory: The storage locker down in the parking area.

Julianne: Okay, I'll start there tonight. Will you do the closets with me on the weekend?

Gregory: I don't know. I'll let you know when I feel like it.

Julianne: Look, I'm just trying to take care of my part of the closets and make space for you. You can do your part whenever you feel like it. I thought that would help you.

Gregory: No! I said I want to do them with you, and we'll do it when I have time.

Julianne feels she's trying to be accommodating—but she's been waiting for him to purge the closets for months. She doesn't know why she can't purge her stuff and he purge his at different times. But she knows that if she purges hers there will be a consequence. He'll complain and go on and on and accuse her of not respecting him.

As we saw in Chapters 4 and 5, Julianne is aware that Gregory is controlling. She's tried talking with him in a direct and clear manner about her experience of how he behaves toward her, and she's worked on her own ability to accept Gregory by using new self-talk and attempting to regulate her

I/ME

Wait, Isn't Julianne Also Trying to Control What Gregory Does by Telling Him How and When to Organize?

It certainly seems that way to Gregory. That's what happens when there is no mutuality. Both people can look like they are trying to control the other: "I want you to change." "No, I want you to change." A battle develops where both people are vying for control.

emotions. Unfortunately, so far none of this has worked. Julianne is aware of her thoughts, feelings, and behaviors, as well as their consequences. She has tried to be aware of Gregory's needs and to communicate hers to him. Yet they haven't been able to engage in mutual problem solving.

An important question for Julianne and Gregory is whether they can unify against the problem (mutuality step 3). Is there any way they could come together in seeing that they both have to work toward acceptance? Like Mia and Corey, Julianne and Gregory see each other's behavior as the problem. They blame and work against one another. They don't really understand each other's needs (insight step 6). To do so, they would have to work to become familiar with each other, care about each other's feelings, and really listen to what each other has to say. Here's how that might look:

Take the example of Julianne wanting the closets and the apartment to be neat and tidy and Gregory wanting to be able to leave his coat and other belongings wherever he likes. Julianne would communicate authentically, using soft feelings and showing her vulnerable side (mutuality step 4), that having the apartment in order helps her feel calm and reduces her anxiety. In an attempt to become familiar with Julianne, Gregory would listen carefully to her (mutuality step 5). He would show his understanding by demonstrating empathy toward her (mutuality step 2), and he would show care by wanting to contribute to her feeling calm. Gregory also would communicate authentically, using soft feelings and showing his vulnerable side (mutuality step 4), that after a long day of having to please difficult clients, he finds it freeing and relaxing to be able to "just be" without any pressure of things having to be a certain way. In turn, Julianne would listen carefully, show understanding by demonstrating empathy, and show care by wanting to reduce his sense of pressure (mutuality steps 2 and 5). This mutual sense of understanding and care would allow them to unify against the problem and commit to trying to meet each other's needs, and this would allow for mutual problem solving.

For example, they could decide to hire a closet organizer so there would be plenty of space to store things. Or they could decide together that Gregory can leave his stuff anywhere he wants in the bedroom where guests would not see his mess and that Julianne can pick up anything he leaves in other places. Or that Gregory can leave things anywhere he wants on work nights, and then together they will tidy up on Saturday morning. Whatever solution they come up with would be fine, as long as they come to it from unity. Moreover, once they really understand each other's needs and preferences (insight steps 2 and 6)—when Julianne sees Gregory not as an inconsiderate slob but as a person who needs to reduce a sense of pressure to perform and when Gregory sees Julianne not as an overorganized neat freak but as a person who feels calmed by a sense of order—they will be able to use that new understanding to develop new self-talk. New self-talk will help them with emotion regulation by reducing their feelings of frustration and anger and allowing them to continue to feel empathic, and it will make them want to make changes to meet the other's need. That's the heart of mutual problem solving.

Of course, this can happen only if both partners understand and aspire to mutuality. Therefore, an important question for Julianne to examine is whether Gregory is capable of mutuality. Can he do it? Although Julianne is aware of Gregory's tendency to be controlling, she must go back to examine the "I know and like him" familiarity need to really understand how it makes him who he is and how it influences the way he acts and the way he gets his needs met. She has to really let herself look at the evidence in his behavior over time and across different situations to determine whether Gregory's being controlling can ever allow for mutuality. She has to consider that the very need to control what she does is a sign of Gregory's being interested in meeting only his own needs. If that is the case, their needs conflict will never be resolved.

I/ME

Can You See How the Skills Help You Understand Your Partner Better?

Have you ever found yourself asking, "Why is he doing that?"

The process described for Julianne and Gregory would allow each to understand the other better—to accurately know why they're doing what they're doing—what their real intentions are. If you take a mutual perspective and use the skills, and if your partner can express soft feelings, you'll be able to figure out his real intention, and you'll be better able to understand him.

We hope this chapter has helped you see how the I/ME skills can be used when needs conflict in relationships. We encourage you to take some time to think through the skills and how you might use them in your own relationship. Write your ideas below.

Skills That I Could Use

Insight:

Mutuality:

Emotion Regulation:

In the next chapter, we bring together, in a big-picture way, all the lessons from Chapters 3–6 to help you determine whether you're in a healthy relationship. Through two of the characters' stories, we'll demonstrate how you can use real evidence to assess whether all the conditions for a healthy relationship are being met.

7

Am I in a Healthy Relationship?

In Chapter 6, you saw how Emily, Mia, and Julianne could use the I/ME skills to navigate needs conflicts that they were well aware of but didn't know how to resolve. The road to a healthy relationship is not, however, always that straight. When you're in a relationship (or considering one) that just doesn't seem to be working but you're not sure what's wrong, you need to step back and do a full needs assessment. This evaluation will help you develop insight into whether you're headed for a healthy relationship and, if not, where the problems lie.

First, remember that you'll know you're in a healthy relationship if all of the following are true—that is, if you have real evidence for them:

1. "I know and like myself." Knowing and liking yourself means knowing what your needs are, respecting those needs, and being able to meet those needs for yourself.
2. "I know and like him." Knowing and liking him means you are confident he is the guy you want, and you treat him in a way that shows you like and respect him.
3. "He knows and likes me." This means you are with a guy who wants what you have to offer and treats you in a way that shows he likes and respects you.

Lexi and Lauren aren't entirely aware that their needs aren't being met in their current relationships, but they're not particularly content either.

Lexi

In Chapters 4 and 5, we saw that Lexi was not getting her need to share an interesting life (among other needs) met with James, and we suggested that the prognosis was not good. Indeed, Lexi ended up breaking up with James—but not before she met someone who seemed to better fulfill her needs. Here's how that went:

Lexi was feeling bored with James, but conflicted as well. She was ambivalent about being with him but couldn't seem to end the relationship. Until she met Ryan.

She was out at a bar with friends one night and happened to notice this very hot guy come in carrying his motorcycle helmet. He took the only open seat at the bar, which was right next to her, and they struck up a conversation. When he offered to take her for a ride, she quickly accepted. This was the adventure and spontaneity she had been craving. As she wrapped her arms around his waist while he drove fast, she felt an amazing rush. She felt alive, and when he put his hand on her leg while they were stopped at a light, she could feel her desire need being met. He asked to see her again, and she agreed.

That next time they were hanging out, he said:

Ryan: So you know I like to ride motorcycles. What do you like to do?

Lexi: Well, I really like hot yoga. I go a couple times a week.

Ryan: Huh, I've never done that. I'd like to try it.

Lexi: (*looking him right in the eye and laughing*) Shut up! Really? You would go with me?

Ryan: Yeah, I've never done it, and if you like it, I want to try it.

She's speechless. James NEVER was interested in doing what she liked. It feels like Ryan really gets her and wants to share in her life!

Lexi and Ryan quickly start spending more time together. She is aware that her feelings for him are really strong—she gets butterflies every time she sees him. They can talk for hours, and they really seem to get one another. But before she makes a decision to break up with James, she wants to define the relationship with Ryan.

Lexi: I need to ask you some questions about you and us.

Ryan: Ask away.

Lexi: Do you go to the bar, pick up girls, and hook up with them?

Ryan: (*laughing*) You mean like I did with you?

Lexi: (*laughing*) Right! Okay (*smiling*), are you seeing any girls casually besides me?

Ryan: I'm not seeing anyone else but you.

Lexi: I want to be with you and have sex with you, but I need to be the only person.

Ryan: Exclusive or committed?

Lexi: Both. Committed and monogamous.

Ryan: Okay, I'm in (*smiling*).

I/ME

The "Define-the-Relationship" Talk

Talking about what type of relationship you both want helps keep you emotionally safe because you can set your expectations accurately and manage your feelings better.

Mia and Corey had the talk when they discussed exclusivity and ended up on the same page. Olivia and Zach didn't have it, and now Olivia's operating on assumptions.

Why wouldn't a woman have a define-the-relationship talk? Maybe she thinks it's the guy's job to bring it up. Maybe she's afraid of what he'll think (that she's needy or chasing him), or maybe she's afraid to learn he doesn't want the same things she does. In all of these cases, a woman is acting from low power and from a place of wanting to be what he wants rather than wanting to figure out whether this is the right relationship for her.

When should you have the talk? It's specific to each person because it's based on what type of relationship you're looking for and your preferences and limits. When an issue comes up that relates to these things, or when there's a relationship decision to be made, you'll want to have the talk to know whether you and he are on the same page. For example, Lexi knows she wants to be the only one, so she would have the talk before she has sex. Also, the talk is not a one-time thing. There can be many of them over the course of a relationship as it develops and changes.

That's all Lexi needed to hear. She breaks up with James in a text the next day (not cool!), and she and Ryan quickly move in together. She feels she's found her Mr. Right. Not everyone agrees, however. Her family thinks she can do better; they feel she's dating down because he works as a security guard. They're concerned she's moving too fast, especially by letting him move in so quickly. But Lexi doesn't care. She and Ryan are interested in sharing in each other's life.

Okay, let's stop and assess what's happened so far. Lexi's found a guy who meets a key need for her (interesting), one that was not being met by James. That's a good thing. It's important to select partners who will meet key needs for us. (Although breaking up with a longtime partner in a text—terrible. James got back at her by posting some very nasty stuff on Facebook.) And Lexi is getting her needs for authenticity (she can be herself) and desire met very well with Ryan. Also a good thing. Jumping in quickly and assuming Ryan is Mr. Right based only on early indicators present in the intensity and passion of a new relationship? Not so good. In Chapter 4, we discussed how it takes time to assess whether needs are really being met. You need evidence—data—and data become clear only over time and across situations. Let's see what kinds of data emerge in Lexi's relationship with Ryan.

A CRAZY CAR RIDE

Lexi and Ryan are out with a group of friends having a good time. Ryan's a little drunk, and when it's time to go home, he gets into the driver's seat of the car. Lexi tries to take the keys, and his friends are saying, "Let Lexi drive! Let Lexi drive!" But Ryan will just not let that happen. Lexi's thinking, "I can't just get out of the car and leave him by himself. What if he goes out and does something stupid or gets hurt? I love him. I have to take care of him. He doesn't know what he's doing. I have to make sure he's okay." So off they go. It's snowing and there's black ice, but he just starts speeding through the side streets. The tires are spinning, the car is fishtailing—all that crazy stuff. Lexi's heart is racing. Her mouth is dry. It's hard to breathe. She's scared, feeling *unsafe*.

Lexi: Stop. The. Car. Let. Me. Out!
    (Ryan ignores her.)
Lexi: If you don't stop this car, I'm going to jump out and roll! That's how much I do not want to be with you right now!
    (Ryan continues to ignore her.)
    (She tries to open the door. Ryan extends his arm across her, pinning her by pushing down on her chest. When they get home, she gets out sobbing.)
Lexi: You hurt me!
Ryan: You were going to jump out of a moving car. I had to hold you down.

During the night, when Ryan tries to cuddle her, she pushes him away because she's still upset. He cuddles up to her anyway. He can be physically imposing like this, but in some ways she likes it because it makes her feel safe. The next morning Lexi is still sad and angry, aware that what happened the night before was not good. She feels betrayed and wonders whether she can trust Ryan to keep her safe. She starts crying.

Lexi: Do you know how unsafe I felt with you last night? (*She looks at his big, beautiful eyes and sees tears flowing. She knows how sensitive he is.*)
Ryan: I know. I made a mistake. I'll never ever let anything like that happen again. Come here. I love you.
Lexi: No!
Ryan: It was a one-time thing. I'll never, ever let anything like that happen again. I

promise. I'm so sorry. I will never do this again. I hate that this happened. I'll make it up to you. I'm so sorry. I'm so sorry.

She feels reassured, and Ryan shows her he is sorry by being sweet and nice to her in the ensuing days. For example, she gets home from work and her favorite, a grilled cheese sandwich, is just off the pan, and tomato soup is simmering on the stove. All the chores are done. He's washed the dishes, and the apartment is even vacuumed. She thinks, "Okay, he's made a mistake, and he's said he's sorry. I can see he really does mean it." So she forgives him and files away "kind" as one of his best traits.

A BRUISE ON THE ARM

A few weeks later, Ryan goes out with his friend Matthew. Lexi wakes up at 4:00 A.M., and Ryan isn't home, so she starts worrying about whether he's okay and whether he's going to be able to make it to her sister's bridal party fitting this afternoon (they're both in the wedding party) and their family dinner afterward. She calls his phone, but he doesn't answer. Then she calls Matthew's phone, and when he picks up she can hear Ryan flirting with some girl in the background. Of course, Matthew hangs up on her. Then Lexi starts thinking about whether or not Ryan's cheating on her. She starts thinking he's probably spent his rent money again. She feels sick to her stomach. He finally gets home in the afternoon, right before they have to leave to get to their fittings on time. He's still drunk:

Lexi: Where have you been? We have fittings and dinner with my family today. What am I going to say to them?
(He goes into the kitchen to make himself a sandwich.)
Lexi: (*She follows him.*) Did you cheat on me?
Ryan: No.
Lexi: (*She can't deal with this right now, so she moves on.*) You're obviously still drunk, so forget the fittings. Do you think you'll be able to make it to dinner?
Ryan: I'll go! Stop going on and on! I'll get some sleep and show up at the dinner. There, you happy?
(Lexi doesn't know what to say. She's not going on and on, and Ryan is not acting like himself at all.)
Ryan: I always give you what you want. Be happy!
(She storms off into the living room. He tries to grab her arm, she pushes him, and he grabs it again, squeezing it hard enough so she can't get away. She pushes him away again, he lets go of her arm, and he tries to hug her.)
Lexi: Let go of me! This should never have happened. There should be no grabbing my arm ever. You left little bruises! (*She starts crying.*)

Ryan: You always blame me. You pushed me. How is it my fault? Stop crying! Grow up. What are you going to do—call your mom? I don't know anyone else at your age that still calls their mommy crying. You're so immature.

Lexi: That's not true! How can you say that? Nobody who knows me would describe me as immature. I call my mom because she helps me work out my feelings.

Ryan leaves to go to bed. Lexi sits there dumbfounded. She wonders whether the crazy car ride was a red flag. She had a sneaking suspicion at the time that it was a bad sign.

Lexi goes to the fitting. Ryan doesn't even show up at the dinner. Lexi finds herself thinking, "I can't believe this is happening. How could he do this? Why is he ruining our relationship? I just don't want this to be happening." The next morning:

Lexi: This is the first time someone's grabbed my arm and left a bruise. No one's ever left a mark on my body. No one.

Ryan: I know what I did was wrong. I'm sorry. I made a mistake. *(pleading)* Don't make it a big deal, though. I just grabbed your arm.

Lexi: Did you spend your rent money?

Ryan: (sheepishly) Yes.

Lexi: Why are you friends with Matthew? There is so much drama every time you go out with him. He does coke, he's single, he flirts with girls. Then you do coke and you flirt with girls.

Ryan: I didn't do anything wrong. But you're right, I'm sorry. Listen, it won't happen again. I love you.

Lexi: It's Matthew. Can't you see that?

Ryan: I know. I'm so sorry. I will never do this again. I hate that this happened. I'll make it up to you. I'm so sorry. I'm so sorry.

Lexi thinks his potential is there. "He's a good person with good intentions. He has a great heart, he does nice things, he's kind to people. If this works out, it's going to be great. If it doesn't, at least I tried. No one knows him like I do."

A CRAZY SAD KITTY STORY

A month later, Ryan's been out drinking again and comes home very late. Lexi is upset. He starts yelling about how she should leave him be, saying he does everything around the house, so why is she complaining? She follows him into the bathroom yelling back at him, and then he gets right in her face, yelling at her. Then he picks up a can of hairspray and throws it at the wall, but it bounces off and hits their cat, Kitty, on the leg. Ryan immediately feels awful, begins apologizing ("I'm so sorry, I'm so sorry! I will never do this again! I hate what I just did!"), trying to soothe the cat and Lexi.

The next morning, Kitty's hobbling on three legs. Lexi picks her up and says she's going to take Kitty to the vet. Ryan apologizes again and says he'll drive. They leave Kitty at the vet, and Ryan drops off Lexi at work. She's so confused. "It's just so not him. I can't believe this is really Ryan." Later Ryan texts, "I love you . . . after work we'll go check on Kitty. Hopefully, they'll let us take her home." Lexi's self-talk is "Okay, our text messages are back to normal. He's back to being himself, the man I love."

A CRAZY PORN STORY

Two weeks later, Lexi wakes up on Saturday morning, and Ryan is still in the living room drinking with Matthew from the night before. She thinks, "I hate Matthew. Whenever Ryan hangs out with him weird stuff happens." She decides to ignore them and go out. The wedding is next weekend, and she has things to do to get ready. She gets dressed, goes into the living room, and hears porn on the computer. She questions Ryan angrily about it, and Ryan yells at her and throws a bowl of noodles that he's eating in her face. "What the fuck, Ryan!" she screams as she runs into the bedroom to get away from him and clean up. She searches for her car keys but can't find them. Sobbing, she calls Emily, home on break from school, who comes to pick her up. They drive for about two minutes when Lexi says, "Pull over please. I have to call him. I don't think I can just leave him there like that." Emily says, "Don't. Just leave it. Tell me the whole story first." Lexi says, "I have to call him. I'll just be a minute. Please." She calls Ryan:

Lexi: If you ask Matthew to leave, I'll come back now and we can talk about what happened.
Ryan: You're the one that left. Don't tell me what to do.
Lexi: I'm right around the corner.
Ryan: You can't tell me what to do.
Lexi: (*exasperated*) Ryan, I can't do this anymore. I can't live with someone I always feel disappointed in.
Ryan: Fine.
Lexi: Do you understand? I. WANT. YOU. TO. LEAVE. MY. APARTMENT.
Ryan: Okay.
Lexi: I want you to remember this day as the date that I told you it was over.
Ryan: You gotta do what you gotta do. I don't know why you're freaking out, but whatever.
Lexi: Are you serious? I don't know what it means when a person throws noodles in your face. I wake up, and you and Matthew are watching porn. I saw you mini-

mize it. What is that? It's weird. When you do coke, you get weird. I can't take it anymore.

Ryan: No porn, no drugs. Stop freaking out.

Lexi: How could you do this? Why are you ruining our relationship? Just ask Matthew to leave and I'll come back.

Her self-talk is "Ah, man, I should have listened to my gut! First the crazy car ride, then my bruised arm, then Kitty, now this. Maybe they're all red flags, not mistakes. Ugh, I just don't want this to be true."

Lexi doesn't listen to her gut. As she's telling Emily everything that happened, Lexi gets a text from Ryan: "I love you. I am in love with you. If you want to move on, tell me. I do not want to move on. I have never loved anyone like I do you. Miss you so much. And I want to be missed . . . I'm ready for whatever . . . Matthew's gone. Come home."

And Lexi does.

THE GOOD STUFF, OR WHY IT'S SO CONFUSING

Why does Lexi stay? She feels confused by Ryan's behavior. It all seems so out of character. All this craziness just can't be real. He can be such a good man.

When Lexi thinks about the kind of person she wants to be involved with, Ryan seems to totally fit the bill. She was looking for someone smart, kind, honest, and affectionate, as well as someone daring, adventurous, and strong, and she experiences Ryan as all of those things. He's the kind of guy who rides a motorcycle and who can go into a forest with nothing but a Swiss Army knife and build a tree house—a strong, manly man. He's also sweetly affectionate, always saying things like "I love you, I need you, I can't imagine my life without you," and surprising her with kisses and cuddles. And Lexi's *never* had a guy meet her desire need like Ryan does. He makes it all about her before it's all about him. He's totally unselfish, and she is able to be open with him about what she wants and likes. She even tells him how she feels when he's inside her. She's never told anyone those things before, and after they make love, she always thinks, "He's the man I've been looking for. I've found the love of my life."

Ryan takes good care of Lexi and is sensitive to her in other ways as well. He brings her water when she feels anxious, rubs her back when she's stressed, and makes her food when she's hungry. They're always willing to help each other with things, like picking up groceries or laundry and taking care of the apartment. He's also always ready to do anything she wants. And they have fun together: they go to sports events, movies, and yoga, and on adventures such as hiking or checking out places neither one of them has ever seen before.

They tell each other everything. She's told him every single little thing that has ever happened to her. He knows that she had problems growing up with her dad (who was so critical) and her brother (who always talked down to her). And Ryan makes Lexi feel as if she's the only person in his life that matters. He's told her everything about his childhood. He's been on his own since he was 15. He's in contact again with his mom and sister, but with Lexi, for the first time in his life he feels as if he has his own family, and he has a chance to build a good life with her. He's also talked about his past relationships, including his last girlfriend, who cheated on him and broke his heart. Lexi and Ryan also share the same values about extended family, inviting their families over for dinner and hanging out with them on holidays and whenever else they can.

Given all of this, it's not surprising that Lexi thinks, "Finally, I have a relationship with a guy who's my best friend, my other half. It's so awesome to have a buddy to do things with, who's on my side, who I'm interested in sharing life with!" It's also not surprising that when they're together, enjoying each other and some fun activity, and talking about their future, Lexi can block out all the crazy stuff that has happened.

IS LEXI IN A HEALTHY RELATIONSHIP?

After the crazy porn incident, Emily was intent on not letting Lexi block out all the crazy stuff. She encouraged Lexi to take a long, hard look at her relationship with Ryan. So Lexi did a needs assessment to see whether her relationship with Ryan met all three criteria for a healthy relationship. What she came up with for "I know and like myself" is shown on the facing page.

As you can see, Lexi believes she's meeting a lot of her needs. As for how she treats herself in this relationship, she believes she cares about her own feelings. She knows she is upset by Ryan's behavior, and she knows her feelings are valid. She accepts her decisions without being self-critical. She doesn't beat herself up for things. And she helps herself by taking care of things that need to be done in her life. She's not relying on Ryan for things she knows she can do herself. She knows she does not easily forgive herself for things, and she is concerned that she would never forgive herself if she left Ryan and his life spiraled out of control. However, she's uncertain about whether she's meeting these needs: Do I pay attention to what my gut/intuition is telling me and use it to help me make choices? Do I consider and value my needs in my choices? Do I trust myself to not engage in behaviors that would betray who I am or what I need? Do I recognize situations that are potentially dangerous for me (emotionally, physically, and practically) and make my safety a priority? She's becoming aware that she's not listening to her gut about Ryan's behavior, and even though

I KNOW AND LIKE MYSELF

Needs	I know and like myself. (I know my needs, I respect them, and I can meet my own needs.)	Yes	No	Not sure
What I need				
Familiar	Do I know my best and worst traits? Do I understand how they make me who I am, influence how I act, and affect the ways I get my needs met?	X		
Authentic	Do I know and understand all aspects of who I am because I face whatever fears I have about doing so?	X		
Attracted	Am I comfortable with the body I have?	X		
Desire	Do I feel comfortable being intimate, do I know what I'm ready for, and do I know what sex and intimacy mean to me?	X		
Interesting	Do I have a life of my own that I feel good about regardless of whether I'm in a relationship?	X		
Support	When I'm faced with challenging or upsetting situations, do I deal with them by actively problem solving rather than avoiding them?	X		
How I treat myself				
Care	Am I aware of how I feel, do I treat my feelings as logitimate, and do I use them to guide my behavior?	X		
Listen	Do I pay attention to what my gut/intuition is telling me and use it to help me make choices?			X
Important	Do I consider and value my needs in my choices?			X
Trust	Do I trust myself to not engage in behaviors that would betray who I am or what I need?			X
Accept	Do I accept who I am? Do I take responsibility for my behavior, without being self-critical, feeling ashamed, or treating myself in a harsh manner?	X		
Forgive	Do I forgive myself for mistakes I've acknowledged and allow myself to stop thinking about them and move on?		X	
Help	Do I take responsibility for what needs to happen in my life and make sure it gets done?	X		
Safe	Do I recognize situations that are potentially dangerous for me (emotionally, physically, and practically) and make my safety a priority?			X

she includes her needs in her choices in many ways, like making sure she engages in activities she enjoys such as yoga and hiking, she sees she's been making some choices that compromise her needs, like getting in the car with Ryan when he was drunk, and now she's not really sure she should trust the decisions she's making with Ryan. In line with this, she's not sure she's keeping herself safe because she stays with him despite the fact that he has put her in danger a number of other times.

If we look at the evidence in Lexi and Ryan's relationship, we can see that Lexi's assessment of whether she's meeting her "I know and like myself" needs is pretty accurate. She has some insight into the needs she's not meeting for herself and the ways in which she is not treating herself well. Let's take a look at the other conditions for a healthy relationship before we talk about how Lexi can use this insight. For "I know and like him," Lexi has come up with the chart shown on the facing page.

As the chart shows, Lexi also believes most of her "I know and like him" needs are getting met, although she's not sure about support. Ryan really is her go-to person, for everything, but not when he's drunk or high.

Lexi believes in most ways she treats Ryan as if she knows and likes him, but she wonders whether she really listens to him well enough. She thinks maybe she's missing something he's trying to tell her—like he's unhappy in some way or there's a need he's not getting met—and that's why he drinks and uses drugs and acts crazy. And she's also no longer sure she trusts him and accepts how he treats her. Those four crazy incidents have certainly eroded some of her trust and acceptance.

As with the prior needs condition, Lexi's answers seem to largely reflect the reality of her relationship. There are data to support why she's not sure her needs are being met. However, Lexi may have missed some things. She believes she is really familiar with Ryan, but does she really know all of his traits and understand how they make him who he is and how they influence how he acts and the way he gets his needs met? Based on his repeated drug and alcohol use and its negative consequences, something may be occurring that Lexi doesn't understand about Ryan's adventurous, spontaneous nature. Perhaps he's more impulsive than she realizes and has less control over his behavior than she hopes? If so, impulsivity does not bode well for reduction of substance use and aggression. In addition, Lexi may be mistaking her lack of familiarity with Ryan's impulsivity for a perceived lack of listening to him.

Lexi also is forgiving Ryan for mistakes he's acknowledged, and she sees this as a healthy thing. However, she has been forgiving him for his behavior toward her when he's drunk and high. She does so because he apologizes in ways that seem sincere. He admits his mistakes. Unfortunately, forgiving him without being clear with herself or him about what she is willing to accept perpetuates the pattern: he treats her poorly, she

Needs	I know and like him. (I am confident that he is the guy I want, and I treat him in a way that shows that I like and respect him.)	Yes	No	Not sure
What I need				
Familiar	Do I know his best and worst traits? Do I understand how they make him who he is, influence how he acts, and affect the way he gets his needs met?	X		
Authentic	Is he fully open to showing all aspects of himself and to facing whatever fears he has about doing so?	X		
Attracted	Do I like his physical appearance just as it is without wanting it to change?	X		
Desire	Do I want to be sexual with him, and do I feel comfortable telling him about my sexual interests and needs?	X		
Interesting	Am I interested in his life (whatever it happens to be), and do I want to be a part of it?	X		
Support	Is he my go-to person in good times and bad times?			X
How I treat him				
Care	Am I attuned to his feelings, and do I respond in a helpful rather than hurtful way?	X		
Listen	Do I try to hear what he is expressing and what he means in order to understand who he is?			X
Important	Do I consider and value his needs in my choices?	X		
Trust	Do I trust in his availability, consistency, and commitment, and do I trust him not to betray me in whatever way would be considered a betrayal in our relationship?			X
Accept	Can I let him be who he is and not try to change him or make him into something he's not, doesn't want to be, or can't be?			X
Forgive	Do I forgive him for mistakes he has acknowledged and move on?	X		
Help	Am I willing to respond to his requests for help with things he has to do?	X		
Safe	Do I make choices to help keep him emotionally, physically, and practically safe?	X		

gets upset, he apologizes and pleads for forgiveness, and she forgives him, and then repeat—with no behavior change on his part. Lexi must consider what she can and cannot accept, make that clear to Ryan, and then base her forgiveness of him on genuine remorse accompanied by behavior change on his part. Bottom line: Lexi needs to pay more attention to her need to accept him than to forgive him.

Lexi also believes she's getting her need to be interested in his life met with Ryan. In many ways, she definitely is. It was his immediate meeting of that very need that led her into Ryan's arms in the first place. However, at this point Lexi needs to consider that there may be parts of Ryan's life that are not so interesting to her anymore, specifically his desire to go out and party all night with alcohol and cocaine and his desire to engage in risky behaviors, like recklessly driving drunk. Lexi sees how these activities have started to erode her support, trust, and acceptance needs. She should also look carefully at whether they are also important for her need to find Ryan's life interesting. Lexi did another assessment. For "He knows and likes me," Lexi came up with the assessment on the facing page.

Lexi's responses show that she believes Ryan truly wants what she has to offer, and there is some validity in that. We reviewed the evidence in our earlier section "The Good Stuff, or Why It's So Confusing." She is authentic, and he's familiar with her. He's attracted to and desires her. He's interested in sharing her life, and she's his go-to person for support. However, even Lexi sees that Ryan is not completely treating her as if he likes her. She believes he trusts her. He's always willing to help her, and he's always been able to forgive her when she's acknowledged her mistakes, but she's not sure whether he cares about her feelings, really listens to her, treats her needs as important, keeps her safe, and always accepts how she treats him. In many ways, she believes he does, and there is evidence that he does, but then there is his drinking and partying and reckless behavior. She wonders, "How could he really care about my feelings if he keeps doing these things? He must not be listening to me about this. He's putting me in unsafe situations, he's not treating my need for him to stop doing these things as important, and he doesn't accept how I treat him when I get upset with him over these things."

Lexi is right to wonder about all of this stuff. So what does this needs assessment mean? What does it tell Lexi? Is she in a healthy relationship?

The answer is no, not at the moment. Don't get us wrong: there are lots of healthy aspects to Lexi and Ryan's relationship. Many necessary aspects of the three conditions are in place, and Lexi has been getting many of her key needs met. However, Ryan's substance use and reckless and aggressive behavior are getting in the way of Lexi's getting other key needs met. (For information on how common substance abuse is, see the sidebar on page 172.)

HE KNOWS AND LIKES ME

Needs	He knows and likes me. (He wants what I have to offer, and he treats me in a way that shows he likes and respects me.)	Yes	No	Not sure
What he needs				
Familiar	Does he know my best and worst traits? Does he understand how they make me who I am, influence how I act, and affect the way I get my needs met?	X		
Authentic	Am I fully open to showing all aspects of myself and to facing whatever fears I have about doing so?	X		
Attracted	Does he like my physical appearance just as it is without wanting it to change?	X		
Desire	Does he want to be sexual with me, and can he comfortably tell me about his sexual interests and needs?	X		
Interesting	Is he interested in my life (whatever it happens to be), and does he want to be part of it?	X		
Support	Am I his go-to person in good times and bad times?	X		
How he treats me				
Care	Is he attuned to my feelings, and does he respond in a helpful rather than hurtful way?			X
Listen	Does he hear what I am expressing and what I mean and use it to understand me?			X
Important	Does he consider and value my needs in his choices?			X
Trust	Does he trust in my availability, consistency, and commitment and trust that I will not treat him in whatever way would be considered a betrayal in the relationship?	X		
Accept	Can he let me be who I am and not try to change me or make me into something I'm not, don't want to be, or can't be?			X
Forgive	Does he forgive me for mistakes I've acknowledged and move on?	X		
Help	Is he willing to respond to my requests for help with things I have to do?	X		
Safe	Does he make choices that help keep me emotionally, physically, and practically safe?			X

I/ME

What's the Likelihood You'll Have to Deal with Substance Abuse?

Higher than you might like to think. According to a report by the Substance Abuse and Mental Health Services Administration, in 2013, among adults ages 18 to 25, the rate of alcohol abuse or dependence was 13%. The rate of drug abuse or dependence was 17%. This means that more than one in ten people that you meet likely has a problem.

And we can see why she is confused and unsure about things. The drunk Ryan is very different from the Ryan she fell in love with. And remember, she jumped in pretty quickly because she was focused on a need that was key at the time (interesting). Now, with time, she's seeing more and more of who Ryan really is—the full picture of Ryan—and that picture is providing her with new information she must take into account.

Lexi is likely to struggle to integrate this new information into her assessment of the relationship. She is in love with Ryan, and, thus far, he has been able to meet lots of her needs. Indeed, she may be tempted to discount all of her "Not sure" answers, but doing so would be a mistake for Lexi—or anyone. There is a reason Lexi is "Not sure." She had plenty of "Yes" answers. A "Not sure" answer should be a red flag. It needs to be looked at carefully and honestly. It also will be hard for Lexi to integrate the new information gained from the needs assessment because she believes that when you love someone you must sacrifice for him. She feels some responsibility for Ryan's well-being. She's afraid he'll get hurt, and she'd never forgive herself if it was because she left him. She believes she knows the person he could be, and she just wants him to be that person—after all, that's who he was when they started dating, right?

Maybe. But no matter what, Lexi also has to look at all of the data about who Ryan is, and all of the data on whether she is getting her needs met, to assess accurately whether she is in a healthy relationship and then make a decision about what to do about it.

Fortunately, the I/ME skills can help Lexi do this. First, just doing the needs assessment can help Lexi develop insight. If she's honest with herself, as we see she largely has been, she will be able to use the real evidence that exists in her relationship to become aware of whether her needs are being met. It can be scary to look at the evidence of unmet needs that exists in a relationship. Sometimes we just can't see it or don't want to see it. But we have to make ourselves look. We cannot let fear or denial stand in our way. The same is true for what we learn from a needs assessment: the reality that our relationship is not fully healthy may be hard to deal with. As Lexi looks at that reality, it may make her scared, sad, angry, or even defensive. Indeed, it is very upsetting to have to acknowledge that there are real problems in your relationship—problems that might mean the relationship will not work. This is where emotion regulation comes in.

It is important for Lexi to identify what she is feeling. She needs to take time to reflect on her feelings, maybe even write them down so she can be clear about them. When she does, she will see she feels both sad and angry that her relationship is not healthy right now, and she will feel scared about the possibility that it might not work.

Next, Lexi needs to examine her self-talk. She finds herself saying things like "No, this can't be! I don't want this to be true!" These kinds of nonacceptance thoughts might lead her into denial of reality. It's very tempting to engage with these thoughts because if we believe them we don't have to feel sad or angry or scared anymore. We can just deny there is a problem. That's not good emotion regulation because, ultimately, the problems do not get solved; in fact, things get worse, and we get sadder, angrier, and more scared.

Lexi also finds herself thinking, "How could he do this? Why is he ruining our relationship?" These kinds of blaming thoughts are likely to increase Lexi's anger and may lead to her lashing out or acting in an extreme way that she will later regret, such as when she told Ryan to move out of the apartment after he threw noodles in her face. Now, we're not saying that asking him to move out is a bad idea. Rather, Lexi needs to make that decision based on a realistic consideration of what is best for her and not from a place of intense anger, which makes objective thought difficult. As we saw, Lexi also has thoughts that will conflict with her anger, such as "I can't leave him like this. I want to take care of him. I want to help him fix this so we can be happy together. I won't be able to live with myself if something bad happens to him." So if Lexi were to make an impulsive, anger-based decision, she would go back on it, as she did before, when her other thoughts took over.

Therefore, Lexi needs to be aware of all of her thoughts and feelings that arise in response to looking honestly at her unmet needs. She must look at how her thoughts and feelings are connected and how they are likely to make her behave. Once she sees this clearly, she can develop new self-talk that will help her regulate her emotions better so she can develop a plan and make healthy decisions. Remember, one goal of emotion regulation is maintaining your self-respect and commitment to your needs in the face of emotional challenges. If Lexi can remember that her needs are important, that it takes two people to make a relationship work (mutuality), and that she can handle her emotions, she is likely to be able to use the information she acquired in her needs assessment to make a healthy decision about how to proceed.

Lauren

As you've seen, Lauren has been struggling with deciding who she wants to be with—Dan or Lucas—not realizing that neither one really meets her needs. She started off dating Dan. Then, when she got concerned about his jealousy and paternalistic behavior, she started seeing Lucas at the same time (which was okay because no commitments had been made). Then, when she got upset by Lucas's ongoing attachment to his ex-wife, she decided to become exclusive with Dan but continued to play the breakup/makeup game every time she got angry at him. The saga continues:

LAUREN AND DAN

Lauren and Dan are still together, and Lauren is still struggling with wanting to change careers and have a life of her own. In an unusual occurrence, they're at home one night as Dan has no social or work commitments. They're spending time talking and reading poetry together, which they both love, and the conversation turns to Lauren's feelings:

Dan: I can see you're not as depressed as you were, but you still don't seem happy. I know you're trying to figure out your life. I know you want to be a wife and a mother, but what else is missing?

Lauren: Every time I read an article on early child development or education I feel working with children is my passion. It's something I would be excited to wake up to. It's just so me. I love the idea of teaching them and helping them grow and develop. I feel like I could really make a difference in the world this way.

Dan: Okay, I'm here to help you. Any connections I have, I'll get you in touch with those people. Any financial support you need, I'll give to you. We just have to start thinking about it. And I'll get more involved in charities for kids; that way we can support them together.

Lauren: What I really want is to go back to school. I'm going to need to get a teaching degree if I really want to be in this field.

Dan: Okay, you're right. Let's do this.

Lauren is so excited. She's thrilled that Dan seems on board with her plans. So she goes ahead and researches what classes she needs to take and then registers for school. That night she tells Dan:

Lauren: I registered today, and classes start next week. I'm so excited.

Dan: That's great that you registered, but hold on a second—how is that going to work? I have a trip next week. You're supposed to go with me. You can't just not come with me.

Lauren: I know you want me to go with you, but then I'd miss class. And you told me that you would support me in going back to school.

Dan: I know, but we didn't discuss the timeline and the details of when classes would be. This won't work. We have to start looking at other options.

Lauren: But you promised. What do you mean other options?

Dan: I don't know. Okay, you're already registered, so let's just go with that. We'll figure it out as we go. Why don't you let the instructor know that you won't be in class until the following week? You won't miss much in the first week.

She does what Dan wants.

Fast-forward two months. Lauren continues to get mixed messages from Dan. He prioritizes her needs one minute—"Of course you can go to school"—and then the next minute he doesn't: "You have to come to Chicago." She's missed 50% of her classes. She's angry, and she starts thinking again, "Maybe there is someone out there who is good husband and father material and will support my going to school. But wait, do I have the time to find him? I'm almost 28. There's no time to find someone else."

But then again—

"I don't want to wake up one day with a baby thinking I missed my chance to have the career I want because Dan needs me to go every place with him."

But then again—

"Dan would be an excellent provider for me and our child."

Ugh. She's confused again.

Over the next few weeks, Lauren's unhappiness and anger grow. One night, when Dan asks her to miss yet another class, she breaks up with him, packs her stuff, and goes back to her apartment. She vows it's over. He texts, he pleads, he implores her to talk with him, to reconsider, but she ignores all of this. Literally doesn't respond. She's afraid she'll give in and go back.

She's trying to live her life, to be independent. She writes in her journal:

I'm heartsick over Dan, my stomach hurts, but I can't go back. I have pushed myself, figured out my own way to build my own life. Buying my apartment was one of the best things I did for me. I've forced myself to go back and renegotiate my interest rate on my mortgage, and I've rented out my extra bedroom, and these things are how I will pay for school, fight for myself, not depend on anyone but me—I don't need Dan to do this. But what about motherhood? Time is running out.

It couldn't hurt to text Lucas. Just to see how he is, right?

LAUREN AND LUCAS

They decide to have lunch at a café next to his favorite art gallery. He excitedly talks about a beautiful painting he's just seen in the gallery's gift shop. After lunch, Lauren finds herself at the gallery buying him that beautiful painting, leaning it up against his doorway, ringing the doorbell and giggling as she's running to the elevator, hoping she makes it before he opens his door. She's so happy to be able to give something to someone again.

She starts seeing Lucas again. Julianne and Anna say in unison, "Are you kidding me? Come on, he treated you so badly the first time, so why would you try it a second time?" She can't explain it. She just feels a powerful connection with him.

After school, Lauren meets up with Lucas at his work. They hold hands, walk back to his apartment. She makes dinner, they make love, and, as before, she goes home. She knows he likes to go to bed early and alone on work nights. She feels she understands Lucas better this time around. He needs "alone time." As it happens, that is exactly what she eventually wanted with Dan, and she can better see Lucas's perspective because of that. She also finds, much to her surprise, she likes not being with someone so much—she has enough time to study, catch up with friends, make fresh almond milk and kale chips for snacks, do whatever she wants to do.

Lauren believes a good relationship is about putting the other person's needs first. She always does that. She's happy that Lucas seems to be doing more of it too, and she's trying to teach Lucas about how they can do this for each other:

Lauren: You know how I say, "Let's go to so-and-so for dinner," and then I ask you, "What do you think about that?"
Lucas: Yeah.
Lauren: I always check how you feel about it. It's like I have your needs in my head.
Lucas: I'm not following.
Lauren: If you say, "I'm craving seafood," I make seafood for you. If I say, "I like you to walk me home," you walk me home. Get it?

Apparently he does. This time around Lauren feels as if Lucas cares more about her. For example, last Sunday she was at Chris's house (one of her new friends from school), and Lucas texted: "Where are you?"

Lauren: At Chris's apartment.
Lucas: Want me to swing by, walk you home?

She loved that. Lucas has always known she doesn't like to walk home alone at night, but he never did that kind of stuff before. He was hands off, no questions asked, I do only what I want to do. That seems to be changing.

And there's more. One night they're talking over dinner (his favorite meal that she's made for him):

Lucas: What's your biggest fear?

Lauren: Not sure. Yours?

Lucas: This job pays me well, but I want to take a leap, change things, do something that would be more right for me, but I'm afraid to let go of stability.

Lauren: You should do it.

Lucas: Why?

Lauren: You want to change how your life is going and do what you love. I think that will make you happier and less angry. When you're happy, you're a different person.

Lucas: You would really support me in that?

Lauren: Absolutely.

Later that night when she's home in bed (it's a weeknight, after all, and she wanted to give Lucas his space), Lauren texts him: "I had an amazing evening with you tonight. The most important message is you will be the best at whatever you choose to accomplish in life. I love you to pieces."

And despite the fact that Lucas still talks about his ex-wife, at least he tries to reassure her now, letting her know how much he appreciates her support:

Lauren: I will forever be second best. Whatever connects you with her is so important to you that I cannot compare.

Lucas: You've got to understand: she was never supportive and loving the way you are. And I am so grateful you're stubborn. If you hadn't put that much effort in, we wouldn't be together. You're good for me.

"Wow," she thinks, *"he's never said that before."*

There are still issues, of course. For instance, she invited Lucas out to celebrate the end of another semester. When she got to his apartment, it was apparent right away he wasn't happy and didn't feel like going. He went into the bathroom to finish getting ready. She heard him slam a bathroom drawer shut. She rolled her eyes, thinking, "He gets so negative about doing anything on a work night. I shouldn't have suggested that we go out for dinner tonight." And although she was upset, she kept it to herself and said, "You know what? We don't have to go tonight. I'm going to leave. I'll see you tomorrow." Kissing him, she shut the door. She texted Julianne, who fortunately was up the street having drinks with friends. Lauren joined them and told Julianne about what just happened:

Julianne: You asked. He could have said no.

Lauren: Everything is so good with us. I shouldn't have asked. I know he doesn't like going out on weeknights.

Julianne: You have to ask for what you want from a guy.

Lauren: I'm happy. I'm satisfied just being with him. Why would I start getting demanding?

Julianne: Asking a guy to go out and celebrate with you is not demanding. Your love story with this guy never sounds epic. Why are you with him?

Lauren: I feel like he's a little troubled. I'm a little troubled. We're good for each other. I want to take care of him, be a better partner to him than his ex-wife was.

Julianne: She probably left because he was so moody.

Lauren: You think he's moody?

Julianne: Hell, yes!

As Lauren thought about this, the tiniest bit of doubt crept into her mind, but she decided that she knew what she was doing.

Lauren's at lunch with Anna the next day:

Anna: Is Lucas still talking about his ex-wife?

Lauren: Yes, but he tells me how much better I am for him than she was.

Anna: And you believe him? I think you just love a challenge. You've never struggled to get attention from a guy, except for Lucas. You're like, "Okay, you don't love me. You love her? We'll see about that."

Lauren: Maybe.

Anna: I don't understand you. You love a guy who is still in love with his ex-wife. You left a guy who wants to marry you, have a baby with you. He's so wealthy that even if it didn't work out he's still going to financially take care of you.

Lauren: I know, but with Lucas I can be myself. I can go to school. It's something very new to me. I can't explain it, but I feel like I need to make my relationship with Lucas work. I can't think about Dan anymore.

But she does keep thinking about him. She wants to call him and share with him that she's still going to school. She starts wondering, "If I still feel this connection with Dan, if I miss him this much, maybe I'm supposed to be with him?" She gets back home, opens her journal, and reads snippets of when she felt as if her life with Dan was draining all the energy out of her. It helps her remember why she left. Yet she can't help asking herself, "If things don't work out with Lucas, would I go back? I had a good life with Dan. It's tempting to go back. When I'm with Dan, all my uncertainty about getting the outcomes I want goes away. I can have a baby tomorrow and be a stay-at-home mom." All of this makes Lauren feel anxious. "I'm with Lucas, and things are working out, but we're not at a point where we'd even start talking about having a baby, and I'm almost 28." She wonders, "Why hasn't Dan texted me? Maybe he doesn't love me anymore."

She texts Dan's personal assistant, Angie, who knows the whole story of Lauren and Dan:

Lauren: I know Dan's back, but I haven't heard from him. Has he fallen out of love with me?

Angie: Isn't that what you wanted?

Lauren: Yes.

Angie: He's leaving for Chicago tomorrow.

Thoughts are running furiously through her head. "Chicago, great! We spent so many wonderful times in that suite together. He won't be able to stop thinking about me. Wait. I cannot go back to Dan. I wasn't happy. Lucas is getting better. He's showing me he cares. But what about having a baby? No, I can't focus on that. I've got to let go of Dan. Refocus on Lucas. He loves me now, not his ex-wife. I'm sure of it. At least I think I am."

WHY IS LAUREN SO CONFUSED?

Why does she keep going back and forth? There are a couple of reasons. First, as with Lexi, it's the good stuff. Both Dan and Lucas provide things that Lauren really wants and needs. The problem, however, is, as we've pointed out, neither one of them provides all (or even most) of what she wants and needs. It's also that Lauren is outcome focused rather than needs focused. She has a clear idea about what her ultimate goal for a relationship is—becoming a wife and mother—but she has no idea that it's really her needs that must figure most into her decision as to who she wants to be with and why. So she keeps going back and forth based on who she thinks will get her to her desired outcome, rather than based on who will be the best relationship partner for her—who will meet her needs best. Given these issues, can either of Lauren's relationships be healthy? Let's see.

IS EITHER OF LAUREN'S RELATIONSHIPS HEALTHY?

Following are Lauren's needs assessments for both Dan and Lucas, starting with the chart on the next page. In addition to Lauren's answers, shown with an X, we have included our answers, where they differ from Lauren's, indicated by an asterisk *. Our answers are meant to reflect a more objective assessment of whether Lauren's needs are being met and, therefore, illustrate places where Lauren had a lapse in insight.

I KNOW AND LIKE MYSELF

Needs	I know and like myself. (I know my needs, I respect them, and I can meet my own needs.)	Yes	No	Not sure	Yes	No	Not sure
			Dan			Lucas	
What I need							
Familiar	Do I know my best and worst traits? Do I understand how they make me who I am, influence how I act, and affect the ways I get my needs met?	X	*		X	*	
Authentic	Do I know and understand all aspects of who I am because I face whatever fears I have about doing so?	X			X		
Attracted	Am I comfortable with the body I have?	X					
Desire	Do I feel comfortable being intimate, do I know what I'm ready for, and do I know what sex and intimacy mean to me?	X			X		
Interesting	Do I have a life of my own that I feel good about regardless of whether I'm in a relationship?		X				X
Support	When I'm faced with challenging or upsetting situations, do I deal with them by actively problem solving rather than avoiding them?		X		X		
How I treat myself							
Care	Am I aware of how I feel, do I treat my feelings as legitimate, and do I use them to guide my behavior?		X		X	*	
Listen	Do I pay attention to what my gut/intuition is telling me and use it to help me make choices?	X	*		X	*	
Important	Do I consider and value my needs in my choices?		X		X		
Trust	Do I trust myself to not engage in behaviors that would betray who I am or what I need?	X	*		X	*	
Accept	Do I accept who I am? Do I take responsibility for my behavior, without being self-critical, feeling ashamed, or treating myself in a harsh manner?	X			X		
Forgive	Do I forgive myself for mistakes I've acknowledged and allow myself to stop thinking about them and move on?	X			X		
Help	Do I take responsibility for what needs to happen in my life and make sure it gets done?		X		X		
Safe	Do I recognize situations that are potentially dangerous for me (emotionally, physically, and practically) and make my safety a priority?	X	*		X	*	

Lauren's answers suggest that her "I know and like myself" needs are being met better in her relationship with Lucas than with Dan. This is particularly evident in a number of key differences. With Lucas, unlike with Dan, Lauren is able to live an exciting, independent life. This rediscovered independence is reflected in the fact that she is solving her own problems and taking care of things she needs to do on her own. She also prioritizes her needs in her choices. This is clearly a much healthier way for Lauren to live. It was these very needs being unmet that contributed to Lauren's depression when she was with Dan.

Lauren's "I know and like myself" needs are not perfectly met with Lucas, however. Although she is living a life she finds interesting with regard to going to school, catching up with friends, and going to yoga, she would find her life more interesting if she had a baby. Her goal to have a baby sooner rather than later is an ongoing concern. It will definitely be later with Lucas, and that worries Lauren. It also contributes to her confusion about whether to go back to Dan.

There also are some important "misses" in Lauren's answers—responses that reflect low insight into herself. For example, Lauren believes she knows her traits and understands how they make her who she is and how they influence how she acts and the way she gets her needs met. Although she may know her traits, she is less insightful about how they influence her. For instance, she doesn't recognize how her competitive nature results in her trying to win people's love; for example, she's trying to make Lucas love her more than he loves his ex-wife, and she will do anything to make him love her. She also thinks she's able to keep herself safe with Lucas, but a relationship where she constantly feels second best in comparison to his ex-wife is definitely not a safe place for her to be emotionally. Similarly, Lauren believes she cares about her feelings in her relationship with Lucas, yet she continues to silence herself about things that bother her, like his unavailability on work nights.

Lauren also believes she's able to keep herself safe in her relationship with Dan. However, because of her desire to put Dan's needs first, she continually allowed herself to be in situations that were emotionally dangerous for her, such as agreeing to do everything he wanted her to do despite the fact that it was making her depressed and compromising her career goals. This is another example of how she doesn't see how who she is affects how she gets her needs met, or doesn't get them met, as the case may be.

Lauren also believes she can trust herself not to engage in behaviors that betray her needs. There is plenty of evidence, however, that Lauren does so all the time, with both Dan and Lucas. For example, if Lauren believes her relationship is threatened, she'll do whatever she thinks she must do to keep it together, even if her actions go against her own needs, such as traveling with Dan and missing many of her classes. Again, by putting the emphasis so strongly on her partner's needs, Lauren constantly betrays her own. In addition, although Lauren thinks she listens to her gut, she is actually driven by emotions and often acts impulsively or without thought. This is very different from the ability to pay deep and careful attention to thoughts and feelings and act intuitively. Unless Lauren develops more insight into herself, she will continue to miss meeting her "I know and like myself" needs. Now she looks at whether she knows and likes Dan or Lucas (see the facing page).

Lauren's answers reflect that, on balance, she "knows and likes" Lucas a little bit more than Dan, although it's close, and there are some things she gets from Dan that she doesn't get from Lucas. For instance, Lauren feels as if Dan lets her see him more deeply than Lucas does. She also sees Dan as her go-to support person and isn't sure Lucas is there for her in that way (and he's not—she'll always go to her girlfriends first when she has a problem). However, she is more interested in and excited about Lucas's life than she is about Dan's. She loves meeting up with Lucas after school, walking home, making him dinner, and so on. She also cares more about Lucas's feelings and has been better at making choices to keep him safe than she has been with Dan.

As before, Lauren has some "misses." By saying she accepts how both Dan and Lucas treat her, she is acting from a place of low personal power. Given that both treat her poorly sometimes, albeit in different ways, in order to be loved she is accepting things that are not good for her. This is not healthy.

The other misses come from her poor understanding of Lucas. Lauren believes she knows and understands Lucas, but she is missing things. For instance, she doesn't fully appreciate how rigidly structured he is. She thinks his being structured is good for her because it helps her be more disciplined, but it also means she and Lucas will never be able to do anything spontaneous. She also believes he is not being authentic with her, and she has some evidence for this. In the past he sent her mixed messages by staying with her while at the same time continuing to express his wish to be with his ex-wife. But in other ways, more recently, he has shown himself pretty plainly, as in his honesty about his feelings for Lauren, his communication of his needs, and his disclosure of his fears. Lauren may experience this as inauthentic because (1) she doesn't always like what she hears and (2) there may not be much more there. That is, perhaps he is not a particularly deep or self-aware person. So he may be being as authentic as he can, at least in some ways. Therefore, Lauren's assumption that Lucas is not being authentic may reflect another way in which she does not know him as well as she thinks she does. Related to this point, Lauren believes she really listens to Lucas and hears what he has to say. She may hear some things, but she has missed important communications that are evident in

I KNOW AND LIKE HIM

Needs	I know and like my him. (I am confident that he is the guy I want, and I treat him in a way that shows that I like and respect him.)	Yes	No	Not sure	Yes	No	Not sure
		Dan			Lucas		
What I need							
Familiar	Do I know his best and worst traits? Do I understand how they make him who he is, influence how he acts and affect the way he gets his needs met?	X			X	*	
Authentic	Is he fully open to showing all aspects of himself and to facing whatever fears he has about doing so?	X				X	*
Attracted	Do I like his physical appearance just as it is without wanting it to change?	X			X		
Desire	Do I want to be sexual with him, and do I feel comfortable telling him about my sexual interests and needs?	X			X		
Interesting	Am I interested in his life (whatever it happens to be), and do I want to be a part of it?			X	X		
Support	Is he my go-to person in good times and bad times?	X				*	X
How I treat him							
Care	Am I attuned to his feelings, and do I respond in a helpful rather than hurtful way?			X	X		
Listen	Do I try to hear what he is expressing and what he means in order to understand who he is?	X			X	*	
Important	Do I consider and value his needs in my choices?	X			X		
Trust	Do I trust in his availability, consistency, and commitment, and do I trust him not to treat me in whatever way would be considered a betrayal in our relationship?			X			X
Accept	Can I let him be who he is and not try to change him or make him into something he's not, doesn't want to be, or can't be?	X		*	X		*
Forgive	Do I forgive him for mistakes he has acknowledged and move on?	X			X		
Help	Am I willing to respond to his requests for help with things he has to do?	X			X		
Safe	Do I make choices to help keep him emotionally, physically, and practically safe?		X		X		

what he says, particularly about his ex-wife. Everything he says about his ex-wife indicates he has not found closure with that relationship, but Lauren does not see that.

Unless Lauren develops more insight into her partner and increases her personal power, she will continue to miss getting important "I know and like him" needs met. Let's see how she assesses the condition "He knows and likes me" (on the facing page).

Lauren's answers pretty clearly reflect that she's much more certain Dan wants what she has to offer more than Lucas does. She's not sure whether Lucas really knows her and wants to be fully intimate with her. She's also not sure whether he's excited about her and her life, and she doesn't think she's his go-to support person. She's confident that Dan meets all of these needs, although we think she's missing the fact that Dan may not really be interested in part of her life—the career part. He's definitely interested in the wife and mother part, but, despite his words, his behavior doesn't provide evidence that he's really interested in her developing a work life.

Lauren's answers also clearly reflect the reality that neither Dan nor Lucas is treating Lauren as if he likes and respects her. The only need Lauren is certain she is getting met with Lucas is that he trusts her. She knows that, unlike Lucas, Dan wants to help her with things (he makes appointments for her, provides transportation, introduces her to people, and so on) and he is very forgiving of her, but she's not sure about much else. She does think Dan trusts and accepts her, but we think these are lapses of insight on her part, and perhaps wishful thinking. Dan has shown himself to be a jealous guy, insisting she can't dance with other people or accept business cards from potential professional contacts. Such behavior does not convey trust. And although Dan says he accepts Lauren for all she is, if he truly did, would he always tell her what to do and ignore her needs? No, he would not. Lauren also is not fully seeing how much Dan does not consider her needs in his choices. She answered Not Sure for this need. If she were to really look at the evidence, she would see that with every choice Dan makes, all of his behaviors clearly show that no matter what he says, he sees his needs as more important than hers.

Let's take stock of this needs assessment. Overall, Lauren is treating herself better in her relationship with Lucas than she did in her relationship with Dan. Score one point for Lucas—and good for Lauren! She also seems to "know and like" Lucas better than Dan. Two points for Lucas. On the other hand, Dan more clearly wants what Lauren has to offer. However, neither Dan nor Lucas is consistently treating Lauren as if he likes and respects her. That's a really bad sign.

So is either of Lauren's relationships healthy? The answer is no. Nei-

HE KNOWS AND LIKES ME

Needs	He knows and likes me (He wants what I have to offer, and he treats me in a way that shows he likes and respects me.)	Yes	No	Not sure	Yes	No	Not sure
		Dan			Lucas		
What he needs							
Familiar	Does he know my best and worst traits? Does he understand how they make me who I am, influence how I act, and affect the way I get my needs met?	X					X
Authentic	Am I fully open to showing all aspects of myself and to facing whatever fears I have about doing so?	X			X		
Attracted	Does he like my physical appearance just as it is without wanting it to change?	X			X		
Desire	Does he want to be sexual with me, and can he comfortably tell me about his sexual interests and needs?	X					X
Interesting	Is he interested in my life (whatever it happens to be), and does he want to be part of it?	X		*			X
Support	Am I his go-to person in good times and bad times?	X					X
How he treats me							
Care	Is he attuned to my feelings, and does he respond in a helpful rather than hurtful way?			X			X
Listen	Does he hear what I am expressing and what I mean and use it to understand me?			X			X
Important	Does he consider and value my needs in his choices?		*	X			X
Trust	Does he trust in my availability, consistency, and commitment and trust that I will not treat him in whatever way would be considered a betrayal in the relationship?	X		*	X		
Accept	Can he let me be who I am and not try to change me or make me into something I'm not, don't want to be, or can't be?	X		*			X
Forgive	Does he forgive me for mistakes I've acknowledged and move on?	X					X
Help	Is he willing to respond to my requests for help with things I have to do?	X				X	
Safe	Does he make choices that help keep me emotionally, physically, and practically safe?			X			X

ther one meets all three criteria for a healthy relationship. The evidence is simply not there.

This may come as no surprise to you; we've been hinting at it all along. In addition, when you're an objective observer, it can be easier to see the writing on the wall than when you're an emotionally involved participant. One of the aims of doing a needs assessment and developing your I/ME skills, particularly your insight and ability to regulate your emotions, is to help you learn how to be more objective in your own relationship so you can look clearly at the evidence and realistically evaluate the relationship. Now that you see how to do that for Lauren and Lexi, you can try it out for yourself.

Let's look at how the I/ME skills can help Lauren understand her confusion, see the reality of her relationships with Dan and Lucas, and think about how to make healthy decisions. Lauren's needs assessment reflects what we've been saying all along. Lauren is getting different key needs met in each relationship, but neither relationship meets all of her key needs. It's no wonder she's confused and can't decide whom to be with. It's as if she's having one whole relationship split between two people. So she has to keep going back and forth to meet all of her different needs. Dan fulfills some, but then she struggles with not getting the others met. So off she goes to Lucas, who meets the unfulfilled ones, but then she misses the others again, and back and forth it goes. What Lauren really needs is one partner who can meet all of her key needs, as well as fulfill the outcome she wants. She needs a guy who wants to be married and have a family *and* who supports her career, who listens and cares and considers her needs, where they have a good balance of independence and intimacy and they keep each other safe, and so on. So what does Lauren need to do to get this?

First, she needs to develop her insight skill. She needs to start with recognizing the three criteria that are necessary for a healthy relationship. Right now, she's still completely focused on her outcome goals and on "Can I be who he wants?" Hopefully, doing the needs assessment will help reinforce for Lauren the necessity that all three criteria be met. Until Lauren sees that neither Dan nor Lucas meets all three criteria for a healthy relationship (especially in the "He knows and likes me" domain), she will continue to be confused and go back and forth, thinking, wishfully, that one of them is the right one. Lauren needs to see the big picture more clearly.

Lauren also needs to develop better insight into herself. She is not fully aware of how her beliefs and values affect her behavior and her ability to get her needs met. For example, she doesn't recognize how she is hurt by her idea that she should always put her partner's needs first or how her belief that love conquers all blinds her to seeing the reality of problems in a relationship. You may have noticed that Lauren had a lot of "Not sure" answers in her needs assessment. Although answering "Not sure" can reflect legitimate uncertainty due to the fact that one's partner meets the need in some ways but not in others (for example, he's interested in sharing one part of my life but not another part), it can also reflect an inability to accurately identify the evidence, that is, to see things clearly for what they are. Such clouded vision may be driven by fear of seeing the reality and its consequences, by a wish that things could be different (an inability to accept the present reality), or even by a deficit in awareness of what to use for evidence. One thing is certain, though: a "Not sure" answer is not a "Yes" answer. A whole lot of "Not sure"s doesn't convey a great deal of confidence that the needs are truly being met. So although Lauren might want to rest in her "Not sure" answers, holding on to hope that maybe the need is or could be getting met, a lot of "Not sure" answers suggests the opposite and calls for strengthening one's insight skills.

Lauren also is going to have to develop and use her emotion regulation skills to face the reality of her needs assessment, just as Lexi (or anyone) needs to do. Despite being with Lucas and, reportedly, being happy, Lauren can barely tolerate the idea that Dan might be over her. Her anxiety about losing his love—about not being the one he wants anymore (another indicator of low personal power)—overwhelms her and sends her into a panic over whether she can win his love again. Anna suggested to Lauren that Lauren likes the challenge of getting someone to love her. Sadly, she does. Lauren's need to be loved, to be what Dan or Lucas wants, completely blocks her ability to assess realistically whether either one of them is the one she wants. Her anxiety about being loved throws her off course and will need to be handled with solid emotion regulation skills, including new self-talk and self-soothing. The same is true for the anxiety Lauren will feel at the thought of being alone and of not meeting her self-imposed pregnancy deadline.

Lauren will also need to call on mutuality skills to help her see that neither Dan nor Lucas represents a healthy relationship. Again, Lauren's belief that she should always put her partner's needs first presents a problem. As we discussed earlier, this belief allows her to accept behavior that hurts her, and it gets in the way of getting her own needs met. Fortunately

I/ME

What Should You Do If You Have a Lot of "Not sure"s in Your Relationship?

Resting in "Not sure" equals giving up your standards. Review your key needs, identify how you want to get them met, reset your expectations and limits, and then make new choices accordingly.

for Lauren, she is starting to get the idea with Lucas, trying to teach him that both partners should be thinking about what the other one wants and needs. If she is able to succeed in this, and they develop a more mutual relationship, there is potential for that relationship to be healthy.

Are You in a Healthy Relationship?

Do your own needs assessment to find out, using the forms starting on the facing page.

Do I Know and Like Myself?

Needs	I know and like myself. (I know my needs, I respect them, and I can meet my own needs.)	Yes	No	Not sure
What I need				
Familiar	Do I know my best and worst traits? Do I understand how they make me who I am, influence how I act, and affect the ways I get my needs met?			
Authentic	Do I know and understand all aspects of who I am because I face whatever fears I have about doing so?			
Attracted	Am I comfortable with the body I have?			
Desire	Do I feel comfortable being intimate, do I know what I'm ready for, and do I know what sex and intimacy mean to me?			
Interesting	Do I have a life of my own that I feel good about regardless of whether I'm in a relationship?			
Support	When I'm faced with challenging or upsetting situations, do I deal with them by actively problem solving rather than avoiding them?			
How I treat myself				
Care	Am I aware of how I feel, do I treat my feelings as legitimate, and do I use them to guide my behavior?			
Listen	Do I pay attention to what my gut/intuition is telling me and use it to help me make choices?			
Important	Do I consider and value my needs in my choices?			
Trust	Do I trust myself to not engage in behaviors that would betray who I am or what I need?			
Accept	Do I accept who I am? Do I take responsibility for my behavior, without being self-critical, feeling ashamed, or treating myself in a harsh manner?			
Forgive	Do I forgive myself for mistakes I've acknowledged and allow myself to stop thinking about them and move on?			
Help	Do I take responsibility for what needs to happen in my life and make sure it gets done?			
Safe	Do I recognize situations that are potentially dangerous for me (emotionally, physically, and practically) and make my safety a priority?			

Is there evidence that you know and like yourself? Write your conclusions here:

Do I Know and Like Him?

Needs	I know and like him. (I am confident that this is the person I want, and I treat him in a way that shows that I like and respect him.)	Yes	No	Not sure
	What I need			
Familiar	Do I know his best and worst traits? Do I understand how they make him who he is, influence how he acts, and affect the way he gets his needs met?			
Authentic	Is he fully open to showing all aspects of himself and to facing whatever fears he has about doing so?			
Attracted	Do I like his physical appearance just as it is without wanting it to change?			
Desire	Do I want to be sexual with him, and do I feel comfortable telling him about my sexual interests and needs?			
Interesting	Am I interested in his life (whatever it happens to be), and do I want to be a part of it?			
Support	Is he my go-to person in good times and bad times?			
	How I treat him			
Care	Am I attuned to his feelings, and do I respond in a helpful rather than hurtful way?			
Listen	Do I try to hear what he is expressing and what he means in order to understand who he is?			
Important	Do I consider and value his needs in my choices?			
Trust	Do I trust in his availability, consistency, and commitment, and do I trust him not to treat me in whatever way would be considered a betrayal in our relationship?			
Accept	Can I let him be who he is and not try to change him or make him into something he's not, doesn't want to be, or can't be?			
Forgive	Do I forgive him for mistakes he has acknowledged and move on?			
Help	Am I willing to respond to his requests for help with things he has to do?			
Safe	Do I make choices to help keep him emotionally, physically, and practically safe?			
Is there evidence that you know and like him? Write your conclusions here:				

Does He Know and Like Me?

Needs	He knows and likes me. (He wants what I have to offer, and he treats me in a way that shows he likes and respects me.)	Yes	No	Not sure
What he needs				
Familiar	Does he know my best and worst traits? Does he understand how they make me who I am, influence how I act, and affect the way I get my needs met?			
Authentic	Am I fully open to showing all aspects of myself and to facing whatever fears I have about doing so?			
Attracted	Does he like my physical appearance just as it is without wanting it to change?			
Desire	Does he want to be sexual with me, and can he comfortably tell me about his sexual interests and needs?			
Interesting	Is he interested in my life (whatever it happens to be), and does he want to be part of it?			
Support	Am I his go-to person in good times and bad times?			
How he treats me				
Care	Is he attuned to my feelings, and does he respond in a helpful rather than hurtful way?			
Listen	Does he hear what I am expressing and what I mean and use it to understand me?			
Important	Does he consider and value my needs in his choices?			
Trust	Does he trust in my availability, consistency, and commitment and trust that I will not treat him in whatever way would be considered a betrayal in the relationship?			
Accept	Can he let me be who I am and not try to change me or make me into something I'm not, don't want to be, or can't be?			
Forgive	Does he forgive me for mistakes I've acknowledged and move on?			
Help	Is he willing to respond to my requests for help with things I have to do?			
Safe	Does he make choices that help keep me emotionally, physically, and practically safe?			

Is there evidence that he knows and likes you? Write your conclusions here:

Are you in a healthy relationship? (circle your answer)   Yes   No

Why or why not? Write your conclusions here:

8

Wow, It's Even Worse Than I Thought!

Honing your I/ME skills, as described in Chapter 6, can help you resolve conflicts between your own needs or between your needs and your guy's needs to see whether this can turn out to be the relationship for you. Sometimes you can't put your finger on specific conflicts and need to step back and see the bigger picture by doing a full needs assessment, as illustrated in Chapter 7. But there's another essential ingredient in all healthy relationships, and that's security.

Secure relationships are ones in which people feel safe and trust their partner, knowing their partner is available in times of need, values and loves them, can help them manage whatever is troubling them, and can also give them the space to be independent. Security yields a healthy balance of closeness and autonomy. Secure relationships also are mutual: both people feel respected and cared for, and intimacy grows as they negotiate to get their needs met. If you don't feel safe, if you can't trust your partner to have your best interests at heart, if you're constantly feeling like the relationship is threatened or you could lose him at any time, you're not in a secure relationship.

Many situations can result in insecurity in a relationship, and insecurity can take a variety of forms. But there are two situations where, for sure, you will never be able to feel secure because they compromise safety and trust and increase a sense of relationship threat. One is when there is repeated lying and betrayals and jealousy. The other is when there is relationship aggression. Because these behaviors make it impossible to feel secure, you need to know how to set limits when you encounter them.

From what you just read, you might think it's easy to identify these unhealthy relationship behaviors and to decide whether they signal exit time. Sometimes it is; sometimes it's not. To help you figure out how to do so, we take you through the stories of Olivia, Mia, Anna, and Lexi, all of whom are dealing with these security-eroding behaviors.

Betrayal and Jealousy

As you are about to see, Olivia and Mia are both facing betrayal and jealousy. Are these behaviors deal-breakers for them? Let's see.

OLIVIA AND ZACH

When we last saw Olivia and Zach, things seemed to be going all right for them, although some potential problems were brewing. Let's look at their Needs Recap.

Does Olivia know and like Zach? She's attracted to him, desires him, and feels safe with him because she's communicated her sexual limits and, so far, he has respected them. She trusts he's committed to some kind of relationship progression, although this trust may be based on hope rather than actual evidence. They haven't had any kind of define-the-relationship talk; instead, Olivia is just using her feelings of love and lust as evidence the relationship must be going somewhere.

Does Zach know and like Olivia? Although she's not sure whether Zach's familiar with her—whether he really knows her—she thinks he's interested in sharing her life. He's said she makes him want to try new things, and often they stay on the phone with each other talking all night, even though they have to get up early the next day, just because it feels so good. She also knows he is attracted to and desires her, but she's not sure he's being fully honest about what sex and intimacy mean to him and about what he needs. He doesn't turn to her for support, but he does care about her feelings, particularly with regard to her concerns about his relationship with his ex-FWB Ashley. As a result, he's made clear to Ashley that he's with Olivia.

Recently, as you saw in Chapter 5, Zach has started pushing Olivia's sexual boundaries a bit, although he backs off when she calls him on it. Still, the mixed messages are starting to upset her. She's confused and doesn't know how to interpret his behavior. She knows his sexual history and his number of past sex partners (40!) because she helped him figure it out. Olivia also is confused about Zach's relationship with other girls, especially Ashley. Olivia believes guys and girls can just be friends, but maybe Zach can't just be friends with a girl given that his number is 40 and he's had FWB relationships.

Olivia decides to talk with Emily and Lexi about her confusion. She asks them, "What if it gets too much for him to wait and he turns to Ashley?" They both say some version of "If he really wants to be with you, he'll wait. If he can't wait, then he's not the guy for you. But if you want to have sex with him, just make sure you know you're both on the same page. You know yourself. You don't want to have sex with someone you're not in a real relationship with."

Olivia believes she and Zach are in a real relationship. They've been together almost six months now, and they get along so well. And last weekend when he was upset he couldn't make it back home to his cousin's wedding, he mentioned he wanted a family someday. He didn't say it would necessarily be with her, but at least she knows his ultimate relationship goals are similar to hers. And he is just so damn sexy. "Maybe," she thinks, "our six-month anniversary could be the night." And she begins to hatch a plan.

In the meantime, Olivia is still concerned about Zach and Ashley. Olivia's actually become friends with Ashley, and Olivia likes her more than she thought she would. She sees what Zach sees in her, although that makes her feel kind of insecure. She secretly fears she's not as pretty or funny as Ashley, and she knows she's not as thin (she hates her hips). She also still doesn't know what to think about Zach and Ashley's relationship. For example, one day Ashley starts casually and confidently talking about a sexual experience a friend of hers had. Zach is clearly interested in the story, and he and Ashley are joking and laughing about it. Olivia doesn't know what to say. She's uncomfortable, and she can't tell if Zach is behaving in a more-than-friends-like way with Ashley. "But you know what," she thinks, "once our anniversary night happens, I won't have to worry anymore."

It's anniversary day, and the plan is in motion. She tells Zach she has a surprise for him, but she won't tell him what, just that he's going to really, really like it. She buys lingerie and gets a bottle of champagne. She arranges to have the dorm room all to herself and sets the mood with candles and music. She tells him to meet her there at 7:00 P.M., and he shows up right on time.

Needless to say, Zach does really, really like the sex. And so does Olivia. She feels even more in love and lust than before, and as their relationship progresses she finds herself feeling really attached to Zach. To her surprise, she also finds herself feeling more jealous of Zach's relationship with Ashley. She had thought that once she and Zach had sex he would become less interested in hanging out with Ashley and would pay less attention to her, but that doesn't turn out to be the case. For example, when Ashley posts a selfie on Facebook and Zach comments on how "hot" she looks, Olivia is overwhelmed with jealousy and anger.

Olivia: (*angry and tearful*) Zach, how could you do that? I know you think Ashley is hotter than me, but you don't have to tell that to everyone!

Zach: What are you talking about? I don't think that. I just thought she looked hot in that picture she posted.

Olivia: But why did you have to say that to her where everyone can read it?

Zach: That's just what I do. You know that. I've always done that. Why are you so upset now?

Olivia: Just because. I mean, I guess I thought that once we had sex things would change. I want you to pay more attention to me than her.

Zach: I do! I'm so happy with us. Things are awesome between us. My relationship with Ashley doesn't change any of that.

Olivia: So you'd rather be with me than with her?

Zach: Yes, you know that. I love you. You're my girlfriend, not Ashley.

Olivia: (*reluctantly*) Okay.

Zach: (*flirtatiously, while kissing and tickling her*) Post some pictures of yourself and I'll comment on how great you look—how's that?

Olivia: (*smiling and kissing him back*) Okay.

Olivia feels more reassured. She also feels kind of guilty, thinking maybe she gave Zach a hard time. She decides to make it up to him by bringing over his favorite ice cream as a surprise. They don't usually get together on Monday nights because Olivia has to study and get to sleep early for an eight o'clock class on Tuesday morning, but she figures she can make an exception this once. Unfortunately, it's Olivia who gets the surprise, when she finds Zach and Ashley together. It's not clear exactly what went on. When she knocked on his door and said, "Hey, Babe, it's me with a surprise for you," she heard a lot of rustling around, and he said, "Oh, hey, I'll be right there. Just give me a minute." When he finally opened the door, Ashley was in the bathroom and Zach looked sort of normal, but not really, and Olivia didn't know what to think.

Olivia: What's going on here? Looks like I came at the wrong time.

Zach: No, what are you talking about? What's the surprise?

Olivia: Me and ice cream, but never mind that. What's going on? Were you and Ashley just having sex?

Zach: No! Of course not. We're just hanging out.

Olivia: I don't know whether to believe you. I'm really confused here, Zach.

Zach: You have to believe me. Everything is fine between us.

(*Ashley comes out of the bathroom and sees Olivia tearful.*)

Ashley: Hey, Olivia. Is everything all right?

Olivia: I don't know. You tell me.

Ashley: Everything's fine here. Listen, I can tell you're upset. I'm gonna head out so you and Zach can talk.

After Ashley leaves, Olivia and Zach talk more. He tells her he loves her, he's really happy with her, and nothing is going on with Ashley. She tells him she doesn't feel comfortable with him and Ashley hanging out alone in his room, and he tells her it won't happen again. They kiss and cuddle and eventually have sex, and Olivia feels happy again. Until the next time.

She and Zach are eating lunch with a group of friends, talking about sports. One guy says to Zach, "Oh yeah, Ashley told me that was such an awesome game you guys saw." What? Olivia nearly chokes on her food. "When was that, Zach?" she asks. "Oh," he says, "the other night, but there was a bunch of us. I would've invited you, but I knew you were studying." "Oh, really," she thinks to herself, as she starts to get the feeling that he might be lying. That everything he's told her might be lies.

She confronts him again that night:

Olivia: Are you cheating on me with Ashley?

Zach: No! I told you I'm not.

Olivia: I'm having a really hard time believing you. You said you wouldn't be alone with her in your room again, but it seems like you were.

Zach: I wasn't. There were other people there.

Olivia: Who?

Zach: Jessie was there.

Olivia: Who?

Zach: Jessie. You know, Ashley's friend Jessie.

Olivia: (*sarcastically*) Oh, the one you're always talking about with the crazy sex stories? Well, that sure makes me feel better.

Zach: C'mon, Olivia, stop this. There's nothing going on.

Olivia: I've told you I've been cheated on before and it really hurt me—just be honest.

Could there really be nothing going on? Olivia is confused. It's true that everything is circumstantial, and his explanations kind of make sense. She wants to trust him, but should she?

Let's cut to the chase here. Zach is, in fact, cheating on Olivia. Olivia found out from Mia, who happened to hear about it through the grapevine. When Mia told her, Olivia was devastated and heartbroken. She felt completely deceived—and she had been. Turns out Zach and Ashley have regularly been hooking up—which they've done for a long time, from well before he and Olivia started dating—and he and Ashley saw no reason to stop. Neither wanted to be in a relationship with the other. They just wanted to be FWBs and were happy with the other having other partners. That's fine for them. What's not fine is that Zach was never honest with Olivia, and he continued to lie about the hookups with Ashley over the course of their relationship, even when he knew Olivia was not comfortable being with someone who was having sex outside of the relationship. Even when he knew that Olivia had been cheated on before and how much it hurt her. He repeatedly lied to her and betrayed her so that he could have the relationship he wanted, knowing it wasn't the relationship she wanted. Repeatedly lying to and betraying your partner to meet your own needs—when you know it would be wrong for him or her—is not a way to build a healthy relationship.

After Olivia found out, she thought, "Again. It happened again. Cheated on twice!" She confronts Zach, and he downplays the significance of his betrayal, offering no real apology except for "I don't want to be with Ashley. I want to be with you. I love you. From now on it's just us." She thinks, "I'm not ready to end things. I love him. He's my soul mate. And yes, he cheated and fidelity is important to me, but everyone I know has either cheated or been cheated on."

I/ME

Is This the Time for Olivia to Be Empathizing with Zach?

Remember in Chapter 6 we told you there were exceptions to mutuality step 2, "Take your guy's perspective?" This is one of them. When you've been repeatedly cheated on and lied to, it's the time to focus on your needs, not his.

Olivia tries to make the relationship work, but she can't help herself—she becomes insanely jealous—snooping his Facebook page, grilling him about his whereabouts, calling his friends to find out where he is. She's out of control. They're fighting all the time, and then she gets caught checking his phone while he's in the bathroom:

Olivia: I only checked your phone to see if Ashley had texted you.
Zach: Stop being stupid. I don't give a fuck about Ashley. I only care about you.
Olivia: (*She doesn't know what to say.*)
Zach: If you want to leave, do it. I don't have time for this bullshit.
Olivia: I hate this (*sobbing*). You know I love you. I want to work this out. Ashley betrayed me. Why are you still friends with her?
Zach: It's just us now. Believe me.
Olivia: I want to. Stop being friends with Ashley, and I will.
Zach: I can't. We're friends. Stop acting so insanely jealous.
Olivia: You and Ashley are a better fit than me and you (*sobbing*). I don't want that to be true, but it kinda is—right? I mean why not choose her over me?
Zach: (*He doesn't know what to say.*)
Olivia: You don't care about me—you care about her. And you don't even want to work

at earning back my trust; you just want to deal with this by me forgetting it ever
happened.

Zach: You're not listening to me! I love you. I can't keep rehashing this shit over and
over again. I'm done.

Olivia didn't realize that, as in her prior relationship, jealousy was
making her crazy, and it was a clear signal that there was no way to rebuild
trust. What was there to trust in? They had wildly different ideas about
what a good relationship is. Zach wanted to live a particular lifestyle (or
wanted a more casual relationship with Olivia), and he lied to get it. Why
wouldn't he keep doing that? Especially when he had no interest in living
any other way? He never even fully fessed up. Given this, Olivia could
never have a relationship with Zach that was based in mutuality. What was
there to trust in? Although she wanted to trust Zach again, she could never
feel safe. The evidence? Her insane jealousy and how she tried to control
Zach's behavior with Ashley. Olivia would always feel jealous and be on
alert for betrayal. Insecurity. It's a deal-breaker.

MIA AND COREY

As you've seen, Mia and Corey are dealing with insecurity as well. Jealousy,
betrayals, breaches of trust. But there are a number of important differences between their situation and that of Olivia and Zach. To begin with,
Mia and Corey have been honest with one another about what they want
and need. Corey was upfront about wanting free passes, and they worked
together to develop a plan and a set of limits. Mia and Corey also had an
initial define-the-relationship talk, and many more of them, all along the
way. They agreed they wanted to be together and made a plan for the
future of their relationship. Mia and Corey also acknowledged their mistakes and apologized. Although they still need to work on treating each
other with respect, their intent has never been to deceive, and both of
them care if the other gets hurt. They've always wanted to have a mutual
relationship where they both feel secure. They just haven't known how to
do it. But they're working on it.

It's only two more months until the end of long-distance. Mia will
graduate and decide what job to take, and Corey will move to be with her.
It's definite. Now they're trying to get through the last phase of free passes
and repair and rebuild security. Mia's still turned on by their open relationship, but at the same time she's looking forward to the return of monogamy.
She loves Corey and wants their relationship to progress, just as he does
with her. They're both tired of feeling jealous.

On FaceTime one night they each admit they have a crush on their
OtherPerson. They talk about how it's not as if either one of them can

reasonably be upset with the other for developing some kind of connection to their OtherPeople. They're trying hard to remember this. To take one another's perspective (mutuality step 2). To be in this together, rather than fighting against one another (mutuality step 3). It's hard.

For example, Mia struggles with the reality that Corey has what he calls a "small" emotional connection with OtherWoman. He's admitted that he goes to her for support, that she helps him deal with his feelings about OtherGuy, that he feels love for her, though he's not "in love" with her. Whether their connection is as small as Corey says has no meaning to Mia. It's still a connection. Does the love he has for OtherWoman amount to cheating? She's not sure. She laughs, thinking, "How do you define cheating in a long-distance open relationship?" She thinks, "At least I know what he's really doing. I don't have to make up stories in my head. I know what's going on." She likes to be in reality about these things. In some ways what Corey is doing is understandable. In some ways it's so hard to accept, but she's working on keeping herself calm, reminding herself of the reality of Corey and his feelings for her, not letting jealousy take over.

She's doing the same with her jealousy about OtherWoman being Corey's go-to person for support. Mia wants to be that person. But then she thinks, "Wait. Emily and Lexi are my go-to peeps for certain things, and Corey is fine with that. Maybe, depending on what the issue is, Other-Woman can serve as Corey's go-to person as well." In fact, Mia appreciates OtherWoman helping Corey with his jealousy. He's been managing better, and that's good for both of them.

Mia and Corey also decide to revisit their limits as a way to deal with jealousy. They want to find a way to earn back each other's trust.

Mia: I've been thinking, and I'm realizing that we're both treating each other as if we're cheating when we're really not. We're each feeling betrayed and getting angry and jealous, but what are we really betraying? A set of arbitrary limits, not really our commitment to one another. Right?

Corey: I don't know. It's so hard for me to imagine you with OtherGuy, even though I know that seems like a double standard.

Mia: I know. I just want to try to help you stop being angry at me. When your first real girlfriend cheated, you told me you were angry because you felt more embarrassed than anything else, like she made a fool out of you. Our free passes are entirely different. I'm not making a fool of you. We've agreed to doing this. Does looking at it that way help?

Corey: Kind of. But I also get angry when I see you put your own interests over mine and our relationship. That's what it feels like when you do things I've asked you not to do. It feels like you're being selfish and I can't trust you.

Mia: Corey, don't you see that I could say the same thing about you? That's my point.

I/ME

Is It Ever Okay to Feel Jealous?

It's normal to experience the occasional pang of jealousy, particularly at the beginning of a relationship when you don't know your partner well. For instance, in watching the guy you like interact with another girl, you might wonder, "Does he like her more than me? He treats her differently than me. What does that mean?" And so on. In a healthy relationship, jealousy should lessen as you build mutuality and security increases. If it doesn't, it's a sign that something is wrong. In those instances you need to ask yourself, "Why am I not feeling secure?"

We either give each other permission to have this open relationship and trust in our commitment to one another, or we don't.

Corey: Or we fully respect one another's limits completely.

Mia: Can you do that?

Corey: I don't know.

Mia: Right. Me too. My limits don't make sense to you, and your limits don't make sense to me, and that's because we both know that breaking those limits is not a breach of our feelings and commitment to one another. But we just can't get each other to see that. So what do we do?

Corey: I'm not sure. I need to think. We should talk more about this.

Mia: I agree. Let's keep trying to help each other feel better.

As you can see, Mia and Corey still have work to do to rebuild security in their relationship, but it's important to see that the potential is there. Even though they've faced betrayals and jealousy, their openness and honesty and legitimate desire to have a mutual, committed relationship makes their situation very different from that of Olivia and Zach. There's insecurity at present, but it's not necessarily a deal-breaker.

Relationship Aggression

Anna and Lexi are both facing aggression in their relationships. Do they need to exit?

ANNA AND ERIC

As you've seen so far, Anna is not getting very many of her needs met with Eric. He's not really interested in being part of her stay-at-home-mom life, nor does he want to help her with taking care of Emma or things at home. Eric also has included Anna's needs in his choices less and less, and he has shown he really doesn't trust her. Despite this, she loves him—all of the fun times, the romance, the chemistry that's still so strong. And she's committed to raising Emma with two parents.

To this point, Anna has thought of each of her unmet needs separately—as isolated incidents. She hasn't recognized that each one was, in fact, a red flag, a warning sign of things to come—the beginning of a pattern of aggression. It's not surprising that Anna missed this. In fact, many women do not recognize the warning signs, and you only may be able to see some of them once a pattern develops. Let's look at Eric's pattern of behavior, starting with the early signs:

- Eric was unhappy because Anna didn't show enough interest in him, so he found someone else.
- When they got back together, Eric immediately suspected that Anna was cheating on him when she asked him to come over so they could talk (when she was going to tell him she was pregnant).
- In response to Anna's selfie postings, Eric made sure to post that she was his.

Any of these things would seem like no big deal, or might even be attractive in a "look how much he loves me and wants me all to himself" kind of way. However, they were the beginning of a pattern of neediness, jealousy, and possessiveness that is common in aggressive relationships. Next:

- Eric refused to allow her to see her family on Thanksgiving.
- When she came home late after a night out with the girls, Eric broke her phone, called her a slut, and lied to her that others had said the same.

These are more significant and clearly were of concern to Anna. As you can see now, they were the next steps in the pattern of jealousy and controlling behavior that also included starting to isolate her from her family—all very common types of relationship aggression. The last incident, when he broke her phone, is the clearest example of verbal aggression and behavior meant to intimidate. Seeing the pattern this way, it's no surprise that things continue to get worse. For example, now every time she's out with friends, Eric calls incessantly. If she doesn't pick up, he'll text constantly, "Pick up the damn phone when I call you! Where the fuck are you? Who are you with? You should be here with me." Anna thinks, "He knows where I am and who I'm with. I don't understand why he wants to talk to me this much when I'm not with him and why he can't just let me do what

I'm doing without interrupting me." When she finally answers the phone or comes home, he angrily calls her names, accuses her of not caring about him, and berates her. They end up in a nasty, emotionally draining screaming match. It's happened over and over. She's always known that Eric likes a lot of attention and support, but she thought he wanted to be with her all the time because she was his go-to person. Now she's not so sure. And she's right not to be sure. Eric's demanding and controlling behavior goes well beyond what is reasonable for being supported in a relationship. It's another indicator of aggression.

Eric's verbal aggression and intimidating behavior are coming up in other areas as well, including in the form of sexual coercion. One night, Anna joins Eric on the couch to cuddle and watch their favorite show. She's just getting into it and Eric starts kissing her. She kisses him back, and it's clear he wants more.

Anna: I just want to unwind a bit, Eric. Let's have sex after.
Eric: You never want to have sex anymore. What's wrong with you?
Anna: Seriously? This is the first time I've sat down today after working and taking care of Emma, and I need to unwind. I've been waiting to watch this episode all week. I want to watch it.
Eric: What the fuck. I have needs, you know that.
Anna: Stop it! (*She pushes him away.*) We'll have sex after.

Eric begins his pressure-to-consent-to-sex rant: "What has happened to you? You don't love me. You're not attracted to me. What is wrong with you? Sex is what married people do—why don't you want to—". He won't drop it. She finally yells at him, "Just leave me alone! You're making things worse!" and they have another nasty screaming match. When it's over, Anna decides that it's best to have sex when Eric wants. She thinks, "I've always loved having sex with him. I'll just rally when I'm tired. I want my marriage to work. We can't keep fighting like this."

But they do keep fighting, and it gets worse.

I/ME

Is There a Difference between Consent in a Casual Relationship and Consent in a Serious Committed One, Even Marriage?

NO! The answer still has to be an enthusiastic YES!

If you haven't yet watched Laci Green's video on consent, "Wanna Have Sex? [Consent 101]" *www.youtube.com/watch?v=TD2EooMhqR*, you might want to do so now.

They go out with friends as a group one evening. (She's not going out alone with her friends anymore because Eric demanded, "We're married now. We do things together." Another example of aggression in the form of control and isolation of her.) Anna is talking and laughing and having lots of fun with their friend Kevin. The whole time Eric is staring at her and giving her dirty looks. He finally pulls her aside:

Eric: What the fuck! You're so insulting the way you're behaving with Kevin; you have no respect for me.
Anna: What? We're just talking and laughing.
Eric: Do you want to fuck Kevin?
Anna: (*surprised*) NO!
Eric: Well, he wants to fuck you—that much is clear.
Anna: We've all been friends forever—you know that! Even if he did, I'm not interested. I love you. I don't want to be with anyone else.
Eric: Yeah, sure you don't.

He ramps it up, causes a scene, and they leave. She's thinking, "I don't understand him. He knows I love to have fun with our friends. Why did he get so upset? And why did he feel it necessary to cause a scene in front of our friends? It's so embarrassing. What must they be thinking? We're married and happy. What is he doing?"

When they get home (and after the babysitter has left), Eric gets right in her face, yelling, "You're just a drunken slut!" Anna tells him to stop. She tries to defend herself and reason with him, but he doesn't want to hear it. He's standing right in front of her, with his face right in hers, continuing to yell and call her names. She pushes him back from her—hard. He immediately grabs her and pushes her into a wall—harder. Then he grabs a lamp, throws it at the wall, and yells, "No being friends with Kevin, at all!" Emma wakes up crying. "Oh great," Eric says sarcastically. "Anna, pull yourself together and go take care of Emma," and then he puts on the TV and flops onto the couch.

The next day Lauren meets her at work for lunch.

Lauren: How's everything going?
Anna: Okay.
Lauren: Kevin called me and told me what happened. Why haven't you returned his texts?
Anna: Eric doesn't want me to be friends with him.
Lauren: Seriously? You've all been friends for so long.
Anna: I know, but he's my husband. I want my marriage to work. I have to respect him.
Lauren: How is giving up your friendship with Kevin respecting Eric? How is that even okay for you?

Anna: I don't want my marriage to be over. Emma needs a home with both a mother and a father to grow up happily. I really want my marriage to work with Eric. I do love him.

Lauren says nothing. She doesn't know what to say to that. Instead, she asks Anna about Emma to sidestep tension. She wanted to ask Anna, "Am I next?" but didn't because she doesn't know how to deal with how Eric is treating Anna and why Anna's okay with it. Meanwhile, Anna talks about Emma because she doesn't know what else to say. She can tell Lauren doesn't understand, and she's certainly not going to tell Lauren about the lamp incident. She thinks, "Lauren so doesn't get my life. It's just easier to give in sometimes. There's no way I can win the stay-friends-with-Kevin fight and keep my marriage."

This is a typical reaction that women can have in response to aggressive, controlling behavior—"If I just give in and do what he wants, everything will be okay." And then they make up, and things are good, and everything seems okay. Until the next time.

Julianne is having a girls' night for her birthday, and Anna wants to go. At first Anna said no. Eric would never agree to it. But then she thought, "I'll tell him I'm going to my mom's house for a visit and sleepover with Emma. He still wouldn't like that, but he'd probably agree to it." Nervously, Anna carried out the plan. She really did want to be with Julianne. They'd always done girls' nights for their birthdays.

This is another typical reaction that women can have in response to aggressive, controlling behavior. Because they lack power to negotiate to get their needs met, they lie about things. It seems like the only way they can get what they want without conflict or without putting themselves in danger. Therefore, lying can also be an attempt to protect themselves from further aggression.

I/ME

Is It Appropriate for Anna to Take Eric's Perspective When He Demands That She Give Up Her Friendship with Kevin?

Definitely not. This is another exception to mutuality step 2, "Take your guy's perspective," that we described in Chapter 6.

Eric's demand is unreasonable and aggressive. Anna needs to see it as such and keep herself clear on this reality rather than buy into his perspective. Lauren is right to say Anna should examine whether Eric has the right to make this demand. Anna should be asking herself, "How is this okay for me?"

Anna's out with the girls, having so much fun, when her phone rings. The display says "Mom" so she picks up. It's Eric. She's busted. When she didn't pick up his call earlier (she was already at the bar and didn't want to answer it there), he got suspicious and went over to her mother's house. He got furious when she wasn't there (her mom said she just went to the store) and insisted on calling Anna from her mom's phone.

Eric: Where the fuck are you?

Anna: Eric, what are you doing calling me from my mother's phone?

Eric: What am I doing? I'm taking Emma home. You better leave wherever you are right now and meet me back at home.

Anna: What? Why?

Eric: (*interrupting her*) You lied to me, Anna! Meet me at home now! (*He hangs up.*)

Anna's angry and scared, but she's afraid things will be even worse if she doesn't go home. When she gets there, Eric launches into his I-do-everything-for-you-you-owe-me rant, yelling and going on and on:

"You're just a lying bitch. It's all about you—whatever makes you happy. You never do anything for me. I bought you a car, a beautiful house, I make way more money than you. You don't bring anything to the table—and then you lie to me."

Anna: Eric, I'm sorry. I'm sorry I lied. I know I shouldn't have lied. I just really wanted to see Julianne, and you've been so unreasonable about not wanting me to go out.

Eric: Unreasonable?! Did you say unreasonable?! FUCK YOU, ANNA! I can't trust you at all. You lie. You're out there being your slutty self, getting drunk, disrespecting me! You are not going anywhere now!

Anna: That's bullshit, Eric, and you know it!

Eric: Don't fucking tell me what I know!

And with that, he pushes her and she pushes him back, both of them screaming. Anna ends up on the living room floor with Eric sitting on top of her, shaking her, while she's slapping him and pulling his hair and trying to get him off her. All of a sudden, there's a knock on the door. It's the police. Eric tells Anna to go to the bathroom and clean up and not say a thing about what happened. When Eric answers the door, the police tell him they were called because someone heard what sounded like a domestic dispute. Eric tells them they were arguing, but everything is okay. They ask to speak to his wife, and Anna verifies that she is fine. The police leave with a warning to them.

The next morning he ignores her, gives her the silent treatment, and she gives him silence right back. At work all day, she's worried about what will happen that night. When he gets home for dinner, she tiptoes around him, trying to assess his mood. Over dinner he says, "Look Anna, if you just don't lie to me anymore, things like last night won't happen again, okay?" "Okay," she says, figuring it's better not to argue with him. And with that, he goes back to acting like everything is fine between them. She, however, was really shaken by what happened. She's not sure what to do or whether to tell anyone. She only knows for sure she doesn't want another fight like that.

Sadly, she gets one.

It's a Thursday night, and Eric has informed Anna he invited his parents for dinner on Friday night. He wants Anna to do the cooking. Normally she loves doing this, but work is crazy busy and she's had extra things to do for Emma, and she's really tired this week. She asks if they can move it to Saturday or the following week. Eric launches into his I-do-everything-for-you-you-owe-me rant again, yelling and going on and on. She tells herself to ignore it, that it just gets worse when you say anything (she's learned from experience). But when he says, "You're just a lazy, selfish bitch, aren't you? What do you have to say for yourself?" she can't take it anymore.

Anna: SHUT THE FUCK UP! Why are you such a bastard? How dare you call me lazy and selfish!

Eric: DON'T YOU DARE SPEAK TO ME THAT WAY! I do everything for you!

Anna: Oh really? Like when you come home after work, asking when dinner is ready, ignoring me and Emma, and turning on the TV? How about coming into the kitchen to talk to me while I'm cooking dinner, or, better yet, helping me out when I ask you? You never help me, and you don't appreciate all the things I do for you!

Eric: You owe me. I work my ass off for this family. I do my job, and you have to do yours. Stop being such a whiny bitch and suck it up!

Anna: Stop it, Eric! Stop it! Why are you so mean to me?! Why can't you be more aware of the small things that are important to me, like paying attention to Emma?

Eric: You're wrong! On Saturdays, I get up with Emma. I feed her, put her in the swing, and turn on cartoons.

Anna: Yes, and then you come back into the bedroom on the pretense to snuggle but it's really to have sex—that's not paying attention to Emma.

Eric: You're not paying attention to her either. You can't get your lazy ass out of bed on Saturday. That's pretty shitty!

Anna: SCREW YOU, ERIC!

(Anna turns to walk out of the room.)

Eric: DON'T YOU FUCKING TALK TO ME LIKE THAT AND THEN WALK AWAY!

Eric grabs her as she's turning around, but she pulls away. He goes after her and punches her hard in the back. She falls to the floor and hits the ground hard. She can't breathe. She starts crying, but can't move. Eric sees that she's not okay. He *takes her to the hospital, and tells her to say that she fell off a ladder at home.*

The doctor in the ER says, "Your ribs are broken." She's scared. She's in pain. She's confused. Anna has always believed that if anyone ever hurt her she'd be out the door immediately, but that was before Emma. "How could this be happening?" she thinks. "How could he be doing this? And what am I doing?" She really doesn't know.

The next day Lauren calls:

Lauren: Hey, how are you? Want to meet for lunch? I can come by your office.

Anna: I can't. I'm at home and I'm not feeling well.

Lauren: What's the matter?

Anna: (*She figures she has to tell Lauren something. It's going to take a while for her* *ribs to heal.*) Well, actually, I broke my ribs.

Lauren: What? Oh my goodness! What happened?

Anna: I was on a ladder in the house last night trying to change that really high lightbulb we have and I fell off.

Lauren: (*skeptically*) You fell off? And you broke your ribs?

Anna: Yes, crazy, right?

Lauren: Very. Where was Eric when that happened?

Anna: He was here. It was a good thing too. He took me to the ER.

Lauren: You know, Anna, this is really bizarre. Are you telling me the truth?

Anna: (*silence*)

Lauren: Anna, what happened?

Anna: (*crying*) It was nothing. Eric and I had a fight.

Lauren: It couldn't have been nothing! You're crying and your ribs are broken. Did Eric do this? What did he *do*?

Anna: We were arguing about something and he got really angry and I tried to walk away from him, and he came after me, and it just happened.

Lauren: Anna, this is not okay! Go to your mom's. You're in danger. He injured you! What's to stop him from doing this again?

Anna: Don't be so dramatic. I know it's a problem, but I don't know what to do. I love him. I don't want my marriage to end. I don't want to do that to Emma. I want to find a way to make it work.

Lauren: That's crazy, Anna. If you stay, Emma could be in danger.

Anna: He would never hurt her, and I'm just not going to let this happen again. I can handle this.

Lauren: That's ridiculous. I'm coming over to get you. Pack your stuff.

Anna: No, don't. I can't.

Lauren: You've got to get out, Anna. Or at least get help.

Anna suggests to Eric they go to marriage counseling. Eric doesn't want to, but he agrees to one session. When the marriage counselor suggests Eric attend anger management classes, he refuses—and refuses to go back to the counselor. He blames Anna for their problems. She doesn't know what to think. She doesn't understand who he is anymore. She just wants her happy family back the way it seemed to be in the beginning.

Unfortunately for Anna, she's unlikely to get it. Why? Because she's in a relationship with an aggressive partner.

DEFINING RELATIONSHIP AGGRESSION

There are three primary forms of relationship aggression (also called intimate partner violence and domestic violence): verbal/emotional aggression, physical aggression, and sexual aggression.

- *Verbal/emotional aggression*: Nonphysical behaviors, including threats, insults, name-calling, blaming, constant monitoring or "checking in," excessive texting, humiliation, intimidation, or isolation.
- *Physical aggression*: Physically forceful behaviors, including hitting, shoving, biting, strangling, kicking, throwing things, or using a weapon.
- *Sexual aggression*: Actions that impact a person's ability to control his or her own sexual activity or the circumstances in which sexual activity occurs. Actions (verbal or physical) intended to coerce a person into engaging in sexual activity. Ignoring someone's refusal to engage in sexual activities by repeatedly using verbal or physical pressure.

These types of aggression (particularly verbal and sexual) can occur separately, but in the worst cases, they occur together, as is the case for Anna.

THE DATA ON RELATIONSHIP AGGRESSION

Reports from the National Violence Against Women (NVAW) Survey and the National Intimate Partner and Sexual Violence Survey indicate nearly 25% of surveyed women in the United States over the age of 18 reported they were physically assaulted by someone with whom they were in a relationship, with approximately 70% of those assaults occurring before age 25. Many of those assaults (15–40%) resulted in physical injury. In addition, the average number of assaults reported with the same partner was approximately seven. Twenty percent of women reporting physical assault reported 10 or more assaults, and 27% of women reported victimization by the same partner over more than five years. These data suggest that not only is physical aggression prevalent in romantic relationships, but it also can be repetitive over long periods of time.

It can also be mutual, which is very common among young adults. Indeed, research shows 20–30% of couples of all types (married, cohabiting, dating) report engaging in "both-partner" (that is, mutual) aggression. Anna and Eric have done this. In the context of major arguments, she's pushed him and fought with him physically. However, all data show that the risk of injury is much greater for women than it is for men, and that's certainly been true for Anna.

The NVAW Survey also showed that women whose partners were jealous, controlling, or verbally abusive were the most likely to report being assaulted. In fact, having a verbally abusive partner was the variable most likely to predict whether a woman would be physically assaulted. Therefore, verbal aggression should be a major warning sign for women. Had Anna known this, she might have better understood what type of risk she was at. Indeed, all of these data illustrate why Anna is unlikely to have that happy family experience she so wants with Eric. Their pattern fits the data. Eric is a jealous, controlling, verbally abusive guy who is engaging in repeated physical aggression and sexual coercion. And, if Anna stays with him, she is putting herself at significant risk for physical and mental health problems.

A recent report by the World Health Organization noted that experiencing physical assault by an intimate partner is associated with alcohol use, depression, suicide attempts, gastrointestinal problems, neurological disorders, chronic pain, anxiety, and posttraumatic stress disorder (PTSD), as well as noncommunicable diseases such as hypertension, cancer, and cardiovascular diseases. There also is evidence linking intimate partner violence with subsequent negative child health and development outcomes, suggesting that if Anna stays with Eric and he continues to be violent, Emma is at risk too.

Research on the treatment of intimate partner violence indicates there are few effective treatments and violence often recurs even after what appears to be successful treatment. Of course, a person has to be willing to attempt treatment for there to be even a chance of change. As you saw, Eric was not willing to try. This effectively means that Anna has little chance of getting her needs met.

Given all of the data, should Anna exit? Yes, she should.

Why wasn't Anna able to see this all along? Like many women, Anna was not recognizing that all of the ways in which Eric was aggressive toward her fit a larger pattern of domestic violence. The jealousy, controlling behavior, insults and name-calling, demanding of her attention and time, isolating her from her friends and family, blaming, physical attacks, sexual pressuring, and coercion all go together. As we noted earlier, Anna saw them as unrelated, isolated incidents. (For more information about how typical it is for women not to see the pattern, see the box below.)

In some relationships there are isolated incidents. For instance, if one night Julianne pressured Gregory to have sex when he didn't feel like it (for example, "C'mon Gregory, you never want to have sex. What's wrong with you? You don't care about my needs!"), and she got angry and distant when he said no but she later apologized, that's not a pattern of domestic violence. That's an isolated incident. Or when Emily repeatedly called Will an asshole when she was upset, that's verbal aggression, but, as you saw in her story, it did not lead to an escalating pattern or to any physical violence. Instead, Emily finally recognized her behavior for what it was and worked on stopping it. Anna may have thought Eric would do the same, but instead he continued to repeat and escalate with no signs of remorse or intention to stop. There is no way for Anna to ever be secure in this situation. It's domestic violence, and it's a deal-breaker.

I/ME

Is It Typical for Women Not to See the Pattern of Domestic Violence?

Yes, it is. For another story where violence seems to come out of the blue, watch Leslie Morgan Steiner's TED Talk "Why Domestic Violence Victims Don't Leave" (*www.ted.com/talks/leslie_morgan_steiner_why_domestic_violence_victims_don_t_leave*).

In her talk she discusses how she didn't know anything about the pattern of domestic violence and talks about why she stayed for so long. Here's a quick excerpt:

> Conor first physically attacked me five days before our wedding. It was 7:00 A.M. I still had on my nightgown. I was working on my computer, trying to finish a freelance writing assignment, and I got frustrated, and Conor used my anger as an excuse to put both of his hands around my neck and to squeeze so tightly that I could not breathe or scream, and he used the chokehold to hit my head repeatedly against the wall. Five days later, the ten bruises on my neck had just faded, and I put on my mother's wedding dress, and I married him. Despite what had happened, I was sure we were going to live happily ever after, because I loved him, and he loved me so much. And he was very, very sorry. He had just been really stressed out by the wedding and by becoming a family with me. It was an isolated incident, and he was never going to hurt me again.

I/ME

You Might Be Tempted to Ask, "What Would Make Eric Behave This Way? What's His Motive?"

Researchers have identified a number of characteristics of violent men that suggest different causes or motives. However, it really doesn't matter. This is no time to try to understand his need (insight step 6) or take his perspective (mutuality step 2). If you find yourself in a domestic violence situation and you're asking the question "Why is he doing this?" tell yourself, "It doesn't matter" and then get out.

To find out more about domestic violence and what to do if it's happening to you, check the following resources:

National Resource Center on Domestic Violence
www.nrcdv.org

National Domestic Violence Hotline
www.thehotline.org

Lexi and Ryan

What about Lexi? Does she need to exit? Clearly, Ryan has been aggressive toward her. He has physically restrained her, grabbed her arm so hard it bruised, thrown a can of hairspray (hitting Kitty), and thrown noodles in her face. He's also said some pretty nasty stuff to her. Importantly, Lexi has seen that Ryan's aggressive behavior occurs only when he's drunk or using drugs (cocaine). The rest of the time, he's the sweet, supportive, awesome, fun guy she loves. Research shows that substance use—alcohol and cocaine in particular—is strongly associated with aggression in relationships; people are more likely to be aggressive when they are under the influence. And remember how we said that Lexi may have missed Ryan's tendency to be impulsive, instead seeing only his adventurous, spontaneous nature (which she totally loves)? Research also shows that impulsivity is associated with both substance use and relationship aggression. So Ryan is definitely at risk for continuing both of these behaviors.

The good news is there is evidence that treatment for substance use—in either individual or couple therapy—reduces both substance use and intimate partner violence. This suggests that if Ryan were willing to get treatment for his substance use problem, and if he were to stay sober, he would be less likely to be aggressive with Lexi, and Lexi would be more able to get her needs met.

What does this mean for Lexi's exit decision? If she wants to stay with Ryan, she must assess whether Ryan is willing to get treatment and keep herself safe until he's sober. People with substance use disorders are notoriously in denial about their problem. It can be very hard to motivate them for treatment. Ryan's refusal to get help and stay sober would not bode well for Lexi. He'd continue to be aggressive with her, and Lexi would need to decide whether she was willing to live with that. As with Anna, we would advocate strongly for "No." A relationship with an aggressive and substance-abusing person is not a healthy relationship. It's dangerous, and Lexi should end it immediately. However, if Ryan was open to getting treatment and accepted responsibility for his own recovery, and he and Lexi engaged in mutual problem solving as they faced the challenges that recovery brings, their relationship would have a chance. All the good stuff about their relationship that you read about in Chapter 7 would be there, and they would have the potential for a happy, healthy relationship where they were both getting their needs met.

So is Ryan's aggressive behavior and substance abuse a deal-breaker? It's not if he gets treatment and stays sober. Plenty of people have successfully recovered from substance abuse and gone on to have secure, healthy relationships. But it definitely is a deal-breaker if he doesn't get sober. The bottom line for Lexi is that, as with Eric, if Ryan doesn't want to do anything to change his behavior, Lexi, like Anna, will never feel secure and will need to exit. In the next chapter, you'll see how Lexi goes about making her stay-or-go decision.

In this chapter, we helped you identify extreme situations where exiting the relationship is the *only* option. To review, these are situations that result in chronic insecurity and danger, where your safety and trust needs are severely compromised, such as ongoing lying and betrayal and relationship aggression. You also may have noticed these are situations in which

---

I/ME

If He's Aggressive When He's Drunk, Isn't He Going to Be Aggressive When He's Sober?

Not necessarily. People may behave quite differently when drunk compared to when sober. Think about it—what's the likelihood you'd send the text you sent while drunk when you're sober? Pretty low, right? The best indicator of what someone is really like is when he's sober, not when he's drunk. The question is whether he can stay sober.

the partner engaging in these behaviors has no interest in changing. That's a sure sign you need to exit.

I/ME

Wait, Are *You* the Lying, Jealous, or Aggressive One?

If you are, you need to develop better I/ME skills, particularly better emotion regulation skills so you can change your behavior, because it's not fair to your boyfriend—he has no security either.

In the next chapter, we help you figure out how to make stay-or-go decisions in situations like Lexi's, where the answer to whether to exit the relationship is not so obvious.

9

Do I Stay or Do I Go?

We all know how difficult making a decision about the future of our relationship can be. Is the love we feel enough to make the relationship work? It can be tough to know, right? "Do I stay in a not-so-great relationship longer to see if things can change? Do I leave now? Does the fact that my relationship is good right now mean I should take it to the next level?"

Research shows that people make stay-or-go decisions based on whether they believe they are getting their needs met and whether they think they have better alternatives. This is why we've focused so much on helping you learn to assess your needs accurately. Now we build on this by showing you how you can use insight into your key needs to consciously make healthy stay-or-go decisions.

This chapter also helps you deal with the emotions that can come up when you're making hard relationship decisions. Uncertainty breeds fear. "What if I make the wrong decision? Am I going to be okay? I don't want to make a mistake! What if our commitment doesn't last?" These thoughts and feelings can hold you back when the evidence suggests that moving forward is a good risk. Fear can also hold you back from exiting when it's clear that you should. "Maybe things can change. I might not be okay on my own. How will I live without him? Maybe I won't find someone better." Uncertainty can paralyze people and lead them to make fear-based decisions.

Other emotions work the same way. Guilt ("I don't want to hurt him") can make you stay in an unhealthy relationship. Love ("We don't want the same things, but I *love* him") can do the same, as can sadness ("I just feel so sad when I think about all the good things I'll miss"). Anger ("Screw him! I'll never give him the chance to disappoint me again!") can make

214

you impulsively leave a relationship that might have potential. Fortunately you can use your emotions to help you stay focused on your key needs and make good relationship decisions. We've already introduced you to emotion regulation in Chapter 6. Here we describe two other ways to regulate emotions using "tolerance of uncertainty" and "wise mind."

Tolerance of Uncertainty

We live in an uncertain world, relationships included. It's just reality, but it's a reality that can be very difficult to accept. The trouble is that being unable to tolerate uncertainty can paralyze us when we need to make a decision. Badgering ourselves with questions like "What if I make the wrong decision?" can keep us from making one at all. Intolerance of uncertainty can also put us into extreme control mode. We get ideas in our head about the way things "should" be, and we start demanding that things be as we say they must be and searching for reassurance from ourselves and others. This never works. Why? Because there is never 100% certainty. About anything.

How can we deal with the reality of uncertainty as we make relationship decisions?

1. *Focus not on how things should be but on how they are.* How many times have you heard someone say something like "He shouldn't treat me that way. If he didn't, everything would be okay and our relationship would work." Have you ever said that? If so, you need to know that the fact of the matter is he *does* treat you that way. You can't be certain that he'll change in the future. All you can do is be clear about your needs and how things really are and determine whether that's acceptable to you. That doesn't mean you don't give someone the opportunity to change. It means you look at the reality of how things are to make your decisions.

Can you think of a time when you were focused on how things should be rather than on how they actually were? Write an example here:

2. *Stay in the present moment and make the best decision you can based on the accumulated reality-based evidence at that moment.* You

cannot live indefinitely in the hopes or fears of what might be. (Well, you could, but it would be a miserable life.) You must take action at some point. Muster up your courage, with all your strength, and use all the evidence you have to bravely make a plan and follow through on it. The next strategy can help you do so.

3. *Recognize that every decision you make is a calculated risk, but you must make a decision and be willing to assume the risk*. Because nothing is certain, all decisions come with risk, and the fact of the matter is you won't be fully able to evaluate your decision until after it's been made and you see the consequences. This means you must be open and willing to take a risk and to learn from doing so. Willingly taking risks is a scary business. It's also liberating, especially if you view all risks as learning experiences, which we encourage you to do.

> Have you ever taken a risk in a relationship? What happened? What about not taking a risk? Why not?

The next strategy provides a great way to face your fears about what might happen when you take a risk.

4. *Figure out your worst-case scenario(s) and make a coping plan for how you will handle it (or them)*. Say you're afraid to move in with your boyfriend because you think, "What if it doesn't work out? What will I tell people? Where will I go?" Those are pretty typical concerns, and all of them can be addressed with problem solving. Look at each concern and figure out a plan for dealing with it. What would you tell people? We recommend the truth. Where would you go? Think ahead about options. For example, do you have a friend or family member you could stay with for a while? Will you have money saved to rent an apartment?

> Is there anything in your relationship that you're afraid of? Write your worst-case scenario by listing what you're afraid of:
>
> 1.
>
> 2.
>
> 3.
>
> 4.

Now see if you can come up with a plan for dealing with each fear:

1.

2.

3.

4.

What if you're also thinking, "How will I cope emotionally if we break up?" That's another good question, and in the next chapter we're going to deal with that issue specifically, so stay tuned. In the meantime, the next strategy can also help with coping.

5. Develop some healthy, reality-based self-statements (new self-talk). To come up with statements that help you tolerate uncertainty, you must be open to looking at your fears and identifying the thoughts that are getting in the way of your making a decision. You must cultivate an attitude of openness to the future and to whatever new experiences—good or bad—may come, trusting that you will figure out how to handle them. For example, if you're thinking, "I have to be certain," remind yourself, "I can't be certain, but that's okay. Certainty isn't possible. I need to be brave and make the best decision I can." If you're thinking, "I have to know for sure whether this relationship is going to work out," tell yourself, "Relationships don't all last, and I will cope with it if mine doesn't." If you're thinking, "I may never find another relationship," tell yourself, "I may or may not. I can't know now, but either way I will be okay, and fear is no reason to stay in an unhealthy relationship."

What are some reality-based self-statements that can help you cope with something you're uncertain about?

Wise Mind

It can be hard to know what information to use to make relationship decisions. Do we use reason to try to do the most logical thing? Do we go solely on the intensity of our feelings? Many people rely on only one of these strategies, but the reality is that both are important. We need both to make fully conscious, healthy decisions. "Wise mind" is a concept that was developed by Dr. Marsha Linehan, an expert in interventions designed to help people regulate their emotions. Linehan teaches us that everyone has three states of mind:

1. **Reasonable mind**—which is a logical, problem-solving, practical approach to things. Examples of this approach might be making a to-do list of things you need to get done or researching and then figuring out what your best job options are. It's all about getting things done in a thoughtful, logical, and effective way, rather than acting on emotion. When it comes to relationships, examples might be planning the details of moving in together, like what to keep and what to pack away, or planning how often you'll see each other in a long-distance relationship.

2. **Emotion mind**—in which thoughts and behaviors are guided by emotions rather than logic. Examples of such behaviors might be buying a new dress just because you love it, even though you already spent your clothing budget this month, or going out and doing something just for the fun of it. It's all about doing things based on what you feel in the moment, whether it's logical to do so or not. In relationships, examples might be staying on the phone with your boyfriend talking all night, even though you have to get up early the next day, just because it feels so good, or taking a motorcycle ride with a guy you just met that you're attracted to.

Reasonable mind and emotion mind can result in both healthy and unhealthy behaviors. The examples above are generally healthy behaviors. When reasonable mind is too much in control or too strong, you might be really strict with yourself and not allow yourself to have any fun or take reasonable risks. Or you may not be able to feel or use emotions that can guide you to know yourself and get close to other people. Or you may get stuck in what you deem logical (you'll see Mia and Julianne struggle with this). When emotion mind is in control or is too strong, you can lose all sense of logic and be blinded to reality (you'll see this with Emily and Lexi). You may get stuck in negative feelings, ruminate a lot, and feel depressed and anxious. You might accept poor behavior from others or make unreasonable demands, and you might stay in an unhealthy relationship. So this is where wise mind comes in.

3. **Wise mind**—which happens when reasonable mind and emotion mind come together in an integrated way. When they do, they create a whole that is greater than the sum of its parts. They provide you with intuition—with a sense of knowing what's right for you. Wise mind is a combination of listening to your emotions (your heart) and thinking about things logically (using your head) to really know what's best for you. It's a calm place that helps you feel centered and secure in your decisions. It's like knowing in your gut that you've made the right decision.

Of course, it's not at all easy to be in wise mind, and no one can be there all the time. It comes only with practice.

- Practice paying attention to both your head and your heart. Ask yourself, "Where is this thought or feeling coming from? Is it coming from my head or my heart? And what's underneath it—what's driving it? Is it healthy?" Or is it driven by a reasonable mind that is too strict or rigid or controlling? Or a fantasy-driven emotion mind that's not in touch with reality? Take your time to figure out the answer (maybe ask a trusted friend to help you). And get to know your typical style. In what relationship situations are you more head driven? More heart driven? When are you head and/or heart driven in healthy ways? Unhealthy ways?

Write your head and heart styles here.
Situations in which I tend to be more head driven in healthy ways:

Situations in which I tend to be more head driven in unhealthy ways:

Situations in which I tend to be more heart driven in healthy ways:

Situations in which I tend to be more heart driven in unhealthy ways:

- Practice making decisions that consider information from both head and heart. Once you're better able to pay attention to both your head and heart, be sure that when you have a decision to make you purposely think about both perspectives. Ask yourself: What would my head say? What would my heart say? What are the healthy messages, and what are the unhealthy ones? And then make a decision that respects and takes care of both head and heart. For example, if your head is providing the healthy message, respect and take care of your heart by soothing your emotions as you let your head guide your decision. If your heart is providing the healthy message, respect and take care of your head by being compassionate with yourself and letting your heart inform a new way of thinking.

- Practice not acting impulsively. Take the time to work on wise mind in the ways we're suggesting. There is no rush. You want to be able to make the best decision you can make. Give yourself the time and space to do so.

- Practice trusting that you will be able to get through whatever pain you are feeling. Use compassionate self-talk, as described in Chapter 6, that affirms your ability to cope with your emotions.

It takes a wise-mind choice—a head and a heart choice—to make a good decision about whether to stay or go.

Let's look now at how Emily, Lexi, Mia, and Julianne can use emotion regulation to help them make their stay-or-go decisions based on whether they're getting their key needs met.

EMILY AND WILL

Emily's got a decision to make. Should she take her relationship with Will to the next level by moving to be with him? She's uncertain. She's not sure she wants to have a lifestyle defined by being a med-school girlfriend. She's worried she'll feel as if her life is on hold if they live together while he's in school and worried about being able to pursue her own career the way she wants to if she moves to be with him. So Emily is really conflicted. She feels like she wants to know for sure how the future will go. She decides to have another talk with Will about this:

Emily: What do you want, if anything, before you settle down?
Will: (laughing) What's up? Get to the point.
Emily: (laughing) You know what I mean!
Will: (laughing) You know I want to get married and have children someday, if that's what you mean.

Emily: I'm just concerned I'll want that sooner than you. When do you think you'll be ready?

Will: I don't know. Just move in with me. We want the same things. I'm just not sure on the timing, and I'm not in any rush to have a family. I'd like to be settled, have some stability, spend time with you first. I don't even know what city I'll do my residency in.

Emily: And what if things are going well for me at work—would you consider doing your residency there so I'm not the one who has to keep moving?

Will: (*laughing*) Yes, of course.

Emily: I'm really glad you're open to that.

Will: I am. But we can't force this, Em. We want to be together. Let's just go with it. Let's just be together and enjoy it and take it from there.

Emily thinks, "Well, that didn't make me more certain!" She kind of sees his point, but she still doesn't know if she's going to be happy living with him. She thinks, "What if I don't like my job? What if I don't make friends? What if my life just revolves around Will's schedule?" She's very focused on what the future should be, so it's hard for her to consider just appreciating the present as Will was suggesting. Consequently, her uncertainty continues as they approach the end of the semester. They had both agreed to miss their last scheduled weekend visit and now they've just agreed to miss the one coming up. It's crunch time for both of them, with exams and papers coming due, and they're both stressed out and needing to work.

It seemed like a good idea at the time, but now Emily misses him and starts thinking (Oh no! Emotion mind is taking over and she's getting ready to repeat her pattern), "This is exactly what it's always going to be like. I'm an absolute idiot to think things will be different if I move there. He'll be in medical school, and there's going to be no time for me. And what if I can't find a job I really like?" She texts him:

Emily: Playing "he loves me, he loves me not" again—haven't played it in so long. Tell me something reassuring.

Will: You are in my head every day. Every night I think about you when I go to bed and every morning I'm thinking about you and wanting to see your face. That happens every day.

Emily: Thank you, Baby. Your words are all I can hold on to right now.

Will's words are helpful, but she's still uncertain about whether she should move to be with him.

The next morning, Will and Emily text each other:

Will: Hope your day is going well. Love you and miss you.

Emily: Me too, but still struggling about the move.

Will calls Emily right away:

Will: Are you okay? What's going on?

Emily: I don't know. I'm afraid that even if I move there I'll still feel the way I feel now.

Will: If you move here we'll be together, and you'll be building your career while I'm in school. Things will be better for us, and you'll be busy too.

Emily: I hope that's the case, but look what we just did—canceled two visits with each other because of how busy we are.

Will: I thought you were okay with that.

Emily: I thought so too, but I guess I was angry that we didn't make time for each other, and I didn't realize how it was affecting me. I'm worried about how this is going to be any different when we're together.

Will: For one thing, we'll wake up each morning together. We can cuddle and kiss before I leave for class, and we'll be able to eat dinner together the nights I don't have class. And then we'll be in bed together every night.

Emily: Huh, I guess I hadn't thought about that.

Will: Plus, you'll be working in a great job, and running out to spin class at the awesome gym we have here, and going for drinks with the new friends you're going to make.

Emily: You're so optimistic. I guess I worry what if those things don't happen for me and then I'm there with no life of my own.

Will: Well, if they don't, I'll help you make whatever changes you need to make to get what you want. I want you to be happy. That will make me happy too. I want you to have your own life. Just like you do now. I love that you have career goals. I love that we spend time with your friends, and we'll make that happen here too.

Emily: Okay—that's sweet of you.

Will: (*He can hear the sadness in her voice.*) Em, tell me what you need right now. If you want me to come out there and spend time together, I will find a way to come this weekend. Maybe I'll come and we can both just study together. Tell me what you need and I'll do it.

Emily: I don't know. I do feel so much pressure from school, but I also want to connect with you.

Will: I don't want to add to all the pressure on you. I don't need an answer right this minute. But if you want me to come this weekend, I'll find a way.

Emily: Yes, I want you to come. I need you to come. Are you angry at me?

Will: No, I can understand. This is the longest we haven't physically seen each other, and I miss you too.

Emily: But you hate drama.

Will: But I love you. I know this is your process sometimes. And I accept that. You're so important to me.

"I'm important to him," she thinks. "That is exactly what I want." But Emily's scared because she doesn't always feel important to Will, and she knows it's a key need for her. When she thinks about whether she should move to be with Will, her heart says, "Yes," but her head says, "I'm not sure." She needs to find that wise mind space, where she can really make sense of what's going on and figure out what to do. To deal with her uncertainty, she also needs to stay in the present moment and make the best decision she can based on the accumulated evidence. She turns to the "He knows and likes me" needs questions and really tries to answer them with evidence using her heart and her head. Here's what she came up with:

Needs	He knows and likes me. (He wants what I have to offer, and he treats me in a way that shows he likes and respects me.)	Yes	No	Not sure
What he needs				
Familiar	Does he know my best and worst traits? Does he understand how they make me who I am, influence how I act, and affect the way I get my needs met?	X		
Authentic	Am I fully open to showing all aspects of myself and to facing whatever fears I have about doing so?	X		
Attracted	Does he like my physical appearance just as it is without wanting it to change?	X		
Desire	Does he want to be sexual with me, and can he comfortably tell me about his sexual interests and needs?	X		
Interesting	Is he interested in my life (whatever it happens to be), and does he want to be part of it?			X
Support	Am I his go-to person in good times and bad times?	X		
How he treats me				
Care	Is he attuned to my feelings, and does he respond in a helpful rather than hurtful way?	X		
Listen	Does he hear what I am expressing and what I mean and use it to understand me?			X
Important	Does he consider and value my needs in his choices?			X
Trust	Does he trust in my availability, consistency, and commitment and trust that I will not treat him in whatever way would be considered a betrayal in the relationship?	X		

Needs	He knows and likes me. (He wants what I have to offer, and he treats me in a way that shows he likes and respects me.)	Yes	No	Not sure
Accept	Can he let me be who I am and not try to change me or make me into something I'm not, don't want to be, or can't be?	Χ		
Forgive	Does he forgive me for mistakes I've acknowledged and move on?	Χ		
Help	Is he willing to respond to my requests for help with things I have to do?	Χ		
Safe	Does he make choices that help keep me emotionally, physically, and practically safe?	Χ		

Answering these questions helped Emily do three things: (1) use her "Not sure" answers as insight to see why she's confused about her decision; (2) describe her relationship as it really is, using clear, concrete language; and (3) be clear on her key needs.

First, Emily's "Not sure" answers are evidence of her confusion, particularly for the need to be important to him. Will is largely attentive to her needs and factors them into his choices, but when school needs arise they always take priority. This is painful for Emily. Her heart tells her this does not feel good. But then her head tells her there is a reality to Will's choices. If he wants to become a doctor, he's got to do what he's doing. Can she tolerate that? And will it be different when they're living together, or will he always put his career ahead of her? That's an important question, and she realizes that when she talked to Will about this what he said made sense. He's right: she'll carve out her own life in a new city instead of relying on him to fill up her time. She'll grab a spin class before work and go for drinks after work with her new friends. That's what she wants for herself anyway. She just forgets it when she gets insecure about Will. As for moving again after medical school, at least she'll have a lot more experience, and maybe at that time they can make some more solid plans for the future. She sees she's kind of obsessed about planning for the future. She has to remember she can't plan everything out now.

As she thinks this through, she remembers that she's actually already made a plan for taking care of herself, at least financially, if her relationship doesn't work out. Having problem-solved one of her worst fears makes her less concerned about being certain that Will can prioritize her and that moving is the right thing. She starts to think maybe it's worth taking the risk. Tolerance-of-uncertainty skills at work!

Next, Emily tries to get really clear on how she would describe her relationship by building a "He knows and likes me" paragraph using her "Yes," "No," and "Not sure" answers, making sure she captures her key needs: a guy who's interested in her life, who cares about her feelings, who wants her to be his go-to person, and especially who shows her she's important to him:

> He knows the best and worst of me—that's for sure! He's attracted to me, desires me, and accepts me; he's interested in sharing in my life—he keeps telling me so and showing me so when we're together—it's only my own insecurities that make me forget this; he listens to me so much better now than before—maybe not always, but I can deal with that; he definitely cares about me; and I mostly let him deeply see me—I guess that's something I need to work on, not him. He's really trying to treat me as if I'm important to him—and it's easier now that I've given up my pet want! Still, it's probably going to be an ongoing issue we both have to work on. And even though I'd like him to turn to me more, I really am his go-to person—I know that if he's going to go to anyone it's going to be me, and I've seen him get better and better at this over time.

She stops there and reads the paragraph. She realizes, "I think my key needs are getting met. Will is definitely investing time to meet my needs. He literally told me he'd do whatever I need, and when I asked him to come visit, he did. He's trying to find that balance between his ambition and his love for me. That's hard work, but it's clear he's working at it, and that really tells me that I am what he wants. That I am important to him." And when she says it, because it's based in the evidence, she says it with personal power. And she says it from wise mind. Her head and her heart have both informed her assessment, and it feels right.

Emily then builds her "I know and like him" needs paragraph to make sure her key needs for this perspective (interesting, trust, and accept) are met:

> I know the best and worst of him. I'm attracted to him and I desire him. I'm interested in sharing his life with him (and I will build my own interesting life so that I'm not just the med-school girlfriend waiting around for him). I listen to him and treat him with care and show him that he's important to me. He mostly lets me deeply see him—he's working on that too. He mostly is available for me when I need support—another thing he's working on and has gotten so much better at. I'm working on trusting him and accepting him. Again, it's my insecurities that get in the way of that, and I have to be better at dealing with them.

"Yes," thinks Emily, "I really do know and like Will. We've both got stuff to work on, but we're doing it, and things keep getting better. Can I be certain of where things will go? No, but at this point all the data [as evidenced in the changes she and Will have made to better meet their own and the other's needs] show that things have gotten better." Her self-talk has personal power again; it comes from the evidence. Emily can now be clear on her key needs and whether they're getting met, and with the kind of self-talk she engaged in above, she's better able to tolerate the uncertainty of the future. Emily recognizes her relationship with Will is growing more mutual, and this lets her develop further insight into whether she can trust him to find that balance between his ambition and his love for her. She can't build a healthy relationship on her own; it takes two people who want to meet each other's needs. She's noticed Will has been opening up to her more, like being honest about how he sees the future going. This helps her feel more secure about trusting that he will prioritize her and also feel more safe in talking with him directly about how he might do that. Emily's plan has always been to be who she is and to let Will be who he is, and then see if they can both feel secure in the kind of relationship they're building. The plan seems to be working. Although she's aware there are no guarantees about the future, Emily now believes the evidence suggests it's worth taking the risk of moving forward with the relationship. She knows that to be emotionally close to Will while retaining her own identity, she'll have to practice regulating her feelings when he needs to study, and she'll need to take care of herself and live her own interesting life so she doesn't feel dependent on him. She knows she'll need to stay grounded in the evidence rather than insecure self-talk and use both her head and her heart to remain clear on what she's feeling with Will. She knows she'll need to enjoy the present, as Will suggested, rather than be so focused on the uncertainty of the future. And she knows if she uses these skills she'll always make the best decision she can. She calls Will and tells him she's going to make the move.

LEXI AND RYAN

Lexi is struggling to figure out what to do about Ryan's reckless and aggressive behavior. Should she stay with him and try to help him? Should she leave him, as Emily is begging her to do? She knows in her gut something is very wrong, but, as you saw in Chapter 7, she loves him and all the good things in their relationship—the affection, the intimacy, the spontaneity, the fun they have together, that sense of family they have. So far, Lexi has been listening only to her heart. She's let her emotions (love of Ryan, fear that he will not be okay without her, and guilt if anything were to happen to him) rule her decisions. Lexi needs to cultivate wise mind. Fortunately, Emily is helping out:

Emily: I'm just trying to understand all of this with you. What are you going to do?

Lexi: Lately, everything's been good. There's only a problem when he gets really drunk or uses coke and it doesn't happen that frequently.

Emily: Have you said, "No drinking, no coke, or you have to go?"

Lexi: No, I don't want to do that.

Emily: Why not?

Lexi: Because I don't really want him to go. I want to be with him.

Emily: You have to set some limits. How can you accept how he treats you—driving drunk, bruising your arm, throwing noodles at you, spending his rent money? What's he going to do next? How are you going to protect yourself?

Lexi: If he could just lay off the coke. I can handle it if he just drinks beer sometimes.

Emily: That's ridiculous. He clearly is not able to control his drinking and drug use. You could get really hurt!

Lexi: Look, he's really sorry when he does crazy stuff, and I see him trying to do his best. Maybe he can control it.

Emily: And maybe he can't. C'mon, think clearly about this. I think you should ask him to move out until he gets his act together. You need to keep yourself safe.

Lexi: I'm not going to do that. I want to be with him, and I want to help him.

Emily: If you really want to help him, you'll make him see a counselor. That way you can find out how serious this is, and maybe he'll be willing to get treatment.

Lexi: Maybe you're right. I think Ryan and I have a chance at making our relationship work, and if it works it's going to be really good. I want to do everything I can to try to make it work, and you're right, it's not working with him the way it is now.

Emily: Will you at least consider staying with your family until you can be sure he's sober?

Lexi: I really don't want to leave him, but I get your point that I need to be safe.

After this conversation, Lexi does some research. She Googles "substance abuse" and finds all kinds of useful information about what it is and how important it is to get treatment. This strengthens her reasonable mind. She doesn't know whether Ryan will go for it, but she realizes she has to try. He gives her the perfect opportunity.

That very night she wakes up in the middle of the night to find Ryan and Matthew in the living room drinking and snorting coke. A screaming match ensues. Recognizing that she needs to keep herself safe, she grabs her purse and keys and goes to her parents' house to sleep. Remembering her conversation with Emily, she sends him a text, saying, "I'm not coming back until this all stops. I mean it."

In the morning Ryan texts: "Honey, I love you so much—I can't make that go away. I'm SORRY. No more drugs, I PROMISE. Without you nothing matters in my life. I miss your touch, your love, and your voice. I can't get you out of my head. Please I still trust you to never stop loving me, nobody leaves, together forever. I belong with you. You belong with me. I love you.

Lexi replies, again remembering Emily's words for strength. She sends a text that she really means: "Well, then you need to stop drinking and using drugs and you need to see a counselor. If you agree, I'll come back. If not, we're done. I'm serious."

Ryan responds: "Anything for you. Please come back!"

And she does, and she holds him to his promise.

They've been going to counseling together weekly, and Ryan's stopped drinking and using drugs and started going to AA meetings. Just as Emily has been doing, the counselor is helping Lexi see that she has to be clear about her limits. She's already told Ryan, on Emily's absolute insistence, that if she sees any evidence of drinking, drugs, or aggressive behavior, she's going to stay with her parents until he stops (she's so hoping she doesn't have to do this). To further define her limits, Lexi has to get clear on her key needs and whether they're being met. She goes back and looks at the needs assessment that Emily encouraged her to do.

She already knows for sure that one of her key needs is to be interested in sharing Ryan's life with him. She is, but not the substance abuse and aggression part of it. "So," she thinks, "I guess that's a limit. I don't want to share that part of his life, so if he's going to do that stuff, I can't stay around for it. When he's doing that stuff, I just feel scared. Huh, that really fits with the fact that he's not really keeping me safe, and I'm not keeping myself safe either. I knew that in my gut, but I didn't listen. I have to listen now. I have to make my safety a priority. I guess that's another reason why if he uses drugs and alcohol I'm going to need to go."

And the list of unmet key needs grows. "He can't support me when he's drunk or high. I really need him to be my go-to person. I need someone who is reliably available. Ryan's not anymore. And it's so important for me to be able to accept the person I'm with. Maybe I'm too accepting? Maybe it's actually bad for Ryan and me for me to be so accepting. I mean, who am I kidding? I can't accept his behavior. I guess that's another reason to set limits."

Lexi now sees her key needs are not being met consistently because of Ryan's drinking and drug use, and she has to make a decision about exactly what limits to set. She really believes if Ryan can stay sober they can have a healthy relationship because of how great things are when he's not drinking or using drugs. She loves him so much and she knows he loves her. Once they took a passionate love test they found online, and this was their result:

> Wildly, recklessly in love. When men and women are wildly in love, they can't stop thinking about the other, their hearts pound, their pulses race, and they find it impossible to keep away from the objects of their desire—even when pursuit is dangerous or foolish.

They both agreed that's them. And they can't keep their hands off one another. Just the other day when she walked in the door from work Ryan was waiting for her:

Ryan: I want to make love to you.
Lexi: I want you to make love to me.
　　(They race each other to the bed.)
Ryan: (*kissing her deeply*) I love you. You're the love of my life.
Lexi: You lying on top of me skin to skin like this—I ache for this all day.
Ryan: Shush (*as he twirls her nipples*), do you like that?
Lexi: Yes!
Ryan: What else?
Lexi: You know what I want! (*laughing*)
　　(He pulls her on top of him.)

Afterwards they order Chinese food, talk about plans for some hiking adventures they want to take, and watch their favorite show while cuddling on the couch. She's thinking, "He's my best friend, my other half, the love of my life—we can do this!"

Indeed, when Ryan's not drinking or using drugs, Lexi's excited to be around him and wants to share in his life. She wants to go to him when she has a problem and she also wants to keep him safe and help him—and she wants to give him a chance.

She also knows she's got to be clear about what behaviors she won't tolerate and what the consequences will be if those behaviors persist. She talks it over with Emily. It's really hard to figure out. She knows this is going to be a difficult journey for Ryan. As much as she wants him to be sober, she understands it's really he who has to want to. She also knows she needs to keep herself safe. She's tried so hard to keep him safe, but she's starting to realize she can't make his choices for him; she can't keep him out of the danger he creates himself. (For more on this, see the sidebar on page 230.) For instance, she can't make him get out of the car when he's drunk. In fact, she can't stop him from drinking before he gets in the car. He's the only one who can do that. And she can only take care of herself, for example, by not getting in the car with him. So her bottom line is "If he does anything where I can't keep myself safe, I'm leaving him."

Lexi now knows for sure her limits include that Ryan stay completely sober—she used to think it would be okay for him to drink beer, but she knows that's not an option anymore. Her limits also include that he continue to go to counseling and AA regularly. He has to show her he is willingly and actively engaging in his own recovery and that they're doing mutual problem solving to meet the challenges of recovery. She is also setting the limit that Ryan not hang out with Matthew anymore because the

---

I/ME

But I Just Want to Keep Him Safe . . .

In a tweet, presumably about her then husband's substance abuse problem, Khloe Kardashian said, "I would surrender my whole being to see you whole once more."

Sounds nice, but really? Surrendering her whole being equates to sacrificing her needs for his. Not a good idea. It's really important to learn how to set limits and keep yourself safe.

---

counselor said one of the biggest reasons for relapse is continuing to hang out with other people who abuse drugs and alcohol. If Ryan does relapse—which could definitely happen—as long as she feels she can keep herself safe in the situation, like not getting into a car with him or leaving the house so he can't hurt her, then she will give him another chance provided he goes right back to being sober.

Lexi's now using her head, as well as her heart, to make decisions.

I/ME

Where Can I Find Out More about Substance Abuse?

To find out more about substance abuse and what to do if you or your partner has a substance problem, check the following sources:

Substance Abuse and Mental Health Services Administration
www.samhsa.gov/atod

National Institute on Alcohol Abuse and Alcoholism
www.niaaa.nih.gov

National Institute on Drug Abuse
www.drugabuse.gov

HelpGuide.org
www.helpguide.org/articles/addiction/drug-abuse-and-addiction.htm
www.helpguide.org/articles/addiction/alcoholism-and-alcohol-abuse.htm

National Council on Alcoholism and Drug Dependence
https://ncadd.org/learn-about-alcohol/alcohol-abuse-self-test

She's using her love and compassion for Ryan to give him a chance, and she's using her awareness of her unmet needs and the dangerous reality of the situation to set clear limits. She's acting from a place of wise mind and feels more confident in her decision. "If he respects my limits by staying sober, I will stay. If he doesn't, I will go."

But she's still scared and having to deal on a daily basis with the uncertainty of the situation. "Will today be the day he has a relapse? What will I actually do if that happens? How will I get him to leave my apartment? Who will help me make this all happen?" These are important questions, and to deal with the uncertainty Lexi needs to make a plan. To problem-solve in advance. To determine the worst-case scenario and figure out how she'll cope. That way, if it happens, she's ready. She also needs to develop and use some healthy self-statements, things like "Worrying about whether he's going to relapse will not make it less likely to happen. I'm doing what I can to support him. His sobriety is his decision. If he relapses, I'll follow my plan. If he can't stay sober, he's not the guy for me. I will make it through this." Doing so will help Lexi tolerate the uncertainty and be prepared to follow through on her decision. Finally, if Ryan does stay sober, Lexi will still need to continually assess whether her needs are being met to make sure all "the good stuff" is still really there and worth staying for, just as she would need to do in any relationship.

Mia and Corey

Corey's moved back, and he and Mia are living together again. In so many ways, it's the way it used to be. They're in love. They're excited to be in each other's life every day, supporting and helping one another with things they have to do. And they're having great sex. Many of Mia's key needs are being met. But they've got past hurts to work through, and the saga of whether to have an open relationship is ongoing. Can Mia make this relationship work for her?

They're working on repairing breaches of trust in a mutual way. For example, when Corey first moved back they had the following conversation:

Mia: Did you always use a condom with OtherWoman?
Corey: Yes.
Mia: C'mon, we both need to be honest here.
Corey: No, toward the end, right before I left, no, I didn't.
Mia: How many times?
Corey: Maybe two or three times. Did you?
Mia: Me too, a couple times at the end.
     (They sit in silence for a minute, upset with themselves and each other.)

Corey: We need to both go get tested.

Mia: I know. This really sucks. Hopefully, neither one of us brought home an STI. How would we know it was me, not you?

Corey: We'd never know, and we can't let that matter.

Mia: You're right. We both didn't practice safe sex, so we both need to take responsibility and be in this together. No blaming.

Corey: Yes, we need to move forward together in this.

The next morning they are both pretty shaken up but happy it's all out in the open so they can really move forward in their relationship. They go together to the free clinic and have their STI/HIV testing done.

They're also working on negotiating whether they will continue to have an open relationship. Neither was sure as they were planning for Corey's move back. They decided not to talk with OtherGuy and Other-Woman for a month to see how that felt and then figure it out from there. OtherGuy totally understood the situation. He and Mia had already planned to message only occasionally once Corey returned, just to see how the other was doing. OtherWoman also thought it was a good idea, although she let Corey know she would be happy to keep the relationship going. During that month, Mia had grown to like the comfort and safety of it just being her and Corey. She missed some of the erotic excitement, but she didn't miss the stress of jealousy and distrust that came with it. Neither did Corey, but he did miss OtherWoman:

Corey: I miss being friends with OtherWoman. Are you comfortable with that or do you want me to not talk to her anymore? She knows I left to be with you. She knows I'm committed to you.

Mia: I'm comfortable with you being friends. She was an important part of your life, and when we were having difficulty she was a great support to us.

Corey: Okay, thank you. I appreciate that. Are you going to stay friends with Other-Guy?

Mia: Yeah, kind of. We're just planning on keeping in touch to see how things are going with each of us. I never had an emotional connection with him the way you did with OtherWoman.

The next month Corey lets Mia know that he and OtherWoman are having a hard time just being friends:

Corey: We can't just be friends. The attraction is still there, and it's hard to manage. And we can't even have the same kind of conversations we used to have because I don't want to hurt you, break a limit, go beyond the boundary of friendship.

Mia: Okay, I'm glad you're being honest with me. I don't know what to say, though.

What do you want here? Are you asking me if you can be in an open long-distance relationship with her?

Corey: Yes.

Mia: Okay. (*She tries to breathe.*) Do you love her?

Corey: Yes.

Mia: You've said in the past that you loved her but weren't in love with her.

Corey: I guess I am in love with OtherWoman. I am absolutely in love with you too.

Mia: What's changed? You've said you don't believe one person can be in love with two people. Are you less monogamous than you believed you were?

Corey: Yes, I guess maybe I am. You're just different women. You have different interests, and I have different conversations and experiences with both of you. She and I have talked about people who have polyamorous relationships, like she does, and I'm starting to realize I have a lot of the same feelings.

Mia: So you want to be with both of us then.

Corey: Yes, but I've told her if you're not happy with that, then I can't do it.

Mia: I appreciate that, but how would you feel if I said no?

Corey: It would be very difficult for me if I had to stop contact with her.

Mia: What would that mean for us? How could I ask you to stop contact with her? I'd be feeling every day you were missing something and unhappy with me. Isn't that how you'd feel?

Corey: I don't know. I know this is hard. Why don't you take a couple days to think about it to see if you're okay with it, and then we'll talk more?

Mia: You know if you asked me to marry you right now, I'd say "No."

Corey: That's why I'm going to wait before I ask you, until I'm sure you'll answer "Yes!"

Mia is confused. She doesn't know what to think. Corey still wants to marry her. It makes her trust in his commitment when he talks like that. But he would want an open marriage. "Could I do that?" she wonders.

As we said in Chapter 6, that's exactly one of the questions Mia needs to answer. It's hard for her. She's been very focused on whether she could give Corey what he wants because she cares about him and he is important to her. For her, it follows logically that she would let him have what he

I/ME

Why Isn't Mia Freaking Out about Corey Loving OtherWoman?

Because she's using the skills. She's regulating her emotions, she's trying to understand Corey, and she's working on being mutual. In addition, Mia may be okay with Corey loving both her and OtherWoman. Someone else might not be okay with this, and that's fine. It's all about knowing what's right for you.

wants (there goes reasonable mind!). She figures they could plan it all out, like they did before, with limits and such. But then she remembers that didn't work the first time. Something has to go differently this time.

Mia turns to her key needs. For "He knows and likes me," she thinks, "He definitely knows me, but my need to be authentic with him has hurt him. I need to talk with him more about that. It's definitely a key need for me, and I need to see where he is with it. He wants to share in my life, and it's clear to me that I'm his go-to person. He's attracted to me, desires me (though not only me—Hmm . . .), and helps me with everything. But he hasn't trusted me. We're working on that, though. We both want to regain trust."

For "I know and like him," she thinks, "I definitely know him, and he's very authentic with me. I really appreciate and respect that. I love having sex with him, and now that he's here he's totally my go-to person. I always consider his needs in my choices—maybe too much even! And I'm always happy to help him out. It's really important that I want to share in his life, and I do, but do I want to share in the open-relationship life, especially one that involves an emotional connection, not just sex? I guess that's the question."

"Do I want an open relationship, a polyamorous one, in fact?" Mia knows she has to figure this out—it's her own "I know and like myself" desire need. She feels like she used to know, but along the way, with new experiences, things have changed. She was always open to casual sex. Then she met Corey, and suddenly monogamy seemed right, but with the free passes—as difficult as they were to negotiate—she learned that she liked the excitement of them. Right now she's feeling more monogamous, but who's to say that won't change again? People evolve, after all. Maybe in the future she'll also want another OtherGuy. She can see how having the option to look, flirt, and do what she wants—even if she doesn't act on it—could make things exciting for her. "But only if Corey and I can both be open and honest with each other so we can stay connected and really trust one another. And I guess I have to figure out whether I'm okay with the emotional connection. I can deal with the sex. In fact, it turns me on. But can I share his love? I better think about that more."

In saying this, Mia knows she needs to pay attention and listen to her gut (she's bringing in emotion mind). "If I'm honest with myself, I know I couldn't handle his emotional connection to OtherWoman before. What makes me think I can do it now? I was so jealous. I guess I need to ask myself what I was jealous of. I think I kept feeling like he would leave me for her, that she was more important than me. But he moved back to be with me. He's living with me and wants to marry me. Maybe I don't really have anything to be afraid of."

Mia is doing excellent insight work and really trying to look at the evidence in her relationship. Rather than go with her impulse to just make a plan to do it for him, she's slowing herself down, considering her feelings, and trying to listen to her gut. She's moving toward a place of wise mind. She decides to talk with Corey about her feelings and questions.

Mia: I'm ready to talk more about you wanting an open relationship. I haven't decided yet whether I can be okay with it. I mean, I want to for you, but I want to be sure that I'm really taking into account what's most important to me. Do you understand?

Corey: Yes, I do.

Mia: I guess my first question is whether you would be okay with me having other relationships too.

Corey: Multiple ones? (*laughing*)

Mia: (*laughing*) No, you know what I mean. I mean looking, flirting, maybe having a casual hookup relationship sometime.

Corey: I don't know. I get so jealous.

Mia: I thought you said you were only jealous because you weren't here with me. That it was hard for you knowing about it because we were far apart.

Corey: You're right. I did say that. I guess I don't know what it would be like for me. Can I think about that?

Mia: Yes, definitely, but I want you to know that I do think it will be important for me to have that freedom if you're going to be in a relationship with OtherWoman. And also—I've really thought about this—it will be very important for me to be able to be open and honest with you about any relationships I have. I need to be with someone who wants me to be authentic. I'm sure of that. I can't imagine that I'm ever going to feel comfortable having to keep quiet about such an intimate part of our lives. If this is going to hurt you, then we're not going to be able to work this out.

Corey: Wow. Okay. I see you've really thought about this. I really don't want to lose you.

Mia: I don't want to lose you either, but I also don't want to repeat what happened with the free passes. We hurt each other. We set limits and broke them, and broke our trust. I don't want to do that again.

Corey: I don't either.

Mia: What kind of relationship do you ultimately want?

Corey: I don't know. I know I want a future with you, though.

Mia: How is this going to work? Are you always going to want to be in a relationship with OtherWoman?

Corey: I don't know. I don't feel I can predict with any accuracy what type of relationship I'll want in the future with you. Can you?

Mia: I see what you mean. We each had a very traditional monogamous view about our relationship prior to the free pass idea.

Corey: (*He pauses, thinking.*) What if we do a trial run? But we try to do it differently this time. What if we both focus on letting each other have what they want and seeing how it feels, rather than setting limits. Like we both can have an open relationship and you tell me everything. And maybe you can help me figure out how to handle it.

Mia: And you help me see that your emotional connection to OtherWoman doesn't hurt our connection and commitment?

Corey: Yes. I don't know what's going to happen, but maybe we can see if we can help each other through this to see if it works.

Mia: I think that's a good idea. It might be hard, Corey. We're going to need to really be on the same page. It's kind of exciting and kind of scary. It's like I want to know for sure what's going to happen, but I guess we can't be certain. Let's just promise each other we're going to listen to what we're feeling and what the other is feeling, and if it doesn't work, we have to just be honest about that.

Corey: Okay. I agree.

Mia: And just one more thing. I want you to always use a condom with OtherWoman. That's a limit for me. I wouldn't be able to be with you if you didn't help keep me safe. I'm serious.

Cory: I totally agree. I'll definitely do that, and you too, okay? I want you to use one too outside of this relationship.

Mia: Agreed.

By examining her key needs and being open to listening to her gut, Mia was able to approach the situation from a place of wise mind. Not only that, she used the I/ME skills very successfully to be direct and clear about her needs and to work with Corey in a more mutual problem-solving manner. Now Mia and Corey will have plenty more work to do and plenty of uncertainty to tolerate. What will they learn about whether they can handle the open relationship? How will their desire needs evolve? Will they be able to stay together? They don't know, and they can't predict. However, they seem committed to focusing on the reality of how things are, staying in the present moment and making decisions on the existing evidence, taking the risk to see if they can make the relationship work, and being prepared to end it if necessary. In an uncertain situation, that's the best they can do, and if they continue to use the I/ME skills they'll be able to make whatever future decisions are needed.

JULIANNE AND GREGORY

The clock is ticking. Julianne has to decide whether she wants to marry Gregory. She's been putting it off (a sign, perhaps?), and Gregory is feeling hurt and impatient. The fact of the matter is that despite all the good things—they're totally on the same page about work, he's so excited to be

─── I/ME ───

What Do You Think about Monogamy?

Different people have different views on it. What's important is that you know what yours are and use the skills if you have to deal with issues of nonmonogamy and jealousy.

If you're interested in learning about different perspectives on monogamy, here are some things to read or listen to:

This American Life, hosted by Ira Glass (*www.thisamericanlife.org/radio-archives/episode/95/transcript*):

> Today in our program, monogamy and its discontents. Stories of people struggling to redefine monogamy, to stay monogamous, and what we should make of these ad hoc experiments in everyday life. Today, we hear case examples. Act One, Scientific Experiment, the story of a couple, the wife got a crush on another man, and how they tried to contain the crush, channel the crushy feeling, and what happens when you apply rational ideas to irrational feelings. Act Two, Love and Happiness. Dan Savage talks to real nonmonogamous couples, who explain whether they're actually happy and why it might be OK to see other partners, but only if it happens in other time zones. Act Three, Istanbul. Ian Brown talks about the experience that most of us have struggling to stay monogamous, and what we should think of that struggle.

Dan Savage, in his talk "Why Monogamy Is Ridiculous" (*www.youtube.com/watch?v=w8SOQEitsJI*), talks about his belief that people need to have more realistic attitudes about sexual exclusivity. An excerpt:

> . . . if you're with somebody for 40 or 50 years and they only cheated on you a few times they were good at being monogamous, not bad at being monogamous . . .

Read the article "Why You Shouldn't [and Should] Be Monogamous" (*http://bigthink.com/against-the-new-taboo/why-you-shouldnt-and-should-be-monogamous*) for a discussion of the difference between nonmonogamy and betrayal.
An excerpt:

> Being nonmonogamous is not about being better or worse than monogamous couples: it's about what works for you as individuals and as a couple. For example, it would be wrong for you to have multiple partners beyond your primary partner without her consent or approval. Again, this would be unethical nonmonogamy and therefore betrayal.

with her, they have fun together—they haven't been able to see that they both have to work toward mutual acceptance.

For example, it's Sunday evening. They both had to work all weekend. They've just had a nice romp (finally, he felt like having sex!) and eaten takeout, and she's helping him pack for his next business trip. He's catching the red-eye later tonight. As she's folding one of his shirts (just so—the way he likes it), she thinks about how much she's going to miss cuddling him all week, until:

Gregory: Look! My suits can't lie flat in the new suitcase you bought me!

Julianne: We have others in the storage area. I'll go grab another one to try.

Gregory: The one you threw out, with the rip on the back—why did you do that?

Julianne: I checked with you before I got rid of it!

Gregory: You shouldn't have done that. You're always so quick to throw things out. My suits will be wrinkled by the time I get there.

Julianne: I hate clutter. You know that. We have a suit bag—take that.

Gregory: Why would I do that? It'll be difficult to walk around the airport with. Why would you even suggest that?

Julianne: Okay, when you get to the hotel, run a tub full of hot water and hang up your suits. It'll take all the wrinkles out.

Gregory: I'm really upset that you threw that suitcase out.

Julianne: (She cuts him off.) Enough! Why is everything my fault? Pack yourself!

As she storms out of the room, Julianne thinks, "And the best part will be the next time we're out with friends he'll nonchalantly drop how he wrapped up the company's merger with a wrinkled suit. They'll ask why, and he'll blame me. I know him. He does it every time."

While Gregory's away Julianne takes a look at their relationship. From the beginning, she didn't know how to tell whether they were meant to be, but she feels that by moving in with Gregory she implicitly committed to a future she's not even sure she wants. That was not a conscious decision. Worse, in hindsight she can see moving in together furthered her own commitment to Gregory's ultimate goal of marriage and children. At this point she feels so much pressure to say yes because saying no would blindside not only Gregory but their families and friends. If they both didn't work so much, maybe they wouldn't be together. If they didn't already live together, maybe they wouldn't still be together. But she thinks getting married is just the next logical step. She's sliding rather than deciding. And yet she's unhappy and she knows it. "What am I going to do?!"

On the one hand, she thinks to herself, "I manage a team, work insane hours to deal with obscene workloads and deadlines. I travel a lot, and I absolutely love my job. I don't even have a lot of time for Gregory. Yet he loves me. He still wants to share in my life. He's as ambitious, engaged, and high-achieving as I am, and we both really like this life–work balance. Who else am I going to get this with?"

On the other hand, she sees that her patience for his critical, controlling behavior is running out. In the past, she's always made sure to treat Gregory's needs as important. Now she finds herself less able to do so. She thinks, "My needs aren't important to him, so why should his be important to me?" For instance, they're supposed to be going to his mother's birthday dinner when he gets back. Normally she would be looking forward to going and would have everything organized. Now she's dreading it, thinking, "I don't care if this is important to him. I'd rather stay home and do what I want." That's not who she is, but it's who she's becoming. Up to now, when she's worked on really listening to what's underneath Gregory's criticisms, she's felt good when she's been able to meet his needs and make him happy, like folding the corners on the bedsheets the way he likes so he sleeps through the night (that's mutuality steps 1 and 2). Now she just feels angry and resentful (she can't get to step 3). Even when he brings something up that makes sense, she doesn't want to do it. She just yells "ENOUGH!" or "Shut the fuck up!" That is not her, but that's how she's been treating Gregory (she's tried to work on mutuality steps 4 and 5, but she's so frustrated because they can't get to step 6!).

Up to this point, Julianne has been stuck on listening to her head— "It's the next logical step to marry him" (reasonable mind gone awry). But that's not fully conscious decision making. She's ignored her feelings to the point where she's behaving in ways that are completely out of character for her (she's the type of person who generally does what's expected of her). She sees that she's acting out of character, but she hasn't yet put two and two together to realize that her emotions and her gut are screaming at her to pay attention to them. Julianne also has gotten caught up in the fears that come with uncertainty—"Who else am I going to get this with?" (in other words, "Who else will ever love and accept my ambition and work life?"). These fears are getting in the way of her making a fully conscious healthy decision based on the evidence of whether she's getting her needs met.

Julianne has a long talk with Lauren, who is surprised by how Julianne has been behaving:

Lauren: I've known you a long time, and you've never treated anyone that way. That's a sign.

Julianne: I guess it's just—I don't know. When he criticizes me or blames me for something I have to say to myself, "He's critical, that's who he is, and it's about him, not me." Maybe I have to try harder, be more patient.

Lauren: Seriously? You think you need to be more patient?

Julianne: Maybe?

Lauren: Why is it you who has to do all the changing?

Julianne: I know. That's how I feel sometimes! But he's impossible. He just won't see things any way but his way. I can never get him to see my perspective.

Lauren: You need to think about what you just said and whether you want to live with that your whole life.

Julianne: Yes, but I do want a relationship, and how will I find someone else? Who's going to want to deal with my working so much?

Lauren: You found Gregory, didn't you? There are other men out there like him.

Julianne: Maybe—but imagine what he's going to say about me.

Lauren: What?

Julianne: He'll blame me for this!

Lauren: Who cares? Let him say what he wants. You're talking about marriage. About a commitment. About the rest of your life. Not his.

Julianne: It's just so hard to make this decision.

Lauren: I know it's hard. I've got to go to class now, but will you promise me you'll think about our conversation? Think about what you really need?

Julianne: Yes, I will.

And so she does. Over the next few days, while Gregory is still away, she thinks, "What do I really need?" She starts with "He knows and likes me" to see if he wants what she has to offer and treats her in a way that shows he likes and respects her. It's hard for her. She goes over and over it in her head, trying to listen and face the things she's afraid of. She finally develops some insight. She thinks, "Well, I'm not sure he really knows me. He's labeled me an overorganized freak. That shows he doesn't understand that part of me. And I'm not sure he really wants to be sexually intimate with me, at least not as much as I'd like. He is interested in my life. He's made that clear. And I am his go-to person. But I don't think he really listens to me, and he certainly doesn't consistently consider my needs in his choices. And he definitely doesn't accept me for who I am, in so many ways. And that's the thing that's really getting to me. That's what's making me treat him so poorly."

For "I know and like him," she thinks, "I definitely know his best and worst traits, that's for sure. He's been authentic with me, which I appreciate, and I'm attracted to him, but I definitely can't share what sex and intimacy mean to me. That was a disaster when I tried, and now I don't feel safe in that arena. Oh, safe, okay, that's another one I forgot about with 'He knows and likes me.' I've always treated him well in all sorts of ways, and I definitely trust he's committed to our relationship, but not to consistently negotiating with me without criticizing or shooting down all of my ideas, and I guess these days I'm not really listening to him or caring about his feelings or considering his needs as much. I guess that's a sign I'm not treating him as if I like him. I also don't feel like helping him anymore. And it's all because I really just can't accept the way he treats me.

"Ugh. He doesn't accept me for who I am. I don't accept him for who he is. I'm not having the sexual relationship I'd really like. And I'm treating him terribly. This is not a healthy relationship. And he doesn't want to do anything to change or fix the problems. He blames it all on me. This has gone on our entire relationship, and I can't stand it. It doesn't seem that he can even have a mutual relationship. He's got to be right. He's got to be in control. If we get married, this is how it's going to be. I can't marry him."

She calls Lauren:

Julianne: I did what you said. I thought about my needs and my relationship with Gregory.
Lauren: What did you decide?
Julianne: I can't marry him. (*She starts crying.*)
Lauren: (*empathically*) Oh, Julianne, it's going to be okay. You're going to be okay. I'm here for you. So is Anna.
Julianne: I know. You're such good friends. I know you'll support me. I'm just so sad, and so upset. I know it's the right decision, though. When I really looked at what was happening, over the whole relationship, and what it's done to me, I saw how bad things are. How unhealthy this relationship is.
Lauren: It's so good you recognized it now. Imagine if you hadn't. How hard it would've been later.
Julianne: You're so right. But now I have to tell him, and he's going to flip out and get angry and blame me.
Lauren: I know. You'll be okay, though. You have to be strong and remind yourself that it will all be history soon and you'll find a guy that's better for you.
Julianne: Okay, but you're going to have to keep reminding me. It's easy for me to get stuck in thinking, "Will I ever find someone? Can I ever get close to someone again?" and all that stuff.
Lauren: Don't worry. You can count on me to help you get through this.

When they get off the phone, Julianne feels a little better. She's able to use healthy self-talk to help her deal with her uncertainty: "It's okay that I don't know what the future will bring for me. What I do know is that what I have in the present is not healthy and I have to get out of it." She also has a sense of personal power. She took stock of whether her needs were being met in this relationship, and she made a decision that felt right in her gut. She was in wise mind space. That's not to say she isn't still sad and nervous about the breakup. She is, but she knows she has to exit.

That night when Gregory gets home from his business trip, she tells him. She tries to explain to him how neither of them is getting their needs met and how a relationship must be based on acceptance and mutuality, but he is too upset to hear her. He reacts as she expected—angry, blaming, trying to convince her she's making a big mistake. But she stays strong in her decision. To deal with uncertainty, she's already done some problem solving. She's planned ahead to stay with Lauren for a few days (even though she and Gregory are living in her apartment—she wants to give him time and space to get his own plans in order), and then she is leaving for a weeklong business trip. He agrees he will move out by the time she comes back. As she drives to Lauren's she feels more and more confident in her wise mind decision.

In this chapter you saw four of the characters use their key needs to make difficult relationship decisions. You saw that although we all have the same needs, we might prioritize them a little differently based on what's most important to us in the context of our current relationship. (For more about this, see the exercise at the end of this chapter.) And you saw how we might not even realize what's key for us until we look carefully and see we're not getting it.

You also saw the characters learn to tolerate uncertainty and come to a place of wise mind to be able to make decisions that felt right to them. These emotion regulation skills are critical to practice when you're faced with hard decisions. Being overly logical, overly emotional, or paralyzed by uncertainty will stop you from being able to see what's best for you and making a fully conscious, healthy decision. Finally, you saw that all the characters made different decisions, but they made ones that were healthy for them in the moment because they focused on the accumulated evidence in their relationships. In the next chapter, we focus on dealing with the aftermath of the hard decisions we make, or that others make for us, and talk about how to cope when your heart is broken.

Exercise: How Do You Prioritize Your Key Needs?

To understand how key needs might differ based on the type of relationship you're in or the status of that relationship, select which needs are priorities for you in the following situations:

1. A casual relationship (for example, hookup, fuck buddy, FWB)

	"I know and like him."	"He knows and likes me."
Familiar		
Authentic		
Attracted		
Desire		
Interesting		
Support		
Care		
Listen		
Important		
Trust		
Accept		
Forgive		
Help		
Safe		

2. A dating relationship in the early stages

	"I know and like him."	"He knows and likes me."
Familiar		
Authentic		
Attracted		
Desire		
Interesting		
Support		
Care		
Listen		
Important		
Trust		
Accept		
Forgive		
Help		
Safe		

(cont.)

3. A committed monogamous relationship where you're planning to marry and have children

	"I know and like him."	"He knows and likes me."
Familiar		
Authentic		
Attracted		
Desire		
Interesting		
Support		
Care		
Listen		
Important		
Trust		
Accept		
Forgive		
Help		
Safe		

4. A committed monogamous relationship with no plans to marry and/or have children

	"I know and like him."	"He knows and likes me."
Familiar		
Authentic		
Attracted		
Desire		
Interesting		
Support		
Care		
Listen		
Important		
Trust		
Accept		
Forgive		
Help		
Safe		

10

Lovesick?

Women need skills to cope successfully with the end of relationships, no matter who initiates the breakup. After a relationship ends we often write and rewrite the story of where things went wrong and whether it had to end. We search for reasons, fault, and mistakes. We question ourselves and our ex's feelings. We get emotional and confused. For some women, this can go on for years. They can get stuck and then repeat the same problematic patterns in the future. This is a terrible outcome. A much better outcome is being able to accept what's happened, learn from it, and move on.

In this chapter, we show you how you can deal with the intense emotions and with the painful lovesickness that accompanies a breakup by:

- Using emotion regulation skills to take care of yourself as you cope with the breakup.
- Using insight skills to focus on what you can learn from your past relationship to use in future decision making.

The deep pain women can feel when a relationship ends is reflected poignantly in an interview about relationship breakups with a woman on the radio program *This American Life* (*www.thisamericanlife.org*). In the first five minutes, as the woman and host Ira Glass take a walk together around her neighborhood, she talks about her experience since the breakup. The transcript on the next page is the first minute or so of their discussion. It will undoubtedly resonate, but even more if, instead of reading the transcript, you listen to the recording at *www.thisamericanlife.org/radio-archives/ episode/339/break-up*.

Woman: It's so embarrassing. I don't want to get upset. But like, he has a car. So the last time I saw him on purpose was just in the car in front of my house. And I don't know. It's just bad.

Ira Glass: Bad like when you walk out of your house you think like, there his car was?

Woman: Yeah. I still look for it. It's crazy.

Ira Glass: Okay. Now, we're about a block from your house.

Woman: Like on that—in front of that building, right there, this like churchy-looking building, was where we were parked when we first had the conversation where we decided we were going to be exclusive, which was a joke. Like I don't really date around. And I don't think he does either. But, you know, it's like kind of a big conversation. But yeah, we were parked in the middle of that block, right where that white car is.

Ira Glass: And so every time you walk down this street, you'll think like, oh yeah, there's the spot?

Woman: I don't walk down this street. I just don't. Like I haven't even seen him for a month. You know what I mean?

We know what she means.

We all do.

Research on the neuroscience of love has provided us with important insights into why we all can relate to this woman's experience. Love can be like an addiction. People in love show activation in the same parts of the brain associated with drug addiction—the reward centers—and people who are in love are motivated to get the reward: their partner's love. So, yes, love is rewarding—it feels *so* good, and we want more of it. When people are rejected, they continue to show activation in these parts of the brain, and also in the same parts of the brain associated with feelings of deep attachment and physical pain. This neurological activity reflects how much they are missing their partner, craving love, and hurting: they want the reward of love, and they are suffering without it. Like going through withdrawal, dealing with the loss of the once rewarding experience of love is physically and emotionally challenging.

That's why the end of a relationship and its consequences can lead to so much negative emotion, emotion that is very difficult to manage. Women can experience anxiety, depression, and even suicidal thoughts and feelings following a breakup. They also may take their feelings as signs that they never should have broken up—"If I feel this way, I must have made the wrong decision. I need to go back/get him back." Remember, in Chapter 7 Lauren says (about Dan), "If I still feel this connection, if I miss him this much, maybe I'm supposed to be with him?" Occasionally these emotions can lead to the insight that the breakup was in fact a poor choice. More often than not, however, acting on these emotions reflects a lack of personal power—a dismissal of unmet needs or violated limits—and will likely prolong the misery as another breakup is almost certain to follow. That's how the breakup/makeup game goes.

If you believe healthy relationships are based on meeting the three needs conditions—the premise of this book—then a breakup means one or both of you couldn't or didn't want to meet the other's needs. *People who can't or don't want to meet each other's needs should not be together. Period.* When you recognize and accept this fact, you can look carefully at which needs weren't met in your relationship and decide on what you really want from the next one. Then you can figure out what you might do differently in the future.

Common Reactions to Lovesickness and How to Deal with Them

Here are seven common reactions to lovesickness that can keep you from healing and moving on, plus ways to use insight and emotion regulation to combat them.

RUMINATING

Rumination involves thinking about what happened over and over, focusing on what-ifs ("What if I hadn't said that? What if I hadn't done that?"), whys ("Why did he break up with me? Why doesn't he care about me?"), and how awful you feel (sad and miserable without him). You think you're going to figure out how to feel better, but ruminating just makes you feel worse by keeping you focused on how bad things are.

Have you ever ruminated after a breakup? What was going through your head?

How did it make you feel?

Combating Rumination

1. *Use mindfulness techniques*. Rumination is all about engaging with one's thoughts. Mindfulness is all about intentionally disengaging—not pushing thoughts away or wishing you didn't have them but simply noticing your thoughts without judging them and then intentionally letting go of them. It's about making a conscious decision not to have the same conversation with yourself over and over again. So every time you find yourself thinking about the what-ifs and whys, and about how bad you feel, you need to catch yourself doing so and just observe. You might say to yourself something like "There I go again, ruminating on why it ended. I just need to let that go. I can't answer that question. All I know is that it's over and thinking about why it ended over and over again is not helping me. It's just making me suffer." This kind of self-talk is hard work and takes lots of practice, but over time it works. In addition, you can choose to direct your attention to something else you want to focus on. The ruminative thoughts may still be in the background, but you can just notice them and return your attention to the task at hand. For example, if you're working or studying and you find yourself having intrusive thoughts, you can catch this happening and tell yourself something like "I'm thinking about him again. I will let those thoughts go and refocus on my work," and then bring your attention back to the task at hand (over and over again as necessary).

2. *Do something else*. Doing something physical, pleasant, or constructive can give you a break from rumination and maybe even help you feel better about yourself. Staying in bed all day won't help you stop ruminating. Getting out and doing other things—working out, showering, seeing friends—just might.

3. *Problem-solve*. Ask yourself, "Is there any problem here that I can solve or any question that I can really answer?" If not—for example, if you're ruminating on what might have happened if . . . —there's no problem to be solved, no question to be answered. If there is a problem to be solved, work on figuring out a realistic solution with clear, feasible steps.

4. *Reflect*. Similar to problem solving, self-reflection involves focusing on concrete aspects of the situation and realistic improvements that you can make. Note that neither self-reflection nor problem solving should involve trying to figure out how to get your ex back. Instead, you should be working on developing insight and learning for the future by reflecting on things you can do differently.

REHASHING WITH FRIENDS

What researchers call *corumination* involves repeating your internal ruminative dialogues out loud with your friends. Your friends can be a great source of support after a breakup, but endless rehashing with them will just keep you focused on how bad things are rather than on how things could change.

Combating the Urge to Rehash

Again, problem solving can help. Recruit a trusted friend or family member who won't let you just go on and on about how bad things are and ask that person to help you figure out realistic solutions to concrete problems—how you're going to get your work done (instead of lying in bed all day), how you're going to deal with seeing him around town (or wherever), and how you're going to pick a better partner in the future.

TRYING TO STOP FEELING BAD

After a breakup, you may feel like you can't possibly stand the sadness and anxiety you're experiencing and that you've got to do something to make those feelings go away. Researchers call this low distress tolerance. You can't make emotions just go away. Trying to do so often amplifies them and makes you feel worse. Now you're not only sad and anxious but also upset about being sad and anxious.

Combating the Urge to Stop Feeling Bad

1. *Use mindfulness.* As with thoughts, you can work toward noticing and accepting the presence of your emotions without judging them or trying to make them go away. You can intentionally direct your attention to other sensations or experiences, letting your emotions recede into the background, even if only momentarily. You can go about your life being aware of your emotions without engaging with them at every moment. And noticing all of your feelings—how your body feels while exercising or how the breeze feels on your skin—can keep your awareness on all of your experience, not just your misery.

2. *Develop new self-talk.* Following from a mindful, accepting approach, you can change "I hate this feeling! I can't live like this! It has to go away!" to "I'm aware of how sad I am. I can't make it go away. Sadness is part of the process for me right now. It's okay. I can live with this." You can remind yourself that feelings are temporary and that you can cope.

3. *Soothe yourself.* You also can take care of yourself and tolerate negative emotion by doing something to engage your senses and make you feel good, comforted, or healthy in the moment—taking a bath, listening to music, exercising, lighting a candle, praying, watching a favorite show. The list of possibilities is endless. What matters is you do something that is

soothing for you, as much as you need to. And remind yourself that you're attending to and taking care of your needs.

SEEKING SUPPORT FROM YOUR EX

It can be tempting to try to make your sadness and anxiety go away by seeking support from your ex. The person who caused your pain in a breakup can never be the person who takes away the pain of the breakup.

Combating the Impulse to Seek Support from Your Ex

Seek support from other trusted people in your life. Support from others improves well-being, and will not only help you better regulate your emotions but also help you develop insight by talking and problem solving with someone who knows you well and cares about you.

ACTING ON IMPULSE

When you feel like you can't bear how bad you feel, you're vulnerable to impulsive decisions and behavior—calling or texting your ex, posting something about him, having sex you'll regret, getting really drunk. There are many things you could do impulsively that would make things a lot worse for you.

Combating Impulsivity

1. **Slow down**. Commit to yourself that you will *not* make any decisions or take any actions unless you've carefully thought them through and talked them over with trusted others. If you're feeling impulsive in the moment, literally step away, put down the phone, or get up from the computer, and do not go back until you can be certain that you will not do the thing you were about to do. Call a friend, leave the house, take a shower. Do whatever it takes to stop your behavior.

2. **Listen to your friends**. If your friends (or other trusted others) tell you not to do something (or to do something healthy), listen to them. They care about you, and they are much more objective about the situation than you are right now. And remember, time is *not* of the essence. You can always decide later, after more discussion and thought, to do the thing you want to do.

3. **Listen to yourself.** Once you slow yourself down, take the time to really look at what you're thinking and feeling. Ask yourself, "What am I feeling right now? What is going on for me? What are my emotions telling

me? Why am I behaving this way?" and take time to consider the answer. Get to know yourself a little better by learning how you react when lovesick. Doing so gives you new insight into who you are, what your needs are, and how you try to get them met, which you can then use to guide you in the future.

IDEALIZING YOUR EX AND DENYING REALITY

After a breakup, it's easy to focus solely on the good things you got from the relationship and actively avoid looking at the bad things. Selective attention does not allow you to assess the situation realistically, and it fuels your feelings of lovesickness because it keeps you thinking you're missing out on something wonderful.

Combating Idealization

Look at all of the data, the good and the bad. Do a full needs assessment so that you can clearly see unmet needs. Recruit a trusted friend or family member who knows you well to help you. And when you find yourself remembering only the positive or romanticizing your relationship with your ex, remind yourself of the reality and let yourself focus on the negatives. The negatives, the unmet needs, are the reason you are no longer together. Keep your eye on them and don't forget them.

CRITICIZING AND BLAMING YOURSELF

It's easy to blame the demise of the relationship solely on yourself and to be highly self-critical ("If I had only listened to him. There must be something wrong with me. It's all my fault"). Self-blame and self-criticism also do not allow for a realistic assessment of the situation, and they keep alive the myth that if you were somehow better the relationship never would have ended. This just reinforces the inaccurate idea that by fixing yourself you could fix the relationship and get him back. *Totally wrong.*

Combating Self-Criticism and Self-Blame

1. ***Look at all of the data.*** In the vast majority of cases, it takes two to create relationship problems that lead to a breakup. Of course, it's important to accept responsibility for things you may have done wrong and commit to learning and growing for the sake of personal development. But bashing yourself and absolving your partner gets you nowhere. Go back to that needs assessment and see what it tells you.

2. *Be kind and compassionate with yourself.* This is extremely important. You just had a breakup. You're hurting. You don't need to hurt yourself further. What you need right now is to be kind and gentle with yourself, to have compassion for your situation—all of it.

Olivia, Lauren, and Anna: Breaking Up Is Hard to Do

Once you start using these strategies to deal with lovesickness, you'll be better able to get over the breakup and move forward in your life. Olivia, Lauren, and Anna's stories illustrate the skills, or lack thereof, in action.

OLIVIA

As you saw in Chapter 8, it's over with Zach. It should have been Olivia who broke up with him after she found out about his chronic cheating and lying, but she couldn't do it. Her rejected-lover brain was missing and craving and hurting. So she hung on and got crazy jealous. Zach wanted to live his college version of the happily married man with a mistress, but when the rewards shrank and the cost grew (why would he want to work through a trust needs conflict when Olivia's trust was not key for him?), he saw no reason to stay and got out. Low impact on him. High impact on Olivia. Now she's knocked flat by lovesickness.

Day 1

Olivia's always been able to control her emotions and behavior, put distractions aside, and focus on what she needs to get done. Not now. She's lying in bed, bawling her eyes out, cycling between thoughts about why he broke up with her when he was the one who made her act like a crazy girlfriend and hoping he'll call her and take "I'm done" back. He doesn't call. All she can think of is "I want him back."

Day 2

Knowing Zach was angry when he said, "I'm done," she wonders, "He's going to regret it, right? He's going to want me back, right?" She makes a frantic call to Mia, who comes over, takes her to the campus clinic to get tested for STIs, and encourages her not to call Zach—but to delete all online connections with him, videos, even his number from her phone. Olivia doesn't want to hear it and doesn't follow her friend's advice.

Day 6

It's Saturday. Olivia's anxiety grows as she pictures Zach with Ashley, blocks and then unblocks him, unfriends Ashley, and stalks him on Facebook, Instagram, and Twitter. Finally, she can't stand how anxious, sad, and desperate she feels. She wants him to take away her pain. Impulsively, she texts Zach:

Olivia: Can we meet up later and talk?
Zach: Watching the game.
Olivia: How about after?

No response. Olivia tries to go about her day but can't concentrate as she obsessively checks her phone every five minutes.
Five hours later. She's starting to feel really anxious.

Olivia: Is Ashley there?

Thirty minutes later.

Olivia: Will you pick up the phone real quick? I really need to talk to you.

She calls him. He doesn't pick up
Five minutes later. She can't stop crying. She resumes texting.

Olivia: I get it—watching football with Ashley is more important than texting me back or missing the game to talk to me. I finally understand—you don't care about my feelings.

One hour later. She's angry now.

Olivia: I really get it now. You always cared more about watching the game with her than you did about me. Well, now you can. You get to spend time with your fuck buddy any night you want now. Yay for you.

One hour later. She's really angry now.

Olivia: Just so you know, I'm going to be just fine. Even after six days, I'm already remembering less of your good qualities and more of your bad ones. You're incapable of honesty, you put your own feelings and needs first. I actually hate you.

Nothing
Olivia checks her Facebook. "What?!"

Olivia: You unfriended me? WTF? So, what—are you not going to speak to me now when we run into each other?

Nothing.

Day 8

Olivia feels ill; her stomach actually hurts. She doesn't want to get out of bed but knows she has to get it together. She doesn't want her GPA to slide. Self-criticism sets in: "I'm so stupid. Clearly Zach cheated on me with Ashley because she's thinner than I am. I hate my hips. I was never attractive enough for Zach. I've got to stop eating."

Day 13

It's been a tough week. Olivia feels as if she's in a thick, sad fog, and she can't shake it. She's writing some of the most important final papers of her life, and she can't concentrate. She saw Zach in the campus book store today. Her stomach dropped and her mind flooded with all the images of how it used to be. She got out before he could see how "horrible" she looked: "I've been eating like a horse. I've gained so much weight, it's embarrassing." She swears to herself that starting tomorrow she's going to eat healthy and work out. "Maybe I can look hot to him again." She's been thinking a lot about how she got so insanely jealous, wishing she'd listened to Zach when he said he just wanted to be with her. She wonders whether he could ever forgive her for not listening to him.

Day 14

She wakes up early, certain that if she apologizes to Zach for getting so jealous and acting so crazy, he'll want to get back together. She meets up with Emily to read her the e-mail she's written.

Emily: Do not send this e-mail, Olivia. This is not what's best for you. No contact is best right now.
Olivia: No. I disagree. I can't act like I don't care when I do. I read a lot of articles on breakups. Some suggest sending text messages to plant good memories in your ex's mind so they remember all the reasons they were with you in the first place.
Emily: Do you want to get back together with him?

Olivia: (*She doesn't answer Emily's question.*) He was angry because I checked his text messages. It wasn't right of me. I was trying to feel confident he wanted to be with me. I didn't understand that at the time. I do now. I want to tell him and apologize.

Emily: Why do you want to get back together with him?

Olivia: (*She doesn't answer Emily's question.*) I want to make things right on my side. I don't want to have regrets for not saying what I want to say. And I just want to get some closure. I deserve that. He dumps me instead of Ashley? I want to understand why. I mean, did he not love me? He said he did, but then why did he dump me?

Emily: Listen, he was quite happy having sex with you and hooking up with Ashley on the side. I think he wanted a more casual relationship than you wanted. When you found out and got jealous, it was too much trouble for him because it wasn't important to him to work to earn your trust. You know? What do you think?

Olivia: (*She doesn't know what to say.*)

Emily: I mean, it's a little twisted you asking him to forgive you—isn't it? Shouldn't it be the other way around?

Olivia's emotion mind trumps Emily's reasonable mind and she sends the e-mail. She feels better, stronger. Yay! Finally, she feels a little better. Or so she thinks.

Day 15

She wakes up, checks her e-mail, and feels sick to her stomach. He didn't reply. She checks her phone. He didn't even text her. She tells herself, "Maybe he hasn't seen it yet. Maybe he needs to think about it." She feels hopeful with this thought, and it makes it easier to write the paper she's working on. Still, every 15 minutes she checks her e-mail and texts to see if he's responded. He hasn't. Her anxiety and despair grow.

Day 17

It feels like the worst day of her life. She's distraught and has no energy. She goes for a walk with Emily.

Olivia: I wanted to be honest, but now I feel worse. I wish I hadn't sent the e-mail. I should be entitled to him meeting up with me, explaining to me why he said he loved me and then broke up with me. I need to know he cares and supports me.

Emily: Why? He's not your support person anymore. In fact, I don't know if he ever was. Look, he doesn't want to be with you. If he did, he'd have gotten back to you. But he doesn't. This is what he's showing you.

Olivia: (*sobbing*) I'm never going to see him again after we graduate. We're not even connected through Facebook.

Emily: I know, Olivia. I know. You might never see him again, but you're going to be
    okay. And listen, sending him the e-mail gave you an opportunity to see if he
    wants to change his mind. You have to assume now that he doesn't. I know it's
    hard, but it's true. Even though you still want to be with him, he doesn't want to
    be with you. And you know what? That alone should make you not want to be
    with him.

Olivia: I want to be with him, I can't help it. I know he cares about me.

Emily: It's hard. I know. But I don't know what you're basing that on. Asking him not to
    hang out alone with Ashley when he cheated on you with her is a pretty reason-
    able expectation and something a guy would do if he cared about your relation-
    ship.

Olivia: But remember early on, when I was uncomfortable about his and Ashley's
    friendship, he showed her we were together.

Emily: You have new information now.

Olivia: Why doesn't he care about me now?

Day 20

Last night she saw him at a party. She knew she would, and she wanted
him to see her looking good after almost starving herself for a week. When
she saw him go to the bathroom, she got on the bathroom line so he would
have to walk past her when he came out. He did and said a surprised kind
of "Hi." She asked him how he was and he said "Good" and that was it.
Then he went back to playing foosball with his friends. Ashley was there
too, and they also said hi to each other. Olivia wanted to make sure they
saw her as calm and together. She noticed that Zach and Ashley acted the
way they used to with each other, just like friends. When she left, she was
proud of herself for having handled the party well and thought maybe it
would get Zach thinking about her again.

Now she can't get this idea out of her mind. She Googles "how to get
your ex back" and watches a video on the subject. The video shows how
to create a text "to get the conversation started." She calls Mia to read her
the text message she wants to send: "Know you're probably feeling stressed
with finals coming. You'll do great. You're on my mind after seeing you last
night." The video was very clear to stop there, but Olivia decides she wants
to say more. She goes on to add: "I'd like to make good on that promise to
celebrate your birthday tomorrow night. It's our last chance. Remember
our anniversary night ☺" "Noooooooooo!" says Mia, who tries to convince
Olivia to see the reality and move on. "He doesn't want a serious relationship, and hooking up one more time isn't going to lead to one. You're
not going to get what you need here. You're going to end up feeling worse
because either he'll ignore your text or you'll hook up and then that will
be it. This won't end well." Olivia thinks it over and decides to ignore Mia.

She sends the text. He texts back, "Thanks, but already have plans." She's crushed.

Day 30

She continues to feel miserable, sad, and angry. "How could he do this to me?" she asks herself over and over. "I don't deserve this. I'm a kind person. Why did he use me and then just throw me away?! I wish he knew how much he hurt me so he would have to deal with that."

Olivia is stuck in lovesickness.

Breaking up really is hard to do, and the pain of losing a relationship is inevitable. Although Olivia still would have felt sadness, anxiety, and anger in the month following the breakup, she might have been able to move on more quickly and prevent it from disrupting her life so much if she had used the skills to combat the common reactions she was having. For example:

- If Olivia found herself having intrusive thoughts about Zach, she could have caught them happening and told herself something like "I'm thinking about Zach again. I'm just going to let those thoughts pass and refocus on what I need to do right now. I want to get into a good graduate school, and ruminating will not help me." This might have helped Olivia get her work done.
- Instead of wondering about how to get Zach back and blaming herself for being jealous, Olivia would have been better off really figuring out why she acted so insanely jealous. There's a clear answer there: she felt insecure. Learning this would lead to the insight that it's not healthy for her to be in a relationship where she feels insecure—information she could use to make healthier relationship decisions in the future.
- Olivia also should have listened to the advice of her friends. She went to them for support, but she ignored everything they had to say.
- She needed to slow herself down, look at the reality of the relationship, and carefully think through her choices.
- If Olivia had done a needs assessment she would have seen that, in the end, Zach was not meeting many of her needs. He was not authentic with her, she didn't trust him, he didn't care about her feelings or support her, and he didn't keep her safe. If she was able to see this truth and remind herself of it every time she felt lovesick, she would have gotten over the breakup much more easily.
- She also needed to deal with her emotions in a more mindful and compassionate way, which would have reduced her self-blame and allowed her to make better decisions.

LAUREN

Lauren is still with Lucas, but struggling to face the reality of her needs assessment, wondering whether Lucas really knows and likes her. She sees the evidence of her unmet needs, but what about her belief that love conquers all? Does it?

She's walking back to Lucas's apartment with him. They pass a store with Halloween window dressings. She starts excitedly making plans:

Lauren: Oooh, let's dress up and go to one of those big parties. I'll buy tickets. What do you want to be? I know what I'd like to be.

Lucas: (*He interrupts her.*) I hate Halloween. It's the saddest day of the year.

Lauren: I don't remember—why is it so negative? There's your wedding anniversary, that's a bad day.

Lucas: I left my wife on Halloween.

Lauren: Are you kidding me? I can't believe you're doing this again.

Lucas: It's not like you don't know this.

Lauren: Everything is going so well. I thought I would never have to hear this again. You even said that she was never supportive and loving the way I was and that I'm so good for you. I don't understand how you can say that and then still regret leaving her. (*She turns around and starts walking away from Lucas toward her apartment. He just watches her walk away.*)

While Lauren's walking home she thinks, "He says he wants to be with me. He says she was never supportive and loving the way I am. Yet he hates Halloween. It has to be because he regrets leaving her. I don't understand. What if I said to him, 'I wish I had never left Dan'? I can't tell whether he wants to be with his ex-wife or me, and I'm so sick of dealing with this." Lauren is struggling with how to deal with Lucas talking about his ex-wife. Yes, it upsets her, but she wants to be his go-to person. She wants him to feel safe enough to tell her anything, and she wants to know what he's thinking. What should she do—not talk to him tomorrow? If she does, what does she say—"I'm sorry"? "But for what?" she thinks. She feels like it's an impossible situation.

She calls Julianne:

Lauren: You just don't say things like that. He has to know it hurts me.

Julianne: Apparently he doesn't care.

Lauren: Why not? Why doesn't he care?

Julianne: I don't know. Obviously it's just who he is, and, really, it doesn't matter why. The fact is he just doesn't and he's hurting you. How long are you going to stand for that?

Lauren: (*She ignores the question.*) His friends have told me his ex-wife wasn't even good for him.

Julianne: It doesn't matter. Clearly Lucas can't see that. So what are you going to do about this?

Lauren: I don't know. I guess I'll just let it go.

Julianne: What do you mean? You're upset about this, and it keeps happening.

Lauren: Not that much.

Julianne: That not's what I'm seeing. Anyway, what does he miss about her?

Lauren: I haven't asked. I guess I've been afraid of hearing what his answer is.

Julianne: Why? I'd want to know.

Lauren: Think about it—what if he tells me about her and then I try to turn myself into her, give him what he misses? And besides, I'm not his psychologist.

Julianne: You're not making sense, Lauren. You're clearly upset about this, and then you say you're not. You want him to stop talking about her, and then you say you don't. You don't want to know what he misses because you're afraid you'll try to become her. You're still trying to make him love you, and you're still focusing only on his needs. What about yours?

It's 6:00 P.M. the next day. Lauren hasn't gotten even a text from Lucas. She hasn't called because she wants to see if he'll call her. She's always the one to initiate and stop the silence, but she's trying to wait it out this time. Surprisingly, at 11:00 P.M. Lucas texts "Good night. Hope you had a great day." She's relieved, but she doesn't respond. She's not sure what to say. She's thinking about her conversation with Julianne.

The next day Lauren is feeling stressed. She gets back a paper with a lower mark than she expected, someone dented her car while it was parked on the street, and she still hasn't come up with what to text back Lucas. Finally she decides on this:

Lauren: I am so sad today—everything is not going well.

Lucas: I'm enormously sad too. Should we meet later?

Lauren: Sure. (*She gets the feeling that something is really wrong.*)

They meet up at his house.

Lauren: What are you sad about?

Lucas: You know when I restarted this relationship with you I said this time I would do my best to make it work. Yet I'm sad about my life as it is right now.

Lauren: (*She's thinking, "Wow, here we go again."*) Why?

He starts talking about his ex-wife. The more he says, the more she thinks, "I am not going to live my life trying to prove to you that I'm better than your ex-wife!" She's angry, and she tries to pay attention to that, again remembering her conversation with Julianne.

Lauren: Okay, stop. I get the point. I can't continue competing with your ex-wife. I'm going to grab my stuff and go home.

He doesn't stop her, and she slams the door on her way out. On her way home she texts Julianne to tell her that she's done with him.

Day 1

Lauren wakes up the next morning thinking, "Okay, this isn't so bad. Now I don't have to live my life trying to prove I'm better than his ex-wife." She deletes his texts, unfriends him on Facebook, makes herself a smoothie, and goes to school. She meets up with her friends that night for drinks. It's what she would have done anyway since Lucas and she rarely got together on work nights. And, she thinks, being with her friends is a good distraction from her feelings, as is the wine.

Day 5

Lauren's been thinking about how things ended with Lucas. She's been feeling more and more anxious over the past few days and thinks maybe she needs more closure, but she's not sure. She calls Julianne:

Lauren: I'm thinking about texting or calling Lucas. I'm feeling anxious, and I don't know exactly why. I'm thinking that I need more closure, but I really don't know why.
Julianne: What would you say?
Lauren: I guess "I still care about you, and I've treasured the moments we've had, but you have to deal with your ex-wife issue or it's going to get in the way of all your relationships." I think this will help me get closure, walk away, and move forward.
Julianne: Okay. Those seem like good things to say. As long as you really do walk away.
Lauren: I will. I mean I am. I have to. (*She starts crying.*) I just don't know how to make a relationship last.
Julianne: What?
Lauren: (*crying more*) Look at what happens to me. Every one of my relationships ends. I know I'm attractive and men like me, and I have power over them in that way, but you know what? It's never gotten me what I really wanted—to make a relationship work. I think it's actually finally hitting me—this is really happening. Lucas and I are over.
Julianne: I know it's hard. You're better off alone than with him, though.
Lauren: Am I really? This is so hard.

Julianne: What else would you tell him?

Lauren: (*still crying*) I would want to be strong and powerful and say things like "You know what, I had a great time, but it's the best for both of us to part ways."

Julianne: Okay, but maybe you also should tell him why.

Lauren: What do you mean?

Julianne: He doesn't support you, care about your feelings, help you with things.

Lauren: Should I tell him that? What good would it do? I don't want to sound mean or demanding.

Julianne: You can say to him, "I wanted to be with you, but I do not feel cared about or supported because of your continued attachment to your ex-wife. I do not feel that you really want to be with me." I don't see that as mean or demanding. You're just telling him about your feelings and what you needed.

Lauren: That doesn't sound like I'm being strong and powerful, though.

Julianne: That's ridiculous. You never really expected or asked for him to meet any of your needs. You've got to stop focusing only on what Lucas needs and start focusing on what you need. Now, with this breakup, and in the future with any guy you're with.

Lauren: Maybe you're right.

Julianne: Don't call him yet, Lauren. Wait and think about things. You can always call another time if you want to. There's no rush.

Lauren: You're right. I'll think about this.

Day 6

Lauren's thinking a lot about her conversation with Julianne, and she's thinking about Lucas. She misses him in certain ways—she felt really sad when she walked by his favorite art gallery this afternoon—but what she's really upset about is now she's alone. This is what her lovesickness is about. She doesn't have a relationship. She's never made one work, and her plan for marriage and kids by 28 is pretty much over (for more information on this, see the box on page 262). Her anxiety is starting to grow. It's Sunday night and she has no plans, so she opens a bottle of wine and settles in to watch movies.

Day 12

It's Saturday morning, and Lauren wakes up relieved that she made it through the week. She was able to get all of her work done but had a hard time concentrating at school. Going out with her friends and classmates each evening helped pass the time, but she didn't tell them how she was feeling. She didn't want to deal with it, so she acted as if she was just fine. But she just can't get the thoughts out of her head: "I'm alone. I have no one to love. No one to love me. What am I going to do? Have I screwed my

---

I/ME

The Ticking Biological Clock

A lot of women feel anxious about fertility issues. That's certainly understandable. However, it's important to remember a couple of things:

1. Women in their 20s, like Lauren, still have time. Women can be fertile well into their 30s and sometimes 40s.

2. A self-imposed deadline, like the one Lauren has, can get in the way of being able to assess realistically whether a relationship is healthy. Lauren was considering trading an outcome for a healthy relationship. Would you want to wake up one day with a baby in an unhappy relationship?

---

life up by ending things with both Dan and Lucas?" A deep sadness starts to take her over, and she calls Julianne for guidance.

Julianne: We know the answer, Lauren. Neither one of them was good for you or met your needs. Lucas didn't support you, care about your feelings, or help you.
Lauren: (*interrupting*) Yeah, but Dan did.
Julianne: (*interrupting*) Yes, but neither one cared about your feelings. You have to remember that.
Lauren: I know, you're right. It's just hard. It's so easy to remember the good things.

Lauren feels lost and overwhelmed.

She feels like she doesn't know how to have a good relationship—she certainly didn't manage it with either Dan or Lucas—but she doesn't know where to begin to figure out why, and that means she's at risk for making the same mistakes in the future. Lauren has been coping with her version of lovesickness—her anxiety about being alone and not having love—by not dealing with her feelings or the reality of what happened in her recent relationships. She lapses into downplaying the problems in her relationship with Lucas, wanting to say only that she had a great time in the relationship rather than telling him directly about her unmet needs. In fact, she barely recognizes her unmet needs, let alone gives them much credence.

Lauren could well benefit from the emotion regulation and insight development strategies we described earlier:

• In particular, to help her tolerate distress on a daily basis, Lauren should approach her negative thoughts and her anxiety in a mindful way rather than using avoidant coping strategies to try to make them go away. Instead of trying to dampen her anxiety by drinking alcohol or downplaying it by pretending everything is okay, she should practice acknowledging it, accepting it, and letting herself know that how she feels is okay and that she will be able to cope with it by learning how to have a healthy relationship.

- She also would benefit from healthy self-soothing activities. Although she already does some of these (she stays active and makes her favorite smoothies and food), she could include additional ones to replace her use of alcohol. For instance, on nights when she is alone she could take an aromatherapy bath and do yoga or meditation (or whatever would feel soothing and healing for her).

- If Lauren thinks that not knowing how to make a relationship work is a problem, she needs to make a plan. Fortunately, Julianne is a trusted friend who can help her. Julianne has identified a key issue—Lauren never expects or asks for her needs to be met—which resulted in her not asserting herself appropriately with both Lucas and Dan.

- Lauren also needs to reflect about the fact that of the three conditions for a healthy relationship, she focuses only on "I know and like him," where she is doing all the caregiving. Lauren doesn't understand, or at least she doesn't act on, the very core of mutuality—that for a relationship to be healthy, both people's needs are important and must be attended to. She hasn't even made it to mutuality step 1.

- Lauren also needs to question her basic assumptions about relationships and evaluate whether acting on them has worked. For example, she believes that love conquers all. Lauren currently has a lot of data about whether that assumption is true in her case, and it all points to "no." Given that, Lauren needs to come up with a more realistic assumption, based on the reality of met and unmet needs.

- In line with this, Lauren needs to look carefully at the data and consider what her needs assessment tells her. One of the reasons Lauren plays the breakup/makeup game—Dan, Lucas, Dan, Lucas—is that she skips the part of lovesickness where she should be working on developing new insight by focusing on what she can learn from her past relationship and using it in future decision making. This results in her continuing to idealize her ex and deny reality. Lauren must learn to stay fully attuned to the evidence of her unmet needs. As we said earlier, a breakup means that one or both of the partners couldn't or didn't want to meet the other's needs. That is the insight Lauren needs to really figure out: "Who do I want to be with and why?"

If Lauren can work through lovesickness in these ways, she'll be able to reduce and manage her anxiety about being alone and will be less likely to repeat old patterns (or go back to Lucas or Dan) because she will know what makes for a healthy relationship and she'll be better equipped to have one in the future.

ANNA

Even though Eric refused to go back to marriage counseling, Anna stayed in and started seeing a counselor specializing in domestic violence. Between the advice of her counselor and the pleading from her friends and family, she realized she had to leave Eric. It was hard for her. She kept wondering where she and Emma would go. Could she afford to move out? Would she be able to work and pay for child care? Could she handle everything on her own? These kinds of thoughts almost made her stay. Indeed, there are real practical and emotional issues involved in leaving an abusive relationship. That's why it was hard for Anna to exit, as it would be for any woman.

When she told Eric she was leaving, he went ballistic, going from crying and begging her to stay, to acting as if he didn't care, to aggressively trying to coerce her to stay, making comments such as "You'll regret it for the rest of your life if you leave me!" But she stayed strong and moved into her parents' house with Emma, and now she and Eric are trying to work out their separation and divorce and a custody agreement. She feels safer now—she's made a safety plan with her counselor—but she's still in acute lovesickness. She's struggling emotionally and deeply conflicted about what happened. She really wanted her marriage to work, and not just for Emma. The love she felt for Eric was intense and strong.

The past couple of months have been day-to-day. She's just been focused on taking care of Emma, going to work, and making it through the day. There has been a lot of crying. A lot of exhaustion. A lot of anger. A lot of sadness. She's been getting up each day, doing what needs to be done, and going back to bed completely wiped out.

I/ME

How Can a Woman Still Feel Love in the Midst of Being Abused?

Anna's love for Eric was based on real aspects of who he is. She loved those parts of him, even though she hated the abuse. It takes time for feelings of love to dissipate. They don't just go away immediately even in the face of violence. Indeed, this can be very confusing and stressful for women in violent relationships. Tolerating the continued feelings of love in the face of leaving a violent relationship is difficult but necessary.

Day 60

Even though it's been a couple months, Anna still wakes up at night thinking, "Where am I? What's the matter?" and then remembers "Oh yeah, Eric and I are not together," and bawls. It's hard. Despite what's happened, she sometimes misses their family—having dinner together, talking about their day, taking care of Emma together, watching movies, cuddling. What's worse is she still sees Eric for planned visitation with Emma. And when she sees how warmly he greets Emma and how he hugs her and says sweet things to her, she wishes things could go back to how they used to be before the violence. Knowing they can't makes it all the more difficult.

Day 75

They're in negotiations about the house. Eric continues to be unpredictable. Today he begs her to come home, for them to try again, but becomes hostile when she refuses:

Eric: Please, Anna, why don't you just come home? We can work this out. Let's be a family together again.

Anna: No, Eric, it won't work. I can't trust you. It's over. Let's just work out what's best for Emma.

Eric: Don't say that. Let's try. Please.

Anna: No, Eric. Please don't ask me again.

Eric: Fine. You're horrible. A horrible person who doesn't want any responsibility. And you're the one who can't be trusted. You're a liar. And I bet you're out drinking and slutting around and that's why you don't want to come home!

Anna: Stop it, Eric. Stop twisting things. I'm not going to have this conversation with you.

Eric launches into his I-do-everything-for-you-you-owe-me rant. She hangs up and jots down some notes on their conversation, as she's been asked to do by her counselor. Then she collapses in tears, thinking, "I can't believe this is still going on. Why did I ever get involved with him?!"

Day 80

Today Eric behaves more appropriately:

Anna: I really do think it would be best for Emma and me to be in the house. My parents have been generous letting us stay here, but we need more space. We need to be in our own environment. Please, can we live in the house and you stay somewhere else until we sort out and finalize everything?

Eric: Yes, okay, I can see why that's better for you and Emma.
Anna: Thank you, Eric. Thank you for being reasonable about this. When can you be
ready to make the transition?
Eric: At the end of the month. Will that work? It's just two weeks away.
Anna: Yes, that's fine.

*"What a relief!" Anna thinks, "Why can't he always be like this?" and although
she rests easy that night, in the back of her mind she's wondering what's next
with Eric. Is he going to change his mind? She lives with massive anxiety every
day until the move happens.*

Day 94

Anna and Emma move back into the house. Julianne comes over. She's just
gotten back from a work trip. Emma's sleeping. They're talking. Julianne's
first goal is to make sure Anna is safe:

Julianne: Why did you feel you had to hide things from me?
Anna: I didn't think you'd understand. Lauren didn't. We barely speak now.
Julianne: Do you feel safe now? I mean, do you think he'll try to physically hurt you?
Anna: I don't think so. It only happened when we were arguing, and we don't have any
in-person discussions or negotiations now. It's all on the phone or e-mail. Plus,
I've changed all the locks on the house.
Julianne: Good, I'm glad to hear that.
Anna: Honestly, the stuff that has been the hardest to deal with is all the awful things
he said. "You're a shitty mom, a drunken slut, you can't be trusted." I know what
he said is not true, but I can't get those things out of my head. I just keep going
over the arguments and what he said. I can't understand how he could have
come up with those things.
Julianne: Because he's a crazy person!
Anna: Don't say that. He's the father of my child.
Julianne: I know. I'm sorry. I just think that trying to figure him out might drive you
crazy. It's not worth it.
Anna: Maybe.
Julianne: Also, I just have to say, the first 18 months after leaving an abusive guy,
that's when women get killed.
Anna: I know it can be dangerous. I'm seeing a counselor. I have a safety plan. We're
living here till we get everything settled. Eric's rented an apartment. And I'm wait-
ing for him to sign a separation and child support agreement.
Julianne: So you're definitely done with him, right?
Anna: Yes. I'm done. Besides, my family, Lauren—even probably you—would disown
me if I went back, right?

Julianne: (*laughing*) Yes, we would! No, we wouldn't disown you, but I can tell you that none of us would be able to be around Eric. I don't know that we could ever accept him again.

Julianne's next goal is pushing Anna on things, trying to help her make sense of what happened:

Julianne: So, what do you think really happened with Eric?

Anna: I don't know. Everything was so good for the first year. We were so busy. The wedding, Emma, the new house. It's as if once we had nothing to plan we started to really get to know each other. I remember thinking, "Who are you?" He probably did the same.

Julianne: What do you mean?

Anna: Well, I thought he was a stable and happy person. He's not. As time went on, I honestly didn't know who he'd be when he walked through the door. I didn't know what to expect. It was like he was two different people sometimes. And he probably thought I was less independent than I was. You know how you show the best of who you are in the beginning? I think we both did that.

Julianne: You totally did that. I mean, of course you have to treat people well in the beginning and not show all of your craziness, but you can't pretend to be something you're not. Otherwise you don't know whether the other person really wants to be with the real you. But that's not what happened here.

Anna: What do you mean?

Julianne: It's not that he didn't want to be with the real you. He's an aggressive, violent person and he would've behaved that way no matter what.

(Anna begins crying.)

Anna: I guess you're right. I kept thinking it was me, but it was him.

Julianne: Yes, it definitely was.

(They sit in silence for a minute.)

Julianne: And I'd like to say something else. Please take this as me trying to help you.

Anna: Sounds serious.

Julianne: It is. Anna, you jumped so quickly into the relationship with Eric. You didn't even know him. You didn't even give yourself the chance to really know him. And you ignored some really important information that he gave you. Do you realize that?

Anna: What do you mean?

Julianne: Remember how he just dropped you? And remember what he said about his other girlfriend and why he liked her better? You kind of ignored that and just jumped right back in with him the minute he flirted with you again. (*Anna starts crying again.*) Anna, I'm not trying to hurt you or blame you for what happened. He is totally to blame for his behavior. I'm just saying that for the future you need to think differently about your approach to getting into a relationship.

Anna: (*tearful*) I guess you're right.

Julianne: (*laughing*) No more what-was-I-thinking boyfriends for you. (*Even through her tears, Anna starts laughing too.*)

Day 100

It's still hard for her not to think about Eric. She's curious about his life and what he's doing. She creeps on Eric's Facebook page. She can't help herself. She sees pictures of him with some woman. "Who is that?" she thinks. "Is he dating?!" Anna doesn't know what to think. She's upset and angry that he might be with someone else. She's sad that it didn't work out for them—"Why does she get to have what I wanted? Is she going to have the relationship with him that I wanted?" She's in tears thinking about it. "Why didn't it work with us? Could it ever? Could I have done something different? Is this woman going to be raising my child now?" She thinks about calling Eric. NO! She knows she's in a bad place. She calls Julianne, who's out of town for work and doesn't pick up. She's feeling desperate and needs to talk to someone. She calls Lauren:

Anna: Lauren, I'm so sorry we haven't been speaking. I just really need a friend right now. I'm struggling.

Lauren: I know. Julianne has kept me up to date. What's going on right now that you're so upset?

Anna: (*crying*) I think Eric is dating someone.

Lauren: How do you know?

Anna: I saw some pictures on Facebook.

Lauren: Well, first of all, you've got to stop looking at Facebook.

Anna: I can't help myself. He's still my husband and the father of my child. I feel like I need to know and see what he's doing. And now I'm upset that he's happy with some other woman. Why couldn't he be happy with me? (*sobbing*)

Lauren: You're just looking at a picture and making assumptions. No one posts pictures of themselves when they're arguing or unhappy. They only post the happy pictures. How do you know he doesn't or won't treat her as badly as he treated you?

Anna: Yeah, I guess, but how can he move on so fast?

Lauren: Why are you surprised? This is exactly what he did when you first started dating him. He was all into you and then dropped you. Why would he have changed?

Anna: I don't know. I just thought things were different.

Lauren: Why? That doesn't make any sense.

Anna: You're one to talk, always thinking that Lucas was going to get over his ex-wife.

Lauren: There's no reason to get mean about things.

Anna: I'm sorry.

Lauren: But you're right. I did think I could make him love me better, that I could win him over, and now it's clear to me that I can't. So yes, I know what you're going through.

Anna: I just wanted so badly for it to work.

Lauren: I know, Anna, I know.

Day 101

She's trying to remember the things she talked about with Lauren and Julianne. Trying to remember who Eric really is—a violent, aggressive person. It's so hard. It takes constant effort.

Day 110

She invited her friend Ian over to watch a movie. They haven't seen each other in a while because of how stressful Anna's life has been, so she's really looking forward to seeing him. They talk about what's happened. He's supportive, understanding, and comforting. They watch the movie— a comedy—so that Anna can take her mind off things and have a good laugh. Out of the blue Ian kisses her. She kisses him back. It feels good. They hook up. After, she thinks, "Oh no, if Eric finds out, he'll freak, probably won't sign the separation/child support agreement." Before he leaves, she says, "Eric cannot find out about this. We have to keep this completely private." Ian agrees.

Day 111

She wakes up thinking about Ian. It was the first time in months that she'd felt good. She can't wait to talk to Julianne later to tell her what happened. She can barely contain herself all day. She's actually kind of giddy thinking about Ian and the possibilities. Her mind is full of "He's so smart and sexy and supportive!" Finally, she calls Julianne:

Anna: You're not going to believe what happened last night. I hooked up with Ian!

Julianne: Wow! I didn't see that one coming!

Anna: Me neither! He came over to watch a movie, and one thing led to another.

Julianne: How was it?

Anna: It was great, and I feel great. It's the first time in months that I've felt good about myself.

Julianne: I'm happy for you.

Anna: I'm just so excited about it. I think there could be a real future with him.

Julianne: Huh? What makes you say that?

Anna: He's really smart and attractive. He has a good job. He was so supportive of me last night. Really understanding and comforting. I'm thinking of inviting him over again tonight.

Julianne: Those are all good things, Anna, but slow down. Remember the conversation we had a couple weeks ago? The one about jumping into things?

Anna: Yes, but this is different. I know him. He's been a friend.

Julianne: It doesn't matter. You're already invested, and all you had was a hookup. You don't even know if he'd want to do it again, let alone whether he wants a relationship.

Anna: I know, but it just feels right.

Julianne: Anna, listen to me, you have nothing in reality to base that on. You've got to do things differently this time. I know it feels good, but you're feeling sad and lonely. A few days ago you were crying about Eric. So feeling good is not a signal that it's going to work or that he's the right guy for you.

Anna: I know. I guess it just feels nice to feel something different. To see the possibility of being over Eric.

Julianne: Yes, and that's really great. You need that. I'm just suggesting that you think of it more like a casual relationship until you know where this is going to go or whether you're going to really want it to go anywhere.

Anna: I just want to be happy again. I'm tired of this.

Anna just wants to move on, already.

Anna's version of lovesickness has taken a number of different forms. Anna initiated the breakup and is aware she really needs to move on, so her lovesickness has involved dealing with a variety of exhausting consequences—the day-to-day stress of dealing with Eric's instability, being a single mother, letting go of the fantasy of happily-ever-after with Eric. She just wants to be done with it and be happy again.

She's dealt with a lot of the same problematic reactions to the breakup as Olivia and Lauren and could benefit from using all of the strategies designed to help with those problems:

• She needs to remind herself to let go instead of ruminating about what Eric has said about her and why he said it, telling herself those are just his distorted, manipulative beliefs that reflect who he is, not who she is.

• When Anna starts missing the things she experienced as positive (for example, family life with Emma), she must look clearly at the evidence and remind herself, "He is a violent, controlling person who has no interest in changing, and I don't want that in my life."

• When she starts criticizing herself for getting involved with Eric, she needs to be compassionate, telling herself things such as "I'm not to blame. I did the only thing I was capable of back then. I may have made a mistake, but I'm learning now. I need to forgive myself and go forward knowing that I will keep taking good care of myself."

- Anna would also benefit from healthy self-soothing to deal with all of her daily stressors. Stress can make people very vulnerable.

- Anna also needs to take a mindful approach to her emotions, especially because they are tied to Eric's unpredictable behavior. It's not healthy for Anna's emotions to be reactive to however Eric is acting. To the extent that she could intentionally disengage from Eric's every little move, as well as work to accept (not condone) the unpredictability over which she has no control (and hence cannot change), Anna would likely feel more calm and less worried about what the next day will bring. For example, Anna would need to catch herself when she's overly focused on Eric and develop new self-talk to help her disengage: "I cannot control what Eric does. I need to focus on my life and what I do have control over. Worrying about what he's going to do doesn't change anything. It just makes me miserable."

- Anna also needs to work on distress tolerance so that she doesn't act impulsively. This is particularly true with regard to Ian. Her desperation to be happy puts her at risk for jumping blindly into another relationship before getting to know the person, just as she did with Eric. Like Lauren, Anna has the benefit of the trusted and wise Julianne, who astutely and lovingly has pointed out to Anna her tendencies to jump in, to fail to be authentic up front, and to rely solely on feelings rather than data to make decisions. Julianne's caution to Anna to slow down and gather data is consistent with the strategies we described for reducing impulsive behavior and for staying in reality rather than fantasy, and Anna would greatly benefit from listening to her friend and doing so. If she is able to, she'll get out of lovesickness in a much better position than she went in, ready to apply what she's learned to having a healthier relationship in the future.

- Finally, if Anna intends to go forward with Ian, she must reflect on what needs she did and did not get met with Eric so that she can use unmet needs for insight in future decision making. When Anna had her bachelorette party, she identified her key needs as interesting (wanting to be part of one another's life), support (being available and reliable), and care (about each other's feelings). If she thinks about this, she will realize that none of these needs got met in her relationship with Eric. This could allow her to gain a deeper understanding of each. For example, she might realize she had a faulty assumption that telling a guy about her feelings and what she's unhappy about will only hurt his feelings and so she shouldn't do it. She could now recognize that it may hurt his feelings, but it also provides her the evidence to see whether he wants to meet her need and is willing to modulate his behavior to do so. If she runs down the needs list to identify the key ones, she would likely see that her key needs include interesting (someone who wants to share in her and Emma's life), accept (someone who accepts her decisions about what she wants to do, when she can go out, who she can be friends with), trust (someone who trusts her and doesn't make unfounded assumptions), and safe (no abuse).

To get through lovesickness in the healthiest way, Anna and all the other women in this book need to commit to making future relationship decisions based on whether their needs get met. Not on feelings of love alone. Not on "chemistry." Not on sex. On met and unmet needs.

11

A Healthy Romance

I f you've made it this far in the book, you now know a lot about how to have a healthy relationship. So does Julianne.

Julianne Moving Forward

Fast-forward six months. Julianne has spent a lot of time taking care of herself post-Gregory. With the help of her friends, she's worked through love-sickness, and she's done a lot of thinking about what happened, how she got to the place she was in with Gregory, and what she wants in the future. She's developed a lot of insight. She's learned the following about herself:

- She needs a guy that, like Gregory, will understand and accept her career focus.
- She needs a guy that, unlike Gregory, will accept her for who she is and not be critical of her or try to control everything she does.
- She needs a guy with whom she can have a mutually fulfilling sexual relationship (a guy who better meets her desire need), and she knows she will need to take the risk to be open and honest about her sexual interests and preferences and not stay with someone who can't meet them.

She also knows she needs to continually assess *all* of her needs in whatever relationship she has—just because a guy may meet her desire and accept needs, he might not meet other important ones—and she has to work on mutual problem solving when needs conflicts arise. She also knows that if those conflicts can't be worked out, especially if her partner isn't interested in doing his part to work them out, she'll need to end that relationship and find a healthier one. Scary, but true. She has committed

to listening to both her head and her heart and to making conscious decisions. No more ignoring her feelings or sliding into things. Perhaps easier
said than done, but she's set her intentions and is willing to do the work to
use her I/ME skills. Fortunately, she gets the opportunity.

The New Relationship: Can Julianne Begin to Use What She Learned?

Julianne is assigned a new client at work. She goes to his office to meet him
for the introductory lunch. Waiting in reception, she's reading a magazine,
and she hears the receptionist on the phone say, "Yes, she's here." Two
minutes later her client comes out, and she's immediately struck by how
attractive she finds him.

At lunch, it's hard for her to keep her mind on work, but she does her
best. Rob seems sufficiently satisfied with their project plan, and over coffee
the conversation turns a little more personal—how long they've worked in
the business, where they're from, what neighborhood they live in. Eventually he looks at his watch and says, "Almost late for the next meeting, gotta
go. Don't want to, but have to," and he heads out as she pays the check. On
her way back to the office, she calls Anna:

Julianne: So I just met with that new client for lunch.
Anna: How'd it go?
Julianne: Great. He loved the project plan, and we had a great lunch.
Anna: Do tell.
Julianne: We had a great conversation over coffee, and then he said he didn't want
to leave.
Anna: Did you want to leave?
Julianne: Definitely not. I was super attracted to him.
Anna: (*teasing*) What about your rule about not dating clients?
Julianne: I know, but eventually he won't be a client.
Anna: Was he wearing a wedding ring?
Julianne: No, I checked right away!

Julianne starts buying new suits and shoes for the project update meetings with the rationale that it's been a while since she's had someone to
dress up for, even if he is a client, and it can't hurt to look good. A few
weeks later she's at a dinner meeting with Rob, and he asks if she can drop
him off at his apartment. Because they had spoken about where they live,
he knows it's on her way. When they arrive, he asks if she'd like to come
up for a drink. She's caught off guard and makes an excuse about needing
to get work done for a morning deadline. When she gets home, she calls
Lauren:

Julianne: I just seriously considered going up to Rob's apartment for a drink.

Lauren: You mean you almost invited yourself up?

Julianne: No. He asked me up, but I made an excuse not to do it. He's still my client. I don't want to screw up the deal or the potential to see him after.

Lauren: Why was he in your car?

Julianne: He asked for a ride home. Anyway, when we were following the waitress to the table, I felt his hand on my back, and he leaned in and whispered, "You look fantastic in that dress." And then at dinner he asked me whether I had a boyfriend.

Lauren: Did you ask if he had a girlfriend?

Julianne: No.

Lauren: Why not? What happened after you told him no boyfriend?

Julianne: Well, it had come up in a conversation about having to travel so much for work, so he went right back to talking about work.

Lauren: Clearly he's attracted to you.

Julianne: I know. I'm so nervous. He's the first guy I've really been interested in since Gregory.

Lauren: I know. Just take your time and keep your cool for now.

The project with the company Rob works for is finally over. They're doing the client exit survey at dinner that night. They definitely have a mutual attraction. She's expecting they'll talk about that tonight. Julianne can barely breathe!

They're nearing the end of dinner and have just wrapped up talking about business. It went really well, but it took longer than expected because they had so much to talk about:

Julianne: (*She raises her wine glass to toast.*) Here's to an on-time project implementation!

Rob: Cheers to that!

Julianne: So, what would you like for dessert?

Rob: (*looking at his watch*) Oh no, it's later than I thought. I'm going to have to pass on dessert. I'm really sorry. I have to meet some friends from work to celebrate how well this all went. It's our work tradition. We always have drinks after the exit interview. I'm sorry we don't have more time. I would have liked to spend more time talking.

Julianne: (*hiding her disappointment*) Me too, but I understand. A tradition is a tradition.

Rob: Yes, gotta do what you gotta do, right?

Julianne: Right, well, have a great time celebrating tonight.

Rob: (*smiling*) Thanks. Last time I had a hard time making it in to work the next day!

Julianne: (*smiling back*) Sounds like you all take your celebrating pretty seriously!

Rob: (*laughing*) We do. I work with a great group of people. They're really good friends.

Julianne: That's really great. Me too. It's nice that you all get along so well. Listen, I know you've got to go. Go ahead. Go have fun.

Rob: Thanks. (*He winks at her as he gets up to leave.*)

Julianne is so disappointed—and confused. She thinks, "Was he being honest with me? Did he really have plans? Maybe he's not interested in me. But what about the wink and him saying he would have liked to talk more? Maybe he was just being nice." Julianne sees herself falling into "I want him to like me" mode and sees she's having trouble dealing with the uncertainty, so she changes her self-talk. "I don't know what he thinks of me, and I'm not going to know for sure right now, so I need to calm down and make a plan. I'll text him tomorrow to see if he wants to get together. If he does, great. If he doesn't, fine, disappointing, yes, but fine. Not every guy I like has to like me. If he doesn't, he's not the guy for me. I'll move on, find someone who does. Plus, I don't even know if I like him yet!"

What Julianne just did is great. She used emotion regulation skills to help her deal with uncertainty and with that internal pressure of wanting him to be the one. She demonstrated personal power by recognizing that it's not about getting a guy to like her; it's about figuring out whether they like each other. She's now ready to take the risk to find out. The next evening she texts: "Hope you made it to work today ;-)" He responds right away.

Rob: Yes, I did. Didn't want a repeat of last time.

Julianne: How responsible of you.

Rob: I'm a responsible guy.

Julianne: You were certainly responsible for me having a nice time last night.

Rob: I'm glad. Care to do it again?

Julianne: Love to!

Rob: Friday?

Julianne: Sure.

Rob: Meet at same place at 8.

Julianne: Great! See you then.

"Hooray!" Julianne texts Anna and Lauren to let them know.

It's Friday night and they go for dinner. She keeps reminding herself, "I'm here to get to know him and find out whether I really like him. I have to listen carefully to what he says and see how he treats me." They talk about all sorts of things. She learns they have things in common. They're both ambitious and hard workers. They like to go out with friends. They like to travel. He talks warmly about his family and about people in general. He seems to have a lot of friends and good relationships with them; he's sociable, and she really likes that. She's aware that he listens to her when she talks. He asks her questions and seems genuinely interested in what she has to say. And not once does he question her choices or say anything remotely critical. She's liking him, and she's so attracted to him. There's an obvious air of flirtation between them the entire dinner. Finally the check arrives:

Rob: So, do you have any pressing work deadlines that you have to meet for tomorrow?

Julianne: No, thankfully, not tonight.

Rob: (*flirtatiously*) Good. That means you can come over to my place for a nightcap this time.

Julianne: Oh, well, I guess I could.

The minute they walk in his door, they begin to kiss passionately. "I've wanted to do this since the first time I saw you," Rob says. "Me too," she replies, and kisses him again. He whispers, "I promised you a nightcap. Come inside and I'll get you a drink and we can get comfortable." He takes her by the hand and she follows him in. As he's making their drinks, she's thinking about what she wants to do next. Does she want to have sex with him? How much of herself is she willing to show right now? She's really turned on. But is she okay with having sex this early on? What if it turns out she doesn't like him or he's not relationship material? Will she be okay with that?

These are good questions she's asking herself. Even in the heat of the moment, Julianne knows to check in with herself. To listen to both head and heart. To make thoughtful decisions. She decides she'll go for it if it feels right to her. It will give her a chance to see whether she thinks she might be able to be open sexually with him. She knows she'll need to be able to do this. If not tonight, then sometime soon.

They settle onto the couch with their drinks. Rob kisses her again. His kisses are wet and deep and delicious, and his hands feel so good caressing her. He gently and slowly slides his hand up her thigh and under her dress, and as he's doing so says, "How are you feeling? Are you okay with this?"

Julianne: More than okay.

Rob: I want to make sure you're comfortable.

Julianne: Thank you. (*She wraps herself around him, and talks into his ear.*) Honestly, I'm never fully comfortable the first time. It takes me some time to open up and to feel safe.

Rob: (*He hugs her tight.*) I want you to feel safe with me, and I want you to be open with me. I love it when a woman tells me what she likes and wants. I want to know. I want to please you. [See the sidebar on the next page for a discussion of how this conversation highlights the seeds of intimacy development.]

I/ME

The Development of Intimacy

The interaction between Julianne and Rob illustrates the initial seeds of intimacy building—not just sexual, but emotional. Intimacy between partners is a sense of closeness and safety that develops through mutual self-disclosure, where we share our innermost selves and where our partners respond in a caring way that conveys understanding and validation. You can see how Julianne is revealing herself and being vulnerable and how Rob is being open and gentle and caring in his response. You'll see this a lot in their relationship. Look for these kinds of instances in all of their conversations.

Julianne: (*giggling*) I'm really glad to hear that.

Rob: I'll tell you what. How about you tell me one thing you like right now and we'll start there, and then next time you can tell me another.

Julianne: I like that there's going to be a next time.

Rob: You better believe there is. (*They're giggling together now.*) Okay, what's your one thing for tonight?

Julianne: (*She's nervous, but she knows this is her chance to start being open and taking a risk.*) You know where your hand was a minute ago?

Rob: You mean here? (*He touches her clit.*)

Julianne: Yes, exactly. I really like being touched there.

Rob: Well that's an easy one. (*They're giggling more as he's gently rubbing her.*) How's that?

Julianne: Perfect.

Rob: Do you want me to keep going?

Julianne: Not tonight. How about we save that for the next time?

Rob: Can the next time be tomorrow?

Julianne: That sounds good to me. How about I make you dinner?

Rob: Deal.

Julianne: (*flirtatiously*) Okay, I better go. I have an early meeting. Come over around seven.

Rob: I'll be there.

He shows up at seven. They immediately start kissing. He suggests they put dinner on hold, and she agrees as she leads him to the bedroom. He says, "Let's pick up where we left off last night. Tell me what you like." "Okay, I'll tell you as we go along," she says, and as she tells him he does exactly what she asks for, all the while telling her how excited it makes him.

She has to keep using her self-talk all along to help herself keep taking the risk to be open with him. She reminds herself that it's scary for her, but after she broke up with Gregory she made a promise to herself to tell her partner what she wants and not to fake orgasms. This is her chance, and she's taking it. She also has to keep using her self-talk not to get caught up in worrying that she's taking too long or that he'll get tired. She reminds herself that he's saying he's excited, and she can feel how hard he is as he presses his body against her side. She reminds herself to stay focused on her body and how it feels. She feels herself getting close to orgasm. She knows what she needs and pushes herself to tell him, "I'm so close, Rob. Rub me the same way you're doing, but use your palm and put some more pressure there." "Like this? Is that what you want?" he whispers. "Yes, yes, it is," and it works.

Not only does Julianne feel amazing physically, she's so proud of herself for being open about her needs and so happy that Rob is the kind of guy who wants to meet them. She thinks, "Already this is better than Gregory."

Things Progress

They start spending more time together. Well, as much as two super-busy business travelers can spend, but they make plans to get together at least once each weekend. It's clear to Julianne that, if nothing else, they are mutually infatuated with one another and they both want to see each other as much as they can. Whenever they get together, they go for dinner, they cook, they go to sporting events (he likes that) and the ballet (she likes that), and they have sex, a lot of great sex.

For example, last Friday night, they met up at Rob's place and had slam-me-against-the-wall, crazy, hot, sweaty sex. Lying next to him, she drifted in and out of sleep, feeling the heat from his body, their legs and arms all tangled up. In the morning, Julianne starts caressing Rob, kissing

---

I/ME

Mutuality—The Root of a Healthy Sexual Experience

For a sexual experience to be healthy it has to be mutual, no matter what the context (hookup, dating, committed relationship). It's got to be about both people communicating their needs and wanting to help each other meet them. In the past, not only did Julianne not communicate her sexual preferences, she didn't even think they were legitimate. She was operating from a place of "Am I worthy enough for him to please me?" Now she's operating from a place of mutuality and personal power.

him, and he immediately responds, leaving her feeling a little shaky (the good kind) and starving. They go to their favorite breakfast place, and when they get back both dive into work. He asks her to look over a letter he's writing to his boss. She walks over to his desk, reaches to turn on the light, and he says, "That's a perfect snapshot for me. You in a white T-shirt, braless, bending over to turn on my light." She smiles. She gives him input on the letter, and then they make love again. It's so intimate. She's fearless. She stares into his eyes while he's inside of her. He stares back. She's so close, and they work together to find a rhythm that sends her over the edge. And then they work together to help him get off. She asks him to show her how he pleases himself. She watches mesmerized. She feels close to him like she's never felt before.

She texts him later that week: "Wearing white T-shirt, braless, bending over table to turn out light. Key under mat! I want your hands on me. Come over." He does.

He wants her to meet his friends. He's always talking about them and how important they are to him, so she's excited to meet them. He's already told her that his best friend is Jessica from work. She was caught off guard by that initially, thinking, "A female best friend—really? How close are they? Can I trust that they're just friends?" She knows they spend a lot of time talking and they go out for drinks after work a lot, which makes her a little jealous. To help herself deal with this, Julianne reminds herself that he is clearly interested in being with her. All the data from their relationship so far point to that, and she's got to stay focused on the data. This is very important work that Julianne is doing. She's using emotion regulation skills to replace potential jealousy-maintaining self-talk with jealousy-reducing self-talk that is objective and based in evidence.

Rob arranges for Julianne to meet him and his friends at one of their weekly after-work-drinks. When she arrives, she can tell he's happy to see her. He jumps up, hugs her, introduces her all around. They had all been talking about something going on at work, and she listens and watches carefully to see what she can learn about Rob and his friends, especially his relationship with Jessica. This is Julianne gathering information that can give her insight into who Rob is, which can help her assess her "I know and like him" needs.

As the evening goes on, it's clear that Rob and Jessica are really close. They know each other well and can even finish each other's sentences. Jessica's been very nice to her, made her feel included, but Julianne feels uncertain about her role in Rob's life. She thinks, "I want to be the one who knows him best." She feels a little jealous, but reminds herself, "They've known each other much longer. It's natural that they're close. It's going to take time for Rob and me. And he's told me how important she is to him." Still, she feels a little uncertain. She decides to continue to observe Rob's relationship with Jessica and to learn more about it and see how it feels to her over time. This is a healthy plan and shows good use of the I/ME skills. Julianne is giving herself the time to develop insight into Rob and his needs, as well as her own. Her recognition that Jessica is important to Rob reflects Julianne's use of mutuality skills—she sees that Rob has needs in the relationship, and she wants to try to meet them. That Julianne is giving herself the time to see if meeting Rob's need is something she can do also shows she is respecting her own needs. And her self-talk reflects good emotion regulation skills—she is keeping her jealousy under control so it won't result in her saying or doing something dramatic or impulsive.

One night, after a particularly fun time in bed together, Rob asks Julianne, "How is it that you're still single? I feel so lucky."

Julianne: That's sweet that you see yourself as lucky. I'm feeling pretty lucky too! (*laughing*)

Rob: I'm serious. Who would've let you go?

Julianne: Actually, I let him go.

Rob: Poor guy. What happened?

Julianne: It's kind of a long story.

Rob: (*He smiles at her.*) I've got all night.

Julianne: We were together about 18 months. His name was Gregory. He had asked me to marry him and I came pretty close to saying yes, but I finally realized the relationship was not good for me.

Rob: How so?

Julianne: He was very critical of me. He was always telling me what to do, how to do things, why my way wasn't right. It was really tough. I tried to let it go. I tried to just accept who he was, but I couldn't. I found myself getting really angry and acting in ways that were totally unlike me. In the end I wasn't even nice to him. And when I finally saw what I was doing I realized I couldn't marry him. It was hard, but it was the best decision I could've made.

Rob: Wow. Sounds like it.

Julianne: It really taught me some important things.

Rob: Like what?

Julianne: Like I can't be with someone who is critical of me. I need the person I'm with to accept me for exactly who I am. I mean, not if I'm doing something truly hurtful, but to basically accept me. To want to be with me, not some version of me he would prefer. And I want to be with someone I can accept too.

Rob: That makes a lot of sense.

Julianne: (*thinking*) And I also learned that I want to be with someone where we can negotiate. Like if there's a decision to make, or if we want different things. I want to be able to talk that out openly. (*pausing*) What do you think of what I'm saying?

Rob: It makes sense. It's better than arguing. I hate arguing.

Julianne: I don't like arguing either. So, what about you? Why are you still single?

Rob: Just didn't find the right girl, I guess.

Julianne: Well, that's vague.

Rob: I know, but it's kind of true. Most women I've met just aren't what I'm looking for. I'm so into my career. I work all the time. I need someone who's my equal in that way. Who doesn't feel neglected when I've got stuff to do. I'm an independent guy, and I want an independent woman who's smart and got a life of her own, and, of course, who likes to do the same kinds of things that I like so when we have time together we can enjoy it.

Julianne: What about Jessica?

Rob: (*laughing*) Fair question. She's attractive, we argue, we laugh, we can truly talk. Initially there was some sexual tension but that dissipated long ago. Now we're just good friends.

Julianne: Does she have a boyfriend?

Rob: No, not right now. Where is this going?

Julianne: Nowhere—just curious.

This conversation is a good example of Julianne and Rob getting to know some of each other's traits and key needs. They're talking openly and asking one another questions and telling each other, at least a little bit, what they think about each other. As time goes on, Julianne can assess whether Rob has heard and understood her needs by seeing how he treats her. Is he accepting and nonjudgmental? Can he talk openly with her when needs conflict? Julianne can also see whether she can comfortably meet his needs for independence. It also will be important for Julianne and Rob to continue these kinds of conversations. It takes time to really get to know someone. New information emerges all the time, and people tend to become more comfortable showing different parts of themselves, especially the more challenging parts, only as the relationship progresses (for more information on this, see the sidebar on the facing page).

Speaking of that, a month later Rob and Julianne meet after work on a Friday night. Julianne's already at the bar chatting with their favorite bartender. Rob comes in all smiles.

Julianne: Hi there, you look happy!

Rob: I am! I just told my boss I'd take her up on her offer to do the training for the new London office!

Julianne: The new London office? You didn't tell me about that.

Rob: Yeah, the company is opening an office in London, and last week my boss asked me if I wanted to run the training. I've been thinking about it all week, and I decided it was too great an opportunity to pass up.

Julianne: Oh, well, congratulations. That does sound exciting. How much time will you be spending there?

```
──────── I/ME ────────
```

Is He the One?

People tend to crave certainty about exactly where a relationship is going. They want to nail down the future, but that's not realistic, especially not early on. For example, at this point, Julianne has reason, based on the evidence of her interactions with Rob, to keep going forward with the relationship. It would be unwise, however, for her to decide now that he's the one, because she simply does not have the data yet. There are so many more things to learn about him, about how he treats her, about how they negotiate their needs, and about whether they share the same goals. If you want to have a healthy relationship that has a good chance of lasting, keep assessing your needs and whether they're being met.

Rob: Initially I'll go for a couple of weeks to get things running, and then for the next few months I'll rotate a week here, a week there to make sure it's going smoothly.

Julianne: I guess I'm kind of surprised that you didn't mention this to me before.

Rob: Oh. I didn't realize that I needed to.

Julianne: It's not that you needed to. It's just that it's such a big thing for you I would've thought you'd want to share it with me.

Rob: I guess I just wanted to make the decision on my own.

Julianne: Why?

Rob: I don't know. I just did.

Julianne: I'm not saying I wouldn't have wanted you to make your own decision. I guess I just feel out of the loop. Did you talk with anyone else about it?

Rob: Yeah, Jessica, because she'd also be going to London to set things up and I wanted to hear her thoughts about this opportunity before deciding.

Julianne: That makes sense, but I still feel kind of bad about not knowing and maybe even worse now because you told Jessica first, worked it out with her, not me.

Rob: (*defensively*) I'm sorry. I just didn't think it would be a big deal. I had to talk to Jessica about it because she was involved in my decision.

Julianne: Hang on. Don't get defensive. It's not a big deal, and I don't want this to turn into a problem between us. Neither of us likes arguing. Can we please just be honest with one another and listen to one another?

Rob: Okay. Yes. I don't want to fight. I hate conflict in my personal relationships.

Julianne: Okay, so listen to my train of thought about this. We always tell each other things about work. We talk about so much, and we spend as much time together as possible. We've even spent a bunch of time together this week. And then tonight I learn about something that's a really big deal for you and you didn't tell me about it at all, even though there was plenty of opportunity. So it's made me wonder why. Why would you choose not to tell me this?

Rob: (*He doesn't say anything.*)

Julianne: C'mon, Rob. Be honest about this. Please.

Rob: Okay. I really wanted to take the position, and I didn't want to hear it if you didn't want me to. I didn't want to disappoint you or have you be upset at me.

Julianne: Okay, I'm glad you're telling me this. So what you're saying is that you hate conflict so much that you'll avoid it at all costs?

Rob: I guess, yes.

Julianne: I get it, but the thing is, we're bound to disagree on some things, and I'd rather be able to be open about this and try to resolve things. If you're worried about me being upset, I can tell you two things. First, I'm more likely to be upset if you don't tell me something than if you do, and second, I can handle disagreeing and I will do my best not to get angry or irrational. Is that part of what you're worried about, my reaction?

Rob: Yes, it is. And my own too. I'm not so great at staying calm.

Julianne: Okay, well, do you think we can work on this, together?

Rob: Yes, I'll try.

Julianne: Okay, if you'll try to be open with me, I promise to be open to hearing what you want and need. And just so you know, I totally would've supported you in taking the job! (*smiling*)

Rob: Really? (*surprised*)

Julianne: Yes!

Rob: I'm really glad to hear that. I really need that.

This is a good example of Julianne behaving from a place of mutuality, taking the risk to express her feelings directly and calmly, which also is evidence of good emotion regulation. Imagine what would have happened if she had gotten angry and yelled at Rob or gone silent and behaved in a passive–aggressive manner. It could have turned into a major conflict, perhaps even a relationship-ending one. Or imagine if she hadn't said anything at all. Rob never would have known how she felt, meaning he never would have had the opportunity to meet her needs. The relationship would have lacked mutuality right from the start.

Julianne also used her insight and mutuality skills to ask questions to try to understand Rob, and she responded to him in a caring manner. Then she proposed a plan for mutual problem solving. Rob was responsive, which suggests he's interested in being mutual and is treating Julianne in a way that shows he knows and likes her. However, if Rob hadn't been responsive, Julianne would need to consider this as she assesses whether he can meet her needs and as she makes decisions about the future of their relationship.

This example also shows how healthy relationships are not problem free—they're relationships in which potential problems are resolved before they become serious repetitive needs conflicts. And the reality is that they're going to come up somewhat regularly.

Julianne's been away all week. She woke up sooo excited this morning because today she flies home and gets to see Rob tonight. When her plane lands, she texts Rob, "Landed! Can't wait to see you!" No reply by the time she gets home, so she calls:

Julianne: (*He picks up; the music's loud.*) Hi, where are you? Didn't you get my text?
Rob: I'm sorry, Babe. I had the phone in my pocket. Jessica and I are celebrating a big win at work. I'll be right over. Ten minutes tops.
Julianne: Okay, see you soon.

Forty-five minutes go by. She's getting annoyed, thinking, "We're supposed to be having this fun night together, and he's out drinking with Jessica." He finally shows up, and she can tell he's drunk. He's all lovey-dovey, but she's not feeling it. It's not how she wanted the night to go. She's not sure what to do. Ask him to leave? Put him to bed? She really wants to talk about why he was out with Jessica getting drunk on the night she was coming home, but she knows it would be unproductive to try to talk with him about that now. So she puts him to bed.

The next morning she says, "How are you feeling this morning?"

Rob: Ugh, not too good.
Julianne: I'm not surprised. You were pretty drunk. Do you remember?
Rob: Kind of. I remember being at the bar celebrating, but I don't remember how I got here.
Julianne: You took a cab.
Rob: Oh.
Julianne: Listen, I was pretty hurt last night. I was so excited to see you, but the night didn't go at all as I had wanted it to. You knew I was coming home, we hadn't seen each other in a week, yet you decided to go to the bar with Jessica and get drunk.
Rob: I didn't intend to get drunk, and I was excited to see you. Things just got out of hand.
Julianne: Apparently.
Rob: I'm so sorry. I didn't mean to ruin our night. I had a tough week too and wanted to blow off some steam before coming over, but I see that was a bad decision.
Julianne: I guess there's a bit more to this for me as well. I'm not a jealous person, but I sometimes feel jealous of Jessica.
Rob: Whaaat?
Julianne: Yeah. You discussed taking on that London project with her. You go out and blow off steam with her. I want to be that person.
Rob: You are. You totally are.

Julianne: I just don't want to feel second to Jessica.

Rob: You're not second, but you have to deal with the fact that Jessica is my coworker and my friend, and I am going to go to her, and I am going to blow off steam with her. That's what we do. I need you to be able to deal with this.

Julianne: You're right. I want to be able to deal with this. I like Jessica, and I know how important she is to you. I just need to know that I'm your priority.

Rob: Understood. If there's anything I'm doing that makes you feel like you're not, just let me know so we can deal with it. I want you to trust me.

Julianne: (*thinking*) I didn't even realize until you said you want me to trust you that I wasn't. I do trust you. I'm sorry. I love you. And yes, I'll point anything out that makes me feel uncomfortable.

Rob: Good. I love you, very much.

The next weekend, Julianne and Rob are about to leave for an over-night getaway. He meets her at her apartment, and they're chatting about their plans as she's finalizing her packing. She had been running late, so she's feeling a bit stressed. She's got everything laid out on her bed just so, and she's rolling up things carefully and putting them in her suitcase. She hands him a printed list of their itinerary and driving directions.

Rob: Wow, aren't you the organized one!

Julianne: (*annoyed*) Yes, I am. Is there a problem with that?

Rob: No, not at all, I'm just—

Julianne: (*She interrupts him and is clearly irritated.*) You can see I'm stressed out here, and you pick this time to criticize me? When I'm only trying to be helpful and make our trip go smoothly!

Rob: Hang on, Julianne. I am not criticizing you.

Julianne: It sure feels like you are.

Rob: I was just teasing. I didn't mean anything by it. In fact, I really like how organized you are. You're much better than me at this kind of stuff.

Julianne: Thanks, but don't tease me about being overorganized. I'm sensitive about that.

Rob: I see that. I didn't realize. (*genuinely*) I'm sorry. I really am. (*goes over and hugs her and says gently*) You know, I'm not Gregory.

Julianne: I know. I do know that.

This last scenario is a great example of Julianne not being able to regulate her emotions in the moment, but then being able to recover. This was facilitated by Rob's ability to keep his emotions in check and their ability to genuinely apologize, forgive one another, and make a mutual plan for doing things differently in the future. This example also demonstrates how it's both difficult and necessary to use insight into who our partner is to guide our understanding of him and our behavior. In the moment, Rob wasn't realizing his comment might trigger Julianne's concerns about being criticized, and Julianne wasn't realizing that Rob actually isn't a critical guy. Once they reminded each other, in a caring way, both were better able to be more sensitive and reality based.

Sometimes it takes a while to develop insight into your partner. You can get caught off guard by something you don't understand and not know what to do. Julianne and Rob found this out the first morning at their seaside rental.

Julianne wakes up, smells coffee, and gets up to see Rob making breakfast. She puts her arms around his waist, kisses the back of his neck, and says, "Go back to bed or go watch TV. I'll finish up breakfast."

Rob: Why are you telling me what to do?
Julianne: (surprised) I'm not telling you what to do.
Rob: Yes, you are.
Julianne: No, I'm not.
Rob: What did you just say?
Julianne: I said I would finish making breakfast.
Rob: No, you told me to go back to bed. That's telling me what to do.
   (Julianne is confused and not sure what to say.)
Rob: I don't like being told what to do. Something inside me goes, "You think I'm stupid." I don't tell people what to do. I discuss what to do and agree on things to do. When I have to tell a person what to do I think less of them.
Julianne: (uncertain) Okay.

She's not sure what to say. She doesn't want to make things worse, so she apologizes and lets him continue making breakfast, but she can't help wondering, "Where did that come from?" They go about their day and enjoy the rest of the weekend.

Julianne is right to wonder "Where did that come from?" It could be a red flag. Is it an unmet need of Rob's? Does it tell her something about his character or his willingness to be mutual? Is it a vulnerability that he has that comes from something earlier in his life? Julianne needs to keep her eyes open to figure out what it is.

A couple of weeks later, she gets the chance. Julianne and Rob were talking one night while Rob was out of town on business. He was describing something that happened with one of his clients that he was upset about, and Julianne suggested he take a different approach.

Rob: (angrily) No kidding, Julianne. As if I didn't think to try that? Really? What am I, stupid?
Julianne: Rob, I didn't say you were stupid! I'm only trying to help.
Rob: Well, that's not helpful.

Julianne: (She remembers this came up before and she didn't know how to deal with it). What's going on, Rob? I don't think you're stupid. In fact, you're one of the smartest, most business-savvy people I know. I always tell you that, don't I?

Rob: Yes, but when you tell me what to do it makes me feel like you think I'm an idiot.

Julianne: First of all, I'm not telling you what to do. I'm trying to help you problem-solve, and I'm doing this because I care about you, not because I think you're an idiot. Why would I ever think that of you?

Rob: I don't know. It just feels that way.

Julianne: (gently) Do you think it might be possible that it's just a feeling, not the reality?

Rob: It always feels to me like when people tell me what to do they must think I'm stupid.

Julianne: Where does that come from?

Rob: I don't know. I guess because my dad was pretty harsh with me. And I'm pretty harsh on myself too.

Julianne: You don't deserve that. You're so awesome!

Rob: (smiling) Thanks.

Julianne: Okay, well what do you want me to do? What do you need? Do you want me to not ever make suggestions? *(playfully)* Do you want me to remind you of how great I think you are?

Rob: (laughing) No, I don't know what I want you to do.

Julianne: How about if when I want to make a suggestion I tell you that and ask you if you want to hear it? Is that a good start?

Rob: Yes, that would be good.

Julianne: And can you try to remember how smart I know you are?

Rob: (smiling) I'll try.

I/ME

Intimacy Builds When You Use the Skills to Negotiate Conflict

Look how Julianne is conveying care and positive regard in response to Rob being vulnerable in the context of a conflict. That's an important way that intimacy can develop. By using the skills you can turn a potentially negative, relationship-damaging situation into a positive, relationship-enhancing situation.

In this example, like the earlier one with Julianne, you can see how Rob was bringing an earlier experience into the current situation and reacting to his own ideas about whether he's stupid, leading him to misperceive Julianne's intention. Julianne used her skills to manage her emotions and help them engage in mutual problem solving, and she did so in a caring and supportive way that conveyed how much she likes and respects Rob.

In these last few examples you can see how conflicts handled skillfully can actually build intimacy—a lot more than if conflict were avoided altogether. This happens partly because both Rob and Julianne show a willingness to acknowledge when they've inadvertently hurt the other one. It's not enough to declare that you never intended to hurt your partner. It's very important to be sensitive to the impact your action had, no matter how unintended, and to show that you care about your partner's feelings and that you don't want to hurt him or her.

The Next Steps: Six Months In

Rob and Julianne's relationship continues to progress. They've been together for about six months now, but it still feels to Julianne like there's a lot more to learn about whether they can work as a couple. It's mainly because of how much they work and travel. Although it's true that they have dealt effectively with the stressors this brings, it reduces the amount of time they can spend together, which means they still have a lot to learn about one another, such as what it would be like to negotiate day-to-day-together kinds of things. Julianne is okay with this, though. She likes how it's developing slowly. She's really enjoying their relationship, and she's not in any rush. But that's not necessarily how other people feel. The questions are all starting: "How long have you two been together? Are you going to get married? Is he the one? When are you getting engaged?" Even Jessica's asked her a few questions. Fortunately, Julianne has learned from the past. Now she's not going to make decisions based on external pressure. She's not going to worry about what people think she "should" do or about what anyone else thinks about what she wants and her decisions. Getting stuck on "should" nearly resulted in her marrying Gregory. She made a commitment to herself not to repeat that mistake.

But what does she want? Julianne needs to figure this out. She and Rob have spoken a little bit about this. For example, they both want to be with someone who supports their career ambitions and can tolerate their work schedules, so they're good on that front. And she knows they're both open to the idea of children, though neither is absolutely committed to having kids, and neither is in any rush to decide. They discussed it one day when Rob was talking about how cute his niece is. She asked him if he wanted children someday, and they both had similar feelings. So, they're okay on that front too, at least for now. They've also agreed to be monogamous. They had that conversation about two months in. Julianne was nervous about bringing it up, but she knew she couldn't let anxiety get in her way, so she marshaled her courage:

Julianne: I want to check in with you about something.

Rob: What's up?

Julianne: We've been dating for about two months now, and I'm really happy with how things are going.

Rob: (*smiling*) Me too.

Julianne: I just want you to know that I'm not seeing anyone else. I wasn't when we started and I wasn't looking to date around, and I was wondering whether you are seeing other people.

Rob: No, I'm not. Once I met you I really wanted to give us a try, and it's worked out. I don't want to date anyone else right now.

Julianne: (*smiling and relieved*) Okay, I'm glad to hear it. I feel the same way. So, does that mean we are agreeing to be monogamous?

Rob: I didn't say I wasn't sleeping with anyone else. No, just kidding! Yes, we're monogamous, of course.

Julianne: Okay, great, and if either of us feels we can't be in the future, can we agree that we'll tell each other and talk about it? I don't believe in cheating.

Rob: Agreed.

This conversation set the stage nicely for open communication about their relationship.

Julianne: I don't know if this is happening to you, but everyone in my life seems very curious about the future of our relationship. They all want to know what's happening. So it got me thinking that I wanted to talk with you about this. Not because I want anything different than what we have right now, but because it seems like each of us should know how the other envisions the future. And I don't even mean necessarily with me. I mean in general, how have you imagined your life would go?

Rob: Most of my thoughts about the future have been about my career. I've always seen that as the most important thing, and all my planning has been to help me achieve my goals. But I've also always wanted to have a relationship, the right one, like I've described to you.

Julianne: Is marriage important to you?

Rob: Yes and no. If I get married, I want it to work, to last. I want it to feel like the right thing to do for the relationship. I don't feel the need to get married just to be married. I think that two people can be committed whether they're married or not. Though I do think that if there were children marriage would be important.

Julianne: For a long time all I did was work. I wanted a relationship, but I couldn't imagine how to have one at the same time as my career. I've worked hard at finding more balance in recent years, and now that's really important to me. I want to make time for both, like we've been doing, and I definitely like the idea of having a true partner. Someone who's there for you. Someone you can count on.

Someone you can imagine growing old with. Do I want to be married? I guess, in some ways, yes. But I want marriage to be a good decision, not just "the next step" that you take because it's "time."

Rob: I agree with that.

Julianne: I also want to say that I'm definitely interested in seeing where our relationship can go. I really am interested in figuring out whether this has the potential to work for the long run. I'm really in love with you, but I also really like who you are.

Rob: Thank you. That feels good, and I feel the same way.

Julianne: I'm glad to hear that. I really feel like my needs are getting met with you. Do you feel like I'm meeting yours?

Rob: I do. You take such good care of me, and you accept my crazy work life, and you let me be me.

Julianne: So, what do you think I should say when people ask me what's happening in our relationship?

Rob: How about that we love each other and are happily committed to being together and continuing to see what's next for us?

Julianne: Yeah, that sounds good. It's really true. I don't think everyone will understand that, but I guess that doesn't really matter.

In this conversation Julianne and Rob openly discussed their ideas about what kind of relationship they want. This is so necessary. Without it, Julianne might have moved forward on inaccurate assumptions and expectations, finding out only later that she and Rob did not want the same things. That they had similar visions suggests it makes sense to continue the relationship. Had they had very different visions, Julianne (and Rob) would have needed to think carefully about whether this was the right relationship for them so that they could make a thoughtful decision about whether to stay together. You also can see in Julianne's statements that she's embraced the idea that one must make such thoughtful decisions rather than "slide" into things. If she can continue to live this out, she will be able to keep making healthy choices. Julianne and Rob also have jointly defined their relationship in a way that feels right for them. They're aware it might not be what others would want, but that doesn't matter. As we've said all along, there are many ways to have a relationship. It's all about finding out what is right or wrong for you, and Julianne has done that.

Julianne also told Rob that she likes him. It might seem that "like" is simply a lower magnitude of "love" and therefore doesn't need to be declared separately once you've confessed your love. That's not entirely true (see the sidebar on page 292). To have a healthy relationship, you have to be able to say "I know and like him," not just "I'm so in love!" The fact that Julianne both loves and likes Rob is a great sign for their relationship.

I/ME

Isn't It More Important to Love Him Than to Like Him?

No, it's not. Both are necessary.

But, if you love someone, isn't it understood that you like him too? Absolutely not.

Loving and liking someone are separate. Typically, we love with our heart. And we can love someone whose behaviors we really don't like (remember Anna and Eric?). As we've been showing, we like with our head. We assess "I know and like him" with evidence, and then we put head and heart together, using wise mind, to make healthy relationship decisions.

The Next Steps: 12 Months In

Julianne and Rob are happily living their "committed to being together, continuing to see what's next" relationship. The more time they share and the more they talk and reveal themselves to one another, and meet each other's needs in a mutual way, the more their sense of respect, good communication, intimacy, security, and positive regard grows—all the components of a healthy relationship.

Julianne also has continued to share her sexual interests (including erotica!) with Rob, who has been an eager participant, and Julianne feels safe in Rob's acceptance of her. Their work schedules continue to limit the amount of time they can spend together, and Julianne starts to think about how much she'd like waking up with him more often, being able to give him a quick kiss as one of them runs out the door, or just having more in-person conversations compared to phone and Skype. "Hmm . . . " she wonders. "Maybe I'm feeling ready to consider living together?"

She knows, however, that doing so is a big step. She slid into it with Gregory at his insistence without preparing for the challenges. She wants to make this decision with more forethought and accurate expectations. In addition, she wants Rob to make it willingly. If she's ready and he's not, she knows she'll need to give him the time he requires. Pressuring him, as Gregory did to her, would be a disaster. "I want Rob to be excited about living with me, looking forward to it, not feeling like he's got to make some difficult decision." She decides to talk with Rob.

Julianne: I want to tell you something. I've been thinking about how happy I am with you and how well our relationship continues to go. I just love being with you. And as I've been thinking about that I realized I would really like to be with you more. I think I would feel really comfortable actually living together.

Rob: (*He smiles but says nothing.*)

Julianne: I'm not actually asking you to live together right now. I just wanted to tell you I realized I would like that, and that's a sign to me of how good things are for me with you. What do you think of that?

Rob: It makes me feel good that you feel that way about me. I think we should think about what it would be like.

Julianne: I do too. If we decide to do it, I want us to be prepared for what it might really be like. For instance, as you know (*smiling*), I'm really neat and organized, and I know you're less so. Gregory and I had the same issue, and it was a disaster because we couldn't find a way to compromise. I know I probably need to ease up a bit. It's probably not fair to hold everyone to my standards.

Rob: (*teasing*) You think?

Julianne: (*smiling*) Very funny! Listen, I'm admitting my part. How do you think you'd handle it?

Rob: I definitely could not be as neat as you. I just know myself. I don't have it in me.

Julianne: Would you get upset if I picked up after you?

Rob: No, that would be awesome actually. (*He laughs loudly.*)

Julianne: If there were really specific things that were important to me, would you be willing to do them?

Rob: Like what?

Julianne: Like wiping up messes from the counter or making sure the trash isn't over-flowing?

Rob: I think I'd be willing to work on that. You might have to remind me, though. If you just ask me, I'll do things.

Julianne: I don't want to feel like I'm nagging you or have you feel that way.

Rob: I know what you mean. I'd let you know if I felt that way.

Julianne: (*smiling*) Okay, well, it seems like we both know this would be a challenge and we'd both have to work on it. As long as we know this going in, we could probably deal with it, right?

Rob: (*laughing*) Yeah, I think we could figure it out.

Julianne: What kinds of things do you think would be hard for you living together?

Rob: I'm really used to coming and going as I please. I'm not used to having to live on another person's schedule, so I wonder what that would be like for me.

Julianne: Like when?

Rob: Like now I eat when I feel like it. Sometimes I just grab something. I don't keep much in my fridge, and if I run out of something, like milk, I'll just get my coffee out rather than buying more and making it at home. Or if I go for drinks with people from work, I come home whenever I want. I wouldn't want to feel like you're home waiting or that you set the time I have to come home.

Julianne: Yeah, I get that your independence is important to you.

Rob: Yeah, and I don't want to disappoint you.

Julianne: We both need different things, and we'll have to figure out our roles and our priorities to make sure things feel equal for us. I know that if I'm the one in charge of keeping the house in order—which is fine for me, I'm happy to do that—I won't feel good if it means that to do so I have to give up things that I like while you're out doing the things that you like.

Rob: I wouldn't want that either. In fact, I'd rather both of us do the things we like— together and separate—and make the house and those kinds of things lower priorities.

Julianne: I see your point. I know that would be hard for me since I'm a neat freak, but it does make some sense. I'd just have to find a way to feel comfortable in our home, which for me means having a pretty neat and clean place.

Rob: Well, I want to help you with that as much as I can, but I don't need that in the same way you do, so I agree that you figuring out what's tolerable for you is a good idea. And you know what? We both make good salaries. Let's just hire a cleaning service. Problem solved!

Julianne: (*teasing*) I hear you talking as if this was really going to happen.

Rob: I'm thinking maybe it should.

Julianne: Then let's keep talking about these things.

Rob and Julianne know it's important to think about what roles they'll each play if their relationship leads to sharing a home (see the box on the facing page). Next they discuss the issue of Rob going out with friends.

Julianne: I'd be perfectly fine with your going out with your friends and staying out late. Yes, Jessica too! I know them, and I trust you all, but if you choose to go out with your friends when we already have plans or something important to do, I know that won't feel good to me.

Rob: I wouldn't do that. I love being with you. In fact, kind of like you're saying, the great thing about living together is that we get to be together. I'm thinking about this as a way for us to spend more time together, not less.

Julianne: Yes, me too.

As Julianne and Rob are thinking about whether and when to move in together, Julianne learns that her team at work is being asked to take over a failing project from another team. It has an obscene deadline and workload. Her boss asked her to sleep on it, tell him tomorrow. She's so excited, but it will take her across the country, away from Rob, and could delay any decisions they make about living together. Later that evening she talks to him about it:

Julianne: I'm going to have to work insane hours, travel a lot, and be away for about the first two months with very little time to come back home. This means I won't have a lot of time for you. Are you okay with this?

I/ME

Have You Thought about What You Want Your Role to Be in a Serious Relationship?

Regardless of whether you want traditional or nontraditional roles in a relationship, both people will need to think about their roles with regard to things like career choices, moneymaking, housework, and child care. Spending time doing so will help you develop insight about what you want and will allow you to negotiate rather than slide into a role.

Rob: I am. When either of us gets these kinds of opportunities we need to take them, and I want us to be understanding and not get mad if we don't have as much time to talk or text.

Julianne: That's what I want too. But this means we'll have to put our plans for moving in together on hold for a bit. We won't have the time to work on it together.

Rob: I know. That's okay. It will give us something to look forward to.

Julianne: You're so amazing. Okay, so just know that I love you so much even if I'm not in as much contact.

Rob: I get it. Don't worry. I know what you're doing. It'll be drama free on my side.

And it is! They call and text as much as they can. They develop their own little text phrases to let each other know what they're thinking and that they feel loved and cared about. They're proud of how well they're managing things, even though it's hard for Julianne as each night she's aware of how much she wants to be able to tell Rob all about her day and everything that's happening and hear all about him as well. She's keeping a running list for the next time they're together and reminding herself, "I'll see him soon. It will be fantastic." And it is. She gets a quick break to go home, and they reconnect and have fabulous sex and then prepare for the next separation.

After another month of this, Julianne is really missing Rob. She's feeling disconnected from him and exhausted from work. He's also super busy, still having to go to London occasionally. For a few days, their time zone differences make it impossible to have any real-time interaction, and the texts are few and far between. Then they keep missing each other's calls. When she and Rob finally get a phone call scheduled, he has to cancel it because of an emergency work meeting. Julianne is so frustrated. She starts thinking, "This is never going to work. We haven't spoken in so long. I can't believe he had to cancel. Couldn't he get out of the meeting just this once?" She catches herself: "Wait, I probably couldn't if it was me. I can't hold him to standards I don't hold myself to." She texts him, "I understand about your meeting. I just miss you so much." She doesn't get a text back. She wonders whether the separation is easier on him than it is on her. "Maybe he doesn't miss me as much? Maybe he doesn't need me as much as I need him? What does this mean about our relationship?" She texts him again: "Do you miss me?" No reply. During the night she tortures herself with these questions and with imagining the worst about why he didn't reply—"He doesn't miss me," "He's not really at a work meeting," "He's with Jessica," and so on. And then the next morning his text comes. "So sorry I couldn't reply. You can't believe what's going on here. Can't wait to tell you. Miss you so much too. Can't go on like this! Will definitely call you later." Relief! "I tortured myself all night for nothing," she thinks. "I've got to keep working on not letting my fears get the best of me."

Julianne is right, although we can empathize with her. We all have fears and insecurities, and sometimes they do get the best of us. We get all sorts of crazy stories in our heads, stories that have nothing to do with reality. And when we do, it's a sign that we need to look to the evidence in our relationship, identify what we need, and then communicate that to our partner.

That night Rob calls:

Julianne: I am so happy to talk to you!
Rob: Me too! How are you?
Julianne: Well, I have to tell you what happened to me last night. I think it's a sign that we've been out of touch too long.
Rob: (*concerned*) What happened?

She explains how her thoughts and emotions got away from her and how she got caught up in a crazy story and could barely sleep.

Rob: I'm so sorry, babe! I never want you to feel like that. You're so important to me. Don't think those crazy things.
Julianne: Thank you, love. Your saying that means a lot to me. I'm going to do my best to stay in reality. It's just that I miss you and I really need to connect with you. I need to feel how much you care again. I need to know I matter and that you need me too.
Rob: I do, Julianne. You matter so much to me. I want you to feel good, and I miss you too. When we get back home together, let's talk more about how we're going to deal with these situations in the future. We've got to figure out a way to make this work for us.
Julianne: Yes, we definitely do. Oh yeah, what's going on with you?
Rob: I got a promotion, a big one!
Julianne: How big?

Rob: My boss's job.

Julianne: Ohhh! I'm so happy for you. Were you and Jessica celebrating last night?

Rob: No, it's being announced next week. I've been asked not to mention it till then. So you're the first one to know.

Julianne: We'll celebrate when I get home.

And just like that, Julianne feels better again. Why? Because Rob responded to her needs. Doing so is a sign of mutuality and, therefore, a sign of a healthy relationship. If he didn't respond, if he got defensive or blaming or just didn't get it, it would have been a sign that Julianne might not be able to get her needs met in this relationship, and she would need to think carefully about whether to stay with Rob.

When Julianne returns to her normal work schedule, she and Rob spend as much time together as they can. They take their missing each other so much as a good sign that they really do want to move forward into living together, and they both feel confident in being able to work out any issues that come up because they have a lot of evidence that they can communicate well, be vulnerable with one another, and trust that they will treat each other with care.

Of course, just as in any relationship, situations continue to arise that require the use of their I/ME skills, and Julianne and Rob continue to negotiate potential needs conflicts.

For example, Rob's out of town for another meeting in London, and Julianne's grandmother dies. She texts him to let him know, and he texts back, "So sorry! Are you okay? Sympathy to your family, send my love." She replies, "Thank you, sad, but okay" and he texts back, "Keep me posted and let me know what you need." She takes a couple days off work to help her mom make preparations for the funeral, and the day before the funeral she realizes she hasn't heard from Rob. She figures he's busy at work, but then thinks, "Wait, this is different. My grandmother died. He should be checking in with me," and she gets angry. She feels like sending him an angry text. She starts to type it out, but deletes it. The last thing she wants is to start a text argument. She knows he hates arguing, and she doesn't want to make things worse than they are. She calculates the time in London and decides to call him.

Rob: (*concerned*) Hi, I'm in a dinner meeting, is everything okay?

Julianne: Yes, it's just that I haven't heard from you. You haven't even called to see how I am, and I feel hurt. The funeral is tomorrow.

Rob: Oh, I'm sorry. I was just trying to give you space. I know when I'm sad, I need space to think and deal with everything, so that's why I didn't call. Besides, I knew you'd be inundated with calls from people, and I figured you probably were tired of talking.

Julianne: I am kind of tired of talking, but not to you. You're the person I most want to talk with. You're the one I need support from.

Rob: I didn't realize that.

Julianne: How could you not realize that?

Rob: I told you—because I would feel differently in your position.

Julianne: Try to use what you know about me, not what you know about yourself. You know you're my go-to person.

Rob: I know, but I didn't realize you wanted me to be checking in with you every day. I don't have a crystal ball, Julianne. I can't read your mind. And I'm so busy here right now that I lose track of time. I am literally working every moment. You have to tell me what you need.

Julianne: Well, in this case I would have liked you to figure it out. I think it's a reasonable expectation that your boyfriend calls you, even every day to check in with you, if you've had a difficult situation in your life. Don't you think that's reasonable? Why should I have to say, "Call me"? I want you to show you care about me by knowing what I need, and if I experience a death again, or I'm away on a project dealing with a tough client, I want you to call me and check in with me for support.

Rob: Look, you know I love you and care about you and want to support you. I'll do my best to do what you're asking. I do see what you're saying, but please, just tell me when you need me, especially when I'm busy. I promise that if you just tell me I will be there for you.

When they get off the phone, Julianne thinks a lot about what they discussed. She believes what she wants is reasonable, but she does see what Rob is saying. She thinks, "If he really wants to meet my expectations, as he says he does, then I'm going to trust in that and give him every opportunity to do so. I'm going to try letting him know and see what happens. If he responds, then it's a win–win situation." Rob also thinks about what they discussed. He does see her point. It's true he can't be a mind reader, but he realizes it is kind of obvious that he should check in with her at times like this. He decides to add a reminder on his phone to call Julianne each day.

In this example, Julianne and Rob try to negotiate a conflict between her needs to feel cared about, supported, and important and his needs to feel listened to and accepted. She wants him to show he cares enough about her feelings and sees her preferences for how she wants to be supported as important enough to make sure to call her every day when she's experiencing something difficult. He wants her to understand and accept that he does care about her, but he can't always anticipate her needs and wants her help with this. Both Julianne's and Rob's needs are valid, and they make valid points to one another. That Julianne and Rob can see this shows they're using mutuality skills to resolve this needs conflict. They're seeing each other's perspective, uniting against the problem, and coming up with strategies to try to meet each other's needs in the way they prefer. More evidence of a healthy relationship.

Moving In

They found a great new place in a neighborhood they love, near where they each work, and today is move-in day. Julianne is so excited. She posts, "Move-in day with the best guy ever. So happy!" along with a sweet selfie of her and Rob standing and smiling in the empty apartment. Julianne is proud of herself for making this decision in a thoughtful way. She feels confident she's selected a guy who meets her key needs and with whom she can have a mutual relationship. Still, she knows that, just like before, she has to keep doing her needs assessment and using the skills to make sure the relationship continues to work. Fortunately, Rob has demonstrated that he's capable of doing so with her. If he wasn't, she wouldn't be moving in with him.

Bringing It All Together: Using the Needs to Put Healthy Relationship Concepts into Practice

In Chapter 1, we discussed how we all know, in theory, that a healthy relationship is characterized by things such as respect, good communication, intimacy, security, and positive regard. To conclude this book we want to make sure you see how the I/ME skills help women make these concepts come to life. For Julianne, this has happened in a variety of ways.

- By taking a mutual approach to her relationship, Julianne has been an effective communicator of her needs and an open listener to Rob's. This type of mutuality also conveys Julianne's respect for Rob's needs, increases intimacy through self-disclosure and willing compromises, leads to greater security because they have one another's best interests at heart and want to meet one another's needs, and fosters a sense of positive regard toward one another.
- Julianne's insight into herself has allowed her to be authentic and genuine with Rob, and her insight into Rob has allowed her to understand his strengths and vulnerabilities, all of which facilitates communication, intimacy, security, and positive regard.
- Julianne's ability to regulate her emotions adaptively does the same. With her emotions in check, she can tolerate situations that are uncertain, talk through potential conflicts successfully (allowing both partners to feel safe in dealing with problems), manage dif-

ficult feelings like anxiety, jealousy, and hurt, and take the risk to ask for her needs to be met.

- Therefore, by using the I/ME skills, Julianne has set in motion a healthy cycle of respect, good communication, intimacy, security, and positive regard, where each component fuels and sustains the others.

Is Julianne in a healthy relationship? Yes, she is. And if you use the skills in this book, you can be too.

Resources

Relationships and Sex

Science of Relationships
www.scienceofrelationships.com

The Anatomy of Love
https://theanatomyoflove.com

Creating Connections
www.drsuejohnson.com

Make Love Not Porn
http://makelovenotporn.com

It's Your (Sex) Life
www.itsyoursexlife.com

SexualityandU.Ca
www.sexualityandu.ca/sexual-health/how-do-i-know-i-am-ready-for-sex/healthy-relationships

Action Canada for Sexual Health & Rights
www.sexualhealthandrights.ca

Relationships Australia
www.relationships.org.au

Connected Space (Australia)
http://connectedspace.com.au

Domestic Violence

National Resource Center on Domestic Violence
www.nrcdv.org

National Domestic Violence Hotline
www.thehotline.org

Love Is Respect
www.loveisrespect.org/dating-basics/healthy-relationships

Domestic Violence Helpline/VictimLink BC
www.domesticviolencebc.ca

Department of Justice Canada
www.justice.gc.ca/eng/cj-jp/fv-vf

National Domestic Violence Helpline (United Kingdom)
www.nationaldomesticviolencehelpline.org.uk

National Centre for Domestic Violence (United Kingdom)
www.ncdv.org.uk

Domestic Violence Prevention Centre (Australia)
www.domesticviolence.com.au

ReachOut.com (Australia)
http://au.reachout.com/what-is-domestic-violence

Notes

Introduction

PAGE XI: Analysis of bestselling dating advice books: Eaton, A. A., & Rose, S. (2011). Has dating become more egalitarian? A 35-year review using *Sex Roles*. *Sex Roles*, *64*, 843–862.

Chapter 1

PAGE 11: Mia finally convinces her to sign up for online dating, but then she gets to this question: Actual question from Plenty of Fish dating site. Retrieved from *www. pof.com*.

PAGE 12: Lexi's online dating profile: Actual profile format from Plenty of Fish dating site. Retrieved from www.pof.com.

PAGE 15: Olivia's read Meg Jay's book: Jay, M. (2012). *The defining decade: Why your twenties matter—and how to make the most of them now*. New York: Hachette Book Group.

PAGE 16: You would all likely name things like *respect*: Gottman, J. M. (2000). *The seven principles for making marriage work: A practical guide from the country's foremost relationship expert*. New York: Three Rivers Press.

Graber, E. C., Laurenceau, J.-P., Miga, E., Chango, J., & Coan, J. (2011). Conflict and love: Predicting newlywed marital outcomes from two interaction contexts. *Journal of Family Psychology*, *25*, 541–550.

Johnson, S., & Sims, A. (2000). Attachment theory: A map for couples therapy. In T. M. Levy (Ed.), *Handbook of attachment interventions* (pp. 169–191). San Diego, CA: Academic Press.

Laurenceau, J.-P., & Kleinman, B. M. (2006). Intimacy in personal relationships. In A. L. Vangelisti & D. Perlman (Eds.), *The Cambridge handbook of personal relationships* (pp. 637–653). New York: Cambridge University Press.

Mikulincer, M., & Shaver, P. R. (2013). The role of attachment security in adolescent and adult close relationships. In J. A. Simpson & L. Campbell (Eds.), *The Oxford handbook of close relationships* (pp. 66–89). New York: Oxford University Press.

Murray, S. L., & Derrick, J. (2005). A relationship-specific sense of felt security: How perceived regard regulates relationship-enhancement processes. In M. W. Baldwin (Ed.), *Interpersonal cognition* (pp. 153–179). New York: Guilford Press.

303

Murray, S. L., Holmes, J. G., & Collins, N. L. (2006). Optimizing assurance: The risk regulation system in relationships. *Psychological Bulletin, 132,* 641–666.

PAGE 17: Three key skills: *insight, mutuality,* and *emotion regulation*: Davila, J. (2010). Romantic competence. In I. B. Weiner & W. E. Craighead (Eds.), *Encyclopedia of psychology* (4th ed., Vol. 3, p. 1475). Hoboken, NJ: Wiley.

Davila, J., Latack, J., Bhatia, V., & Feinstein, B. A. (March, 2015). *Romantic competence among female emerging adults: Construct validity and associations with relationship behaviors and individual difference variables.* Paper presented at the biennial meeting of the Society for Research in Child Development, Philadelphia, PA.

Davila, J., Steinberg, S. J., Ramsay, M., Stroud, C. B., Starr, L., & Yoneda, A. (2009). Assessing romantic competence in adolescence: The Romantic Competence Interview. *Journal of Adolescence, 32,* 55–75.

Shulman, S., Davila, J., & Shachar-Shapira, L. (2011). Assessing romantic competence among older adolescents. *Journal of Adolescence, 34,* 397–406.

For *mutuality* and *insight* specifically: Murray, S. L., & Holmes, J. G. (2011). *Interdependent minds: The dynamics of close relationships.* New York: Guilford Press.

Chapter 2

PAGE 23: July 2013 *New York Times* **article:** Taylor, K. (2013, July 12). Sex on campus, she can play that game too. *New York Times.* Retrieved from *www.nytimes.com/2013/07/14/fashion/sex-on-campus-she-can-play-that-game-too.html?_r=0&adxnnl=1&pagewanted=all&adxnnlx=1387225305-pB446Iz/CvYsCxS4O/zVbQ.*

PAGE 24: One woman voiced her concerns: Wolken, A. (2013, July 15). What hooking up at Penn is really about. *Philadelphia Magazine.* Retrieved from *www.phillymag.com/news/2013/07/15/penn-females-hook-up-culture-kate-taylor.*

PAGE 24: Sheryl Sandberg's talk: Sandberg, S. (2013). *Lean in: Women, work, and the will to lead.* New York: Knopf.

PAGE 24: "What would I do if I weren't afraid?": Sandberg, S. (2013, December). So we leaned in . . . now what? TED Talk. Retrieved from *www.ted.com/talks/sheryl_sandberg_so_we_leaned_in_now_what?language=en.*

PAGE 25: She felt as if she were breaking a social taboo: Taylor, K. (2013, July 12). Sex on campus, she can play that game too. *New York Times.* Retrieved from *www.nytimes.com/2013/07/14/fashion/sex-on-campus-she-can-play-that-game-too.html?_r=0&adxnnl=1&pagewanted=all&adxnnlx=1387225305-pB446Iz/CvYsCxS4O/zVbQ.*

PAGE 26: Do You Internalize Pressure?: Adichie, C. N. (2013, April 12). We should all be feminists. TEDxEuston. Retrieved from *http://tedxtalks.ted.com/video/We-should-all-be-feminists-Chim.*

PAGE 27: Thirty-six percent of adolescents: Carver, K., Joyner, K., & Udry, J. R. (2003). National estimates of adolescent romantic relationships. In P. Florsheim (Ed.), *Adolescent romantic relationships and sexual behavior: Theory, research, and practical implications* (pp. 291–329). New York: Cambridge University Press.

PAGE 27: Rates of involvement continue to grow into adulthood: Copen, C. E., Daniels, K., Vespa, J., & Mosher, W. D. (2012). *First marriages in the United States: Data from the 2006–2010 National Survey of Family Growth* (National Health Statistics Reports No. 49). Hyattsville, MD: National Center for Health Statistics.

PAGE 27: Average age of first intercourse in the United States: Chandra, A., Mosher, W. D., Copen, C., & Sionean, C. (2011). *Sexual behavior, sexual attraction, and sexual identity in the United States: Data from the 2006–2008 National Survey of Family Growth* (National Health Statistics Reports No. 36). Hyattsville, MD: National Center for Health Statistics.

Martinez, G. M., Chandra, A., Abma, J. C., Jones, J., & Mosher, W. D. (2006).

Fertility, contraception, and fatherhood: Data on men and women from Cycle 6 (2002) of the National Survey of Family Growth (Vital and Health Statistics, Series 23, No. 26). Hyattsville, MD: National Center for Health Statistics.

Martinez, G., Copen, C. E., & Abma, J. C. (2011). *Teenagers in the United States: Sexual activity, contraceptive use, and childbearing, 2006–2010, National Survey of Family Growth* (Vital and Health Statistics, Series 23, No. 31). Hyattsville, MD: National Center for Health Statistics.

PAGE 27: Recent data on hookups: Fielder, R. L., Carey, K. B., & Carey, M. P. (2013). Are hookups replacing romantic relationships? A longitudinal study of first-year female college students. *Journal of Adolescent Health, 52,* 657–659.

Owen, J., Fincham, F. D., & Moore, J. (2011). Short-term prospective study of hooking up among college students. *Archives of Sexual Behavior, 40,* 331–341.

PAGE 27: Average age at which women first marry: U.S. Decennial Census (1930–2000); National Center for Health Statistics. (1995). Advance report of final marriage statistics, 1989 and 1990. *Monthly Vital Statistics Report, 43*(12, Suppl.), Table 9.

United States Census Bureau, American Community Survey. (2013). Retrieved from *http://factfinder.census.gov/faces/tableservices/jsf/pages/productview. xhtml?pid=ACS_13_1YR_B12007&prodType=table.*

PAGE 27: Marriage is becoming obsolete: Pew Research Center. (2010, November 18). The decline of marriage and the rise of new families (executive summary). Retrieved from *www.pewresearch.org/data-trend/society-and-demographics/marriage.*

PAGE 28: Over 50% of women ages 15–44: Copen, C. E., Daniels, K., & Mosher, W. D. (2013). *First premarital cohabitation in the United States: 2006–2010 National Survey of Family Growth* (National Health Statistics Reports, No. 64). Hyattsville, MD: National Center for Health Statistics.

PAGE 28: About 25% of those cohabiting couples: Copen, C. E., Daniels, K., & Mosher, W. D. (2013). *First premarital cohabitation in the United States: 2006–2010 National Survey of Family Growth* (National Health Statistics Reports, No. 64). Hyattsville, MD: National Center for Health Statistics.

PAGE 28: Greater risk for relationship problems and divorce: Rhoades, G. K., Stanley, S. M., & Markman, H. J. (2009). Couples' reasons for cohabitation: Associations with individual well-being and relationship quality. *Journal of Family Issues, 30,* 233–258.

PAGE 28: "Slide, rather than decide": Stanley, S. M., Rhoades, G. K., & Markman, H. J. (2006). Sliding versus deciding: Inertia and the premarital cohabitation effect. *Family Relations, 55*(4), 499–509.

PAGE 28: Lots of people get divorced: Stevenson, B., & Wolfer, J. (2011). Trends in marital stability. In L. R. Cohen & J. D. Wright (Eds.), *Research handbook in the law and economics of the family* (pp. 96–108). Northampton, MA: Edward Elgar.

PAGE 29: Risk factors for divorce: Gottman, J. M. (1994). *What predicts divorce?: The relationship between marital process and marital outcomes.* Hillsdale, NJ: Erlbaum.

Gottman, J. M. (2000). *The seven principles for making marriage work: A practical guide from the country's foremost relationship expert.* New York: Three Rivers Press.

Gottman, J. M., Coan, J., Carrere, S., & Swanson, C. (1998). Predicting marital happiness and stability from newlywed interactions. *Journal of Marriage and the Family, 60,* 5–22.

Lavner, J. A., & Bradbury, T. N. (2012). Why do even satisfied newlyweds eventually go on to divorce? *Journal of Family Psychology, 26,* 1–10.

Lawrence, E., & Bradbury, T. N. (2001). Physical aggression and marital dysfunction: A longitudinal analysis. *Journal of Family Psychology, 15,* 135–154.

Pasch, L. A., & Bradbury, T. N. (1998). Social support, conflict, and the development of marital dysfunction. *Journal of Consulting and Clinical Psychology, 66,* 219–230.

Rodrigues, A., Hall, J. H., & Fincham, F. D. (2006). What predicts divorce and relationship dissolution? In M. A. Fine & J. H. Harvey (Eds.), *Handbook of divorce and relationship dissolution* (pp. 85–112). Mahwah, NJ: Erlbaum.

Sullivan, K. T., Pasch, L. A., Johnson, M. D., & Bradbury, T. N. (2010). Social support, problem solving, and the longitudinal course of newlywed marriage. *Journal of Personality and Social Psychology, 98,* 631–644.

PAGE 29: Eighty-five percent of women have a child: Martinez, G. M., Daniels, K., & Chandra, A. (2012). *Fertility of men and women aged 15–44 years in the United States: National Survey of Family Growth, 2006–2010* (National Health Statistics Reports, No. 51). Hyattsville, MD: National Center for Health Statistics.

PAGE 29: Individuals ages 18–29 are less likely to link marriage: Wang, W., & Taylor, P. (2011, March 9). For millennials, parenthood trumps marriage. Pew Research Center. Retrieved from *www.pewsocialtrends.org/2011/03/09/for-millennials-parenthood-trumps-marriage.*

PAGE 31: Is Mia Normal?: Joyal, C. C., Cossette, A., & Lapierre, V. (2015). What exactly is an unusual sexual fantasy? *Journal of Sexual Medicine, 12,* 328–340.

PAGE 31: Meg Jay's . . . very first client: Jay, M. (2013). Why 30 is not the new 20. TED Talk. Retrieved from *www.youtube.com/watch?v=vhhgI4tSMwc.*

PAGE 31: Risk for subsequent divorce: Bramlett, M. D., & Mosher, W. D. (2002). *Cohabitation, marriage, divorce, and remarriage in the United States* (Vital and Health Statistics, Series 23, No. 22). Washington, DC: National Center for Health Statistics.

PAGE 33: Those in a committed relationship or a marriage: Horn, E. E., Xu, Y., Beam, C., Turkheimer, E., & Emery, R. E. (2013). Accounting for the physical and mental health benefits of entry into marriage: A genetically informed study of selection and causation. *Journal of Family Psychology, 27,* 30–41.

PAGE 33: Being in a bad relationship: Cano, A., & O'Leary, K. D. (2000). Infidelity and separations precipitate major depressive episodes and symptoms of nonspecific depression and anxiety. *Journal of Consulting and Clinical Psychology, 68,* 774–781.

Christian-Herman, J. L., O'Leary, K. D., & Avery-Leaf, S. (2001). The impact of severe negative events in marriage on depression. *Journal of Social and Clinical Psychology, 20,* 25–44.

Davila, J., Capaldi, D. M., & La Greca, A. (in press). Adolescent/young adult romantic relationships and psychopathology. In D. Cicchetti (Ed.), *Developmental psychopathology* (3rd ed., pp. 631–664). Hoboken, NJ: Wiley.

Davila, J., Stoud, C. B., & Starr, L. (2014). Depression in couples and families. In I. H. Gotlib & C. L. Hammen (Eds.), *Handbook of depression* (3rd ed., pp. 410–428). New York: Guilford Press.

Peterson-Post, K. M., Rhoades, G. K., Stanley, S. M., & Markman, H. J. (2014). Perceived criticism and marital adjustment predict depressive symptoms in a community sample. *Behavior Therapy, 45,* 564–575.

Sbarra, D. A., & Whisman, M. A. (2013). Marital and relational discord. In L. G. Castonguay & T. F. Oltmanns (Eds.), *Psychopathology: From science to clinical practice* (pp. 393–418). New York: Guilford Press.

Whisman, M. A., & Baucom, D. H. (2012). Intimate relationships and psychopathology. *Clinical Child and Family Psychology Review, 15,* 4–13.

Whitton, S. W., & Kuryluk, A. D. (2012). Relationship satisfaction and depressive symptoms in emerging adults: Cross-sectional associations and moderating effects of relationship characteristics. *Journal of Family Psychology, 26,* 226–235.

PAGE 33: Women who report satisfaction with their sex lives: Davison, S. L., Bell, R. J., LaChina, M., Holden, S. L., & Davis, S. R. (2009). The relationship between self-reported sexual satisfaction and general well-being in women. *Journal of Sexual Medicine, 6,* 2690–2697.

Rosen, R. C., & Bachmann, G. A. (2008). Sexual well-being, happiness, and satisfaction in women: The case for a new conceptual paradigm. *Journal of Sex and Marital Therapy, 34,* 291–297.

PAGE 33: Being able to communicate successfully with one's partner: Ferroni, P., & Taffe, J. (1997). Women's emotional well-being: The importance of communicating sexual needs. *Sexual and Marital Therapy, 12,* 127–138.

PAGE 33: Approximately 20 million new cases of sexually transmitted infections: Centers for Disease Control and Prevention. (2014). *Reported STDs in the United States* [CDC fact sheet]. Atlanta, GA: U.S. Department of Health and Human Services. Retrieved from *www.cdc.gov/nchhstp/newsroom/docs/std-trends-508.pdf.*

PAGE 34: Approximately 20% of all pregnancies were unwanted: Finer, L. B., & Zolna, M. R. (2014). Shifts in intended and unintended pregnancies in the United States, 2001–2008. *American Journal of Public Health, 104,* S44–S48. Retrieved from *www. guttmacher.org/pubs/FB-Unintended-Pregnancy-US.html.*

PAGE 34: Over 70% of all first pregnancies are unplanned: National Campaign to Prevent Teen and Unplanned Pregnancy. (2012). *Briefly: Unplanned Pregnancy among unmarried young women.* Washington, DC: Author. Retrieved from *http://thenationalcampaign.org/sites/default/files/resource-primary-download/briefly-unplannedpregnancy-among-unmarried.pdf.*

PAGE 34: FWBs represent a diverse set of relationship experiences: Mongeau, P. A., Knight, K., Williams, J., Eden, J., & Shaw, C. (2013). Identifying and explicating variation among friends with benefits relationships. *Journal of Sex Research, 50,* 37–47.

PAGE 34: Positive emotions in response to FWB relationships: Owen, J., & Fincham, F. D. (2011). Effects of gender and psychosocial factors on "friends with benefits" relationships among young adults. *Archives of Sexual Behavior, 40,* 311–320.

PAGE 34: Being more committed to the friendship part: Lehmiller, J. J., VanderDrift, L. E., & Kelly, J. R. (2011). Sex differences in approaching friends with benefits relationships. *Journal of Sex Research, 48,* 275–284.

PAGE 34: Majority of FWB relationships continued as friendships: Owen, J., Fincham, F. D., & Manthos, M. (2013). Friendship after a friends with benefits relationship: Deception, psychological functioning, and social connectedness. *Archives of Sexual Behavior, 42,* 1443–1449.

PAGE 34: Sex can be a more common motivation: Lehmiller, J. J., VanderDrift, L. E., & Kelly, J. R. (2011). Sex differences in approaching friends with benefits relationships. *Journal of Sex Research, 48,* 275–284.

PAGE 35: People in FWB relationships tend to avoid talking: Bisson, M. A., & Levine, T. R. (2009). Negotiating a friends with benefits relationship. *Archives of Sexual Behavior, 38,* 66–73.

PAGE 35: An FWB relationship was associated with greater alcohol use: Owen, J., & Fincham, F. D. (2011). Effects of gender and psychosocial factors on "friends with benefits" relationships among young adults. *Archives of Sexual Behavior, 40,* 311–320.

PAGE 35: As to hookups, both male and female college students: Owen, J., & Fincham, F. D. (2011). Effects of gender and psychosocial factors on "friends with benefits" relationships among young adults. *Archives of Sexual Behavior, 40,* 311–320.

PAGE 35: No differences in psychological well-being: Eisenberg, M. E., Ackard, D. M., Resnick, M. D., & Neumark-Sztainer, D. (2009). Casual sex and psychological health among young adults: Is having "friends with benefits" emotionally damaging? *Perspectives on Sexual and Reproductive Health, 41,* 231–237.

PAGE 35: There may be emotional downsides to hooking up: Bersamin, M., Zamboanga, B. L., Schwartz, S. J., Donnellan, M. B., Hudson, M., Weisskirch, R. S., et al. (2014). Risky business: Is there an association between casual sex and mental health among young emerging adults? *Journal of Sex Research, 5,* 43–51.

PAGE 35: These associations are even greater for women: Fielder, R. L., & Carey, M. P.

(2010). Predictors and consequences of sexual "hookups" among college students: A short-term prospective study. *Archives of Sexual Behavior, 39,* 1105–1119.

PAGE 35: Women find hooking up a positive emotional experience: Owen, J., & Fincham, F. D. (2011). Effects of gender and psychosocial factors on "friends with benefits" relationships among young adults. *Archives of Sexual Behavior, 40,* 311–320.

   Owen, J. J., Rhoades, G. K., Stanley, S. M., & Fincham, F. D. (2010). "Hooking up" among college students: Demographic and psychosocial correlates. *Archives of Sexual Behavior, 39,* 653–663.

PAGE 35: Women show a stronger association between hooking up: Fielder, R. L., & Carey, M. P. (2010). Predictors and consequences of sexual "hookups" among college students: A short-term prospective study. *Archives of Sexual Behavior, 39,* 1105–1119.

   Owen, J. J., Rhoades, G. K., Stanley, S. M., & Fincham, F. D. (2010). "Hooking up" among college students: Demographic and psychosocial correlates. *Archives of Sexual Behavior, 39,* 653–663.

PAGE 35: Alcohol use predicted engaging in hookups: Owen, J., & Fincham, F. D. (2011). Effects of gender and psychosocial factors on "friends with benefits" relationships among young adults. *Archives of Sexual Behavior, 40,* 311–320.

PAGE 35: Situational triggers . . . predicted engaging in hookups: Bersamin, M. M., Paschall, M. J., Saltz, R. F., & Zamboanga, B. L. (2012). Young adults and casual sex: The relevance of college drinking settings. *Journal of Sex Research, 49,* 274–281.

   Fielder, R. L., & Carey, M. P. (2010). Predictors and consequences of sexual "hookups" among college students: A short-term prospective study. *Archives of Sexual Behavior, 39,* 1105–1119.

   For a review of research on hooking up, see Garcia, J. R., Reiber, C., Massey, S. G., & Merriwether, A. M. (2012). Sexual hookup culture: A review. *Review of General Psychology, 16,* 161–176.

PAGE 36: "It's by hooking up": Wade, L. (2013, May 30). Hookup culture: College kids can handle it [Blowback column]. *Los Angeles Times.* Retrieved from *www.latimes.com/news/opinion/opinion-la/la-ol-college-hook-up-culture-blowback-20130530,0,5957732.story.*

Chapter 3

PAGE 51: This list contains a sampling of traits: Anderson, N. H. (1968). Likableness ratings of 555 personality-trait words. *Journal of Social Psychology, 9,* 272–279.

   Cherry, K. The big five personality dimensions. Retrieved from *http://psychology.about.com/od/personalitydevelopment/a/bigfive.htm.*

   McCrae, R. R., & Costa, P. T. (1987). Validation of the five-factor model of personality across instruments and observers. *Journal of Personality and Social Psychology, 52,* 81–90.

   McCrae, R. R., & Costa, P. T. (1997). Personality trait structure as a human universal. *American Psychologist, 52,* 509–516.

   McCrae, R. R., Terracciano, A., & members of the Personality Profiles of Cultures Project. (2005). Universal features of personality traits from the observer's perspective: Data from 50 different cultures. *Journal of Personality and Social Psychology, 88,* 547–561.

PAGE 54: A 2011 poll in Glamour magazine: Dreisbach, S. (2011). Shocking body-image news: 97% of women will be cruel to their bodies today. *Glamour Magazine.* Retrieved from *www.glamour.com/health-fitness/2011/02/shocking-body-image-news-97-percent-of-women-will-be-cruel-to-their-bodies-today.*

PAGE 55: Tend to compare themselves to others: Leahey, T. M., Crowther, J. H., & Ciesla, J. A. (2011). An ecological momentary assessment of the effects of weight and shape social comparisons on women with eating pathology, high body dissatisfaction, and low body dissatisfaction. *Behavior Therapy, 42,* 197–210.

PAGE 55: Most likely to be negatively affected: Ferguson, C. J. (2013). In the eye of the beholder: Thin-ideal media affects some, but not most, viewers in a meta-analytic review of body dissatisfaction in women and men. *Psychology of Popular Media Culture, 2,* 20–37.

PAGE 57: "Can Hormones Released after Sex": Carter, C. S., & Porges, S. W. (2013). The biochemistry of love: An oxytocin hypothesis. *EMBO Reports, 14*(1), 12–16.

For a review of oxytocin in sexual functioning: Meston, C. M., & Frohlich, P. F. (2000). The neurobiology of sexual function. *Archives of General Psychiatry, 57,* 1012–1030.

PAGE 58: Associated with stress in relationships: Bornstein, R. F. (2012). Illuminating a neglected clinical issue: Societal costs of interpersonal dependency and dependent personality disorder. *Journal of Clinical Psychology, 68,* 766–781.

PAGE 59: Evidence points to the fact that active coping: Compas, B. E., Connor-Smith, J. K., Osowiecki, D., & Welch, A. (1997). Effortful and involuntary responses to stress: Implications for coping with chronic stress. In B. H. Gottlieb (Ed.), *Coping with chronic stress* (pp. 105–130). New York: Plenum Press.

Grant, D. M., Wingate, L. R., Rasmussen, K. A., Davidson, C. L., Slish, M. L., Rhoades-Kerswill, S., et al. (2013). An examination of the reciprocal relationship between avoidance coping and symptoms of anxiety and depression. *Journal of Social and Clinical Psychology, 32,* 878–896.

Moos, R. H., & Schaefer, J. A. (1993). Coping resources and processes: Current concepts and measures. In L. Goldberger & S. Breznitz (Eds.), *Handbook of stress: Theoretical and clinical aspects* (2nd ed., pp. 234–257). New York: Free Press.

Roth, S., & Cohen, L. J. (1986). Approach, avoidance, and coping with stress. *American Psychologist, 41,* 813–819.

PAGE 59: Receiving assistance from others: Seeman, T. (2008). Support and social conflict (summary). MacArthur Foundation, Research Network on SES and Health. Retrieved from *www.macses.ucsf.edu/research/psychosocial/socsupp.php.*

PAGE 60: All engaging in self-silencing: Harper, M. S., & Welsh, D. P. (2007). Keeping quiet: Self-silencing and its association with relational and individual functioning among adolescent romantic couples. *Journal of Social and Personal Relationships, 24,* 99–116.

PAGE 63: Do You Use Traditional Gender Role Stereotypes: Eaton, A. A., & Rose, S. (2011). Has dating become more egalitarian?: A 35-year review using *Sex Roles. Sex Roles, 64,* 843–862.

PAGE 66: Perfectionism and self-criticism are unhealthy: Holle, C., & Ingram, R. (2008). On the psychological hazards of self-criticism. In E. Chang (Ed.), *Self-criticism and self-enhancement: Theory, research, and clinical implications* (pp. 55–71). Washington, DC: American Psychological Association.

Holm-Denoma, J. M., Otamendi, A., & Joiner, T. E. (2008). On self-criticism as interpersonally maladaptive. In E. Chang (Ed.), *Self-criticism and self-enhancement: Theory, research, and clinical implications* (pp. 73–86). Washington, DC: American Psychological Association.

Lo, A., & Abbott, M. J. (2013). Review of the theoretical, empirical, and clinical status of adaptive and maladaptive perfectionism. *Behaviour Change, 30,* 96–116.

PAGE 68: People who are less self-forgiving: Pelucchi, S., Paleari, F. G., Regalia, C., & Fincham, F. D. (2013). Self-forgiveness in romantic relationships: It matters to both of us. *Journal of Family Psychology, 27,* 541–549.

PAGE 69: Involvement with a critical partner: Gottman, J. M. (1994). *What predicts* *divorce?: The relationship between marital process and marital outcomes.* Hillsdale, NJ: Erlbaum.

    Peterson-Post, K. M., Rhoades, G. K., Stanley, S. M., & Markman, H. J. (2014). Perceived criticism and marital adjustment predict depressive symptoms in a community sample. *Behavior Therapy, 45,* 564–575.

Chapter 4

PAGE 72: What kind of person do I wish to have as a partner?: Arnett, J. J. (2000). Emerging adulthood: A theory of development from the late teens through the twenties. *American Psychologist, 55,* 469–480. The question referenced is on p. 473.

PAGE 76: Being with someone who is authentic: Wickham, R. E. (2013). Perceived authenticity in romantic partners. *Journal of Experimental Social Psychology, 49,* 878–887.

PAGE 80: Partners feel less close to one another: Gere, J., & Schimmack, U. (2013). When romantic partners' goals conflict: Effects on relationship quality and subjective well-being. *Journal of Happiness Studies, 14,* 37–49.

    Gere, J., Schimmack, U., Pinkus, R. T., & Lockwood, P. (2011). The effects of romantic partners' goal congruence on affective well-being. *Journal of Research in Personality, 45,* 549–559.

PAGE 80: People who are bored in their relationships: Tsapelas, I., Aron, A., & Orbuch, T. (2009). Marital boredom now predicts less satisfaction 9 years later. *Psychological Science, 20*(5), 543–545.

PAGE 80: Self-expansion theory: Aron, A., Aron, E. N., Tudor, M., & Nelson, G. (1991). Close relationships as including other in the self. *Journal of Personality and Social Psychology, 60,* 241–253.

    Aron, A. A., Lewandowski, G. W., Mashek, D., & Aron, E. (2013). The self-expansion model of motivation and cognition in close relationships. In J. A. Simpson & L. Campbell (Eds.), *The Oxford handbook of close relationships* (pp. 90–115). New York: Oxford University Press.

    Aron, A., McLaughlin-Volpe, T., Mashek, D., Lewandowski, G., Wright, S. C., & Aron, E. N. (2004). Including others in the self. *European Review of Social Psychology, 15,* 101–132.

PAGE 81: When couples actively engage in novel, exciting activities: Aron, A., Norman, C. C., Aron, E. N., McKenna, C., & Heyman, R. E. (2000). Couples' shared participation in novel and arousing activities and experienced relationship quality. *Journal of Personality and Social Psychology, 78,* 273–284.

PAGE 82: Support from one's partner: Pasch, L. A., & Bradbury, T. N. (1998). Social support, conflict, and the development of marital dysfunction. *Journal of Consulting and Clinical Psychology, 66,* 219–230.

    Lakey, B. (2013). Social support processes in relationships. In J. A. Simpson & L. Campbell (Eds.), *The Oxford handbook of close relationships* (pp. 711–728). New York: Oxford University Press.

PAGE 84: Why does someone engage in excessive care-giving?: Feeney, J. A. (1996). Attachment, caregiving, and marital satisfaction. *Personal Relationships, 3,* 401–416.

    Kunce, L. J., & Shaver, I. R. (1994). An attachment theoretical approach to caregiving in romantic relationships. In K. Bartholomew & D. Perlman (Eds.), *Advances in personal relationships: Vol. 5. Attachment processes in adulthood* (pp. 205–237). London: Jessica Kingsley.

PAGE 87: Trust in your partner is at the core: Boon, S. D. (1994). Dispelling doubt and uncertainty: Trust in romantic relationships. In S. Duck (Ed.), *Dynamics of relationships* (pp. 86–111). Thousand Oaks, CA: Sage.

Gottman, J. M. (2011). *The science of trust: Emotional attunement for couples.* New York: Norton.

Murray, S. L., & Holmes, J. G. (2011). Trust as motivational gatekeeper in adult romantic relationships. In L. M. Horowitz & S. Strack (Eds.), *Handbook of interpersonal psychology: Theory, research, assessment, and therapeutic interventions* (pp. 193–207). Hoboken, NJ: Wiley.

PAGE 89: Acceptance of one's partner is a key factor: Jacobson, N. S., & Christensen, A. (1996). *Integrative couple therapy: Promoting acceptance and change.* New York: Norton.

McGinn, M. M., Benson, L. A., & Christensen, A. (2011). Integrative behavioral couple therapy: An acceptance-based approach to improving relationship functioning. In J. D. Herbert & E. M. Forman (Eds.), *Acceptance and mindfulness in cognitive behavior therapy: Understanding and applying the new therapies* (pp. 210–232). Hoboken, NJ: Wiley.

PAGE 91: Being able to forgive one's partner: Fincham, F. D. (2009). Forgiveness: Integral to a science of close relationships? In M. Mikulincer & P. Shaver (Eds.), *Prosocial motives, emotions, and behavior: The better angels of our nature* (pp. 347–365). Washington, DC: American Psychological Association.

PAGE 91: Sincere amends lead to greater forgiveness: Pansera, C., & La Guardia, J. (2012). The role of sincere amends and perceived partner responsiveness in forgiveness. *Personal Relationships, 19,* 696–711.

PAGE 96: "Identity fit": Arnett, J. J. (2007). Emerging adulthood: What is it and what is it good for? *Child Development Perspectives, 1,* 68–73.

Chapter 5

PAGE 101: You'll end up feeling misunderstood: De La Ronde, C., & Swann, W. B. (1998). Partner verification: Restoring shattered images of our intimates. *Journal of Personality and Social Psychology, 75,* 374–382.

Weger, H. (2005). Disconfirming communication and self verification in marriage: Associations among the demand/withdraw interaction pattern, feeling understood, and marital satisfaction. *Journal of Social and Personal Relationships, 22,* 19–31.

PAGE 105: Couples who perceive themselves to have lower sexual compatibility: Mark, K. P., Milhausen, R. R., & Maitland, S. B. (2013). The impact of sexual compatibility on sexual and relationship satisfaction in a sample of young adult heterosexual couples. *Sexual and Relationship Therapy, 28*(3), 201–214.

PAGE 107: Responding in active, validating, helpful ways is good for relationships: Collins, N. L., Ford, M. B., Guichard, A. C., Kane, H. S., & Feeney, B. C. (2010). Responding to need in intimate relationships: Social support and caregiving processes in couples. In M. Mikulincer & P. R. Shaver (Eds.), *Prosocial motives, emotions, and behavior: The better angels of our nature* (pp. 367–389). Washington, DC: American Psychological Association.

Gable, S. L., & Reis, H. T. (2010). Good news! Capitalizing on positive events in an interpersonal context. In M. P. Zanna (Ed.), *Advances in experimental social psychology* (pp. 195–257). San Diego, CA: Academic Press.

Gable, S. L., Reis, H. T., Impett, E. A., & Asher, E. R. (2004). What do you do when things go right? The intrapersonal and interpersonal benefits of sharing positive events. *Journal of Personality and Social Psychology, 87,* 228–245.

Reis, H. T., Smith, S. M., Carmichael, C. L., Caprariello, P. A., & Tsai, F. (2010). Are you happy for me? How sharing positive events with others provides personal and interpersonal benefits. *Journal of Personality and Social Psychology, 99,* 311–329.

PAGE 117: The desire for the partner to change: Sullivan, K., & Davila, J. (2014). The problem is my partner: Treating couples when one partner wants the other to change. *Journal of Psychotherapy Integration, 24,* 1–12.

Chapter 6

PAGE 133: Partners will be more successful: Jacobson, N. S., & Christensen, A. (1996). *Integrative couple therapy: Promoting acceptance and change.* New York: Norton.

PAGE 134: Strategies that allow you to communicate: Jacobson, N. S., & Christensen, A. (1996). *Integrative couple therapy: Promoting acceptance and change.* New York: Norton.

PAGE 140: Learning how to tolerate these feelings: Linehan, M. (2015). *DBT skills training manual.* New York: Guilford Press.

Zvolensky, M. J., Bernstein, A., & Vujanovic, A. A. (2011). *Distress tolerance: Theory, research, and clinical applications.* New York: Guilford Press.

PAGE 141: Getting in touch with them: Elliot, R., Watson, J. C., Goldman, R. N., & Greenberg, L. S. (2004). *Learning emotion-focused therapy: The process-experiential approach to change.* Washington, DC: American Psychological Association.

Johnson, S. M. (1996). *Creating connection: The practice of emotionally focused marital therapy.* Philadelphia: Brunner/Mazel.

Chapter 7

PAGE 172: Higher than you might like to think: Substance Abuse and Mental Health Services Administration. (2014). *Results from the 2013 National Survey on Drug Use and Health: Summary of national findings* (HHS Publication No. 14–4863, NSDUH Series H-48). Rockville, MD: Author.

Chapter 8

PAGE 208: Three primary forms of relationship aggression: "Is This Abuse?: Types of Abuse," loveisrespect.org, *www.loveisrespect.org/is-this-abuse/types-of-abuse.*

Warning signs and red flags. National Domestic Violence Hotline. Retrieved from *www.thehotline.org/is-this-abuse/abuse-defined.*

Forms of intimate partner violence (Box 1). (2012). In *Understanding and addressing violence against women.* World Health Organization. Retrieved from *http:// apps.who.int/iris/bitstream/10665/77432/1/WHO_RHR_12.36_eng.pdf.*

PAGE 208: Nearly 25% of surveyed women: Black, M. C., Basile, K. C., Breiding, M. J., Smith, S. G., Walters, M. L., Merrick, M. T., et al. (2011). *The National Intimate Partner and Sexual Violence Survey: 2010 summary report.* Atlanta, GA: National Center for Injury Prevention and Control, Centers for Disease Control and Prevention. Retrieved from *www.cdc.gov/violenceprevention/pdf/nisvs_report2010-a.pdf.*

Tjaden, P., & Thoennes, N. (2000). *Full report of the prevalence, incidence, and consequences of violence against women: Findings from the National Violence against Women Survey.* Washington, DC: U.S. Department of Justice. Retrieved from *www. ncjrs.gov/pdffiles1/nij/183781.pdf.*

PAGE 209: Research shows 20 to 30% of couples: Berger, A., Wildsmith, E., Manlove, J., & Steward-Streng, M. A. (2012, June). Relationship violence among young adult couples. Child Trends research brief, publication no. 2012–14. Retrieved from *www. childtrends.org/wp-content/uploads/2012/06/Child_Trends-2012_06_01_RB_CoupleViolence.pdf.*

PAGE 209: Experiencing physical assault by an intimate partner: Violence against women: Intimate partner and sexual violence against women (Fact sheet No. 239). (2014). World Health Organization. Retrieved from *www.who.int/mediacentre/factsheets/fs239/en.*

Understanding and addressing violence against women. (2012). Geneva, Switzerland: World Health Organization. Retrieved from *http://apps.who.int/iris/bitstream/10665/77432/1/WHO_RHR_12.36_eng.pdf.*

PAGE 209: Violence often recurs: O'Leary, K. D., & Smith Slep, A. M. (2012). Prevention of partner violence by focusing on behaviors of both young males and females. *Prevention Science, 13,* 329–339.

PAGE 210: Violence seems to come out of the blue: Morgan Steiner, L. (2012, November). Why domestic violence victims don't leave. TED Talk. Retrieved from *www.ted.com/talks/leslie_morgan_steiner_why_domestic_violence_victims_don_t_leave.*

PAGE 211: "What Would Make Eric Behave This Way?": Ehrensaft, M. K. (2009). Family and relationship predictors of psychological and physical aggression. In K. D. O'Leary & E. M. Woodin (Eds.), *Psychological and physical aggression in couples: Causes and interventions* (pp. 99–118). Washington, DC: American Psychological Association.

Hamberger, L. K., & Holtzworth-Munroe, A. (2009). Psychopathological correlates of male aggression. In K. D. O'Leary & E. M. Woodin (Eds.), *Psychological and physical aggression in couples: Causes and interventions* (pp. 79–98). Washington, DC: American Psychological Association.

PAGE 211: Strongly associated with aggression in relationships: Fals-Stewart, W., & Klostermann, K. (2009). Substance abuse and intimate partner violence. In K. D. O'Leary & E. M. Woodin (Eds.), *Psychological and physical aggression in couples: Causes and interventions* (pp. 251–269). Washington, DC: American Psychological Association.

Mattson, R. E., O'Farrell, T. J., Lofgreen, A. M., Cunningham, K., & Murphy, C. M. (2012). The role of illicit substance use in a conceptual model of intimate partner violence in men undergoing treatment for alcoholism. *Psychology of Addictive Behaviors, 26,* 255–264.

World Health Organization intimate partner violence and alcohol fact sheet. (n.d.). Retrieved from *www.who.int/violence_injury_prevention/violence/world_report/factsheets/ft_intimate.pdf.*

PAGE 211: Impulsivity is associated with both substance use: Fergusson, D. M., Boden, J. M., & Horwood, L. J. (2008). The developmental antecedents of illicit drug use: Evidence from a 25-year longitudinal study. *Drug and Alcohol Dependence, 96,* 165–177.

Finkel, E. J., DeWall, C. N., Slotter, E. B., Oaten, M., & Foshee, V. A. (2009). Self-regulatory failure and intimate partner violence perpetration. *Journal of Personality and Social Psychology, 97,* 483–499.

Moeller, G. F., Dougherty, D. M., Barratt, E. S., Oderinde, V., Mathias, C. W., Harper, R. A., & Swann, A. C. (2002). Increased impulsivity in cocaine dependent subjects independent of antisocial personality disorder and aggression. *Drug and Alcohol Dependence, 68,* 105–111.

Schafer, J., Caetano, R., & Cunradi, C. B. (2004). A path model of risk factors for intimate partner violence among couples in the United States. *Journal of Interpersonal Violence, 19,* 127–142.

PAGE 211: Evidence that treatment for substance use: O'Farrell, T. J., & Schein, A. Z. (2011). Behavioral couples therapy for alcoholism and drug abuse. *Journal of Family Psychotherapy, 22,* 193–215.

Chapter 9

PAGE 214: Make their stay-or-go decisions: Drigotas, S. M., & Rusbult, C. E. (1992). Should I stay or should I go?: A dependence model of breakups. *Journal of Personality and Social Psychology, 62,* 62–87.

Kelley, H. H., & Thibaut, J. W. (1978). *Interpersonal relations: A theory of interdependence.* New York: Wiley.

PAGE 215: Tolerance of uncertainty: Leahy, R. L. (2005). *The worry cure: Seven steps to stop worry from stopping you.* New York: Three Rivers Press.

PAGE 217: Wise mind: Linehan, M. (2015). *DBT skills training manual.* New York: Guilford Press.

PAGE 228: Passionate love test: Hatfield, E., & Sprecher, S. (1986). Measuring passionate love in intimate relations. *Journal of Adolescence, 9,* 383–410. Passionate Love Scale. Retrieved from *www.elainehatfield.com/Passionate%20Love%20Scale.pdf.*

Chapter 10

PAGE 245: The transcript below is the first minute or so: Reprinted with permission from WBEZ Chicago, *This American Life:* Episode #339, Break Up, August 24, 2007.

PAGE 246: Love can be like an addiction: Fisher, H. E., Brown, L. L., Aron, A., Strong, G., & Mashek, D. (2010). Reward, addiction, and emotion regulation systems associated with rejection in love. *Journal of Neurophysiology, 104,* 51–60. For further discussion of this research see *www.theanatomyoflove.com.*

PAGE 246: Women can experience anxiety, depression, and even suicidal thoughts: Kessler, R. C., Berglund, P., Demler, O., Jin, R., Koretz, D., Merikangas, K. R., et al. (2003). The epidemiology of major depressive disorder: Results for the National Comorbidity Survey Replication (NCS-R). *Journal of the American Medical Association, 289,* 3095–3105.

Monroe, S. M., Rohde, P., Seeley, J. R., & Lewinsohn, P. M. (1999). Life events and depression in adolescence: Relationship loss as a prospective risk factor for first onset of major depressive disorder. *Journal of Abnormal Psychology, 108,* 606–614.

PAGE 248: Combating Rumination: For techniques related to the ones we describe in this section: Tartakovsky, M. (2011). Why ruminating is unhealthy and how to stop. PsychCentral. Retrieved from *http://psychcentral.com/blog/archives/2011/01/20/why-ruminating-is-unhealthy-and-how-to-stop.*

PAGE 248: Use mindfulness techniques: Germer, C. K. (2009). *The mindful path to self-compassion: Freeing yourself from destructive thoughts and emotions.* New York: Guilford Press.

Kabat-Zinn, J. (2011). *Mindfulness for beginners: Reclaiming the present moment and your life.* Boulder, CO: Sounds True.

PAGE 248: What researchers call corumination: Rose, A. J. (2002). Co-rumination in the friendships of girls and boys. *Child Development, 73,* 1830–1843.

Rose, A. J., Carlson, W., & Waller, E. M. (2007). Prospective associations of co-rumination with friendship and emotional adjustment: Considering the socioemotional trade-offs of co-rumination. *Developmental Psychology, 43,* 1019–1031.

Chapter 11

PAGE 278: The Development of Intimacy: Laurenceau, J.-P., & Kleinman, B. M. (2006). Intimacy in personal relationships. In A. L. Vangelisti & D. Perlman (Eds.), *The Cambridge handbook of personal relationships* (pp. 637–653). New York: Cambridge University Press.

Index

About the Authors

Joanne Davila, PhD, is Professor of Psychology at Stony Brook University, a clinical psychologist in private practice, and an internationally recognized expert on young women's romantic relationships. She lives in Stony Brook, New York, with her partner.

Kaycee Lashman is an organizational change specialist who focuses on relationship dynamics within companies. Married with two children, she lives in Vancouver, Canada.